CHILDREN ACT 1975

by

HUGH K. BEVAN, J.P., LL.M.

of the Middle Temple and North Eastern Circuit, Barrister, Professor of Law at the University of Hull

and

MARTIN L. PARRY, LL.B.

Solicitor, Lecturer in Law at the University of Hull

LONDON

BUTTERWORTHS

1978

This book is also available as part of Butterworths Annotated Legislation Service

---

ENGLAND:
Butterworth & Co. (Publishers) Ltd.
London: 88 Kingsway, London WC2B 6AB

AUSTRALIA:
Butterworths Pty. Ltd.
Sydney: 586 Pacific Highway, Chatswood, NSW 2067
Also at Melbourne, Brisbane, Adelaide and Perth

CANADA:
Butterworth & Co. (Canada) Ltd.
Toronto: 2265 Midland Avenue, Scarborough, M1P 4SI

NEW ZEALAND:
Butterworths of New Zealand Ltd.
Wellington: 77–85 Customhouse Quay, Wellington

SOUTH AFRICA:
Butterworth & Co. (South Africa) (Pty.) Ltd.
Durban: 152–154 Gale Street, Durban

U.S.A.:
Butterworth & Co. (Publishers) Inc.
Boston: 19 Cummings Park, Woburn, Mass. 01801

ISBN 0 406 11702 0

Printed in Great Britain by
Billing & Sons Limited, Guildford, London and Worcester

PREFACE

In the words of Dr. David Owen, "A nation's children represent a nation's future. How society treats its own children is a good reflection of the overall health and stability of that society. There is much good evidence for concern at the present state of child care in Britain." In this book we have looked at the ways in which The Children Act 1975 seeks to meet some of the needs of children.

We initially intended to publish our comments on the Act contemporaneously with its enactment, but, when it became clear that implementation of much of it was to be postponed, we took the opportunity of subjecting it to closer scrutiny. In so doing we have confined our analysis to the law as it affects England and Wales.

Since Part I of the Act is to be repealed by the Adoption Act 1976, we have felt it desirable to add a concluding chapter drawing attention in outline to the the later Act's consolidation of adoption law. In other respects the book deals with the provisions of the 1975 Act largely in the order in which they appear in the legislation.

In writing the text we have tried to bear in mind the needs of lawyers both practising and academic, as well as social workers and students of child law and child care, with a view to attempting a comprehensive explanation of the law, whilst at the same time criticising those areas of the Act which we consider to be deficient.

We wish to express our thanks to Miss Kathryn Thorpe for always finding time to type out the manuscript in the face of the idiosyncrasies of not one author but two and to our colleague, Miss Deborah Rudkin for reading and checking the whole of the proofs. We similarly thank our publishers for their patience in awaiting submission of the manuscript.

We have tried to state the law as at January 1st 1978.

February 1978

H. K. Bevan
M. L. Parry

CONTENTS

PART II CUSTODIANSHIP

PART III CARE

PART IV MISCELLANEOUS

TABLE OF CASES

In the following Table references are given to the English and Empire Digest where a digest of the case will be found

Table of Cases

PARA.

Table of Cases

PARA.

TABLE OF STATUTES

References in this Table to "*Statutes*" are to Halsbury's Statutes of England (Third Edition) showing the volume and page at which the annotated text of the Act will be found.

Paragraph numbers printed in bold type indicate whether the Children Act 1975 is set out.

PART I

ADOPTION

CHAPTER 1

INTRODUCTION

All the major enactments affecting children over the past fifty years have been preceded by one form or another of governmental inquiry,[1] but none can be said to have endured such a protracted and painful gestation as was the fate of the Children Act 1975. Its history is now well known. Its origin is traceable to the Report of the Standing Conference of Societies Registered for Adoption.[2] Published in 1968, the Report directly led to the appointment of the Departmental Committee on the Adoption of Children under the chairmanship first of Sir William Houghton and then, on his death in December 1971, of his Honour Judge Stockdale. The Committee published a widely disseminated Working Paper in 1970[3] and its Final Report in 1972.[4] Dr. David Owen's Private Member's Bill,[5] which sought very largely to give effect to the Report, was aborted by the Dissolution of Parliament in February 1974, the day before its proposed Second Reading. Its publication did, however, give fresh impetus at a time when public interest in the Report was tending to wane.[6] It also served as a useful "working paper" for the Government's own Children Bill. [**1**]

Although the Houghton Committee was primarily directed to consider "the law, policy and procedure on adoption", their inquiry inevitably involved examination of matters closely connected with the adoption process, especially long-term fostering and the needs of children in long-term residential care. As will be seen,[7] the Act also deals with a number of other important topics. It would therefore have been surprising if over a period of some six years opinions had not wavered and changed. The latter part of that period saw greater attention being paid by researchers to the need for psychological, as opposed to biological, parenthood, with the emphasis on the right of the child to loving care and the duty to provide a caring home for him rather than on the blood tie and

---

[1] Most notably, the Hopkinson Report ((1921) Cmd. 1254) and the Tomlin Report ((1925) Cmd. 2401 and Cmd. 2469) culminated in the Adoption of Children Act 1926; the deliberations of the Curtis Committee ((1946) Cmd. 6922) produced the Children Act 1948; the Report of the Ingleby Committee on Children and Young Persons ((1960) Cmd. 1191) was the major reason for the Children and Young Persons Act 1963; and the two controversial White Papers, *The Child, the Family and the Young Offender* ((1965) Cmd. 2742) and *Children in Trouble* ((1968) Cmd. 3601) led to the Children and Young Persons Act 1969.

[2] The predecessor of the present Association of British Adoption and Fostering Agencies.

[3] *Adoption of Children*, H.M.S.O. (1970).

[4] Cmd. 5107. Strict accuracy would require reference to the "Houghton Working Paper" and the "Stockdale Report", but the Report is most commonly described as the "Houghton Committee Report". Footnote references herein are to "H.C.R.".

[5] Subsequently referred to as "the Owen Bill".

[6] Cf. the sustained flow of research which the setting up of the Houghton Committee directly or indirectly inspired. See, e.g., *A Survey of Adoption in Great Britain* (Home Office Statistical Studies No. 10 (1971)); Seglow, Kellmer Pringle and Wedge, *Growing up Adopted* (1972); Rowe and Lambert, *Children Who Wait* (1973); Kellmer Pringle, *The Needs of Children* (1975).

[7] Chap. 13, *post*.

the rights of the natural parents to treat him as though he belongs to them.[1] The case for substitute care was advanced by the increasing publicity given to "tug of love" cases between natural parents and foster parents, by the publication of the report of the Maria Colwell tragedy[2] and by the timely appearance of Goldstein, Freud and Solnit's *Beyond the Best Interests of the Child*. However, by the time the Children Bill had reached Parliament a powerful lobby in defence of biological parenthood had emerged. Shortcomings of long-term fostering, especially private fostering,[3] and institutional care were highlighted and the inflexibility of some of the proposals in *Beyond the Best Interests of the Child* was criticised. Particularly open to question was the suggestion that "all child placements, except where specifically designed for brief temporary care, shall be as permanent as the placement of a newborn with its biological parents."[4] A strong contrary case was argued for "inclusive fostering" whereby the child remains in contact with the natural parent and continuity of affection is preserved and encouraged.[5] Such conflicting views much influenced Parliamentary debate with the ultimate result that in certain respects the Act creates an uneasy compromise between the rights of the natural parent and the welfare of the child. [**2**]

In assessing the implications of the Act a caution must be lodged against generalities. With respect, it is as unwise to see it as "anti-mother and anti-family"[6] or "in effect . . . a foster parents' charter"[7] as it is to welcome it wholly as "a new charter of children's rights".[8] Certainly in some respects it shows a distinct shift of balance towards the foster parent and away from the natural parent. Thus, by creating the new status of custodianship[9] it enables, *inter alios*, the foster parent to establish a legal relationship with the child. Indeed, where he has been providing a home for the child for at least three years he can apply for a custodianship order without the consent of the natural parent, who will not be allowed to remove the child pending the hearing of the application.[10] If this provision is thought to be "anti-family", it should be remembered that in deciding whether or not to make a custodianship order the court must treat the child's welfare as the paramount consideration.[11] Many will therefore see custodianship in the different light that it promotes the child's interests rather than as an attenuation of the rights of the natural parent or the creation of rights in favour of the foster parent. Equally, it is with the child's interests in mind that the Act imposes a restriction on removing a child from a foster parent pending the hearing of an adoption application by him if he has provided

---

[1] Kellmer Pringle, *The Needs of Children*, pp. 69–70.
For the view that the parent–child relation should be seen as one involving parental duties and not parental rights see the Report of *Justice* (the British Section of the International Commission of Jurists) on *Parental Rights and Duties and Custody Suits* (1975).

[2] *Report of the Committee of Inquiry into the Care and Supervision Provided in relation to Maria Colwell* (D.H.S.S. (1974)).

[3] Holman, *Trading in Children* (1973) had already pinpointed weaknesses.

[4] At p. 35.

[5] Holman, *The Place of Fostering in Social Work*, 5 Br. J. of Social Work, p. 3.

[6] Samuels, *The Children Act 1975*, 6 Family Law, p. 5.

[7] Freeman, *The Children Act 1975*, p. v.

[8] H. C. Official Report, **1975**, Vol. **898**, No. **187**, col. 1546 (Third Reading; Mr. Bowden).

[9] Part II, Chaps. 9 and 10, *post*.

[10] S. 41, paras. [**254**]–[**258**], *post*.

[11] S. 33 (9).

a home for the past five years.[1] *Prima facie* a stable relationship will have been established over such a lengthy period and ought not to be disturbed until the court decides whether or not it should be made permanent by adoption. [3]

Similarly, the enlargement of certain powers of local authorities should be seen as affording greater protection to the child. Where he has been received into the care of an authority under section 1 of the Children Act 1948 and has remained in care for at least six months the natural parent must give twenty-eight days' notice of his intention to take his child out of care.[2] Undeniably this is a serious restriction on the rights of the natural parent, but it is more than counterbalanced by the risk that "a suddden move, without preparation, can be damaging to the child and may have long-term repercussions".[3] Some, indeed, have argued that for that reason once a child is in care there must in all cases be notice of intended removal. The new rule is a compromise between that view and the *Houghton* proposal of a minimum of twelve months' care—a compromise between the child's welfare and the rights of the parent. More controversial is the new ground entitling a local authority to assume parental rights under section 2 of the Children Act 1948. This they may do once the child has been in their care for at least three years, without any need to prove parental misconduct or disability.[4] There is a modest concession made to the parent in that his right to challenge the authority's resolution is strengthened by giving him a right to appeal from the juvenile court to the High Court.[5] [4]

While the rules referred to in paragraphs 3 and 4 aim to promote the child's welfare, through their time limits they run the risk of being counter productive. The reluctance of the natural parent to place his child with a local authority, voluntary organisation, adoption agency, prospective adopters or private foster parents or the chances of his removing him before effluxion of the relevant statutory period will depend partly on how well informed he is, but the possibilities should not be overstated. It is, for example, very doubtful whether the rule relating to the giving of twenty-eight days' notice will seriously inhibit placement in short-term care. The exigencies of the moment, not a prospective restriction, will usually determine the decision to place the child. The number of cases where the natural parent will remove the child before completion of the five-year period of caring by the foster parent so as to prevent the latter from relying on the restriction on removal is likely to be small.[6] Because the period

---

[1] Adoption Act 1958, s. 34A, as enacted by the Children Act 1975, s. 29 (Adoption Act 1976, s. 28); see paras. [**134**]–[**142**], *post*. (Operative since 26th November 1976.)

[2] S. 1 (3A), as enacted by the Children Act 1975, s. 56; see paras. [**318**]–[**328**], *post*. There is a similar provision affecting children in the care of a voluntary organisation. (Operative since 26th November 1976.)

[3] H.C.R., para. 152.

[4] S. 2 (1) (*d*), as substituted by the Children Act 1975, s. 57; see paras. [**329**]–[**341**], post. (Operative since 26th November 1976.)

The three years may have been spent partly in the care of a local authority and partly in the care of a voluntary organisation.

[5] Children Act 1948, s. 4A, as enacted by the Children Act 1975, s. 58. (Operative in part since 26th November 1976.)

[6] Cf. the sample collected by *Houghton*. During 1970 only 38 children who had been in the care of 25 local authorities and voluntary societies for more than five years were discharged from care. At that time the authorities and societies had some 3,465 children who had been boarded out with the same foster parents for more than five years. See H.C.R., Appendix D, paras. 6–9.

is shorter there may be slightly more cases where a natural parent may forestall a custodianship application by retaking the child before the end of the three-year period, but even then the foster parent may be able to counter by wardship proceedings. **[5]**

A major concession to the interests of the natural parent is to be found in section 3 of the Act, which goes to the heart of adoption law. In reaching any decision relating to adoption both the adoption agency and the court must regard the child's welfare as the first consideration, but it is not paramount as it is in custody, custodianship, guardianship and wardship proceedings. As will be seen,[1] in relation to one aspect of adoption law this principle is probably declaratory of the former law, but otherwise it is novel, and in practice, it is suggested, will create a sea of uncertainty. The same principle will also normally regulate the decision making of local authorities with regard to children in their care.[2] However, having committed itself to this new principle in these two important areas of child law, the Act omits to tackle the problem of the "welfare" test in relation to proceedings governed by the Children and Young Persons Acts 1933–1969. The omission is remarkable in view of the fact that juvenile courts spend most of their time administering those Acts. The scope of the present principle is notoriously uncertain.[3] In practice courts seem to apply the paramountcy test when exercising their civil jurisdiction under the Acts, but are divided on whether or not it should apply in criminal proceedings.[4] **[6]**

It might be objected that any amendment of section 44 (1) would have been outside the scope of the 1975 legislation, but it is difficult to defend that argument given that the Act contains substantial amendments of the Children and Young Persons Act 1969.[5] Indeed, having opened its doors to changes in the law outside those matters examined by *Houghton*, where was the line to be drawn? In particular there was a strong feeling in many quarters that some at least of the recommendations of the admirable (Finer) Report of the Committee on One-parent Families should be implemented; for example, those relating to the establishment of a system of family courts with a supporting family service, day nurseries and a guaranteed maintenance allowance. There was ample opportunity for implementation, since the Report appeared in June 1974.[6] In the event the Government decided against it, essentially on the ground of lack of resources. Since the Children Act itself is subject to piecemeal implementation depending upon the availability of resources, that ground loses much of its validity. The failure to give effect to the Report makes the need for reliance on the preventive and rehabilitative measures under section 1 of the Children

---

[1] Chap. 3, *post*.

[2] Children Act 1948, s. 12, as substituted by the Children Act 1975, s. 59. (Operative since 1st January 1976.) This provision, too, may create uncertainty and inconsistency.

[3] Children and Young Persons Act 1933, s. 44 (1). This provides:

"Every court in dealing with a child or young person who is brought before it, either as an offender or otherwise, shall have regard to the welfare of the child or young person and shall in a proper case take steps for removing him from undesirable surroundings and for securing that proper provision is made for his education and training."

[4] See Cavenagh, *Juvenile Courts, the Child and the Law*, pp. 189–190; Bevan, *The Law Relating to Children*, pp. 16–17.

[5] See Chaps. 12 and 13, *post*.

[6] Cmd. 5629.

and Young Persons Act 1963 all the greater. These are available to the local authority in order to diminish "the need to receive children into care or keep them in care . . . or to bring children before a juvenile court". Regrettably the section in practice is of very variable efficacy. Far more could be done under it to provide supportive services to the family at risk and thus reduce the number of children in care. For example, much more use could be made of it to maintain contact between the parent and the child after separation and so long as there is a real possibility of rehabilitation. As it stands, the Children Act 1975 should be seen as complementary to such measures. Dealing mainly with adoption, fostering, and children in care it aims primarily to improve some of the methods for rescuing children from unsatisfactory homes where prevention and rehabilitation have failed. That aim needs to be repeated loudly and clearly. The Act is not, it is respectfully suggested, "a reversal of the social policy of supporting the child in his family".[1] **[7]**

On the legalistic plane, the Act thickens rather than clears the jungle of child law. This is partly explained by the intrinsically complex nature of some of its subject-matter; for example, the proprietary effects of adoption and legitimation, where, in spite of the modern technique of using illustrations as an aid to clarification, there is still some obscurity. However, subject-matter is not the only reason for complexity. The lawyer's pen runs heavily through the Act[2] and, notwithstanding extensive Parliamentary scrutiny, the implications of some provisions were not explored and their correct interpretation is uncertain.[3] There are many miscellaneous amendments, whose importance is not to be underestimated, hidden in the interstices of the Schedules, and the Act teems with examples of legislation by reference. These are particularly serious defects, since this Act, more than most, will have to be used by laymen as much as, if not more than, lawyers. Happily some relief will be afforded by the Adoption Act 1976 which consolidates the adoption provisions in the 1975 Act and the Adoption Acts 1958–1968.[4]

Because of its complexity and because of the implications of some of its provisions the need for explanatory publicity cannot be urged too strongly. There ought particularly to be issued to parents when their children are received into care leaflets concerning adoption and custodianship and the effects on their parental rights.[5] One of the most satisfactory features of the Act has been the degree of consultation undertaken in the course of its enactment, both by the Houghton Committee and by the Government. It is intended to continue this practice and also to issue circulars of guidance to practitioners as provisions are brought into operation. This is especially desirable in view of the extensive legislative powers which the Act delegates. **[8]**

---

1 Freeman, *The Children Act 1975*, p. vi.

2 See, e.g. ss. 85 and 86. (Operative since 1st January 1976.)

3 If the courts do use the Houghton Report as an aid to interpretation, it will not answer many of the problems raised.

4 The appropriate references to the Adoption Act 1976 are indicated in the footnotes.

5 Measures along these lines are intended; see the Circulars issued by the Department of Health and Social Security, paras. [**10**], [**11**], *post*. In particular L.A.C. (76) 15 Annex A sets out models of two explanatory leaflets for general guidance to parents; see Chap. 11, *post*. Compare a similar recommendation of the House of Commons Select Committee on Expenditure in its Eleventh Report on the Children and Young Persons Act 1969 (H.C. Paper no. 534, Rec. 34).

In these dark economic days there must be serious doubts about the availability of the requisite resources of finance and personnel for implementing the Act. Mindful of the lessons to be learnt from the Children and Young Persons Act 1969, the Government plans a cautious implementation, as indicated by the Circulars issued by the Department of Health and Social Security, which are printed in part below.[1] It is immensely difficult to estimate the long-term demands to be made on resources. A major factor will be the extent to which local authorities will fulfil their duty under sections 1 and 2 of the Act to provide a comprehensive adoption service. This is bound to raise large questions; for example, the extent to which voluntary societies forming part of that service will expect the local authority to provide grant aids. One early note of caution needs to be expressed. If the Act is to fulfil, as has earlier been suggested, the proper function of complementing preventive and rehabilitative work, it is essential that present resources available for the latter purpose (and themselves often inadequate) are not directed to implementation of the Act: there must be additional resources. The very limited implementation of some of the provisions governing separate representation of children in care and related proceedings and the postponement of the appointment of a panel for guardians *ad litem* and reporting officers indicates the cautious approach to the problems to be tackled.[2] **[9]**

DEPARTMENT OF HEALTH AND SOCIAL SECURITY LOCAL AUTHORITY CIRCULAR (75) 21
(December 1975)

1. This letter outlines the effect of the main provisions of the Children Act 1975 and advises you of the arrangements for the first phase of implementation. Its terms have been agreed with the Home Office and the Lord Chancellor's Office.

MAIN PURPOSES OF CHILDREN ACT 1975

2. The Children Act 1975 carries out the Government's intention to reform the law relating to the adoption, guardianship and fostering of children. The main purpose of the Act is to give effect to the recommendations of the Departmental Committee on the Adoption of Children (the Houghton Committee) and certain related matters arising from the report of the Maria Colwell Inquiry.

PHASED IMPLEMENTATION

3. Agreement has been reached in discussions between the Minister of State (Health) and representatives of Local Authority Associations on the programme for the first phase of implementation covering the financial year 1976/77. This takes full account of the Associations' assessment of the financial and human resources that will be required. The Associations have shown a strong commitment to do all they can, within the resources available to them, to implement the

---

[1] We are obliged to the Department for their kind permission to publish them.
[2] See Chap. 12, *post*.

Act and they share the Government's view of the relative importance of the various provisions. Obviously the timetable has been dictated by the necessity to contain expenditure though there are many sections of the Act which do not carry any financial commitment. Discussions will continue on the detailed timetable and future decisions will depend on the resource outlook in the summer of 1976 for the financial year 1977/78. We envisage that it will take local authorities at least a full year to prepare for the statutory requirement to provide a comprehensive adoption service and quite probably a further period before the necessary high standards are achieved to justify bringing in some sections of the legislation.

COMMENCEMENT

4. Section 108 (3) of the new Act sets out the provisions that came into operation at Royal Assent on 12th November 1975; and subsections (4) and (6) set out those that came into operation on 1st January 1976. Subject to what is said in paragraph 3 of this letter, other provisions can be brought into force on days appointed by Order.

5. The provisions which came into force in England and Wales on Royal Assent or on 1st January 1976 are listed below.

(*a*) *The new welfare principle.* Section 3 for Part I relating to adoption and section 59 for Part III for children in care.

(*b*) *Status of adopted and legitimated children.* Section 8 (9) brings in Schedule 1 relating to the status of adopted and legitimated children.

(*c*) *Serious ill-treatment as an additional ground for dispensing with parental consent.* Section 108 (6) is a transitional provision applying to any adoption applications made after 31st December 1975 a new ground for dispensing with parental consent to adoption. This will apply until section 12, which deals with parental agreement to adoption generally in the new terms of the Act, can be brought into force.

(*d*) *Religious upbringing of adopted child.* Section 13.

(*e*) *Grants in respect of secure accommodation in England and Wales.* Section 71.

(*f*) *Explanation of concepts.* Sections 85–89 define certain terms used throughout the Act, namely, "the parental rights and duties", "legal custody", "actual custody", and "child in the care of a voluntary organisation". Section 89 amends the Interpretation Act 1889 to take account of these definitions.

(*g*) *Procedure in guardianship and matrimonial proceedings.* Sections 90 and 91.

(*h*) *Secretary of State's power to hold inquiries in England and Wales.* Section 98.

(*i*) *Authorised courts for the purposes of the Act.* Section 100.

(*j*) *Regulation-making power for establishing panels for guardians* ad litem *and reporting officers.* Section 103.

(*k*) *Saving for powers of High Court.* Section 104.

(*l*) *Regulation-making power of the Secretary of State.* Section 106.

(*m*) *Interpretation of terms used in the Act.* Section 107 contains the interpretation provisions of the Act.

(*n*) *Minor and consequential amendments of related legislation.* Section 108 brings into force certain paragraphs of Schedule 3 and Parts I–III of Schedule 4. Attention is drawn in particular to paragraph 67 of Schedule 3 which adds a new primary condition for orders under section 1 of the Children and Young Persons Act 1969.

PROPOSALS FOR 1976/77

6. See Local Authority Circular (76) 15.
7. See Local Authority Circular (76) 15.

PERSONS ADOPTED AFTER THE PASSING OF THE CHILDREN ACT 1975

8. . . . persons adopted after the passing of the Act (i.e., with effect from 12th November 1975) will be able to obtain their birth certificates when they are 18 years old.[1] It will therefore be necessary for adoption agencies to make clear to parents and adopters alike that adoption does not guarantee anonymity for the natural parents, particularly after the child is 18; and to discuss the implications of this with both parties.

ADDITIONAL PROVISIONS FOR IMPLEMENTATION IN 1976/77

9. See Local Authority Circular (76) 15.

FURTHER GUIDANCE

10. Further guidance circulars will be issued as necessary as more provisions are brought into operation. The Department will also be considering, in consultation with those concerned, the form and content of comprehensive guidance for practitioners on various parts of the Act. **[10]**

DEPARTMENT OF HEALTH AND SOCIAL SECURITY
LOCAL AUTHORITY CIRCULAR (76) 15
(September 1976)

1. This letter advises you of the arrangements agreed between the Department and Local Authority Associations for the implementation of further provisions of the Children Act 1975; and encloses detailed guidance on the provisions relating to "time limits". Its terms have been agreed with the Home Office and the Lord Chancellor's Office.

2. For the most part, the implementation programme follows closely the proposals for 1976/77 set out in Local Authority Circular (75) 21 which described the arrangements agreed with the Local Authority Associations for the phased implementation of the Act. As part of this agreement, a sum of £100,000 was included in the rate support grant settlement for the current financial year to meet the small additional demand on local authority resources which was expected to arise from the three important provisions described in paragraph 4 (ii) to (iv) below. The other provisions bring about relatively minor changes and

[1] S. 26 came into force on 26th November 1976; see L.A.C. (76) 15, para. **[11]**, *post*.

it was agreed that these would be within the capacity of existing local authority staff and resources.

COMMENCEMENT

3. It is proposed that two main groups of provisions should be brought into effect in England and Wales in the financial year 1976/77.

4. The first group of provisions is planned to come into force on 26th November 1976 and consists of:

(*i*) *Minor changes in adoption law and procedure and other minor changes*

Adoption orders and their effects	Sections 8 (1)–(8)
Qualifications for an adoption order (age, status and domicile)	Sections 10 and 11
Parental agreement to adoption	Section 12
Power to make supervision or care orders on refusal of adoption order	Section 17
Hearing of applications, etc., in private	Section 21 (1) and (2)
Restriction on further applications and prohibition on making of adoption order where unlawful payments have been made	Section 22 (4) and (5)
Increase in penalty for making unlawful adoption arrangements	Section 28 (c) (ii)
Return of child on refusal of adoption order	Section 31
Recovery of children in care of local authorities	Sections 67 and 68
Appeals to High Court	Section 101
Grants to voluntary organisations	Schedule 3, paragraphs 46 and 47
Extension of legal aid provisions	Schedule 3, paragraph 82 (a)

(*ii*) *The "time limit" provisions*

Adoption. Restrictions on removal of a child pending adoption
Sections 29 and 30

Care. Restrictions on removal of a child from care
Section 56

Additional grounds for the assumption of parental rights and duties.
Section 57

Right of appeal to the High Court against a juvenile court decision on a parental rights and duties resolution. Section 58 (part)

(*iii*) *Separate representation in certain care and related proceedings*

As foreshadowed in paragraph 7 (b) of Local Authority Circular (75) 21, the provisions for separate representation contained in sections 64 and 65 of the Children Act 1975 will be only partly implemented in 1976/77. The provisions which are planned to take effect on 26th November 1976 will cover proceedings arising from unopposed applications for the discharge or variation of care or supervision orders made in care proceedings.

(*iv*) *Access to birth records*

Enabling adopted persons over 18 to obtain their birth record Section 26

Enabling adopted persons under 18 who are intending to marry to seek information from the Registrar General on whether they and the person they propose to marry may be closely related
Section 26

5. It is proposed that the second group of provisions will come into operation on 1st January 1977. This consists of:

Registration of births of abandoned children
Section 92

Registration of father of illegitimate child
Section 93

CERTIFICATES OF UNRULY CHARACTER

6. It is expected that a further provision will come into operation in the financial year 1976/77:

Certificates of Unruly Character Section 69

This section will be effective from a date yet to be determined. Separate guidance dealing with certificates of unruliness will be issued later in the year.

COMMENCEMENT ORDER

7. It is the intention of the Secretary of State, in exercise of his powers conferred upon him by section 108 (2) of the Children Act 1975, to make an order to bring the provisions described in paragraphs 4 and 5 above into operation on the dates mentioned.

SUBORDINATE LEGISLATION

Adoption

8. Most of the provisions in group (i) require changes to be made to Court rules and adoption agency regulations. The adoption provisions in particular require three new sets of rules: for the High Court, county court and magistrates' court. The new rules and regulations will take account of changes made on 1st January 1976 as well as those scheduled for later this year.

Separate representation

9. The provisions in group (iii) also require Court rules governing procedure and the appointment of guardians *ad litem*.

Access to birth records

10. Applications for information about birth records will need to be made in a form to be prescribed by the Registrar General; the appropriate forms are being prepared.

ADDITIONAL GUIDANCE

(a) "Time limit" provisions

11. It will be necessary for social workers in the field to consider now what action should be taken in individual cases in advance of the operative date of the time limit provisions. Additional guidance on these provisions is given in the Annex accompanying this letter.

(b) Other provisions

12. Comprehensive guidance on access to birth records, on separate representation, and on the other provisions listed in paragraphs 4 and 5 will be given in further circulars to be issued before the appointed day.

IMPLEMENTATION AFTER 1976/77—THE STATUTORY ADOPTION SERVICE

13. It has been agreed that at least one year's notice will be needed for the introduction of a statutory adoption service, so that standards can be brought to the required level. It is unfortunately already clear that sufficient resources will not be available in 1977/78 to make it possible to introduce a statutory service in April 1978.

14. Meanwhile it may be helpful to give an indication of the intention behind Section 1 of the Children Act 1975, which is that local authorities should establish an adoption service as an integral part of their social services provision in partnership with adoption societies operating in their area. The Act does not lay down the form that this partnership should take; it will vary according to the needs of the area—of children, prospective adopters and natural parents—and according to the adoption societies operating in the area, the particular category of clients they serve (e.g., whether they have to be of a particular religious faith) and the extent to which they are likely to meet the new criteria for approval. Each authority will have to consider and assess which groups are not covered by voluntary agencies; ideally, where authorities are not already acting as adoption agencies, the local authority service and the voluntary service should be complementary, with the minimum of duplication or parallel working. (Some overlapping will be inevitable if natural parents and prospective adopters are to be allowed an element of choice, e.g., between a local authority or a voluntary society or between a local authority and a society offering a service to persons of a particular religious faith.) It will be necessary for each authority to ensure oversight of the service available in the area. This will involve at least one senior, experienced officer with a recognised executive responsibility for adoption who should have access to the Director's management team to ensure that an adequate adoption service is provided in conjunction with their other social services for families and children and in liaison with voluntary agencies. The officer involved will need to have direct links with the area teams to ensure that:

(a) the social workers are knowledgeable about the adoption service;
(b) they receive advice and guidance; and
(c) the service is available to local families and children, including children in care.

15. The concept of partnership was recommended by the Houghton Committee in their report and the Government regard the pooling of available skills, resources and local knowledge as central to the proper working of the Act. They recognise that extra money will need to be made available to enable the joint service to be set up, and to enable local authorities not only to establish or improve their own adoption service but also to help voluntary societies who are likely to make a valuable contribution to the service in their area. The Department's Social Work Service is already involved in some regions in discussions with local authorities and voluntary adoption societies about setting up a joint adoption service and it is clear that a good deal of preparatory work can be done by way of assessing needs and resources to anticipate the coming into force of section 1 of the Act and the new provisions in section 4 for the approval of adoption societies. It is hoped that it will be possible to make further progress along these lines in consultation with the local authority and other professional associations. [**11**]

CHAPTER 2

THE ADOPTION SERVICE

THE SCOPE OF THE SERVICE

The provision of adoption services in England and Wales has been spasmodic and haphazard. They have been supplied partly by voluntary adoption societies, operating locally or nationally, and partly by some, but no means all, local authorities. The standard of the services and the availability of resources have varied markedly. Moreover, in the absence of any national service, local authorities have made no systematic attempt to assess the adoption requirements of their respective areas. It came as no surprise, therefore, when the Houghton Committee drew attention to the need for a "service which is comprehensive in scope and available throughout the country".[1] **[12]**

Section 1 of the Act[2] in principle goes a long way to achieving this object by requiring every local authority[3] to establish and maintain a service to meet the needs of children[4] who have been or may be adopted, their parents and guardians,[5] and prospective or actual adopters. To discharge this duty the authority either must itself provide the requisite facilities or ensure that they are provided by adoption societies approved in accordance with the Act.[6] This does not go as far as the Houghton Committee's recommendation[7] that local authorities themselves should provide such a service as part of their general child care and family casework provision, but it does meet the recommendation[8] that there should be a statutory duty on them to ensure, in co-operation with voluntary societies, that a comprehensive adoption service is available throughout their area. In this way a national service, known as the Adoption Service,[9] will be provided. **[13]**

The Act soes not explicitly define the scope of a local adoption service, but potentially it can be very wide, since it must not only be available for those who may adopt, e.g., foster parents, but also remain available after an adoption order has been made. The child, the natural parent, the adopters or any of them may still need help. Indeed, it is expressly enacted[10] that one of the facilities

---

[1] H.C.R., para. 34.

[2] Adoption Act 1976, s. 1. Implementation is not likely before April 1979.

[3] The appropriate local authorities are, in relation to England and Wales, the council of a county (other than a metropolitan county), a metropolitan district, a London borough or the Common Council of the City of London (s. 107 (1); Adoption Act 1976, s. 72 (1)).

[4] A child, except where used to express a relationship, means a person who has not attained the age of 18; see *ibid*.

[5] Defined in s. 107 (1): (Adoption Act 1976, s. 72 (1)); see para. [**48**], *post*.

[6] See *paras*. [**19**]–[**31**], *post*.

[7] Rec. 2.

[8] Rec. 3.

[9] S. 1 (4); (Adoption Act 1976, s. 1 (4)). As at May 1976 the number of local authorities in England and Wales not acting as adoption agencies was 26. There were 58 adoption societies in England and 8 in Scotland.

[10] S. 1 (2); (Adoption Act 1976, s. 1 (2)).

to be provided as part of a service is counselling for persons with problems relating to adoption. This will include those refused an adoption order. An adoptive parent may also, for example, wish to avail himself of this facility in the immediate post-adoption period, if problems over the upbringing of the child should arise.[1] **[14]**

Wide though the potential scope may be, the Act gives no indication of the circumstances which would constitute a breach of the duty imposed by section 1. Nor does it enable the Secretary of State to make regulations or orders which will ensure fulfilment. The most it does is to empower him to cause an inquiry to be held into, *inter alia*, (a) the functions of the social services committee of a particular local authority, in so far as those functions relate to children and (b) the functions of a particular adoption agency.[2] Section 1 is skeletal in its terms. Apart from counselling, the only other facilities expressly mentioned which must be provided as part of an adoption service are (a) temporary board and lodging where needed by pregnant women, mothers or children and (b) arrangements for assessing children and prospective adopters and placing children for adoption.[3] What other facilities are to be regarded as "requisite" for the proper discharge of the general duty? The section is illustrative and not exhaustive. The Houghton Committee considered[4] that a comprehensive service "should comprise a social work service to natural parents, whether married or unmarried, seeking placement for a child (which would include channels of communication with related community resources); skills and facilities for the assessment of the parents' emotional resources, and their personal and social situation; short-term accommodation for unsupported mothers; general child care resources, including short-term placement facilities for children pending adoption placement; assessment facilities; adoption placement services; after-care for natural parents who need it; counselling for adoptive families. In addition, it should have access to a range of specialised services, such as medical services (including genetic, psychiatric and psychological assessment services, arrangements for the examination of children and adoptive applicants, and a medical adviser) and legal advisory services." Local authorities will find different answers and consequently standards will continue to vary from one area to another. What needs to be achieved is a minimum national standard. It is submitted that the Act will not ensure this except in so far as it controls adoption societies by its rules for approving them.[5] One is reminded of the variable efficacy of section 1 of the Children and Young Persons Act 1963.[6] Much will depend on the influence exerted by Departmental Circulars and the guidance offered to local authorities. **[15]**

The facilities for temporary board and lodging are discriminatory in that

---

[1] For counselling where an adopted person seeks a copy of his birth certificate after he ceases to be "a child" see s. 26; (Adoption Act 1976, s. 51); see paras. [**195**]–[**199**], *post*.

[2] S. 98; see para. [**429**], *post*.

[3] S. 1 (2); (Adoption Act 1976, s. 1 (2)). The placement of the child for adoption is perhaps the most important part of the adoption process. For restrictions on arranging adoption and placing of children see paras. [**108**]–[**110**], *post*.

[4] Para. 38. For a fuller description see *A Guide to Adoption Practice, Advisory Council on Child Care, No. 2* (1970) H.M.S.O. (London).

[5] See paras. [**19**]–[**31**], *post*.

[6] See para. [**18**], *post*.

they extend to mothers or children but not fathers. The restriction ignores the plight of motherless families which has been recognised recently by such bodies as the National Council for One Parent Families.[1] It is to be expected that this facility will be interpreted widely in accordance with the spirit of the section[2] and it is to be remembered that the facilities in subsection (2) are to be provided as part of the authority's adoption service and not for other purposes. [**16**]

A keynote of section 1 is the importance it attaches to co-operation. It is essential for an effective adoption service not only that there should develop a partnership between local authorities and approved adoption societies, but also that close links are maintained with departments of local and central government. Section 1 requires that the facilities of the service be provided in conjunction with the local authority's other social services and with the adoption societies in their area, so that help may be given in a co-ordinated manner, without duplication, omission or avoidable delay.[3] [**17**]

Section 2[4] defines "other social services" as those functions which are referred[5] to the local authority's social services committee. These include, e.g., support for homeless persons, but the section spells out particularly those relating to (a) the promotion of the welfare of children by diminishing the need to receive children into care or keep them in care, including (in exceptional circumstances) the giving of assistance in cash; (b) the welfare of children in the care of a local authority; (c) the welfare of children who are foster children within the meaning of the Children Act 1958; (d) children who are subject to supervision orders made in matrimonial proceedings; (e) the provision of residential accommodation for expectant mothers and young children and of day-care facilities; (f) the regulation and inspection of nurseries and child-minders; (g) care and other treatment of children through court proceedings and children's hearings. Each of these calls for brief comment.

(a) This deals with the powers under section 1 of the Children and Young Persons Act 1963 which requires a local authority "to make available such advice, guidance and assistance as may promote the welfare of children by diminishing the need to receive children into or keep them in care . . .". Assistance may be given in kind (e.g., food or clothing) or in exceptional circumstances in cash (e.g., to pay arrears of rent or fuel bills).[6] It may be given directly by the local authority or through voluntary organisations or "other persons". The most effective methods of advice may be through family advice centres or the individual social worker, depending upon the circumstances. The Seebohm Committee in its Report on Local Authority and Allied Personal Social Services[7] was "impressed by the amount of preventive work amongst families accomplished by children's departments since the Children and Young

---

[1] Formerly National Council for the Unmarried Mother and her Child. See Freeman, *The Children Act 1975*, 72/1–/2.

[2] See also s. 2 (*e*) and (*f*); (Adoption Act 1976, s. 2 (*e*) and (*f*)).

[3] S. 1. (3); (Adoption Act 1976, s. 1 (3)). See H.C.R., para. 37.

[4] Adoption Act 1976, s. 2.

[5] Under the Local Authority Social Services Act 1970, as amended by Children Act 1975, Sch. 3, para. 74 and Housing (Homeless Persons) Act 1977, s. 20 (2).

[6] For the growth in the numbers of applications for the various kinds of help available under s. 1 see Jordan, *Poor Parents, Social Policy and the Cycle of Deprivation*, pp. 87 *et seq.*

[7] Cmd. 3703.

Persons Act 1963";[1] but section 1 is wide in its terms and it seems that policies and practices of local authorities in giving effect to it vary considerably.[2]

(b) This refers to the general duty of a local authority under section 12 of the Children Act 1948, as amended by section 59 of the 1975 Act,[3] when reaching any decision relating to a child in their care to give first consideration to the need to safeguard and promote the child's welfare, subject to s. 12 (1A) and the Children and Young Persons Act 1969[4] which enable them and the Secretary of State to act inconsistently with those objects in order to protect members of the public; for example, by restricting the child's liberty in a community home. The powers conferred by the Acts of 1948, 1969 and 1975 are very wide, but the local authority should always subordinate them to their duty of trying to bring the period of care to an end if the child's welfare is likely to be best served in that way.[5] However, so long as he is in their care, their main specific duty is to provide accommodation and maintenance for him.

(c) The third function is concerned with private fostering. The Children Act 1958 as amended by the Children and Young Persons Act 1969[6] provides for the supervision of foster children by giving the local authority powers with regard to inspecting and controlling the use of premises as foster homes. For the purposes of the 1958 Act a foster child is widely defined as a child below the upper limit of the compulsory school age whose care and maintenance are undertaken by a person who is not a relative, guardian[7] or custodian.[8] The responsibility for ensuring the well being of foster children falls upon the local authority within whose area the children are,[9] and if they are to exercise their powers effectively it is obviously essential that they know which homes are being used for private fostering. A foster parent must give notice when he becomes, and when he ceases to be, a foster parent.[10] There are doubtless many informal fostering arrangements, however, where no such notification has occurred.[11]

(d) This refers to the fact that, in matrimonial proceedings in the Magistrates' Courts where custody is granted to an individual, the court can, in exceptional circumstances, order the child to be placed under the supervision of a local authority until he is 16.[12] There is a similar power of supervision on

---

[1] Para. 182.

[2] Research into the operation of the section has been undertaken by some University Departments of Social Administration. See, e.g., Heywood and Allen, *Financial Help in Social Work*. See also Stroud, *Services for Children and their Families*.

[3] See para. [**320**], *post*. The amendment has operated since 1st January 1976.

[4] S. 27 (3), as amended by the Children Act 1975, Sch. 3, para. 71 (*a*).

[5] See Bevan, *The Law Relating to Children*, pp. 156–157.

[6] Ss. 51–57 and Sch. 7. For further amendments by the Children Act 1975, see *infra*, n. 9.

[7] S. 2 (1), as amended by Children and Young Persons Act 1969, s. 52 (1) and Sch. 6.

[8] Children Act 1975, s. 108 and Sch. 3, para. 16.

[9] Children Act 1958, s. 1, as substituted by Children and Young Persons Act 1969, s. 51 and amended by Children Act 1975, s. 95, see paras. [**416**]–[**418**], *post*. See generally Bevan, *op. cit.*, pp. 380 *et seq.* and ss. 95–97, paras. [**416**]–[**419**], *post*.

[10] Children Act 1958, s. 3, as amended by Children and Young Persons Act 1969, s. 53. S. 96 of Children Act 1975 will enable provision to be made for similar notification by parents whose children are, or are going to be, fostered; see para. [**418**], *post*.

[11] See Holman, *Trading in Children, A study of private fostering*.

[12] Matrimonial Proceedings (Magistrates' Courts) Act 1960, s. 2 (1) (*f*).

the granting of a decree of divorce, nullity or judicial separation.[1]

(e) A local authority, through their social services department, must make arrangements for the care of expectant and nursing mothers and for children under 5 who are not attending primary schools.[2] The welfare clinic is one kind of arrangement. The day nursery is another, but the day care of children is mainly provided in local authority nursery schools and nursery classes in infants' schools under the Education Act 1944 or, much more frequently, in private day nurseries or by child minders.

(f) This refers to the Nurseries and Child-minders Regulation Act 1948, which controls private nurseries and child minders. The Health Services and Public Health Act 1968 amended the earlier Act and attempts to remove some of its deficiencies, but it fails to solve the problem of securing effective registration. By the Local Authority Social Services Act 1970[3] the responsibility for registration and inspection was transferred from the local health authority to the social services department of the local authority, who may refuse registration or allow it subject to conditions.[4]

(g) This relates to care and treatment resulting from proceedings under Part I of the Children and Young Persons Act 1969.

By particularising in this way, the Act stresses that adoption should be seen in the context of a comprehensive child care service which itself should ensure that wherever possible children do not come into the care of local authorities unless it is in their interests to do so. **[18]**

APPROVAL OF ADOPTION SOCIETIES

Voluntary organisations[5] will, therefore, continue to play a significant part in the adoption service once they have been approved as an adoption society.[6] Responsibility for approval will be transferred from local to central government. The present defects are well known. Local authority approval is sometimes little more than a formality and has failed to impose adequate standards. Moreover, there has long been a widely held opinion that it is invidious to ask local authorities to exercise control over adoption societies when they themselves are acting as adoption agencies. **[19]**

---

[1] Matrimonial Causes Act 1973, s. 44, as amended by Children Act 1975, Sch. 3, para. 78. This amendment, which took effect on 1st January 1976, has the effect of extending the court's power to make supervision orders in divorce, nullity or judicial separation proceedings to cases where it has made a care and control order.

[2] National Health Service Act 1946, s. 22. These functions were transferred from local health authorities to social services departments by the Local Authority Social Services Act 1970, s. 2 and Sch. 1. See Bevan, *op. cit.*, pp. 390–391.

[3] S. 2 and Sch. 1, as amended by Children Act 1975, Sch. 3, para. 74.

[4] For a full consideration of registration and inspection see Bevan, *op. cit.*, pp. 391–393.

[5] For the meaning see s. 107 (1); (Adoption Act 1976, s. 72 (1)). For the year ending 31st March 1974 the number of children placed by local authorities in England and Wales is quoted by the Department of Health and Social Security as 3,703, although the figure is difficult to assess accurately and the Association of British Adoption and Fostering Agencies think the figure is approximately 2,630. The Association gives the number of placements by voluntary agencies in England and Wales as 3,557. These are latest known figures.

[6] This has the same meaning as in the 1958 Act (Adoption Act, 1976, s. 72 (1)), i.e., a body of persons whose functions consist of or include the making of arrangements for the adoption of children. An adoption agency is defined as a local authority or approved adoption society (s. 1 (4); Adoption Act 1976, s. 1 (4)). For transitional provisions see s. 108 (5).

Under the new power[1] the Secretary of State will have to take into account a number of specified matters in addition to any other relevant considerations.[2] These are (a) the applicant's adoption programme, including in particular its ability to make provision for children who are free for adoption,[3] (b) the number and qualifications of its staff, (c) its financial resources, and (d) the organisation and control of its operations. Adoption societies existing when the new procedure comes into operation will have to apply for approval, as well as bodies wishing to act as adoption societies. In the case of applications by existing societies the Secretary of State will also have to pay regard to the applicant society's record and reputation in the adoption field and the areas within which it is operating or has operated. Similarly, these will be relevant matters whenever thereafter an approved society seeks further approval.[4] [**20**]

In one kind of situation a local authority will, to some extent, still be involved in approval. Where the applicant is a society which is likely to operate extensively within the area of that authority, the authority must be asked by the Secretary of State whether or not it supports the application.[5] This requirement is eminently desirable, because the authority will have a far clearer appreciation of the needs and resources of its own area than will the Secretary of State, particularly in view of the duty of the authority to ensure that an effective adoption service is being provided in its area. [**21**]

If, after considering the application, the Secretary of State gives his approval, he will serve a written notice to that effect on the society. The notice will be effective from a date specified therein or, in the case of a renewal, from the date of the notice.[6] If the Secretary of State is not satisfied that the society is making, or is likely to make, an effective contribution to the Adoption Service, he must give it written notice that he intends to refuse approval, setting out his reasons therefor and informing it of its right to make written representations to him within twenty-eight days. He must then take into account any such representations before reaching his final decision.[7] If he still decides to refuse approval for reasons already communicated, no further notice of proposed refusal must be served,[8] and he must then give notice that the application is refused in accordance with section 4 (6). [**22**]

Continuing central control is ensured by the rule that, unless withdrawn earlier, approval is for a period of three years, when fresh approval has to be sought.[9] Approval can be withdrawn at any time if it appears to the Secretary

---

[1] See s. 4; (Adoption Act 1976, s. 3).

[2] Sub-s. (2) and (3); see H.C.R., Rec. 8.

[3] On freeing for adoption see Chap. 5, *post*.

[4] Sub-s. (1) and (5); (Adoption Act 1976, s. 3 (1) and (5)).
The Secretary of State is empowered to make regulations relating to an approved society's exercise of its functions; see Sch. 3, para. 27 (*a*); (Adoption Act 1976, s. 9 (2)).

[5] Sub-s. (4); (Adoption Act 1976, s. 3 (4)).

[6] Sub-s. (2); (Adoption Act 1976, s. 3 (2)).

[7] S. 6 (1) and (2); (Adoption Act 1976, s. 5 (1) and (2)).

[8] S. 6 (5); (Adoption Act 1976, s. 5 (5)). The subsection is not very elegantly worded. Its effect is that a further notice informing the applicant of proposed refusal is necessary where (i) no representations have been made by the society or (ii) there are such representations and in the light of them there are new reasons for the refusal.

[9] S. 4 (7); (Adoption Act 1976, s. 3 (7)); see H.C.R., Rec. 6. If the reapplication is pending at the time the earlier approval would otherwise expire, approval will continue until the reapplication is granted or refused.

of State[1] that the society is not making an effective contribution to the Adoption Service, or if it fails to provide him with, or to verify, the information necessary to determine whether or not it is making the requisite contribution.[2] The rules governing the giving of notice of refusal of approval apply *mutatis mutandis* to notices of withdrawal of approval.[3] [**23**]

The most important practical problem created by the withdrawal of approval of a society will be the question of the welfare of the children in its care. It is vital that the best possible alternative arrangements be made as quickly as possible. The Act merely provides, however, that on withdrawal of approval the Secretary of State may direct the society to make such arrangements concerning the children and such other transitional matters as seem to him expedient.[4] One might have expected a duty to have been imposed rather than a discretion granted. [**24**]

Whether or not approval has been withdrawn from a society, if it appears to the Secretary of State that it is inactive or defunct, he may direct an appropriate local authority to take any action which the society could have taken, whether acting alone or with the local authority.[5] Thus the authority could apply to a court for an order freeing the child for adoption,[6] thus vesting parental rights and duties in the authority, or apply to a court for an order transferring such rights which were vested in the society under a section 14 order.[7] As with section 5 (3), no duty is imposed on the Secretary of State, merely a discretion granted. When is a society inactive or defunct? A defunct society is presumably one which has ceased to exist and an inactive society one which still exists but ceases to operate. There could therefore be a society from which approval has been withdrawn but which is neither defunct nor inactive, in which case the Secretary of State would have to rely on his powers under section 5 (3). [**25**]

Section 7 is likely to be most useful in respect of a society from which approval has not been withdrawn. Where approval has been withdrawn under section 5 it will be leaving matters too late for action to be taken after withdrawal and such action ought to have been taken on withdrawal. In such cases the children are most likely to have been taken into the care of the local authority. The duty to meet the needs of such children will revert to the local authority under the general duty imposed by section 1, as the requisite facilities in respect of the children will no longer be provided by an approved adoption society. [**26**]

Before directing the local authority under section 7 (1) the Secretary of State must, if practicable, consult both the society and the authority.[8] He is under a duty to do no more than consult and, unlike a case of refusal to approve or withdrawal of approval,[9] the society does not have the right to make repre-

---

[1] The decision is therefore an executive one and the test is subjective.
[2] S. 5 (1) and (2); (Adoption Act 1976, s. 4); see H.C.R., Rec. 7.
[3] See ss. 5 (1) and 6 (3)–(5); (Adoption Act 1976, ss. 4 (1) and 5 (3)–(5)).
[4] S. 5 (3); (Adoption Act 1976, s. 4 (3)).
[5] S. 7 (1); (Adoption Act 1976, s. 8).
[6] On freeing for adoption see Chap. 5, *post*.
[7] On transfer of parental rights and duties see s. 23; (Adoption Act 1976, s. 21). Such a transfer can normally only be made on the joint application of the transferor and the transferee.
[8] S. 7 (2); (Adoption Act 1976, s. 8 (2)).
[9] On refusal to approve and withdrawal of approval see s. 6, paras. [**22**]–[**23**], *ante*. The Secretary of State must state his reasons for the refusal or withdrawal.

sentations to him. The justification for this is that the power under section 7 is for emergency situations where the need to make new arrangements for the children's care is urgent.[1] If the need is so urgent that, even to consult the society and authority would be prejudicial to the children's welfare, the Secretary of State on the ground of impracticability need not do so. **[27]**

By consulting the local authority an opportunity is given to it, if it sees fit, to make some financial arrangement with the society in order to maintain the society's contribution to the adoption service within its area and to promote the welfare of children by diminishing the need to receive them into care.[2] **[28]**

There is no right of appeal against refusal to approve or withdrawal of approval under sections 4 to 6 or against a direction under section 7. The only means of redress will be to seek an order of mandamus or certiorari. **[29]**

The new rules for approval may well lead to the eventual disappearance of unincorporated bodies as adoption societies because the Secretary of State is empowered to make regulations prohibiting them from applying for approval under section 4.[3] **[30]**

The rules do not extend to local authorities. They will be covered by the overall responsibility which the Secretary of State has over them. Whilst it is not suggested that they will have the difficulty that some voluntary adoption societies might have in meeting the requirements, some form of scrutiny would have been useful to ensure that standards are being met and maintained. **[31]**

---

[1] H.C. Official Report, 1975, Standing Committee A (Third Sitting), cols. 119–120 (Dr. David Owen).

[2] See s. 2 (*a*), para. [**18**], *ante*. The giving of assistance in cash is limited to exceptional cases. Arguably cases under s. 7 are only likely to arise in exceptional circumstances.

[3] See Sch. 3, para. 27 (*a*); (Adoption Act 1976, s. 9 (1)).

CHAPTER 3

THE WELFARE OF THE CHILD

THE RATIONALE OF SECTION 3

One of the inadequacies of the former law was its failure to provide positive guidance on the weight to be given to the child's welfare when reaching decisions which might ultimately lead to his adoption. The Adoption Act 1958 merely stated that, when deciding whether or not to make an adoption order, the court had to be satisfied that the adoption would be for the welfare of the child.[1] In particular, the Act was silent on the importance to be attached to his welfare when the court was considering whether or not to dispense with the parent's consent to the making of an adoption on the ground that it was unreasonably being withheld. Consequently, it was left to the courts to try to solve that vexed problem. The judicial solution played a crucial part in the enactment of the new provision, a "keynote section"[2] in the law governing adoption. [**32**]

Section 3 provides:[3]

> "In reaching any decision relating to the adoption of a child, a court or adoption agency shall have regard to all the circumstances, first consideration being given to the need to safeguard and promote the welfare of the child throughout his childhood; and shall so far as practicable ascertain the wishes and feelings of the child regarding the decision and give due consideration to them, having regard to his age and understanding."

The test of "first consideration" is a compromise between the Government's original proposal requiring "full account" to be taken of the need to safeguard and promote the child's welfare and the view that, as in custody and guardianship matters, his welfare should be the "first and paramount consideration".[4] The weakness of the former of these alternatives is that it tends to beg the question.

> "I venture to regard the guidance given in Clause 2 as it stands as being of very little assistance to the courts and very little protection to the child. All courts are presumed to take full account of every fact which is relevant in the hearing of a case. Indeed, if they fail to take full account of a matter which is relevant it might, in certain circumstances, be a ground of appeal. To invite courts or adoption agencies simply to take full account of the need

---

[1] S. 7 (1) (*b*). In *Re G. (D.M.) (an infant)*, [1962] 2 All E.R. 546, Pennycuick J. thought that the principles regarding the welfare of children acted on by the court in guardianship and custody cases appeared to be equally applicable to adoption.

[2] H.L. Official Report, 1975 Vol. 356, No. 32, col. 18 (Second Reading; The Lord Chancellor.)

[3] Adoption Act 1976, s. 6.

[4] See Guardianship of Minors Act 1971, s. 1.

to safeguard and promote the welfare of the child is doing no more than to remind the courts that they are not to forget that the welfare of the child is one of the issues that they are considering."[1]

The essential reason advanced for the rejection of the paramountcy test was that an adoption order means the irrevocable severance of the tie between the child and the natural parent. Its finality therefore justifies special weight being given to the interests of the natural parent. It is respectfully submitted that this outright rejection of paramountcy was based upon misconceived Parliamentary reasoning and an excessive significance attributed to the case law governing the dispensation of parental consent where it is being unreasonably withheld. [**33**]

This matter, more than most concerning the parent–child relationship, demonstrates plainly the futility of trying to maintain a fair balance between their conflicting interests. It took the courts two decades to try to come to terms with this reality. It took the Houghton Committee a lot of heart-searching before it reached an agreed suggested solution. [**34**]

The position by the beginning of 1970 was that in deciding whether or not a parent is unreasonably withholding consent the primary consideration was the parent's attitude to the child's welfare and that attitude had to be tested by what a reasonable parent would do in all the circumstances of the case.[2] Moreover, "a reasonable mother surely gives great weight to what is better for the child. Her anguish of mind is quite understandable; but still it may be unreasonable for her to withhold consent."[3] These rules laid down by the Court of Appeal suffered a setback in 1970 when in *Re W.* (*an infant*)[4] the Court held that parental conduct could only be unreasonable if there were some element of culpability. This ruling proved to be only temporary, but it came inopportunely because the conflicting decisions of the Court of Appeal left the Houghton Committee in doubt about the extent to which the child's welfare was to be taken into account in applying the test of unreasonableness on the parent's part. If the test was one of culpability, it weighed heavily against the child, and it seems that it was this consideration which led the Committee in its Working Paper to propose that the interpretation of what was reasonable or unreasonable should be made subject to the principle that the child's welfare was the first and paramount consideration. Then the House of Lords resolved the judicial conflict in favour of the earlier view and affirmed the principle that a parent may be acting unreasonably even if there is no element of culpability or of reprehensible conduct in his decision to withhold consent.[5] [**35**]

In the light of this decision and that of the House in *O'Connor* v. *A. and B.*[6]

---

[1] H.L. Official Report, 1975, Vol. 357, No. 54, cols. 1057–1058 (Report Stage; Lord Wigoder).

For the view of the Parliamentary draftsman on the background to the enactment of s. 3 see Bennion, "*First Consideration*": *A Cautionary Tale*, 126 New Law Jo. 1237.

[2] *Re L.* (*an infant*) (1962), 106 Sol. Jo. 611 (C.A.); *Re C.* (L.) (*an infant*), [1965] 2 Q.B. 449; [1964] 3 All E.R. 483 (C.A.). For the earlier judicial approach see Bevan, *op. cit.*, pp. 342–343.

[3] *Per* Lord Denning M.R. in *Re L.* (*an infant*), *supra.*

[4] [1970] 2 Q.B. 589; [1970] 3 All E.R. 990.

[5] *Re W.* (*an infant*), [1971] A.C. 682; [1971] 2 All E.R. 49.

[6] [1971] 2 All E.R. 1230; [1971] 1 W.L.R. 1227.

the Committee changed their mind on the paramountcy principle and recommended[1] that statutory effect be given to the line followed by the House of Lords, namely, to accept the objective test of parental reasonableness and, in applying it, to have regard to all the circumstances giving first but not paramount consideration to the effect of the parent's decision on the long-term welfare of the child. The Committee was much impressed by Lord Reid's reasoning in *O'Connor* v. *A. and B.*[2]

> "The test is an objective test—would a reasonable parent have withheld consent? I think that a reasonable parent or, indeed, any other reasonable person would have in mind the interests or claims of all three parties concerned—the child, the parents and the adopting family. No doubt the child's interests come first and in some cases they may be paramount. But I see no reason why the claims of the natural parent should be *ignored.*[3] If the mother were deeply attached to the child and had only consented in the first place to adoption because of adverse circumstances it would seem to me unjust that on a change of circumstances her affection for the child and her natural claim as a parent should be *ignored.*[3] And the adopting family cannot be *ignored*[3] either. If it was the mother's action that brought them in, in the first place, they ought not to be displaced without good reason."

Yet, if the paramountcy principle were accepted, none of these other claims would need to be ignored. It has always been possible when giving effect to that principle in custody cases to take account of other interests and this remains so, notwithstanding the recent ruling of the Court of Appeal that the court must not balance the welfare of the child against the wishes and interests of a parent or against the justice of the case as between the parents.[4] Although those interests must yield to those of the child, they are still a factor to be put into the scales in applying the paramountcy test, as formulated by Lord MacDermott in *J.* v. *C.*[5] However, the difference of emphasis between "first consideration" and "first and paramount consideration" was indicated by Lord Reid in the same passage:[6]

> "So, to balance these claims is no easy task. Often no ideal solution is possible. We are dealing largely with future probabilities, for the decision once made is irrevocable. So, we cannot be certain what will be in the child's interests in the long run. That seems to me to be an additional reason for giving considerable weight in proper cases to the claims of the natural parents and of the adopting family."

---

[1] Rec. 51.

[2] [1971] 2 All E.R. at p. 1232; [1971] 1 W.L.R. at pp. 1229–1230.

[3] Authors' italics.

[4] *Re K. (minors)*, [1977] Fam. 179; [1977] 1 All E.R. 647; *S.(B.D.)* v *S.(D.J.)*, [1977] Fam. 109; [1977] 1 All E.R. 656. See also *B.* v. *B.* (1975), 119 Sol. Jo. 610 (C.A.).

[5] See para. [**41**], *post*.

It was in the light of this formulation that the Court of Appeal refused to follow its earlier decision in *Re L.*, [1962] 3 All E.R. 1; [1962] 1 W.L.R. 886, in which the claims of the parent who was found not to be responsible for the break-up of the matrimonial home were allowed to prevail.

[6] [1971] 2 All E.R. at p. 1232; [1971] 1 W.L.R. at p. 1230.

The paramountcy principle would ensure that in all cases the balance was "considerably weighted" in the child's favour. [**36**]

However, in the light of debate within and outside Parliament, it seems that the test prescribed by section 3 would command wide support in those cases where a parent is unwilling to agree to adoption. Moreover, the test accords with the increasing recognition of the need to strengthen, where possible, the natural family unit. Nevertheless, it by no means follows that the paramountcy principle should have been totally rejected. On the contrary, the Parliamentary discussion of the relevant clause was almost wholly influenced by judicial decisions concerned with circumstances which form a very small minority of cases.[1] It was too readily assumed that the law of adoption necessarily involves conflicting interests. A parent who, after full advice on the effects of adoption and with full consideration of the consequences, decides to allow his or her child to be adopted no longer sees it as a conflict of interests. The argument about conflict is overstated. In practice a much higher degree of conflict is involved in custody cases. [**37**]

In one respect section 3 is to be welcomed, because for the first time it lays down a directive not only for the courts but also for adoption agencies. Yet, this extension pinpoints the inherent weakness of a formula which makes the child's welfare the first consideration at all stages of decision making in the process leading to adoption. Indeed, at the initial stage the whole emphasis of the agency's role should be on ensuring that the rights of the natural parent are properly safeguarded. Under the present law the agency has certain responsibilities to him before the child is placed for adoption. It must see that he is given a memorandum explaining in ordinary language the effect of adoption on his parental rights and calling attention to the process which culminates in the making of the adoption order and to the statutory provisions relating to parental consent or, as the 1975 Act now calls it, agreement. The parent must then sign a certificate to the effect that he has read and understood the memorandum.[2] Any written agreement to adoption given at the time is, of course, not strictly binding since the parent can change his mind up to the hearing of the application, unless the court dispenses with his agreement. It has, however, recently been stressed by the Court of Appeal[3] that once the parent has given formal agreement it becomes progressively more difficult for him to show that his change of mind is reasonable. All the more reason therefore that the memorandum should explicitly point out the possible effect of the passage of time. This method of giving agreement to the making of an adoption order continues under the new law, but there will be the alternative procedure of freeing for adoption before there has been placement of the child.[4] Similarly here the agency ought to have firm responsibilities to the natural parent to see that he fully understands the effect of agreeing to the child's being freed for adoption. The Act is defective in failing specifically to impose these obligations. For this

---

[1] See Grey and Blunden, *A Survey of Adoption in Great Britain* (1971), showing that only in 2% of applications by non-relatives was there a request to dispense with consent (quoted in H.C.R., para. 167).

[2] Adoption Agencies Regulations 1976, reg. 7 (*a*) and Sch. 3.

[3] In *Re H.*, [1977] 2 All E.R. 339; [1977] 1 W.L.R. 471.

[4] See Chap. 5, *post*.

reason the role of the reporting officer is of immense importance[1] and it is equally to be regretted that the Act is not explicit about his obligations, leaving it to rules to prescribe his detailed functions.[2] It is to be hoped that the rules will (1) require him to see that the parent understands the consequences of giving agreement, and (2) make it obligatory for him to be appointed before, or on receipt of, the application for adoption or, as the case may be, freeing for adoption.[3] [**38**]

Once the parent's provisional agreement to adoption or agreement to freeing for adoption has been given,[4] then in caring for the child until placement, in choosing the placement and in the exercise of its subsequent functions the agency should be concerned solely with doing what is best for the child. During these stages in the process it is not concerned with any posslble conflict between the welfare of the child and the interests of the parent. For example, even if the parent should, in accordance with the existing procedure, change his mind over agreeing to an adoption order, that is a problem which the court will have to deal with when hearing the adoption application. So, as far as the agency is concerned, no question arises of the child's welfare merely being given priority as the first consideration. It is to be treated as paramount. The Act[5] accepts that in custodianship proceedings[6] the local authority must apply the paramountcy test when investigating the matters on which it is required to report to the court. It is difficult to see how any other test can be appropriate where an adoption agency is investigating before and after placement and the parent is willing for the child to be adopted. The respective objects of the local authority and the adoption agency are, it is submitted, the same, namely, to regard the child's interests as paramount when trying to determine whether or not the prospective custodians or the prospective adopters are persons likely to promote and protect those interests. The Act should have recognised this reality. [**39**]

Apart from the question of parental agreement, the recurrent theme throughout the Houghton Report was that the long-term welfare of the child must be the first and paramount consideration. This ought to have been accepted by the Act as the general principle in adoption law but made subject to the rule that his welfare was not paramount (a) where the parent's agreement is in issue, i.e., where the court has to decide whether or not to dispense with it under section 12 or section 14 of the Act, and (b) where the parent is applying for revocation of an order freeing the child for adoption.[7] The existence of the two tests would have had the further advantage of emphasising the distinction between them. Support for section 3 revealed contradictory reasoning. It was asserted that there was only "a very fine distinction".[8] Admittedly, "it is impossible to find

---

[1] For reporting officers see paras. [**127**]–[**128**], *post.*

[2] S. 20 (1) (*b*); (Adoption Act 1976, s. 65 (1) (*b*)). S. 20 is not yet operative.

[3] Cf. s. 20 (3).

[4] Or dispensed with by the court; see s. 14, paras. [**60**]–[**72**], *post*; (Adoption Act 1976, s. 18).

[5] S. 33 (9).

[6] Chaps. 9 and 10, *post.*

[7] S. 16, paras. [**76**]–[**83**], *post*; (Adoption Act 1976, s. 20).

[8] H.C. Official Report, 1975, Vol. 893, No. 142, col. 1826 (Second Reading; Dr David Owen).

a form of words which calibrates and quantifies in exact terms",[1] but, if the distinction were only very fine, it is difficult to see how the test of first consideration could fulfil the object which inspired section 3, namely, to give proper emphasis to the interests of the parent. [**40**]

THE SCOPE OF THE TEST OF FIRST CONSIDERATION

The distinction between the two tests was explained by Lord MacDermott in the following well-known passage in *J.* v. *C.*[2]

> "The second question of construction is as to the scope and meaning of the words '... shall regard the welfare of the infant as the first and paramount consideration.' Reading these words in their ordinary significance and relating them to the various classes of proceedings which the section has already mentioned, it seems to me that they must mean more than that the child's welfare is to be treated as the top item in a list of items relevant to the matter in question. I think they connote a process whereby, when all the relevant facts, relationships, claims and wishes of parents, risks, choices and other circumstances are taken into account and weighed, the course to be followed will be that which is most in the interests of the child's welfare as that term has now to be understood. That is the first consideration because it is of first importance and the paramount consideration because it rules upon or determines the course to be followed . . ."

The distinction has been put extra-judicially in a different way but in one which, it is respectfully submitted, distils the essence of Lord MacDermott's *dictum* in relation to those cases of possible conflict of interests of the parent and child and which also gives some practical guidance to the different kinds of persons involved in administering adoption law. "First and paramount" means that "when there is any conflict the considerations of the parents should not be excluded but the welfare of the child is to prevail"; it must "overweigh all other considerations". The test of "first consideration" "merely directs the court, welfare officer or local authority to consider specifically the welfare of the child and to give its welfare greater weight; but it does not say it must prevail over other considerations".[3] [**41**]

Although Lord MacDermott's *dictum* was directly related to the application of section 1 of the Guardianship of Infants Act 1925[4] to a custody issue, it was held in *In re B.* (*an infant*) (*Adoption: Parental Consent*)[5] that the expression "first consideration" in section 3 of the 1975 Act was to be construed in the sense Lord MacDermott declared. That case was concerned with the possible effect of section 3 on the power to dispense with parental agreement because it was being unreasonably withheld. The House of Lords had already established

---

[1] H.C. Official Report, 1975, Standing Committee A (Second Sitting), col. 82 (Dr. David Owen).

[2] [1970] A.C. 668, 710; [1969] 1 All E.R. 788, 820–821.

[3] Lord Simon of Glaisdale. See respectively H. L. Official Report, 1975, Vol. 356, No. 40, col. 793 (Committee); 1975, Vol. 357, No. 54, col. 1061 (Report Stage); 1975 Vol. 359, No. 76, col. 544 (Third Reading).

[4] Now Guardianship of Minors Act 1971, s. 1.

[5] [1976] Fam. 161; [1976] 3 All E.R. 124.

that that power did not entitle the court to substitute its own view for that of the parent. The question was whether or not the parent is being unreasonable, "whether [his] veto comes within the band of possible reasonable decisions and not whether it is right or mistaken".[1] It was argued in *Re B.* that section 3 has not changed the law laid down by the House of Lords because it does not impose any new duty on the parent, who has only to be reasonable. That argument was rejected by Cumming-Bruce J. on the ground that, in making an objective appraisal of the reasonableness of the parent, the section had changed the law since the court had now to regard the child's welfare as the first consideration when weighing the conflicting factors to be taken into account. In *Re P.*,[2] on the other hand, the Court of Appeal, disapproving of *Re B.*, accepted that argument. Section 3 had not changed the relevant law because the section bore no relevance to it. The section related to decisions of courts and adoption agencies and not to a decision whether a parent was withholding agreement unreasonably. The requirements governing agreement or dispensing with it were not factors in the exercise of the court's discretion to make or refuse an adoption order, but conditions precedent to the exercise of the discretion. It is respectfully submitted that this conclusion is difficult to reconcile with the wording of the section which refers to *any* decision relating to adoption reached by a court or agency. It is the court which has to decide whether the parental agreement can be dispensed with on the ground of its being unreasonably withheld. The correct explanation of section 3, it is submitted, is that it is declaratory of the law formulated in *Re W.* (*an infant*) and *O'Connor* v. *A. and B.* and that in applying the objective test the reasonable mother would give first consideration to her child's welfare.[3] Otherwise, if the reasoning of the Court of Appeal is valid, it leads to the strange consequence that the section does not apply to the matter (i.e., unreasonably withholding parental agreement) which was the very source of its own enactment. **[42]**

In submitting that section 3 is declaratory it must be stressed that this is its effect in relation to unreasonably withholding parental agreement, but, as pointed out at the beginning of this chapter, in all other respects it is to be regarded as amending the former general provision relating to the welfare of the child. **[43]**

Since the first consideration must be the need to safeguard and promote the welfare of the child throughout his childhood, the investigations by the adoption agency before and during placement should be wide ranging and the maximum relevant evidence should be adduced to assist the court in making its orders.[4]

---

1 *Per* Lord Hailsham L.C. in *Re W.*, [1971] A.C. 682, 700; [1971] 2 All E.R. 49, 56.

2 [1977] Fam. 25; [1977] 1 All E.R. 182. So too *Re S.* (1976), 120 Sol. Jo. 819.

3 In *O'Connor* v. *A. and B.*, [1971] 2 All E.R. at p. 1232; [1971] 1 W.L.R. at p. 1230, Lord Reid said "*No doubt the child's interests come first* and in some cases may be paramount." (Italics supplied.)

In *Re P.*, Ormrod L.J. concluded ([1977] 1 All E.R. at p. 191) that s. 3 "does apply to the decision to dispense with consent, but I do not think it materially alters the law as it stood before it came into force". In *Re D.*, [1977] 1 All E.R. 145 at p. 161, Lord Simon of Glaisdale expressed the view, *obiter*, that the section was "no more than elucidatory and confirmatory of the pre-existing law".

4 "We cannot be certain what will be in the child's interests in the long run." (*Per* Lord Reid in *O'Connor* v. *A. and B.*, [1971] 2 All E.R. at p. 1232.)

"... One must look at the whole future of the child; not to mere temporary unhappiness or grief, however acute, if it is transient; not to mere material affluence in childhood or a better chance, through educational advantages, to achieve affluence later."[1] **[44]**

The kinds of relevant matters may therefore be as varied as they are in custody cases. We do no more than indicate those which may have particular significance with regard to adoption.[2] Essentially they relate to "material and financial prospects, education, general surroundings, happiness, stability of home and the like".[3] Specifically they include:

(1) *The comparative character and conduct of the parent and the prospective adopter, including past conduct towards other children as well as the child to be adopted.*[4] Conduct has special relevance when considering whether to dispense with parental agreement.[5]

(2) *The strength of the natural tie between the father and mother and the child.* Regard should be given to this "not on the basis that the person concerned has a claim which he has a right to have satisfied, but only if, and to the extent that, the conclusion can be drawn that the child will benefit from the recognition of this tie".[6] Parliamentary discussion of the Children Bill showed how sharply opinion can be divided on the likely benefit. Problems over the natural tie have become more frequent ever since the putative father's right to claim custody was strengthened,[7] and the tie may lead to a custody order in his favour and the refusal of an adoption order.[8] *Prima facie*, however, since an adoption order legitimises an illegitimate child,[9] an order should be made if the natural father has nothing to offer the child in comparison,[10] even if it should mean depriving him of a present right of access.[11]

---

[1] *Per* Diplock L.J. in *Re C.* (*L.*), [1965] 2 Q.B. 449, 471; [1964] 3 All E.R. 483, 495.

[2] The reader is referred to textbooks on custody and adoption; see, e.g., Bromley, *Family Law*, (5th Edn.), Chap. 10; Cretney, *Principles of Family Law* (2nd Edn.), pp. 361–368 and pp. 397–399; Freeman, *op. cit.*, 72/3; Bevan, *op. cit.*, Chaps. 9 and 10.

[3] *Per* Davies L.J. in *Re B.*, [1971] 1 Q.B. 437, 443; [1970] 3 All E.R. 1008.

[4] In *Re G.* (*D.M.*) (*an infant*), [1962] 2 All E.R. 546, it was held that it was not always detrimental to a child to be adopted by a person who has been convicted of indecent assault, but it has been doubted whether "in the changed atmosphere of today that view would be followed"; Freeman, *op. cit.*, 72/3.

[5] See Chap. 4, *post*.

[6] *Per* Wilberforce J. in *Re Adoption Application No. 41/61* (*No. 2*), [1964] Ch. at p. 53; [1963] 2 All E.R. at p. 1085. See also Lord Denning M.R. in *Re O.* (*an infant*), [1965] Ch. 23 at p. 28; [1964] 1 All E.R. 786 at pp. 788–789.

[7] By the Legitimacy Act 1959; see now the Guardianship of Minors Act 1971, ss. 9 and 14.

[8] *Re C.* (*M.A.*), [1966] 1 All E.R. 838; [1966] 1 W.L.R. 646 (C.A.), which was much criticised on the ground of undue emphasis of the blood-tie.

[9] It is now expressly enacted that an adopted child is not illegitimate; Children Act 1975, Sch. 1, para. 3 (3); (Adoption Act 1976, s. 39 (4)).

[10] *Re C.* (*an infant*) (1969), 113 Sol. Jo. 721 (C.A.). The natural father of a legitimate child may similarly have little or nothing to offer; *Re B.* (*a minor*), *S.* v. *B.* (1974), 4 Family Law 75.

[11] *Re E.* (*P.*) (*an infant*), [1969] 1 All E.R. 323; [1968] 1 W.L.R. 1913 (C.A.). The court may, however, feel when making an adoption order that, as an exceptional measure, continued or resumed access by the natural mother or father is in the child's best interests; *Re J.* (*Adoption Order: Conditions*), [1973] Fam. 106; [1973] 2 All E.R. 410; *Re S.* (*a minor*) (*Adoption Order: Access*), [1976] Fam. 1; [1975] 1 All E.R. 109.

(3) *Cultural, racial and religious factors.* The weight given to the respective cultural, racial and religious backgrounds of the natural parents and the applicants for adoption is very variable. Applications for adoption of coloured children are now more common, and in such cases the agency and the court should be particularly careful in satisfying themselves that the applicants appreciate the additional responsibilities and difficulties which absorption into a different cultural environment may create. This is a matter of special importance where the court is considering making an order under section 25 of the Act[1] when it is intended to adopt the child under a foreign law.[2] As for religious upbringing of the child, the 1975 Act requires an adoption agency when placing a child to have regard to the wishes of the parent on the subject,[3] but no longer can he impose conditions concerning it when agreeing to adoption or consenting to freeing for adoption. Only in exceptional circumstances is a court likely to regard this factor as decisive.[4]

(4) *Health of applicant and child.* Unlike its predecessor,[5] the 1975 Act does not expressly direct the court to take account of the health of the applicant, but the Adoption Rules provide for this and the child's health to be considered.[6] Medical evidence to show the risks arising from a change of parentage can be important but rarely decisive. There appears to have been some increase in the use of such evidence,[7] but its acceptance as a general rule has not gained judicial support.[8]

(5) *The wishes and feelings of the child.* The agency or the court "shall so far as practicable ascertain the wishes and feelings of the child regarding the decision and give due consideration to them, having regard to his age and understanding".[9] The practicability of ascertainment will depend much on the degree of skilled investigation. In this regard, with their available resources, the agency has an advantage over the court, particularly since eventually the appointment of a guardian *ad litem* is not likely to be obligatory in all adoption applications. What section 3 obviously intends, though does not say so accurately, is that the wishes and feelings of the child are to be taken into account

---

[1] Adoption Act 1976, s. 55.

[2] Compare wardship and custody cases where it is sought to take the child abroad; *Re L*, [1974] 1 All E.R. 913 (C.A.); *Re E.O.* (1973), *Times*, 16th February (C.A.); *Re O.* (1973), *Times*, 27th February (C.A.). For s. 25 see paras. [**165**]–[**171**], *post.*

[3] S. 13; (Adoption Act 1976, s. 7); see further, para. [**53**], *post.*

[4] Cf. *Re G. (an infant)*, [1962] 2 Q.B. 141; [1962] 2 All E.R. 173 (C.A.).

[5] Adoption Act 1958, s. 7 (2).

[6] Adoption (High Court) Rules 1976, r. 9; Adoption (County Court) Rules 1976, r. 8; Magistrates' Courts (Adoption) Rules 1976, r. 7. These respectively require an application for an adoption order to be accompanied by a medical certificate relating to the applicant's health and a medical report on the child, except where the applicant or one of them is the child's mother or father or where the child has reached the upper limit of the compulsory school age. *Quaere* the exceptions are justified in view of the general duty imposed on the court by s. 3 of the Act.

[7] See Michaels, *The Dangers of a Change of Parentage in Custody and Adoption Cases*, 83 L.Q.R. 547.

[8] See Lord Reid in *O'Connor* v. *A. and B.*, [1971] 2 All E.R. at p. 1232; [1971] 1 W.L.R. at p. 1230 (cited with apparent approval by Cumming-Bruce J. in *In Re B.*, [1976] 2 W.L.R. 755 at p. 759); Pearson L.J. in *Re C. (an infant)*, [1964] 3 All E.R. 483, 494; [1964] 3 W.L.R. 1041, 1054. For the view that there should be wider use of medical evidence see Bevan, *op. cit.*, p. 346.

[9] See formerly Adoption Act 1958, s. 7 (2).

before the decision is reached; but the agency or the court may test the child's reactions to a particular course of action which it has in mind. It by no means follows that effect will be given to them: the child's welfare may require otherwise. In custody cases the practice of interviewing a child varies considerably, but the Court of Appeal has recently held[1] that reliance ought not to be placed on an interview unless he is more than 8 years old. It may, however, be possible to ascertain his feelings, at least if he is younger. It is submitted that for the purpose of adoption the rule is too restrictive, given the terms of section 3. Moreover, it is to be noted that in adoption proceedings there are firmer rules about the attendance of the child. If the proceedings are in the Family Division he must be made a respondent:[2] if in the county court or juvenile court and the guardian *ad litem* reports that the child is able to understand the nature of adoption, he must be given an opportunity to express his wishes and feelings and his personal attendance is also normally required.[3] **[45]**

---

1 *Ingham* v. *Ingham* (1976), 73 Law Soc. Gaz. 486.
2 Adoption (High Court) Rules 1976, r. 4 (2).
3 Adoption (County Court) Rules 1976, rr. 14 and 16; Magistrates' Courts (Adoption) Rules 1976, rr. 13 and 15.

CHAPTER 4

AGREEMENT TO ADOPTION

One of the major changes in the Act relates to the granting of parental agreement to adoption. The past and present inadequacies of the law are well known. First, the agreement must be in relation to a specific application for adoption,[1] even though the identity of the applicants can be, and more often than not is, withheld from the parent. Secondly, the rule that the agreement must be operative at the moment when the adoption order is to be made (notwithstanding the fact that written consent usually has already been given)[2] may place a strain on the parent and encourage indecisiveness on his or her part. Correspondingly, it may create in the applicants the anxiety that agreement may be withdrawn, so that they may hesitate to give total commitment to the child. In turn the child's welfare is at risk since his future remains in doubt.[3] To help avoid these consequences the Act gives effect generally to the proposals of *Houghton*[4] that a new procedure be introduced enabling the parent to give his agreement at an early stage in the adoption process. Section 14[5] provides for a preliminary hearing at which the court can declare the child free for adoption, and, if it does, the parental rights and duties vest in the adoption agency until the adoption order is made. In spite of its defects the old procedure is retained as an alternative. It is dealt with hereunder. The new procedure, which is likely to become the normal practice, is examined in Chapter 5. It has not yet been brought into operation. [**46**]

In the absence, then, of an order freeing for adoption, an adoption order cannot be made unless the court is satisfied either (1) that each parent or guardian of the child freely, and with full understanding of what is involved, agrees unconditionally to the making of an order (whether or not he knows the identity of the applicants) or (2) that his agreement should be dispensed with on a ground specified in the Act.[6] [**47**]

---

[1] See Scrutton L.J. in *Re Carroll*, [1931] 1 K.B. 317, 329. The forms of agreement prescribed by the present Adoption Rules 1976 intend a specific applicant.

[2] *Re Hollyman*, [1945] 1 All E.R. 290 (C.A.); *Re F. (an infant)*, [1957] 1 All E.R. 819.

[3] H.C.R., para. 168.

[4] Recs. 37–45. There are, however, a number of detailed differences between the recommendations and the statutory provisions.

[5] Adoption Act 1976, s. 18.

[6] S. 12 (1); (Adoption Act 1976, s. 16 (1)). (Operative since 26th November 1976.)

AGREEMENT[1] OF THE PARENT OR GUARDIAN

This requirement substantially re-enacts the law but with certain significant amendments. For the purpose of adoption law the term "parent" is still not expressly defined, but by the normal rules of construction it means the father and mother of a legitimate child and the mother of an illegitimate child, and by statutory implication includes the adopter of an adopted child.[2] The putative father is not a parent,[3] but the Act now includes him as a guardian if he has custody of the child by virtue of an order under section 9 of the Guardianship of Minors Act 1971.[4] Apart from that special inclusion, a guardian has its commonest meaning, namely a person who has been appointed guardian by deed or will under the former provisions of the Guardianship of Infants Acts 1886 and 1925 or the present ones of the Guardianship of Minors Act 1971 or by a court of competent jurisdiction.[5] **[48]**

Under the Adoption Act 1958[6] the term "parent" did not include a local authority having the "powers and duties" of a parent by virtue of a care order[7] or having the parental "rights and powers" as the result of a resolution passed under section 2 of the Children Act 1948. The 1975 Act re-enacts the latter limitation[8] and extends it to a voluntary organisation in whom the parental rights and duties are vested under section 60 of the Act.[9] Thus, if the child is with foster parents, who, with the approval of the local authority or voluntary organisation, apply to adopt, the agreement of the parent or guardian is essential, unless it can be dispensed with on one of the specified grounds. It is far from clear why the rule relating to care orders has not correspondingly been re-enacted. Where adoption is sought in this kind of case, the 1976 Adoption Rules still provide for the parent or guardian to be notified of the application as in other adoption applications where the child has not already been freed for adoption,

---

[1] The Act substitutes "agreement" for "consent". In *Re B. (an infant) (Adoption: Parental Consent)*, [1976] 3 All E.R. at p. 127; [1976] 2 W.L.R. at p. 759, Cumming-Bruce J. stated that he was "not sensitive to the implication of that change of language". It seems that the Act wishes to distinguish between a person's agreeing to the making of an order and his consenting to an application for it; see s. 14 (1) and (2); (Adoption Act 1976, s. 18 (1) and (2)); and s. 33 (3). Nevertheless, it is difficult to see any intrinsic distinction.

[2] See cumulatively s. 8 (1) and Sch. 1, paras. 3 and 4; (Adoption Act 1976, ss. 12 (1), 39 and 41).

[3] *Re M. (an infant)*, [1955] 2 Q.B. 479; [1955] 2 All E.R. 911.

[4] Children Act 1975, s. 107 (1); (Adoption Act 1976, s. 72 (1)).

[5] *Ibid.* Nothing in the Act restricts or affects the jurisdiction of the High Court to appoint or remove guardians (Children Act 1975, s. 104).

[6] S. 4 (3) (*a*) and (*c*).

[7] Under the Children and Young Persons Act 1969, s. 24.

[8] See Children Act 1948, s. 2 (11), as substituted by Children Act 1975, s. 57 (operative since 26th November 1976).

The appropriate term is now "parental rights and duties", for the meaning of which see Chap. 9, *post*.

[9] On s. 60 see paras. [**357**]–[**360**], *post*. The section is not yet operative.

Rules under the new Act provide for the local authority or voluntary organisation to be notified of the hearing, as the former Adoption Rules provided in respect of local authorities. See Adoption (High Court) Rules 1976, r. 18 (*b*), (*c*) and (*d*); Adoption (County Court) Rules 1976, rr. 4 (2) (*b*), (*c*) and (*d*) and 12 (2); Magistrates' Courts (Adoption) Rules 1976, rr. 4 (2) (*b*), (*c*) and (*e*) and 11 (1) (*b*).

and when the application is heard the court will be likely to take account of any parental objection. However, the agreement of the parent or guardian or the dispensing with it on specified grounds will not be a *sine qua non* to the making of an adoption order. Subject to the general duty imposed by section 3, the court will have a wide discretion in the weight it gives to any parental objection. From the child's point of view his interests will be protected, because, if an adoption order is not made, the care order will remain in force; but that is not the point at issue. The same kind of home circumstances and parental conduct may justify the passing of a section 2 resolution or the making of a care order. Yet, ironically and illogically, in the one case the law does not automatically deprive the parent of his normal right to grant or to withhold his agreement to adoption, in the other it does. [**49**]

The putative father who is guardian will, of course, be entitled to be notified of the hearing of the adoption application. The 1976 Rules for notifying a putative father who is not a guardian correspond to those in the former Adoption Rules. If he is liable under an order or agreement to contribute to his child's maintenance, he must be notified.[1] If he is not so liable, the guardian *ad litem* is under no duty to seek him out,[2] but, if he does learn of anyone claiming to be the father who wishes to be heard by the court, he should inform it.[3] The court may then give notice.[4] It would seem that eventually this latter limited duty will be given to the reporting officer. [**50**]

The putative father can frustrate an adoption application, temporarily or sometimes permanently, by applying for an order for custody of the child.[5] It is therefore highly desirable, if possible, that his intentions be ascertained. There is, however, no provision on the application for an adoption order, as there is in the case of an application for an order freeing a child for adoption, that the court must satisfy itself that the putative father does not intend applying for custody or that if he did so apply the application would be likely to be refused.[6] If he does apply, it is desirable that the custody and adoption applications be heard together.[7] Strictly that should involve the court in the application of two standards, that of the paramountcy of the child's welfare in deciding whether to grant the father custody and that of the welfare being "first consideration" but not paramount in deciding whether to make an adoption order if custody to the father is refused. It is suggested that, since both issues in this context

---

[1] Adoption (High Court) Rules, r. 18 (*e*); Adoption (County Court) Rules, r. 4 (2) (*e*); Magistrates' Courts (Adoption) Rules, r. 4 (2) (*d*). In the case of High Court jurisdiction the registrar may be directed (presumably by the judge) not to notify any person who is liable to maintain the child.

[2] See Wilberforce J. in *Re Adoption Application No. 41/61* (*No. 2*), [1964] Ch. at p. 58; [1963] 2 All E.R. at p. 1088.

[3] Adoption (High Court) Rules, r. 13 (1) and Sch. 2, para. 10; Adoption (County Court) Rules, r. 11 (1) (*a*) and Sch. 2, para. 10 Magistrates' Courts (Adoption) Rules, r. 10 (1) (*a*) and Sch. 2, para. 10.

[4] See *ibid.*, rr. 18 (*j*), 4 (3) and 4 (3) respectively.

[5] Guardianship of Minors Act 1971, ss. 9 and 14; H.C.R., Rec. 47.

[6] S. 14 (8); (Adoption Act 1976, s. 18 (7)).

[7] See generally *Re Adoption Application No. 41/61*, [1962] 2 All E.R. 833; (on appeal), [1963] Ch. 315; [1962] 3 All E.R. 553; *Re C.* (*M.A.*) (*an infant*), [1966] 1 All E.R. 838 [1966] 1 W.L.R. 646 (C.A.).

are closely interrelated, the court will in practice determine them in the light of the paramountcy principle.[1] [**51**]

Because of the irrevocable and comprehensive effect of an adoption order, the agreement must be given freely and with full understanding of what is involved. Whereas this prerequisite has hitherto been implied,[2] it is now expressly enacted,[3] and in view of the positive wording it seems that the burden of satisfying the court will be on the applicants and not on the parent or guardian to prove otherwise. [**52**]

The parent or guardian must agree unconditionally. It is no longer possible to agree subject to any condition with respect to the religious upbringing of the child.[4] The former rule[5] was criticised on the grounds that (1) the control retained by the parent was anomalous in view of the virtually complete severance of the legal relationship between the parent or guardian and the child, (2) the condition could militate against the child's best interests in that the adopters may have been selected for their religious persuasion rather than their suitability as parents or there may have been considerable delay in the selection process, and (3) in any event it was unenforceable.[6] Yet, the removal of the condition met with strong opposition and by way of compromise section 13 provides that in placing a child for adoption the adoption agency must have regard (so far as it is practicable)[7] to any wishes of the parents or guardians about the child's religious upbringing. This positive direction is not given to the court, but the latter must, it is submitted, still take account of the parental wishes in accordance with its duty under section 3 "to have regard to all the circumstances", just as those wishes are considered in custody cases when the paramountcy principle is applied in accordance with section 1 of the Guardianship of Minors Act 1971. Under both sections effect will not be given to the wishes if to do so would be harmful to the child.[8] On the other hand the court may choose to include in the adoption order a condition concerning the child's religious upbringing,[9] although this is uncommon because of the practical difficulties of supervision and enforcement,[10] the appropriate methods being injunction or, preferably, making the child a ward of court.[11] It is suggested that the fact that the court

---

[1] This kind of case demonstrates the inadequacy of s. 3 of the Act (Adoption Act 1976, s. 6) where there is no issue over the giving or withholding of agreement by the parent or guardian; see Chap. 3, *ante*.

[2] Cf. *Re P. (an infant)* (1954), 118 J.P. 139.

[3] S. 12 (1) (*b*) (i); (Adoption Act 1976, s. 16 (1) (*b*) (i)).

[4] Children Act 1975, Sch. 4, Part III, partly repealing the Adoption Act 1958, s. 4 (2).

[5] The partial repeal and s. 13 have operated since 1st January 1976; see s. 108 (4) (*a*) and (*d*).

[6] H.C.R., paras 228–230; Rec. 55.

[7] Not the same as "reasonably practicable"; cf. *Marshall* v. *Gotham Co. Ltd.*, [1954] 1 All E.R. 937 at p. 942.

A parent who is anxious that effect be given to his wishes is advised to place his child with a voluntary adoption agency which is sympathetic to his religious views.

[8] *Re C. (an infant)* (1964), *The Times*, 1st August; *T.* v. *T.* (1974), 4 Fam. Law 190.

[9] In accordance with the general power to impose terms and conditions; see s. 8 (7); (Adoption Act 1976, s. 12 (6)); para. [*193*], *post*.

[10] See *Re G. (an infant)*, [1963] 2 Q.B. 73, 89; [1963] 1 All E.R. 20, 23, *per* Ormerod L.J.

[11] It is submitted that the parent or former guardian to whose wishes the court gave effect by imposing the condition would have sufficient interest to entitle him to institute wardship proceedings.

is contemplating the inclusion of such a condition should cast added doubts on the desirability of granting adoption to the applicants. [**53**]

An agreement will continue to be ineffective if given by the mother less than six weeks after the child's birth,[1] the purpose of this rule being to avoid the risk of the mother's succumbing to pressure (e.g., from her parents) to allow adoption before she has recovered from the child's birth. The Act also retains the rule that it is not necessary for the parent or guardian to know the identity of the applicants,[2] but it will no longer be the rule[3] that, if he agrees without knowing the identity and later withdraws his agreement for that reason alone, he is deemed to be unreasonably withholding it. [**54**]

DISPENSING WITH AGREEMENT

The grounds for dispensing with agreement are set out in section 12 (2),[4] which, subject to the addition of one new ground, re-enacts the previous law. The grounds are as follows:

(*a*) *The parent or guardian cannot be found or is incapable of giving agreement.* Agreement may only be dispensed with on this ground if the court is satisfied that either every reasonable step by reasonable means has been taken to trace the parent[5] or there are no practical means of communicating with him, because, for example, for political reasons it would be dangerous to him to try to do so.[6]

(*b*) *The parent or guardian is withholding his agreement unreasonably.* This ground has already been considered at length when examining the scope of section 3 of the Act,[7] and the conclusion was reached that in relation to it the section is declaratory of the earlier law. The enactment of section 3 will not remove the uncertainty to which this ground gives rise, but a decision such as that in *Re Application 41/74*[8] would, it is submitted, be the same if heard today. In that case the Court of Appeal refused to disturb the decision of a county court judge that the 25-year-old unmarried Indian mother of a 14-month-old girl had not in the circumstances unreasonably withheld her agreement to adoption. The girl was taken to foster parents ten days after birth and placed with the prospective adopters before she was 3 months old. The mother came

---

[1] S. 12 (4); (Adoption Act 1976, s. 16 (4)). S. 6 of the Adoption Act 1958 (which deals with evidence of parental agreement) will cease to have effect (Children Act 1975, Sch. 4, Part VIII), but it is expected that its provisions will be absorbed into Rules and that any written agreement given by the mother within the six-week period will, in accordance with s. 12 (4), be inadmissible.

[2] S. 12 (1) (*b*) (i); (Adoption Act 1976, s. 16 (1) (*b*) (i)).

[3] Adoption Act 1958, s. 5 (3).

[4] Adoption Act 1976, s. 16 (2).

[5] *Re C. (an infant)* (1957), *Times*, 2nd April (C.A.) *Re F. (R.) (an infant)*, [1970] 1 Q.B. 385; [1969] 3 All E.R. 1101 (C.A.). If an adoption order is made without all reasonable steps having been taken and the parent later comes forward, he may be given leave to appeal out of time, but the longer the delay in the application the less likely is it to be granted, since it may not be in the child's interests to set aside the order.

[6] *Re R. (adoption)*, [1966] 3 All E.R. 613.

[7] Chap. 3, *ante;* (Adoption Act 1976, s. 6).

[8] (1975) 5 Fam. Law 181.

to an early decision that she wanted her daughter back, firmly believing that this was best for the girl's long-term welfare.[1]

(*c*) *The parent or guardian has persistently failed without reasonable cause to discharge the parental duties in relation to the child.* In order to achieve uniformity of terminology in the Act the re-enactment of this ground is subject to the formal substitution of the words "parental duties",[2] for the expression "obligations of a parent or guardian". In *Re P.* (*infants*)[3] it was held that that expression must include:

> "first the natural and moral duty of a parent to show affection, care and interest towards the child; and secondly, as well, the common law or statutory duty of a parent to maintain his child in the financial or economic sense."

The most likely instances of this ground being successfully invoked are those where the child is in the care of a local authority either by virtue of a care order[4] or by a resolution of the authority[5] made because of parental failure in bringing up the child. Where the parent has directly parted with the child to the prospective adopters his conduct ought to be tested against the kind of criteria which are relevant to such care orders and resolutions.[6] The courts have shown some caution in relying on this ground. Thus, in *Re M.* (*an infant*)[7] it was held that failure to visit one's child after deliberately placing him for adoption does not *per se* constitute persistent failure to discharge one's parental duties. Indeed, this ruling is to be welcomed, for, as the Court of Appeal recognised, not visiting the child may well be best for him in the circumstances.[8] However, more recently the decision in *Re D.* (*minors*) (*Adoption by Parent*)[9] indicates a much firmer emphasis in favour of the parent or guardian. The word "persistently" was construed in the sense of permanently, so that the ground is not established unless it is shown that the parent or guardian washed his hands of the child.[10]

---

[1] For other recent cases where, it is submitted, the decision would have been the same if s. 3 (Adoption Act 1976, s. 6) had been operative, see *Re B.* (*a minor*): *S.* v. *B.* (1973), 4 Fam. Law. 75 (C.A.) *Re L.* (*an infant*) (1974), 5 Fam. Law 24 (C.A.) *Re B.* (*a minor*) (*Adoption by Parent*), [1975] Fam. 127 [1975] 2 All E.R. 449; *Re D.* (*an infant*) (*Parent's Consent*), [1977] A.C. 602; [1976] 2 All E.R. 342 (C.A.).

[2] See s. 85 (1), paras. [**208**]–[**230**], *post*.

[3] [1962] 3 All E.R. 789; [1962] 1 W.L.R. 1296 (Pennycuick J.).

[4] Under Children and Young Person Act 1969, s. 1.

[5] Under Children Act 1948, s. 2, as substituted by Children Act 1975, s. 57.

[6] For instances of persistent failure *see Re P.* (*infants*), *ante*; *Re G.* (*an infant*), [1963] 2 Q.B. 73; [1963] 1 All E.R. 20 (C.A.); *Re B.* (*S.*) (*an infant*), [1968] Ch. 204; [1967] 3 All E.R. 629.

[7] (1965), 109 Sol. Jo. 574 (C.A.).

[8] In *Re M.* (*an infant*) an 18-year-old mother handed over her baby a few days after birth to foster parents with a view to adoption by them. She had done so because she wanted to conceal the birth from her parents. Within six weeks she withdrew her earlier written consent to adoption. It was held that there had not been persistent failure.

On the other hand, continued inactivity on the parent's part can eventually lead to such failure.

[9] [1973] Fam. 209; [1973] 3 All E.R. 1001.

[10] In that case the husband, after separating from his wife and two children (then aged 4 and 5 years), saw the children at irregular intervals. He sent them Christmas and Easter presents and some clothes but did not provide maintenance for them. Held that there was not "persistent failure".

Will the enactment of section 3[1] lead to an ease of this construction in favour of the child?

(*d*) *The parent or guardian has abandoned or neglected the child.* This and the next ground are unchanged. The conduct must be such as to give rise to criminal liability,[2] although it is tentatively suggested that the civil standard of proof applies. It is doubtful whether emotional rejection of the child could be brought under this ground of neglect,[3] but it could, it is submitted, be brought under ground (*c*).[4]

(*e*) *The parent or guardian has persistently ill-treated the child.* It seems that here, too, the conduct must be of a kind and degree that would render the parent or guardian criminally liable. In the light of the strict meaning given to the word "persistently" in ground (*c*),[5] it is arguable that a series of acts will have to be proved and that analogy should not be drawn from the matrimonial jurisdiction over persistent cruelty where two assaults on separate occasions may exceptionally suffice.[6] However, it may be possible to rely on the following new ground for dispensation.

(*f*) *The parent or guardian has seriously ill-treated the child.*[7] This ground, which gives effect to a recommendation of *Houghton*,[8] raises uncertainties. It seems clear, however, that if grounds (*c*), (*d*) and (*e*) require conduct of a criminal nature, this must equally do so, especially since the ill-treatment has to be serious. If it is serious, then one act may even be enough. It is such a possibility that particularly led to the introduction of the proviso that this ground does not apply unless the rehabilitation of the child within the household of the parent or guardian is unlikely.[9] The reason for the unlikelihood can be either the ill-treatment itself or other factors. Thus, the ill-treatment may have been so grave that the high risk of harm to the child if rehabilitation took place makes rehabilitation unlikely; or the mental condition of the parent may be so deteriorating as to create the unlikelihood. These are comparatively straightforward illustrations, but in many instances the proviso will place a heavy onus on adoption agencies, guardians *ad litem* and reporting officers when assessing the likelihood of rehabilitation, especially since there is no time limit against which the likelihood has to be set. This omission will, it is suggested, be especially relevant in those cases where the ill-treatment can be related to poor housing accommodation and its attendant pressures on the parent. Given the increasing and understandable practice of local authorities since the Maria Colwell tragedy to institute care proceedings where there is some evidence of child abuse on only one, two or a few occasions (so that there may be difficulty

---

1 Adoption Act 1976, s. 6.

2 E.g., under s. 1 of the Children and Young Persons Act 1933. See *Watson* v. *Nikolaisen*, [1955] 2 Q.B. 286; [1955] 2 All E.R. 427. *Quaere* this is a too restricted interpretation; see Bevan, *op. cit.*, p. 342.

3 Cf. Freeman, *op. cit.*, 72/12.

4 See Pennycuick J. in *Re P.* (*infants*), *ante*.

5 See *ante*.

6 Matrimonial Proceedings (Magistrates' Courts) Act 1960, s. 1; *Broad* v. *Broad* (1898), 78 L.T. 687.

7 This additional ground is already in operation, applying to applications made after 31st December 1975; see Children Act 1975, s. 108 (6).

8 Rec. 52.

9 S. 12 (5); (Adoption Act 1976, s. 16 (5)).

in proving persistent ill-treatment), it seems likely that this ground for dispensation will quite often be invoked. [**55**]

The provisions governing freeing for adoption and parental agreement to adoption in section 12 (1)[1] do not apply to applications for a Convention adoption where the child is not a United Kingdom national.[2] In such a case any consent required for adoption is governed by the internal law of the Convention country of which the child is a national and the court must be satisfied that each person who consents to the order in accordance with the internal law does so with full understanding of what is involved.[3] [**56**]

If, in accordance with section 12, the requirements relating to freeing for adoption or agreeing to adoption or dispensing with agreement are satisfied, the court will have a choice not merely between making and refusing an adoption order but making instead a custodianship order in favour of the applicant, should this be considered more appropriate.[4] The same possibilities will be available where there is an application for a Convention adoption order and the requirements of section 24 (6) are met.[5] These options illustrate the importance, which has already been stressed,[6] of giving full and clear advice to the parents or guardians. For example, in giving agreement to adoption the parents may not realise that, if a custodianship order is made, they may be required to make periodical payments to the custodian for the child's maintenance.[7] Similarly they should be told of the court's exceptional powers to make a supervision order or an order committing the child to the care of a local authority when an adoption order is refused.[8] [**57**]

AGREEMENT OTHER THAN PARENTAL

Under the former law when spouses were not living apart an adoption order could nevertheless be made in favour of only one of them, provided the other was able and willing to consent to adoption.[9] This is no longer possible.[10] The change, which was not recommended by *Houghton*, is designed to encourage joint applications. However, it will be possible for one spouse alone to adopt in certain circumstances, namely those which under the former law were grounds for dispensing with the other's consent. Provided he or she is 21 years old the court may make an adoption order if it is satisfied that:

(i) the other spouse cannot be found, or
(ii) the spouses have separated and are living apart, and the separation is likely to be permanent, or

---

[1] Adoption Act 1976, s. 16 (1).
[2] *Ibid.*, sub-s. (3).
[3] S. 24 (6); (Adoption Act 1976, s. 17 (6)). See generally on Convention adoption orders, Chap. 7, *post*.
[4] S. 37, paras. [**273**]–[**282**], *post*. This provision is not yet operative.
[5] *Ibid.*
[6] See para. [**38**], *ante*.
[7] S. 34 (1) (*b*), para. [**299**], *post*.
[8] S. 17; Adoption Act 1976, s. 26); see paras. [**146**]–[**148**], *post*. (Operative since 26th November 1976.)
[9] Adoption Act 1958, s. 4 (1) (*b*).
[10] S. 11; (Adoption Act 1976, s. 15); see further paras. [**94**]–[**105**], *post*.

(iii) the other spouse is by reason of ill health, whether physical or mental, incapable of making an application for an adoption order.[1]

With regard to (i) and (ii) the 1975 Act re-enacts the provisions of the Adoption Act 1958[2] in identical terms. The meaning of the words "cannot be found" has already been considered. The concept of living apart is well known in matrimonial causes[3] and decisions thereon are relevant by analogy.[4] The parties may have separated in the physical sense but may still be living together, for example, where the husband's work requires him to be away for long periods at a time; or they may not have separated in the physical sense but may still be living apart as two separate households. The circumstance of incapacity is specifically limited by the 1975 Act to ill health, whether physical or mental, and relates to joining in the application for, rather than agreeing to, an adoption order. It was included late in the Act's Parliamentary history[5] to meet the rare case where one spouse is incapacitated by ill-health and the spouses are physically separated (e.g., because the one is in a mental hospital) but it cannot be said that they "have separated and are living apart" in the legal sense. The subparagraph is, however, more extensive, because it also operates where the spouses are living together. The Act thus creates the strange anomaly that a spouse who is living with the other spouse can alone apply to adopt provided the other is incapacitated, but not if he is in good health. In these kinds of circumstances for which section 11 (1) (*b*) provides the court is likely to be cautious before it decides to make an adoption order, especially where the other spouse suffers ill health. However, if an order is made and the other spouse should reappear or his health improve or the spouses resume living together, the spouses could apply for a joint adoption order. [**58**]

The Act does not extend to English law the Scottish rule[6] which requires a child who is a minor to consent to his being adopted, unless the court dispenses with it where he is incapable of giving his consent.[7] For the purpose of this rule a minor is a girl between 12 and 18 years of age and a boy between 14 and 18.[8] However, as already noted[9] the English court is subject to the duty imposed by section 3 to give due consideration to the wishes and feelings of the child having regard to his age and understanding. Although the practical difference between the rules may not be marked, the English rule has the merit of greater flexibility. [**59**]

---

[1] S. 11 (1) (*b*); (Adoption Act 1976, s. 15 (1) (*b*)).

[2] S. 5 (4).

[3] See especially Matrimonial Causes Act 1973, s. 2 (6); Denyer, *Living Apart*, 124 New Law Jo. p. 735.

[4] E.g., *Mouncer* v. *Mouncer*, [1972] 1 All E.R. 289; [1972] 1 W.L.R. 321; *Fuller* v *Fuller* [1973] 2 All E.R. 650; [1973] 1 W.L.R. 730; *Santos* v. *Santos*, [1972] Fam. 247; [1972] 2 All E.R. 246, (C.A.).

[5] H.C. Official Report, 00000, Vol. 898, No. 00, col. 1451 (Report Stage).

[6] Adoption Act 1958, s. 4 (1), re-enacted in Children Act 1975, s. 8 (6).

[7] Law Reform (Miscellaneous Provisions) (Scotland) Act 1966, s. 4.

[8] Freeman *op. cit.*, 72/8 doubts the justification of the distinction in view of the Sex Discrimination Act 1975.

[9] See paras. [**44**]–[**45**], *ante*.

CHAPTER 5

FREEING FOR ADOPTION

A child will be free for adoption if he is the subject of an order under section 14.[1] The general purpose of the order has already been mentioned.[2] Application for it is to be made by an adoption agency[3] and, if it is granted, the parental rights and duties relating to the child will thereafter vest in the agency[4] until either the order is revoked or an adoption order is made. Consequently any parental right or duty which immediately before the date of the section 14 order was vested in a parent or guardian or, by virtue of an order of the court, in any other person[5] will be extinguished. So, too, will any duty under an agreement or the order of a court to provide maintenance for the child (e.g., by the putative father) except a duty arising by virtue of an agreement which constitutes a trust or which expressly provides that the duty is not to be extinguished by the making of a section 14 order.[6] A section 14 order does not however, affect the parental rights and duties so far as they relate to any period before the making of an order.[7] [**60**]

Where a child has been freed for adoption it is possible, albeit exceptionally, for the court to invoke section 37 of the Act and make a custodianship order instead of an adoption order.[8] For example, the applicants for adoption may be relatives of the child; the parent's agreement to adoption may have been dispensed with on the ground of mental ill health when the freeing order was made but it has subsequently been found that the chances of ultimate recovery of health cannot be discounted. A custodianship order might therefore be more appropriate. If it is, the effect will be that the parental rights and duties relating to the person of the child will vest in the relatives as custodians,[9] but the residuary rights and duties remain vested in the adoption agency. The making of a custodianship order would then raise the question whether the mother or father could be ordered to pay maintenance, even though they no longer have parental rights and duties.[10] Moreover, they will be able to apply for access [10] The legal

---

[1] S. 12 (6); (Adoption Act 1976, s. 16 (1) (*a*)). S. 14 has not yet been brought into operation.

[2] See paras. [**46**]–[**47**], *ante*.

[3] *Houghton* recommended that the application be made jointly by the parents and the adoption agency (H.C.R., Rec. 37).

[4] S. 14 (6); (Adoption Act 1976, s. 18 (5)).

[5] E.g., a person who has been granted custody or, under Part II of the Act when it becomes operative, custodianship.

[6] Ss. 14 (6) and 8 (3) and (4); (Adoption Act 1976, ss. 18 (5) and 12 (3) and (4)).

[7] Ss. 14 (6) and 8 (2); (Adoption Act 1976, ss. 18 (5) and 12 (2)).

[8] See paras. [**273**]–[**282**], *post*.

[9] See paras. [**231**]–[**236**], *post*.

[10] Under s. 34.

complexity that can arise from a case of this kind is likely to dissuade the court from relying on section 37. [**61**]

MAKING A SECTION 14 ORDER

The freeing process involves two distinct acts: agreeing to the making of an adoption order and consenting to the application for a section 14 order. The general principle is that each parent or guardian must give his agreement to the former, unless it is dispensed with on one of the grounds specified in the Act,[1] and one of them at least must, apart from one exception, consent to the application. Section 14 (1) and (2) cover three possibilities where a freeing order can be made. They are illustrated by taking the case of two parents. [**62**]

The first, which may be described as one of full agreement and consent, is where both parents agree to adoption and one or both consent to the section 14 application.[2] In the second there is partial agreement and consent. One of them agrees to adoption and the other does not. A section 14 application can be made with the consent of the former and the court, if satisfied, can dispense with the other's agreement to adoption, his consent to the application not being necessary.[3] Thirdly, where neither parent agrees to the making of an adoption order and therefore *ipso facto* neither will consent to a section 14 application, no such application can be made except where the child is in the care of the adoption agency. If he is and the agency applies, the agreement of each parent to an adoption order will have to be dispensed with before the court can make a section 14 order.[4] [**63**]

This third possibility has particularly in mind children in long-term care[5] and will enable them to be freed for adoption instead of spending their entire childhood in care. How far it will deter parents from putting their children in care because of the risk of their later being placed for adoption against parental wishes is difficult to predict. There is no minimum period for which the child must have been in care before a section 14 application can be made. In view of time limits imposed elsewhere in the Act, there is some strength in the argument that a minimum period here would help dispel some of the parental fears when wishing to place their children in care and would accord with the intention of *Houghton*[6] that the provision should only be used:

> "where a child is in care with no satisfactory long-term plan in mind and lacking the possibility of long-term stable relationships . . .".

Moreover, the provision is another illustration of the need for parents to be fully informed of the consequences of their actions. It is submitted that the Act is defective in this respect because it does not itself ensure, or allow for rules to ensure, that parents are so informed, whereas rules will provide for the appointment of a reporting officer when there is an application under section 14[7]

---

[1] S. 12 (2); (Adoption Act 1976, s. 16 (2)); see Chap. 4, *ante*.
[2] S. 14 (1) (*a*) and (2) (*a*); (Adoption Act 1976, s. 18 (1) (*a*) and (2) (*a*)).
[3] S. 14 (1) (*a*) and (*b*) and (2) (*a*); (Adoption Act 1976, s. 18 (1) (*a*) and (*b*) and (2) (*a*)).
[4] S. 14 (1) (*b*) and (2) (*b*); (Adoption Act 1976, s. 18 (1) (*b*) and (2) (*b*)).
[5] See Rowe and Lambert, *Children Who Wait*.
[6] H.C.R., para. 224.
[7] S. 20; (Adoption Act 1976, s. 65). No such rules have yet been made.

and his functions will, it seems likely, include telling parents about the implications of a section 14 order. [**64**]

The Act does, however, provide some safeguards. First, there are those which apply as they do to agreements to adoption under the alternative procedure.[1] So, the parent or guardian must freely, with full understanding and unconditionally agree to the making of an adoption order, the distinction here being that his agreement is given generally for his child to be adopted and not with a specific adoption in mind. The mother's agreement is ineffective for the purpose of section 14 as it is for the alternative procedure if given less than six weeks after the child's birth.[2] [**65**]

Secondly, the parental agreement cannot be dispensed with under section 14 (1) (*b*)[3] unless the child is already placed for adoption or the court is satisfied that it is likely that the child will be placed for adoption.[4] Although it is not explicitly stated that this restriction applies as much to a case covered by section 14 (2) (*b*)[5] as to the others, cumulatively subsections (1)–(3)[6] seem to lead to that conclusion. Even so, the terms of subsection (3) are far from precise. A child in care, living with foster parents who now decide that they want to adopt him, can hardly be said to be already placed for *adoption*. Nor literally will there be such a placement, since he is already with them. To satisfy the subsection in such circumstances it seems necessary to hold that there is a notional placement for adoption when the agency notifies the foster parents that it will support them in an adoption application. [**66**]

Thirdly, the new "freeing" procedure seeks to provide a special safeguard for the child. While a section 14 application is pending in respect of a child in the care of the applicant agency and the application was not made with the consent of *each* parent or guardian, no parent or guardian who did not so consent is entitled, against the will of the person with whom the child has his home, to remove the child from the custody[7] of that person except with the leave of the court.[8] [**67**]

This is a curious and defective provision. Its object seems to be to prevent the child being suddenly removed and thereby to avoid the risk of emotional disturbance, but the Act does not logically and fully pursue that object. The child may well be in a temporary foster home or with someone who may not be

---

[1] Chap. 4, *ante*.

[2] S. 14 (4); (Adoption Act 1976, s. 18 (4)); cf. para. [**54**], *ante*.

However, there is no time limit on the giving of consent to the s. 14 application. This omission tends to undermine the value of the restriction on agreeing to an adoption order. There is nothing to prevent influences and pressure being brought on the mother to give her consent within the six-week period or even before birth. Having so committed herself she may be reluctant later to refuse to agree to adoption. Here, again, the reporting officer could play a critical role in advising her.

[3] Adoption Act 1976, s. 18 (1) (*b*).

[4] S. 14 (3); (Adoption Act 1976, s. 18 (3)).

[5] Adoption Act 1976, s. 18 (2) (*b*). I.e., where the child is in the care of the agency and parental agreement has to be dispensed with.

[6] Adoption Act 1976, s. 18 (1)–(3).

[7] This means "actual custody", as defined by Children Act 1975, s. 87, para. [**237**], *post*.

[8] Adoption Act 1958, s. 34 (2), as substituted by Children Act 1975, s. 29; (Adoption Act 1976, s. 27).

Wrongful removal is an offence punishable with imprisonment for not more than three months or a fine of up to £400 or both; *ibid.*, s. 34 (3); (s. 27 (3)).

the eventual applicant for adoption. His interests may not be served by requiring only that person's consent. That of the agency should, it is suggested, also have been made a prerequisite and the matter should not have been left, as seems intended, to guidance by way of Departmental Circular.[1] Because the child is in care, the agency is inextricably involved. If it is a local authority and the child is in its care under a care order[2] or by virtue of a resolution under the Children Act 1948,[3] or if the agency is a voluntary organisation to whom the parental rights and duties have been transferred in accordance with section 60 of the Children Act 1975,[4] the parent or guardian is not entitled to remove the child without the authority of the local authority or voluntary organisation.[5] It might therefore be argued that in those circumstances to have added a rule in the provision under consideration to the effect that the agency's permission for removal is necessary would have been superfluous; but is such implied reference adequate? In any event the point does not meet those cases where the child has been received into care. The parent may at any time remove the child from the local authority or voluntary organisation.[6] [**68**]

Another unsatisfactory feature of the restriction on removal is its limitation to the parent or guardian who has not consented to the section 14 application. Supposing the consenting parent changes his mind. As already seen, he will not be entitled to remove the child if there is a care order, a section 2 resolution or a transfer of parental rights and duties to a voluntary organisation: in cases of voluntary care he will. Yet, viewed more widely, is removal at this juncture likely to be in the child's interests? The very fact that consent to the section 14 application was given is some indication of the need for inquiry by the court and therefore, until the application is heard, the position should be frozen. Indeed, for this reason it is difficult to justify a distinction between cases of children in care and those who are not. [**69**]

It has already been pointed out[7] that the putative father can frustrate adoption applications by applying for an order for custody. Section 14 (8)[8] therefore provides that before a freeing order is made the court must satisfy itself that he does not intend to apply for custody or that, if he did, his application would be likely to be refused. This requirement is a wise precaution in view of the need to ensure that the result of freeing the child for adoption will be an

---

[1] Persons with custody (temporary foster parents etc.) will be told to consult the adoption agency before allowing the child to be removed; see H.C. Official Report, 1975 Standing Committee A (Eighth Sitting), col. 410 (Dr. David Owen).

[2] Under the Children and Young Persons Act 1969.

[3] S. 2, as substituted by the Children Act 1975, s. 57.

[4] See paras. [**357**]–[**360**], *post*.

[5] Where there is a care order wrongful removal would be contempt of court; where there is a section 2 resolution or a transfer of parental rights and duties to a voluntary organisation such removal is an offence (Children Act 1948, s. 3 (8), amended by the Children Act 1975, Sch. 3, para. 4, so as to bring the penalty into line with the penalty for wrongful removal where an application for a freeing order is pending; see p. 44, n. 8, *ante*).

[6] The rule, which is open to criticism, that s. 1 of the Children Act 1948 does not impose on the local authority an absolute duty to return the child to the parent regardless of the circumstances (*Re K.R. (an infant)*, [1964] Ch. 455; [1963] 3 All E.R. 337; *Krishnan* v. *London Borough of Sutton*, [1970] Ch. 181; [1969] 3 All E.R. 1367 (C.A.)) does not, it is submitted, mean that the parent does not have the right to remove the child.

[7] See paras. [**50**]–[**51**], *ante*.

[8] Adoption Act 1976, s. 18 (7).

unchallengeable transfer of parental rights and duties. If it is found that the father does wish to apply for custody and it cannot be said that refusal of custody would be likely, then it is desirable that the section 14 application be adjourned so that it and the custody application may be heard together by the same court.[1] If this should be a magistrates' court, both applications will be "domestic" proceedings.[2] [**70**]

Section 14 (8) raises two specific problems. The first is the extent of the duty on the court to notify the putative father of the section 14 application. As already mentioned,[3] the former rules for notifying him of an application for an adoption order have been retained. This being so, they ought to be extended to section 14 applications and there seems no justification for a different set of rules.[4] The second problem concerns the depth of inquiry which the court should undertake to assess the likelihood of refusal of custody to the father if he were to apply for it. Strictly it should apply the principle of paramountcy of the child's welfare in accordance with section 1 of the Guardianship of Minors Act 1971. That principle requires a full inquiry into all the circumstances. Will the courts undertake this? If so, into what kinds of matters will they direct inquiry? A major factor will obviously be the father's past interest in the child, particularly the financial provision, if any, which he has been making for him. [**71**]

Section 14 (7) provides that before making an order freeing a child for adoption the court must be satisfied that each parent or guardian *who can be found* has been given an opportunity of making, if he so wishes, a declaration that he prefers not to be involved in future questions concerning the child's adoption. The court must record any declaration made. The Act does not, however, impose a duty on a specific person to ensure that the opportunity is provided or that the consequences of a declaration are explained.[5] Clearly the adoption agency or a reporting officer are the most suitable persons.[6] Section 14 (7) is in such terms that even a parent or guardian who is not agreeing to an adoption order would have to be given the opportunity. Exceptionally he might take the view that, if the court hearing the section 14 application should decide to dispense with his agreement, he would thereafter prefer not to be involved, that in the child's interests their relationship should then be irrevocably severed. The Legislature has had second thoughts about this. The Adoption Act 1976 will amend the rule so that the persons entitled to be given the opportunity to make a declaration are each parent or guardian who agrees to the adoption of the child.[7] [**72**]

---

[1] There may be a preliminary issue of paternity to determine; see Freeman, *op. cit.*, 72/15.

[2] The jurisdiction of the domestic court is to be extended to include proceedings relating to adoption (Children Act 1975, Sch. 3, para. 12) and the juvenile court will no longer have jurisdiction.

[3] See paras. [**50**]–[**51**], *ante*.

[4] Compare s. 22 (Adoption Act 1976, s. 66), which explicitly provides for the making of rules to notify persons whose agreement or consent is required. These will apply to the putative father as guardian if he has custody by an order under the Guardianship of Minors Act 1971; (Children Act 1975, s. 107 (1); Adoption Act 1976, s. 72 (1)).

[5] Especially the forfeiture of the right to apply for revocation of a s. 14 order.

[6] Cf. s. 15 (4) (Adoption Act 1976, s. 19 (4)), para. [**74**], *post*, where the declaration must be made to the adoption agency.

[7] Adoption Act 1976, s. 18 (6).

A parent or guardian "who was required to be given an opportunity of making a declaration under section 14 (7) but did not do so" (whether or not the opportunity was in fact given to him) is entitled to progress reports on the child and eventually will have the right, within limits, to apply for revocation of the freeing for adoption order.[1] [**73**]

A progress report must be made to "the former parent", as the Act describes him, by the adoption agency within 14 days following the first anniversary date of the making of the section 14 order, unless it has already notified him that an adoption order has been made. This first report must tell him whether an adoption order has been made and, if not, whether the child has his home with a person with whom he has been placed for adoption.[2] Thereafter he must be notified of any adoption order (if not already made) or any placement for adoption or cessation of a placement, as the case may be.[3] It is open to the former parent at any time to make a declaration to the agency that he no longer wishes to be involved in future questions concerning the adoption of his child.[4] [**74**]

The declaration under section 14 or section 15[5] relates to non-involvement in future questions concerning the *adoption* of the child. Suppose a parent makes such a declaration, a section 14 order is then made but eventually on hearing the adoption application the court is minded to make a custodianship order instead of an adoption order.[6] It is submitted that a parent who has made a declaration must first be notified of the court's intention, since the question is no longer one of adoption. The need to notify is especially important since the court has powers[7] to make other orders affecting the mother or father when it makes a custodianship order. [**75**]

REVOCATION OF AN ORDER FREEING FOR ADOPTION

The duty of the adoption agency to make progress reports is linked with the right of the former parent to apply, on the ground that he wishes to resume the parental rights and duties, to the court for the revocation of the section 14 order which it made.[8] Application is not allowed within the first twelve months after the date of the order, because the agency must be given an adequate opportunity to place the child for adoption. A limit of twelve months is reasonable. If a placement has not been made within that period, it is likely that difficulties have been encountered and placement may be a lengthy, perhaps impossible, process; e.g., in the case of a mentally sub-normal child. [**76**]

Obviously no application can be made once an adoption order has been granted, since the parental rights and duties have already been irrevocably vested in the adopters. Nor can it be made while the child has his home with

---

[1] S. 15 (1); (Adoption Act 1976, s. 19 (1)).
[2] S. 15 (2); (Adoption Act 1976, s. 19 (2)).
[3] *Ibid.*, sub-s. (3); (sub-s. (3)).
[4] *Ibid.*, sub-s. (4); (sub-s. (4)). The agency must then see that the declaration is recorded by the court which made the s. 14 order. The agency is released from making further progress reports once the declaration has been made.
[5] Adoption Act 1976, ss. 18 and 19 respectively.
[6] In accordance with s. 37, paras. [**273**]–[**282**], *post*.
[7] S. 34, paras. [**298**]–[**311**], *post*.
[8] S. 16 (1); (Adoption Act 1976, s. 20 (1)).

a person with whom he has been placed for adoption.[1] On the other hand, if the child is not currently placed when the application for revocation is made, the agency must not place him without the leave of the court[2] and, in view of section 3 of the Act,[3] with the child's interests not being made paramount, it is unlikely that leave will be granted. The court will want first to hear why the former parent is seeking revocation. That approach would, it is submitted, be consistent with the *raison d'etre* of section 3, that where parental agreement to adoption is involved proper weight is to be given to the parental wishes. **[77]**

However, when it comes to hearing the application for revocation its very nature tends to weaken the significance of those wishes. One cogent factor will be any delay in seeking revocation after the minimum twelve-month period. The longer the former parent and child have been apart the less inclined will the court be to revoke, especially if there is a likelihood of immediate placement for adoption. If the former parent agreed to adoption and consented to the section 14 application, much will depend on the reason for so doing. Was it, for example, inspired by a selfish disregard of his child or was it the consequence of explicable pressures such as poverty or inadequate accommodation or, in the case of the mother of an illegitimate child, pressures from her parents to agree to adoption? If the section 14 order had been made after dispensing with the former parent's agreement to adoption, are there now fresh circumstances which, if the section 14 application were being heard *de novo*, would not justify such dispensation? These are the kinds of matters which courts are likely to have to consider when applying section 3 on an application for revocation. **[78]**

Section 16 (4)[4] enigmatically states that "subject to subsection (5) if the application is dismissed on the ground that to allow it would contravene the principle embodied in section 3" the applicant is barred from making any further application for revocation and the adoption agency is released from the duty of giving to him any further progress reports under section 15 (3).[5] This provision implies that an application may be dismissed on other grounds, but it is submitted that these, whatever they may be, must not be inconsistent with section 3 and the primacy (though not paramountcy) of the child's welfare. A possible example is the case where the application is dismissed because it was inadvertently brought within the twelve-month period. The former parent would not be barred from a fresh application. **[79]**

Subsection (5) empowers the court dismissing the application to give leave to reapply where, because of a change in circumstances or for any other reason, it is proper to allow a further application. This provision corresponds to those which respectively allow for reapplication by the same persons for an adoption order or a custodianship order after dismissal of the application for those respective orders.[6] **[80]**

---

[1] *Ibid.*
[2] S. 16 (2); (Adoption Act 1976, s. 20 (2)).
[3] Chap. 3, *ante*.
[4] Adoption Act 1976, s. 20 (4).
[5] Adoption Act 1976, s. 19 (3).
The other former parent will not be prevented from making an application and the agency will still have to provide him with progress reports.
[6] See s. 22 (4); (Adoption Act 1976, s. 24 (1)) and s. 35 (2).

If revocation is allowed, the parental rights and duties will normally revest in the person or persons in whom they were vested immediately before the section 14 order was made.[1] In practice this is most likely to be the applicant himself, but there are various possibilities. For example, the effect may be that there will be revesting in him and the other parent. However, supposing that they are now living apart or that the other parent had made a declaration that he no longer wished to be involved in future questions concerning the child's adoption. Will the fact of separation in the one case and the lack of interest of the parent in the other influence the court against revocation or will it grant it and leave either parent to seek a custody order? It is suggested that in cases of that kind the court revoking the section 14 order should be ready concurrently to entertain an application for custody.[2] [**81**]

In those cases where the parental rights and duties, or any of them, vested in a local authority[3] or a voluntary organisation[4] immediately before the section 14 order was made, they will revest in the person or persons in whom they were vested immediately before they were vested in the authority or organisation.[5] It is suggested that where the vesting in either of those bodies was due to the misconduct or inadequacies of the parent the court is not likely to be ready to grant revocation. [**82**]

The revocation of the freeing order revives any duty relating to payment towards the child's maintenance, for example, by a putative father, which was extinguished when the freeing order was made.[6] [**83**]

---

[1] S. 16 (3) (*a*); (Adoption Act 1976, s. 20 (3) (*a*)).
Revocation does not affect any right or duty so far as it relates to any period before the date of the revocation.

[2] Compare the power of the court to consider together a custody application by a putative father and an adoption application; see paras. [**50**]–[**51**], *ante*.

[3] By virtue of a care order (under the Children and Young Persons Act 1969) or a resolution of the local authority (under s. 2 of the Children Act 1948).

[4] Under the Children Act 1975, s. 60.

[5] Children Act 1975, s. 16 (3) (*b*); (Adoption Act 1976, s. 20 (3) (*b*)).

[6] S. 16 (3) (*c*); (Adoption Act 1976, s. 20 (3) (*c*)).

CHAPTER 6

THE MAKING OF ADOPTION ORDERS

AUTHORISED COURTS

Until the creation of a system of family courts the Family Division of the High Court, county courts and magistrates' courts will continue to be the courts authorised to make orders for adoption and other orders connected therewith,[1] but the Act introduces a number of detailed changes. Jurisdiction very largely depends upon the presence of the child in England or Wales when the application for an order is made and no longer on a test of residence.[2] So far as concerns the jurisdiction of a county court or magistrates' court he must further be in the district or area[3] respectively of those courts at the date of application. **[84]**

There are two extensions to this general jurisdictional rule. First, the County Courts' Rule Committee is empowered[4] to prescribe other county courts as "authorised courts" to make not only orders relating to adoption but others permitted by the Act. The power thus allows for flexibility as it becomes apparent that additional courts are needed. Secondly, where there is an application to free a child for adoption under section 14 of the Act,[5] any county court or magistrates' court, within whose district or area a parent or guardian of the child is, also has jurisdiction. The purpose of this extension is to provide maximum convenience. **[85]**

Both the general rule and the two additional ones are subject to the following special provisions:

(a) If the application is for an adoption order or a section 14 order and the child is not in Great Britain when the application is made, only the High Court has jurisdiction in England and Wales.[6]

(b) Similarly where there is an application for a Convention adoption order[7] and the child is in England and Wales the High Court alone has jurisdiction.

---

[1] Ss. 100 and 107 (1); (Adoption Act 1976, ss. 62 and 72 (1)). The sections of the Children Act are already operative. For appellate jurisdiction see para. [**440**], *post*.

[2] For the further requirement concerning the domicile of the applicant for an adoption order see paras. [**90**]–[**91**], *post*.

[3] "Area" in relation to a magistrates' court means the commission area (within the meaning of s. 1 of the Administration of Justice Act 1973) for which the court is appointed (Children Act 1975, s. 107 (1)). Consequently the court need no longer be the local magistrates' court of the petty sessions area.

[4] By the County Courts Act 1959, s. 102.

[5] Adoption Act 1976, s. 18.

[6] In Scotland the Court of Session has sole jurisdiction.

[7] Under Children Act 1975, s. 24; (Adoption Act 1976, s. 17). For Convention adoption orders see Chap. 7, *post*.

(c) Magistrates' courts cannot hear applications under section 25[1] relating to children in England and Wales whom it is intended to adopt abroad.

(d) In the case of an application under section 30[2] for a child who has been wrongfully removed to be returned to the applicant, the High Court, the county court within whose district the applicant lives and the magistrates' court within whose area he lives are the authorised courts, except that where there is already pending an application for an adoption order or a section 14 order the court in which that application is pending is the authorised court. [**86**]

The cumulative complexity of these rules illustrates the need for a system of family courts along the lines advocated by the Finer Committee.[3] The Act does no more than accept the *Houghton* recommendation[4] that magistrates' jurisdiction over adoption be transferred from the juvenile court to the domestic court.[5] Complete privacy of these domestic proceedings is ensured by excluding the normal rule that representatives of newspapers and newsagencies may be present.[6] The rules relating to privacy in county courts and the High Court, formerly contained in Adoption Rules,[7] are embodied in the Act.[8] Thus, proceedings in the former must be heard in camera, while those in the High Court may be, and usually are, disposed of in chambers, except when there is some point of law of significance for the future. [**87**]

The jurisdictional rules also lend themselves to administrative complications. For example, a section 14 order may have been made by a magistrates' court for the area in which the natural parent was then living. The child may later be placed for adoption with a person living in another area and application for an adoption order is made to a magistrates' court in that area. It will not, it is suggested, be sufficient for the latter court to be furnished with a copy of the section 14 order. That order may have been made after dispensing with parental agreement to adoption.[9] It is clearly desirable that the court hearing the adoption application should be fully seised of the circumstances which warranted the dispensation. [**88**]

ELIGIBILITY OF THE PARTIES

Domicile, residence, age and marital status have been the main legal conditions governing eligibility to adopt. Except for domicile they have also been relevant in determining a person's eligibility to be adopted. The Act makes

---

1 Adoption Act 1976, s. 55.

2 Adoption Act 1976, s. 29. See paras. [**143**]–[**144**], *post*.

3 Cmnd. 5629. Cf. para. [**7**], *ante*.

4 Rec. 64.

5 S. 21 (3) and Sch. 3, para. 12; (Adoption Act 1976, s. 64 (c) and Sch. 3, para. 4). (Not yet operative.)

6 Magistrates' Courts (Adoption) Rules 1976, r. 18. The *Houghton* Committee saw this change as an interim measure, justified by the fact that all other family cases in the magistrates' courts go to the domestic courts. The Act does not, however, provide, as *Houghton* recommended, for suitably qualified magistrates to sit.

7 Adoption (County Court Rules) 1959, r. 16; Adoption (High Court) Rules 1971, r. 3.

8 S. 21 (2) and (1) respectively; (Adoption Act 1976, s. 64 (*b*) and (*a*)). (Operative since 26th November 1976.)

9 See Chap. 5, *ante*.

changes with regard to each. It does not alter the rule that, apart from a joint adoption by a married couple, only one person is allowed to adopt, but it does impose certain restrictions on adoption by married persons, natural parents, relatives and step-parents. Except where otherwise indicated, the changes have operated since 26th November 1976. [**89**]

Domicile

Under the former law the applicant or joint applicants must have been domiciled in England or Scotland.[1] The rule is extended to include domicile in any part of the United Kingdom or in the Channel Islands or the Isle of Man.[2] In the normal case of an application by a married couple it is enough if only one of them has the requisite domicile. This change takes account of the rule that a married woman may now acquire her separate domicile,[3] but the chances of joint adopters having separate domiciles is very remote. However, if they should and an adoption order is made, it might not be recognised by the foreign *lex domicilii*. [**90**]

The Act does nothing to remove another possibility of "limping adoption", for the child's domicile continues to be ignored, except in so far as the court is prepared to take it into account when discharging its duty under section 3[4] to have regard to all the circumstances. This requirement should, it is submitted, include "consideration of the effect of the order, if made, on the child's status".[5] [**91**]

Residence

The Act[6] abolishes the former requirement[7] that the applicant or joint applicants and the child must reside in England.[8] For jurisdictional purposes all that is needed is the presence of the child, or, as an alternative in the case of an application for a section 14 order, of the parent or guardian.[9] Nevertheless, while this change will relieve the courts of the difficulty of construing the concept of residence[10] and of distinguishing it from "ordinary residence",[11] in practical terms some residential conditions will have to be met because of the requirements, when they come into force, (a) that sufficient opportunities must be afforded to the adoption agency which placed the child or, if he was not

---

[1] Adoption Act 1958, s. 1 (1).

[2] Children Act 1975, ss. 10 (2) (*a*) and 11 (2) (*a*); (Adoption Act 1976, ss. 14 (2) (*a*) and 15 (2) (*a*)). (The sections of the Children Act have been operative since 26th November 1976.) The domiciliary rule will not apply where there is an application for a Convention adoption order. Then section 24 (Adoption Act 1976, s. 17) will have to be complied with. See Chap. 7, *post*.

[3] Domicile and Matrimonial Proceedings Act 1973, s. 1.

[4] Adoption Act 1976, s. 6.

[5] *Per* Goff J. in *Re B. (S.) (an infant)*, [1968] Ch. 204 at p. 211; see Cheshire, *Private International Law* (9th Edn.), p. 466; Bevan, *Law Relating to Children*, p. 316.

[6] Sch. 4, Part IV.

[7] Adoption Act 1958, s. 1 (5).

[8] Or Scotland if the adoption order is to be made there.

[9] Para. [**85**], *ante*.

[10] See Bevan, *op. cit.*, pp. 313–314.

[11] The Act (Sch. 4, Part IV) repeals not only s. 1 (5) but also s. 12 of the Adoption Act 1958.

placed by an agency, to the local authority[1] to see the child in the home environment,[2] and (b) that he must have had his home with the applicant for prescribed periods.[3] [**92**]

Age of applicants

The complex provisions of the Adoption Act 1958 regarding the minimum age requirements of applicants[4] have been repealed.[5] In all cases the applicant or joint applicants must be at least 21.[6] Thus, for the first time an age limit is imposed on the natural parent as a prospective adopter. The new rule is a compromise between the old and the proposal in the Houghton Working Paper that there should be no minimum age. In view of the high incidence of breakdown of marriages entered into by persons under 21 it is wise not to have left capacity simply to the attainment of majority. [**93**]

Status of applicants

There are restrictions on the right of a sole applicant who is married to apply. It is no longer possible to do so with the consent of the other spouse. The court has to be satisfied that (i) the other spouse cannot be found or (ii) the spouses have separated and are living apart and the separation is likely to be permanent or (iii) the other spouse is by reason of ill health, whether physical or mental, incapable of making an application for an adoption order.[7] The implications of these changes have already been considered.[8] [**94**]

Restrictions are also imposed on the mother or father alone to apply. While the number of joint adoptions by natural parent and step-parent has been increasing, that of adoption by a mother alone has been declining. The Act further discourages the latter and checks the former. An application by a mother or father is only possible where the court is satisfied that (*a*) the other natural parent is dead or cannot be found or (*b*) there is some other reason justifying the exclusion of the other natural parent.[9] A crepuscular haze hangs over this subsection. [**95**]

Although the Act is not explicit on the point, it is submitted that the provision applies to the illegitimate child as well as the legitimate. Indeed, it primarily affects the former. It is highly unlikely that the natural parent alone will want to adopt his or her legitimate child. Take the case of the mother as sole applicant. If the father is dead, she will be able to rely on her rights of

---

[1] I.e., the authority within whose area the applicant or applicants have their home.
[2] S. 9 (3); (Adoption Act 1976, s. 13 (3)); see para. [**111**], *post*.
[3] S. 9 (1) and (2); (Adoption Act 1976, s. 13 (1) and (2)); see para. [**107**], *post*.
[4] S. 2.
[5] Children Act 1975, Sch. 4, Part IV.
[6] *Ibid*., ss. 10 (1) and 11 (1), adopting a recommendation of *Houghton* (Rec. 11); (Adoption Act 1976, ss. 14 (1) and 15 (1)).
[7] S. 11 (1) (*b*); (Adoption Act 1976, s. 15 (1) (*b*)).
[8] Para. [**58**], *ante*.
[9] S. 11 (3); (Adoption Act 1976, s. 15 (3)); see also H.C.R., Rec. 18.

guardianship as surviving parent[1] as well as on any existing order granting her custody. In circumstances other than his death there will, in addition to section 11 (3), be the provisions concerning the father's agreement to an adoption order to comply with; but the two will be closely interwoven. Thus, if the mother is relying for the purpose of section 11 (3) on the fact that he cannot be found, that will enable the court to dispense with his agreement.[2] It is submitted that "some other reason" justifying the exclusion of the father must be a reason relating to the child's welfare[3] and section 11 (3) primarily contemplates the circumstances which would justify dispensing with the father's agreement;[4] for example his persistent or serious ill-treatment of the child. There is a faint possibility of the mother's wishing to adopt alone where she is no longer married to the father, but just as the Act encourages relatives and others to seek custodianship rather than adoption, so the court will expect the mother to rely on her right to claim custody under the Matrimonial Causes Act 1973. It will be even more reluctant to grant adoption where the parents are still married to each other and there will in such a case be the further restriction imposed by section 11 (1) (*b*).[5] For all these reasons the chances of adoption of a legitimate child by a natural parent alone are minimal. **[96]**

Although the application of section 11 (3) to the father of an illegitimate child has been doubted,[6] it is submitted that the presumption that the term "parent" does not include such a person[7] is excluded by the context. While it is clear that he continues in adoption law not to be a "parent"[8] but a "relative",[9] he is still the natural father and subsection (3) refers to "the other natural parent" and not merely to the other parent.[10] Indeed, one circumstance where section 11 (3) could be particularly relevant would be where the mother is dead and the father wishes to adopt. Otherwise he should be expected to turn to his right to claim custody under the Guardianship of Minors Act 1971. **[97]**

---

[1] Guardianship of Minors Act 1971, s. 3 (1).

Semble this rule of survivorship applies even if at the date of death the father had custody by an order of the court. Surprisingly the relevant statutes enabling the making of custody orders (Matrimonial Causes Act 1973; Guardianship of Minors Acts 1971 and 1973 and Matrimonial Proceedings (Magistrates' Courts) Act 1960) are silent on this basic point and there is much to be said for the view that in the child's interests the surviving mother should be obliged to seek guardianship and custody. After all, it was the paramountcy of the child's welfare which led the court to deprive her of custody.

There are three possible qualifications to the survivorship rule. It has been held that the divorce court can on the death of the parent to whom it had granted custody give the custody to a person other than the surviving parent; see *Pryor* v. *Pryor*, [1947] P. 64; [1947] 1 All E.R. 381; *B.* v. *B. and H.* (*L. Intervening*), [1962] 1 All E.R. 29. Similarly the Guardianship of Minors Act 1971, s. 9 (4), allows for variation after the death of a parent. It also seems that the rule is qualified by any declaration made earlier by a divorce court, under the Matrimonial Causes Act 1973, s. 42 (3) that the parent, who survived, was unfit to have custody.

[2] S. 12 (2) (*a*); (Adoption Act 1976, s. 16 (2) (*a*)).

[3] Cf. *Houghton*, para. 102.

[4] S. 12 (2) (*c*)–(*f*); (Adoption Act 1976, s. 16 (2) (*c*)–(*f*)).

[5] Para. [**94**], *ante*.

[6] Cretney, 126 New Law Jo. 57. See also s. 33 (4), paras. [**262**]–[**263**], *post*.

[7] *Butler* v. *Gregory* (1902), 18 T.L.R. 370; *Re M.* (*an infant*), [1955] 2 Q.B. 479; [1955] 2 All E.R. 911 (C.A.).

[8] See para. [**48**], *ante*.

[9] S. 107 (1), incorporating Adoption Act 1958, s. 57 (1); (Adoption Act 1976, s. 72 (1)). He may also be a guardian; see *ibid.* and para. [**98**], *post*.

[10] *Houghton*, paras. 98–102, clearly intended that he should be included.

Where the mother is relying on "some other reason justifying the exclusion" of the father, from what precisely is it being sought to exclude him? In the case of the legitimate child, at least, it cannot be exclusion from receiving notice of her application to adopt. He must be given the opportunity to be heard on the adoption application before the court can invoke its powers of dispensing with his agreement.[1] The same will apply to the father of the illegitimate child where he is a guardian by virtue of a custody order made under the Guardianship of Minors Act 1971 (or the former Guardianship of Infants Acts 1886 and 1925). However, the case of the putative father who is not guardian is uncertain. Supposing, for example, that the reason advanced by the mother is that, in the child's interests, she wants to sever his links with the father because of the latter's repeated and allegedly vexatious applications for custody? Should he be allowed to challenge this? The possible but limited rules of seeking him out and notifying him of the adoption application where a person other than the mother is applying have already been suggested.[2] It would be anomalous if he were entitled to less where she herself is the applicant. Is he entitled to more? Where she wishes to rely on the fact that he cannot be found and not on some other reason for exclusion, he certainly is, since she will have to show that all reasonable steps have been taken to find him.[3] The deeper the analysis of section 11 (3) the less apparent its meaning. Unfortunately the new Adoption Rules 1976 do not shed light on this. One point, however, is clear. When the court makes the adoption order it must record its reason for excluding the other parent.[4] The duty should ensure that orders under the subsection are not lightly made. **[98]**

Over half of the adoption orders made annually have been joint adoptions by a parent and a step-parent. This means of establishing a full legal relationship between the step-parent and the child is achieved at the cost of changing the legal relationship between the parent and the child from a natural to an adoptive one and at the same time of severing the child's links with the other natural parent and thus with the other half of his family with whom he will usually have spent part of his life. An adoption order granted to a step-parent alone will not only have the latter effect but will also sever the child's links with the natural parent who is or was the spouse of the step-parent. To avoid these consequences and to reduce the number of adoptions by step-parents the Act imposes two kinds of restrictions of which only the second is currently in force. First, as will be seen,[5] section 37 (1) obliges the court under certain conditions to make a custodianship order instead of an adoption order.[6] Secondly, the Act expects the step-parent in certain circumstances to turn to the divorce court for relief by way of a custody order.[7] Where a step-parent applies, whether jointly with

---

[1] S. 22 (1), para. [**116**], *post*; (Adoption Act 1976, s. 66 (3)). This provision is not yet operative, but the current Adoption Rules 1976 provide for notice.

[2] Paras. [**50**]–[**51**], *ante*; but see also para. [**128**], *post*.

[3] Para. [**55**], *ante*.

[4] S. 11 (3); (Adoption Act 1976, s. 15 (3)).

[5] Para. [**274**], *post*.

[6] The restriction equally applies to relatives.

[7] See similarly the restriction on a step-parent to apply for a custodianship order; s. 33 (5), para. [**259**], *post*.

his spouse or alone, for an adoption order the court must dismiss the application if it considers that "the matter" would be better dealt with under section 42 of the Matrimonial Causes Act 1973.[1] [**99**]

This duty will usually arise on a joint application and is illustrated by reference to the mother who marries the step-father after the divorce or annulment of her earlier marriage. That, indeed, was the case in *Re S.* (*infants*), where the Court of Appeal examined the scope of section 10 (3).[2] As a result of the earlier divorce proceedings the mother had been granted custody of her three children (all boys) and the father access. Subsequently he had taken little interest in them and consented to their being jointly adopted. The boys were pleased to accept the step-father as a father and he regarded them as his sons. In dismissing the appeal from the refusal of the county court judge to make adoption orders, the Court of Appeal stated that the effect of section 10 (3), read with section 3, was to ask: "Will adoption safeguard and promote the welfare of the child better than either the existing arrangements or a joint custody order under section 42?" Since in cases of this kind the child will already have acquired all the material advantages that adoption could provide, "the advantages of adoption will have to be found, if at all, in the intangible results which might flow from it". In the majority of cases, therefore, the emphasis lies firmly against making adoption orders. Accordingly, it would have been preferable if section 10 (3)—and similarly section 11 (4)—had reflected this by providing that "the court shall dismiss the [adoption] application, unless it considers that the matter would not be better dealt with under section 42". [**100**]

Because of the need to consider carefully the choices open where there is an application under section 10 (3), considerably more investigation and information will be needed than in other adoption cases. The Court of Appeal pointed out in *Re S.* (*infants*) that in many cases the judge should hear evidence from the other natural parent, even if his agreement to the making of an adoption order has been obtained, or should at least have from the guardian *ad litem* a detailed statement of that parent's present attitude to, and past relationship with, the child. The guardian *ad litem* should also draw the attention of the court to the disadvantages as well as the advantages of adoption, and the motives of the applicants should be carefully examined. For example, if the real purpose of the application is to enable them to change the child's surname, that object can effectively be achieved by proceedings under section 42.[3] [**101**]

One clear effect of *Re S.* (*infants*) will be that the Rules which will prescribe the kinds of cases where guardians *ad litem* are to be appointed will include applications under section 10 (3) and, it seems, section 11 (4). Another and wider effect of the decision may well be to dissuade parents and step-parents

---

[1] Children Act 1975, ss. 10 (3) and 11 (4); (Adoption Act 1976, ss. 14 (3) and 15 (4)).
[2] [1977] 3 All E.R. 671.
Although s. 10 (3) had no direct application because it only came into effect after the hearing at first instance, the Court considered that it had to apply the philosophy behind the subsection. See also *Re W.* (1976), 120 Sol. Jo. 857.
[3] See p. 108, n. 4, *post*.

from relying on section 10 (3).[1] It seems highly probable that they will be legally advised to proceed straight to the divorce court under section 42[2] rather than risk dismissal of an adoption application, because in the latter event fresh proceedings under section 42 will have to be instituted.[3] The policy of local courts will be crucial when giving advice. If the spouses do decide to seek adoption, for example in a magistrates' court, and their application is dismissed in accordance with section 10 (3), and if they then turn to the divorce court, the decision of the latter court will, subject to any appeal, mean the end of the matter. Should the divorce court refuse to vary its earlier custody order, the parties will scarcely be permitted to return to the magistrates' court with a new adoption application. Such an application is not permitted save where the court on its earlier refusal otherwise directed or where it now appears that there has been a change in circumstances or some other reason making it proper to proceed with the application.[4] It seems that disappointed natural parents and step-parents will rarely be able to rely on any of these exceptions. **[102]**

In some cases the mother will have custody by virtue of an order which was made in the magistrates' court, either under the Matrimonial Proceedings (Magistrates' Courts) Act 1960 or the Guardianship of Minors Act 1971, before her former marriage was dissolved. This fact should not deter the court which is hearing the adoption application from dismissing it and leaving the mother and step-father to rely on an application for custody under section 42. A custody order made by an inferior court does not oust the matrimonial jurisdiction of the High Court. It is established practice that the latter Court can make its own order notwithstanding the existence of a magistrates' court order,[5] and, as a matter of law, there seems to be no objection to a divorce county court following the same practice. **[103]**

The power to dismiss the application for adoption, it must be stressed, is equally available where the step-father is alone the applicant. This could happen

---

[1] The adoption monitor published by the Office of Population Censuses and Surveys in July 1977 showed that 2,902 adoptions were registered in the June quarter 1977, 1,538 fewer than in the June quarter 1976. Section 10 (3) was given as the likely cause of the drop. See (1977), *The Times*, 28th July.

[2] Either the mother or the step-father or both could apply. The Matrimonial Causes Rules 1977, r. 92 (3) now expressly includes the step-parent as a person who can apply without having to obtain leave to intervene.

[3] The report of *Re S. (infants)* states that "the court is now expressly required to make a deliberate choice between making an adoption order, refusing to disturb the status quo, or making an appropriate order under . . . section 42". If that statement accurately records the judgment of the Court of Appeal, then, with respect, it inaccurately states the law.

Even where the court hearing the adoption application is a county court and it happens to be the court which exercised jurisdiction over the former marriage and made an order under s. 42, it would not, it is submitted, be proper for the court to proceed to deal with the matter under s. 42 without adjourning the case for the other natural parent to be given an opportunity to be present. Any other action would be inconsistent with the Matrimonial Causes Rules 1977, r. 92 (4) ,which provides that the respondent shall not be entitled to be heard on an application for custody, unless he is available at the hearing to give oral evidence or the judge otherwise directs. The fact that he might have chosen not to be present at the adoption hearing does not necessarily mean that he would not wish to be heard on the issue of custody, including access, if the court were minded to find a solution in that direction.

[4] Children Act 1975, s. 22 (4); (Adoption Act 1976, s. 24); see para. [**118**], *post*.

[5] See *Re D.*, [1973] Fam. 179, 193; [1973] 2 All E.R. 993, 1005–1006.

if the natural mother has died or even though they are still married, but in the latter circumstances the step-father's right to apply for adoption will be restricted by the terms of section 11 (1) (*b*).[1] [**104**]

It will come as no surprise to find that the Act abolishes the much criticised rule that a sole male applicant cannot, save in special circumstances, adopt a female child.[2] There are sufficient safeguards in section 3 to prevent any undesirable applications from succeeding, without any need for a presumption against such applications. [**105**]

Age and status of child

With regard to the eligibility of the child to be adopted, the Act re-enacts the limitations that he must be under the age of 18[3] and must not be, or have been, married.[4] There is no such marital restriction in respect of custodianship orders,[5] and, although the making of custody orders for children who have attained 16 have been rare, the possibility of younger children, who are married under their foreign personal law, needing custodianship is by no means fanciful.[6] The Act[7] also positively reaffirms the eligibility of an adopted child to be further adopted or even readopted by the natural parents, whether the earlier adoption is by virtue of an adoption order made by an English court or another court or otherwise.[8] [**106**]

LIVING TOGETHER

Section 9 (1) of the 1975 Act[9] provides that, where the applicant, or one of them, is a parent,[10] step-parent or relative[11] of the child or the child has been placed with the applicants by an adoption agency or in pursuance of an order of the High Court,[12] an adoption order cannot be made unless the child is at least 19 weeks old and at all times during the preceding thirteen weeks had his home with the applicants or one of them. This period corresponds in substance to the present rule[13] requiring "actual custody" for three months, not counting the first six weeks of the child's life. Under section 9 (2),[14] in the case of any other

---

[1] See para. [**94**], *ante*.

[2] Sch. 4, Part IV, repealing Adoption Act 1958, s. 2 (3) (operative since 26th November 1976). See also H.C.R., Rec. 11.

[3] Ss. 8 (1) and 107 (1); (Adoption Act 1976, ss. 12 (1) and 72 (1)).

[4] S. 8 (5); (Adoption Act 1976, s. 12 (5)).

[5] For custodianship see Chaps. 9 and 10, *post*.

[6] See Freeman, *Children Act 1975*, 72/8.

[7] S. 8 (8); (Adoption Act 1976, s. 12 (7)).

[8] See further Freeman, *ibid*.

[9] Adoption Act 1976, s. 13 (1); see H.C.R., Rec. 58.

[10] This does not include the putative father; see para. [**48**], *ante*.

[11] As defined by the Adoption Act 1958, s. 57 (1); (Adoption Act 1976, s. 72 (1)).

[12] Presumably this means in pursuance of either its prerogative or its statutory jurisdiction. If the latter is included it creates anomalies. E.g., a third person who is granted care and control by a divorce county court under the Matrimonial Causes Act 1973 could not bring himself within s. 9 (1) of the 1975 Act (assuming he is not a parent, step-parent or relative) whereas he could if the order has been made by the High Court.

[13] Adoption Act 1958, s. 3 (1), as amended by the Children Act 1975, Sch. 3, para. 21 (4).

[14] Adoption Act 1976, s. 13 (2); see H.C.R., Rec. 15.

application the prerequisite is that the child is at least twelve months old and at all times during the preceding twelve months had his home with the applicants or one of them.[1] [**107**]

There are a number of points to note about these subsections.[2] One of these relates to subsection (2) and independent placements. The Act amends section 29 of the Adoption Act 1958 so as to make it an offence for a person other than an adoption agency[3] to make arrangements for the adoption of a child or place him for adoption unless the proposed adopter is a relative of the child or he is acting in pursuance of a High Court order.[4] Equally it is an offence for a person to receive a child who has been placed with him in breach of that rule.[5] Invariably there will be a mutual intention to evade section 29, but, even where the recipient receives the child and at that date does not have adoption in mind, he will be in breach of the section, since it imposes strict liability. Neither of the exceptions to the rule is likely to have a marked impact. High Court orders[6] are rarely made for this purpose, while it is the policy underlying the Act to encourage relatives to seek custodianship rather than adoption.[7] [**108**]

A possible ban on independent placements has long been a controversial issue. Those opposed to it ha e objected mainly on three grounds, namely, that (1) it would be an unwarranted interference with the parental right to determine the child's upbringing, (2) the risks and prejudicial effects of such placements are too readily assumed and overlook the control exercised through the investigations by the guardian *ad litem* and the court before the decision to make an adoption order is reached and (3) a ban would lead to evasion by way of unsatisfactory *de facto* adoptions. Such objections did not prevail with the Houghton Committee. Since adoption is of such profound importance to the child, parental liberty must yield to the child's welfare. Since the decision to place the child is the most vital stage in the adoption process, it is essential to ensure adequate safeguards at that stage and not rely merely on subsequent investigations. Many will find these latter arguments convincing. Less so may be that which minimises the risk of *de facto* adoptions on the ground that private

---

[1] If the child had his home there for twelve months, he must be at least twelve months old! Apparently sub-s. (2) is expressed in this way to emphasise that the first six weeks of the child's life can be included for the purpose of calculating the twelve-month period.

[2] They are not yet operative.

[3] Where the agency is an approved adoption society as respects England and Wales, it cannot act as such in Scotland except so far as the society considers it necessary in the interests of a child who has been or may be adopted, his parents, and guardians or those who have adopted or may adopt him. The restriction applies *mutatis mutandis* to a society approved for Scotland. See Adoption Act 1958, s. 29 (2) and (2A), as inserted by the Children Act 1975, s. 28 (*b*); (Adoption Act 1976, s. 11 (2); Sch. 3, Part II, para. 28).

[4] Adoption Act 1958, s. 29 (1) and (3) (*b*), as amended by the Children Act 1975, s. 28 (*a*); (Adoption Act 1976, s. 11 (1) and (3)).

[5] The new penalties, which operate from 26th November 1976, are a maximum term of three months' imprisonment (formerly six) or a maximum fine of £400 (formerly £100) or both. The same penalties attach to the offence of taking part in the management or control of a body which exists to arrange adoptions but is not an adoption agency. See Adoption Act 1958, s. 29 (3), as amended by the Children Act 1975, s. 28 (*c*); (Adoption Act 1976, s. 11 (3)).

[6] See p. 58, n. 12, *ante*.

[7] See Chaps. 9 and 10, *post*.

fostering is, in any event, controlled. Although the Act does something to strengthen that control, its efficacy remains questionable.[1] [**109**]

Section 9 (2) allows for a backdoor compromise between these conflicting views. The general prohibition will not totally prevent the independent placement,[2] because it will be possible for a child to be placed with private foster-parents ostensibly on a temporary basis but then after twelve months for the foster-parents to rely on the subsection and seek an adoption order. While there is much to be said for exceptionally allowing the door to adoption to remain open to private foster-parents in those cases where an application would be in the child's interests,[3] it is doubtful whether the period of twelve months will prove a sufficient safeguard against fraudulent placements. There is, however, the possible further discouragement against adoption applications following private placements which is provided by the special duty to investigate imposed upon the local authority.[4] The authority's report to the court hearing the adoption application must state whether the child was placed with the applicants in contravention of section 29 of the 1958 Act. If there has been contravention but criminal proceedings have not yet been instituted,[5] the court will, it is suggested, adjourn the hearing pending the outcome of the criminal proceedings, although the Act is silent on the point and open to the construction that the court could proceed with the application The Act is also far from clear about what may happen to the child if criminal proceedings are taken before the hearing of the adoption application and the applicant is convicted of receiving the child in contravention of section 29. It is expressly provided that where a person is so convicted section 17 of the 1975 Act is to apply as it applies where an application for an adoption order is refused.[6] This means that the convicting court can invoke the powers of that section. The section enables a court either (1) to make an order placing the child under the supervision of a local authority or probation officer if it considers that exceptional circumstances make it desirable or (2) to commit the child to the care of a local authority if exceptional circumstances make it impracticable or undesirable for the child to be entrusted to either of the parents or to any other individual. Is it implicit in the conferment of these powers that, if there are no such exceptional circumstances, the convicting court has the power to return the child to the parent[7] or to allow him to continue to live with the intending adopter, even though both parent and recipient may have been convicted, or to place him with some other individual? If so what is the precise nature of the order to be made?

---

[1] Paras. [**415**]–[**419**], *post*.

[2] I.e., apart from the two recognised exceptions, para. [**108**], *ante*.

[3] See H.C. Official Report, 1975, Standing Committee A (Third Sitting), cols. 133–134 Dr. David Owen). Cf. H.C.R., Rec. 15.

[4] See s. 18, especially sub-s. (3) (*b*), para. [**115**], post; (Adoption Act 1976, s. 22).

[5] The illegality of the original placement may not have been discovered until shortly before the date of the hearing of the adoption application.

[6] Adoption Act 1958, s. 29 (5), as substituted by the Children Act 1975, s. 28 (*d*); (Adoption Act 1976, ss. 11 (5) and 26).

[7] Compare the former enactment in the Adoption Act 1958, s. 29 (5) which expressly enabled a convicting court to do this; and see *ibid.*, s. 50 (2); (Adoption Act 1976, s. 57 (2)), which gives a court convicting for an offence relating to unlawful payments power to remove the child to a place of safety until he can be restored to the parent or guardian or until other arrangements can be made.

It is suggested that the scope of the convicting court's powers ought to have been clearly spelt out, especially in view of the fact that, being an adult criminal court, it will have had little experience of making orders affecting children. If, on the other hand, it is *not* implicit that the court has these powers when it does not make an order under section 17, it seems to follow that the court hearing the adoption application would have to determine the child's future. Although there is, it is submitted, nothing in the Act to prevent it from making an adoption order, notwithstanding the conviction,[1] there would have to be cogent reasons, based on the child's welfare, before it would do so. Instead, it would be likely to rely on the powers it has when refusing adoption [2] [**110**]

In any case of a joint application it will be sufficient if the child has had his home with only one of the applicants during the relevant period, thus facilitating adoptions where, for example, the husband's job requires him to be away for periods at a time, particularly overseas.[3] The child's interests are, nevertheless, substantially protected by virtue of section 9 (3),[4] which requires the court to be satisfied that sufficient opportunities to see the child with both applicants together in the home environment have been afforded to the adoption agency which placed the child or, in non-agency cases, to the local authority within whose area the applicants have their home. The same opportunities must be given in the case of adoption by one person. No time limit is imposed by the subsection, but it envisages a number of opportunities and their actually being taken up. "Home environment" is not defined, but essentially, it is submitted, it signifies the household of which the applicants and the child form part: its location, its size and the interrelationship of its members. [**111**]

The Act does, on the other hand, explain what is meant by a child's having a home with a person, but the substitution in section 9 (1) and (2) of this test for that of "care and possession"[5] does not, it is submitted, materially change the nature of the legal relationship of the parties during the relevant period or the nature of the requisite continuity of that period. Section 87 (3) provides that references to the person with whom a child has his home refer to the person who has "actual custody", which in turn is defined as "actual possession".[6] As with the former law this latter term cannot be construed literally, but the 1975 Act expressly recognises this reality by enacting that actual custody continues notwithstanding absence of the child at a hospital or boarding school or any other temporary absence.[7] The principle of whether the applicant stands *in loco parentis* to the child, which the English courts eventually accepted under the former law,[8] continues to operate. There may, however, be a slight modification of the former law. It seems that under that the continuity was not broken even

---

[1] Compare the express prohibition on making an order where the applicant has contravened the rules relating to payments in relation to adoption; see Children Act 1975, s. 22 (5); (Adoption Act 1976, s. 24 (2)); para. [**119**], *post*.

[2] See para. [**146**], *post*.

[3] The change in effect implements a *Houghton* recommendation (Rec. 59).

[4] Adoption Act 1976, s. 13 (3); cf. H.C.R., Rec. 88.

[5] For the former rule (Adoption Act 1958, s. 3 (1)) see Bevan, *op. cit.*, pp. 328–331.

[6] *Ibid.*, sub-s. (1). See further para. [**237**], *post*. The transitional provision (Sch. 3 para. 21 (4)), which is already operative, substitutes "actual custody" for "care and possession".

[7] S. 87 (3).

[8] Beginning with *Re B. (an infant)*, [1964] Ch. 1; [1963] 3 All E.R. 125.

though the child might have been absent from the applicant during the whole of the relevant period, e.g., in hospital.[1] The 1975 Act will not, it is submitted, permit that possibility. If it did, it would not be possible to comply with the requirement of section 9 (3) that opportunities be afforded to see the child with the applicant in the home environment. [**112**]

The primary object of requiring the child to live with the adopters for a prescribed period before an adoption order can be made is to ensure that they are suitably matched. The object is only properly achieved by keeping the child away from the natural parent during that period so that none of the parties, particularly the child, should suffer unnecessary emotional disturbance.[2] The decision in *Re C.S.C.* (*an infant*)[3] is therefore intrinsically sound. There it was held that continuity had been broken by the fact that during the relevant period the applicants allowed the mother to take the child away to her own home, on one occasion for two consecutive nights and on the other for a night and a day. However, by virtue of section 87 (3) such temporary absences would not break the continuity. Yet, they should, it is submitted, be taken into account in applying section 3 when deciding whether to make an adoption order, and in those cases where the child has been placed with a stranger with a view to adoption, as opposed to those where he has had his home with a relative or a long-term foster parent, such an absence should be a cogent factor against the making of an order. [**113**]

NOTIFICATION TO LOCAL AUTHORITY

No adoption order can be made in respect of a child who was not placed by an adoption agency unless the applicant has given at least three months' notice to the local authority within whose area he has his home that he intends to apply for the order.[4] On giving of the notice the child becomes a protected child and the authority must then investigate and submit a report to the court.[5] The Act will abolish the exceptions under the present law to the giving of notice where the child is above the maximum compulsory school age or where the applicant is the parent whatever the child's age. It does, however, create its own exception. Where the child has been placed with the applicant by an adoption agency the agency is responsible for submitting a report to the court and must assist it in any manner it may direct.[6] This division of responsibility logically follows from the division of functions for which section 9 (3) provides. One of the defects in past adoption practice has been the duplication of supervision by the local authority and the adoption agency between the time of placement of the child by the agency and the making of an adoption order.

---

[1] Bevan, *op. cit.*, p. 329. Cf. *G. Petitioner*, 1955 S.L.T. (Sh. Ct.) 27.

[2] Bevan, *ibid.*

[3] [1960] 1 All E.R. 711; [1960] 1 W.L.R. 304.

[4] S. 18 (1); (Adoption Act 1976, s. 22 (1)). (Not yet operative.) The notice must be in writing; s. 107 (1) and s. 72 (1) respectively.

[5] S. 18 (2); (Adoption Act 1976, s. 22 (2)).

Invariably this will be a written report, but the Act does not exclude an oral report at the hearing of the application. For "protected children" under adoption law see paras. [**448**]–[**450**], *post*.

[6] S. 22 (3); (Adoption Act 1976, s. 23). (Not yet operative.)

Since section 9 (3), in removing this defect, provides for supervision by the agency alone where there is an agency placement but otherwise by the local authority, the agency is obviously the appropriate body to report to the court in the one case and the local authority in others.[1] [**114**]

The report of the local authority or, as the case may be, the agency must deal with the suitability of the applicant and any other matters relevant to the operation of section 3.[2] Since that section requires the court to consider all the circumstances, the report must be wide ranging.[3] It should, for example, deal with any matter which might assist in deciding whether a custodianship order is more appropriate than an adoption order[4] or any special circumstances which, if an adoption order were refused, might justify making a supervision order or an order committing the child to the care of a local authority.[5] A further duty is placed on the reporting local authority in non-agency placements to investigate whether an illegal placement or an illegal reception of the child has taken place in contravention of section 29 of the Adoption Act 1958.[6] [**115**]

THE HEARING

Notification of hearing

In applications both for an adoption order where the child is not free for adoption and for a section 14 order[7] every person who can be found[8] and whose agreement or consent respectively to the making of the order is required or may be dispensed with must be notified of a date and place where he may be heard on the application. Attendance is not necessary unless he so wishes or the court requires it.[9] Rules will doubtless prescribe the appropriate procedure for fulfilling these requirements when they come into force. Meanwhile the Adoption Rules 1976 meet the point that those whose agreement to an adoption order is necessary should be notified by requiring notice to be given to each parent or guardian, other than one who is an applicant for the order. [**116**]

Although the Act does not require notification to any other person, the 1976 Rules substantially re-enact the former Rules requiring other persons to be notified.[10] As already noted, the point is of special significance to the natural

---

[1] See H.C.R., paras. 237 and 244, and Rec. 60.

[2] Ss. 18 (3) (*a*) and 22 (3) respectively; (Adoption Act 1976, ss. 22 (3) (*a*) and 23).

[3] Whereas the limit of the agency's duty is to report on the applicant's suitability and matters relevant to s. 3, under s. 18 (3) these are matters "in particular" for investigation and report. Although the inference is that other matters concerning the adoption application may be investigated, it is difficult to visualise any (apart from that dealt with by s. 18 (3) (*b*)) which are not relevant to s. 3.

[4] In accordance with s. 37.

[5] Under s. 17 (1); (Adoption Act 1976, s. 26 (1)).

[6] Adoption Act 1976, s. 11. The efficacy of this penal sanction has been doubted; see Freeman, *op. cit.*, 72/18.

[7] Adoption Act 1976, s. 18. See Chap. 5, *ante.*

[8] See para. [**55**], *ante*, for the extent of the obligation to trace.

[9] S. 22 (1); (Adoption Act 1976, s. 66 (3)). For the procedure on applications for adoption of children abroad under s. 25 see para. [**167**], *post.*

[10] Adoption (High Court) Rules 1976, rr. 18 and 19; Adoption (County Court) Rules 1976, rr. 4 (2) and 12 (2); Magistrates' Courts (Adoption) Rules 1976, rr. 4 (2) and 11 (1) (*b*). For the former Rules relating to notification see Bevan, *op. cit.*, pp. 357–358.

father of the illegitimate child where he is not his guardian,[1] to the parent or guardian whose child is the subject of a care order[2] and to local authorities and voluntary organisations.[3] [**117**]

Restriction on further applications

Once applicants have been refused an adoption order no further application by them can be heard in respect of the same child unless the court directed otherwise when refusing the previous application or it appears to the court that there has been a change in circumstances or some other reason making it proper to proceed with the application.[4] The discretion given is a wide one,[5] and in exercising it the court must discharge the duty imposed by section 3. It would appear that, if on the earlier application the court chose to make a custodianship order, treating the application as though it had been an application for custodianship, its action would constitute a refusal of an adoption order within the meaning of the above rule. This would mean that the custodians would not have an unfettered right later to apply for adoption. This restriction on further application extends to a British adoption order, which means an adoption order made by a court in England and Wales or Scotland authorised by the Act to make an adoption order or any provision for the adoption of a child effected under the law of Northern Ireland or any British territory outside the United Kingdom.[6] [**118**]

Payments by or to applicants

Under the former law the court before making an adoption order had to be satisfied that the applicant had not received or agreed to receive, and that no one had made or given or agreed to make or give to him, any payment or other reward in consideration of the adoption except such as the court might sanction.[7] The 1975 Act goes further and bars the making of adoption orders not only where applicants are the recipients of unlawful payments but also in those cases where they have made the payments. That apparently is the effect of section 22 (5), which provides that no adoption order can be made unless the court is satisfied that the applicant has not contravened section 50 of the Adoption Act 1958.[8] Under subsection (1) of the latter section[9] it is unlawful to make or give to any person any payment or reward for or in consideration of:

(a) the adoption by that person of a child;
(b) the grant by that person of any agreement or consent required in connection with the adoption of a child;

---

[1] Para. [**48**], *ante*; paras. [**50**]–[**51**], *ante*.
[2] Para. [**49**], *ante*.
[3] See *ibid*. and p. 34, n. 9, *ante*.
[4] S. 22 (4); (Adoption Act 1976, s. 24). (Operative since 26th November 1976).
[5] Cf. a similar restriction and discretion allowing further applications to revoke a s. 14 order (s. 16 (5); Adoption Act 1976, s. 20 (5)) or to revoke a custodianship order (s. 35 (2)).
[6] S. 107 (1); (Adoption Act 1976, s. 72 (1)); see *ibid*. for the meaning of British territory.
[7] Adoption Act 1958, s. 7 (1) (*c*). Repealed by Children Act 1975, Sch. 4, Part IV. (Repeal operative since 26th November 1976).
[8] Operative since 26th November 1976.
[9] As amended by the Children Act 1975, Sch. 3, paras. 21 (2), 21 (4) and 34 (*a*).

(c) the transfer by that person of the actual custody of a child with a view to the adoption of the child; or
(d) the making by that person of any arrangements for the adoption of a child.

Under subsection (2) both the person making or agreeing or offering to make the payment or reward and the one who receives or agrees to receive or attempts to obtain it commit an offence. Thus the effect of section 22 (5) of the 1975 Act is that an applicant for adoption who provides a payment contrary to any of paragraphs (b), (c) or (d) cannot be granted an order. By the nature of things where paragraph (a) applies he must be the recipient. Nevertheless, by virtue of subsection (2) he will have contravened section 50 and therefore equally will be barred from adopting. However, as matters stand, this last rule will only continue to operate until the Adoption Act 1976 comes into force, because section 24 (2) of that Act expressly limits the bar to the person making the unlawful payment:

> "The court shall not make an adoption order in relation to a child unless it is satisfied that the applicants have not, as respects the child, made any payment or given any reward to a person in contravention of section 57."[1]

So, the effect of the 1976 Act, a consolidating Act no more, will be to provide a complete reversal of the bar which originally operated under the 1958 Act in that it makes paying or giving by the applicant, and not his receiving, the relevant test. Nevertheless, when section 24 (2) comes into force, the applicant who receives an unlawful payment will still be criminally liable,[2] and the court ought, it is submitted, to take this into account in accordance with section 3 of the Children Act,[3] when deciding whether to grant or refuse an adoption order. However, it may well be that provision has already been made for the child. Where an offence has been committed the convicting court may order the child to be removed to a place of safety until he can be restored to his parents or guardian or until other arrangements can be made for him. **[119]**

A payment *to* an adoption agency by the parent or guardian or by the applicant for adoption which is made to meet expenses reasonably incurred in connection with adoption is already exempt from the general prohibition. So are payments sanctioned by the court, although these are not frequent.[4] The Act introduces a further exception allowing for payments to be made *by* an adoption agency to actual or intended adopters, provided that the Secretary of State has approved a scheme for such payments being made by the agency.[5] **[120]**

This new and hotly[6] controversial provision is intended for a minority of children whose chances of being adopted need special encouragement; for

---

[1] S. 57 of the 1976 Act will replace s. 50 of the 1958 Act.
[2] Adoption Act 1976, s. 57 (2).
[3] Adoption Act 1976, s. 6.
[4] Adoption Act 1958, s. 50 (3); (Adoption Act 1976, s. 57 (3)).
[5] Adoption Act 1958, s. 50 (4)–(10), as inserted by the Children Act 1975, s. 32; (Adoption Act 1976, s. 57 (4)). (Not yet operative.)
[6] See especially the debate in Standing Committee A (Ninth Sitting), cols. 447–480, where the chairman's casting vote saved the provision.

example, the child in long-term institutional care whose links with his natural family have long been tenuous or the handicapped child whose particular needs will impose additional financial burden on his adopters. Strong objection was raised to this kind of financial dependence principally on the ground that it discriminates against the natural parents. "It would be an intolerable situation if financial resources were made available to subsidise adoption when an allocation of similar resources to the natural parents may have prevented the break up of the family in the first place."[1] Moreover, "those voluntarily assuming the rights of parenthood should assume all the financial obligations of parenthood."[2] A prospective adopter who insists on payment should automatically be suspect as a suitable adoptive parent.[3] The cogency of these arguments is self-evident, but they are not likely to commend themselves to "Children Who [Already] Wait". Their special needs ought not to be denied because of the undoubted desirability of the general need to provide supportive measures to prevent family breakdown and the particular need to expand child benefit schemes, whether the child be the natural, foster or adopted child. [**121**]

The concern which the new provision occasioned is partly reflected in the control to be exercised by the Secretary of State. A scheme is not only subject to his initial approval but may at any time be altered or revoked by him. He may also approve the agency's making alterations. His power to approve schemes is experimental[4] and will come to an end after seven years,[5] unless meanwhile he makes an order by way of statutory instrument continuing his power. The making of that order is, however, subject to Parliamentary approval by resolution of each House and the Secretary of State must have published a report on the operation of schemes since the provision came into force.[6] If it is to continue to operate, reports must thereafter be published every five years. Surprisingly, these are not the subject of specific Parliamentary scrutiny, but it is likely that the Secretary of State would refer to them in the quinquennial reports on the working of the Act which he is obliged to lay before Parliament.[7] [**122**]

The Act offers no guidance on the criteria which agencies should follow in submitting schemes for approval, but it seems that they will be expected to indicate any priorities which they may have in mind in operating the scheme; for example, whether precedence is to be given to children in community homes rather than those living with foster parents. Nor does it expressly prescribe a maximum age beyond which payments cannot be made. The absence of express provision probably supports the conclusion that payments must cease on the attainment of majority, even though the child in fact remains financially dependent upon the adopters.[8] Allowances paid under an approved scheme will continue to be made even if the scheme is later revoked by the Secretary of State

---

[1] British Association of Social Workers, *Analysis of Children Bill*, at p. 22.

[2] Samuels, *The Children Act 1975*, (1976) 6 Fam. Law at p. 7.

[3] See *ibid*.

[4] *Houghton* recommended pilot schemes; see H.C.R., Rec. 17.

[5] I.e., from the date when the new provision comes into operation. This is unlikely to be before 1979 in view of the present intention to postpone the introduction of the statutory adoption service beyond April 1978.

[6] This report is equally necessary where it is decided to terminate the power to approve.

[7] S. 105.

[8] Cf. the court's powers under the Matrimonial Causes Act 1973, ss. 23 and 52.

or his power to approve expires. This ensures that adopters who have been given financial assistance and adopted a child on that basis will not find financial support suddenly being withdrawn. [**123**]

GUARDIAN AD LITEM AND REPORTING OFFICER

The Act introduces two basic changes concerning the role of the guardian *ad litem* in the adoption process. When they take effect his appointment will no longer be mandatory in all cases and some of his present functions will be entrusted to the new office of the reporting officer.[1] [**124**]

The guardian ad litem

The first of these changes takes account of the criticisms that where there has been a placement by an adoption agency the appointment of a guardian *ad litem* leads to unnecessary duplication of work and that in any event the important decisions about the child's welfare will already have been taken by the agency. Moreover, the interests of the child will be further protected by the new rule[2] which will require the agency to submit a report to the court on the suitability of the applicants and on any other matters relevant to the operation of section 3. Guardians *ad litem* will be appointable for the purpose of an application for an adoption order or a freeing for adoption order or a revocation of the latter or an order vesting parental rights and duties in a case where it is intended to adopt abroad.[3] "Rules shall provide for appointment in such cases as are prescribed." This is an open-ended delegation of statutory powers, and it remains to be seen whether appointment in some prescribed cases will be mandatory, in others discretionary or in all mandatory or in all discretionary. It is to be hoped that the following, at least, will be included: (1) all contested adoption applications; (2) applications for a freeing for adoption order where section 14 (1) (*b*) or section 14 (2) (*b*)[4] is applicable; (3) all applications under section 25; and (4) all cases involving a point of law, difficulty or conflict; for example, where the court considers that it is more appropriate to make a custodianship order[5] or that the matter would be better dealt with under section 42 of the Matrimonial Causes Act 1973.[6] This last class of cases may require adjournment of the hearing so that a guardian may be appointed and investigate. [**125**]

Where a guardian is appointed his sole duty is to safeguard the interests of the child in the manner prescribed by Rules. Although these are likely to differ in points of detail from the present Adoption Rules,[7] there seems no reason why

---

[1] S. 20; (Adoption Act 1976, s. 65). (Not yet operative.) Meanwhile the Adoption Rules 1976 continue to require appointment in all cases.

[2] S. 22 (3); (Adoption Act 1976, s. 23). (Not yet operative.) See para. [**114**], *ante*.

[3] S. 25; (Adoption Act 1976, s. 55); see paras. [**165**]–[**171**], *post*.

[4] See paras. [**62**]–[**63**], *ante*.

[5] See s. 37, paras. [**273**]–[**282**], *post*.

[6] See ss. 10 (3) and 11 (4); (Adoption Act 1976, ss. 14 (3) and 15 (4)); paras. [**99**]–[**103**], *ante*. In the light of *Re S. (infants)*, [1977] 3 All E.R. 671, appointments for this purpose seem highly probable; see paras. [**100**]–[**102**], *ante*.

[7] See Adoption (High Court) Rules 1976, r. 13 (1); Adoption (County Court) Rules 1976 r. 11 (1); Magistrates' Courts (Adoption) Rules 1976, r. 10 (1); and the Second Schedule to each of these Rules.

they should not very largely follow the same lines, with the guardian investigating all the circumstances relevant to the application and interviewing all the interested parties.[1] [**126**]

The reporting officer

Reporting officers will be appointable in respect of the same kinds of applications as guardians ***ad litem*** but for purposes other than directly safeguarding the child's interests. Section 20 itself refers only to his responsibility of witnessing agreements to adoption. Strangely the Act does not require such agreements to be in writing, but invariably they will be. Indeed it encourages written agreement, because section 102[2] provides that, if the document signifying the agreement is witnessed in accordance with rules, it will be admissible in evidence without further proof of the signature of the person by whom it was executed.[3] Presumably the rules will include witnessing by the reporting officer. Section 20 does not, however, refer to witnessing consents to applications for freeing for adoption orders,[4] although section 102 equally applies to them. It is, therefore, uncertain whether all the other duties of a reporting officer, which are to be prescribed by rules, could include witnessing consents.[5] Section 20 (3) enables rules to provide for appointment of a reporting officer before an application is made. The main object of this provision is to allow the continuance of the present procedure whereby a written agreement to adoption may be attached to the application and, where appropriate, for enquiries to be made before the application is lodged, for example, during the first six weeks of the child's life. However, the subsection may support the conclusion that witnessing consents is an appropriate duty to give to the reporting officer. If he can be appointed before application, it would mean that before the adoption agency applied for a freeing for adoption order he could witness the parent's consent to the application. Unfortunately the Adoption Act 1976 may cast doubt on this conclusion because it does not re-enact subsection (3). On the other hand, it is arguable that the power to make rules imposing duties on reporting officers is sufficiently wide to include the rule in subsection (3). Otherwise it would be surprising if a consolidating Act could effect what would be a substantial amendment. [**127**]

Section 20 is open to the wider criticism that it fails to define the scope of the reporting officer's rôle in the adoption process, but it appears likely that the rules will require him to fulfill an advisory as well as a reporting function.[6] Almost certainly he will be called upon to ensure that a parent fully understands what adoption or freeing for adoption involves and the alternative possibilities, such as custodianship, that are available. This may involve the

---

[1] See Bevan, *op. cit.*, p. 353.

[2] Adoption Act 1976, s. 61. S. 102 is not yet operative.

[3] A document which purports to be witnessed in accordance with rules is presumed to be so witnessed and to have been executed and witnessed on the date and place specified in the document, unless the contrary is proved (s. 102 (2)). Cf. the present Rules; Adoption (High Court) Rules 1976, r. 7; Adoption (County Court) Rules 1976, r. 6; Magistrates' Courts (Adoption) Rules 1976, r. 6.

[4] See s. 14 (2); (Adoption Act 1976, s. 18 (2)); paras. [**62**]–[**63**], *ante*.

[5] *Houghton* recommended that this function should be included; see H.C.R., Rec. 40.

[6] See H.C. Official Report, 1975, Standing Committee A (Sixth Sitting), col. 287 (Dr. David Owen).

officer in discussion with the adoption agency. If these be part of his functions, it is essential that the rules allow for his appointment before any application is made.[1] Probably he will also be responsible for seeing that other interested parties, such as the putative father, are informed and consulted.[2] Like the guardian *ad litem* the reporting officer is to be appointed in such cases as are prescribed by rules. Given the nature of his likely duties it is not easy to visualise cases where his appointment is not necessary. [**128**]

Appointment of guardian ad litem and reporting officer

Because the functions of the guardian *ad litem* and the reporting officer call for impartiality, the Act ensures that both are independent of the adoption agency involved in the application. Thus, a person cannot act in either capacity for the purpose of a particular application if he is employed (a) in the case of an application for an adoption order, by the agency which placed the child or (b) in the case of an application for a freeing for adoption order, by the applicant agency or (c) in the case of an application to revoke a freeing for adoption order, by the agency in which the parental rights and duties have been vested.[3] There are no other restrictions and, if the court thinks fit, the same person may be both guardian and reporting officer. This latter rule may be justified on the ground that in the majority of applications the respective functions of the guardian *ad litem* and the reporting officer will be complementary and not involve any conflict of interests. Therefore, the rule avoids unnecessary duplication, an important consideration in view of the likely shortage of experienced persons suitable to discharge either office. However, since the Act provides for appointment of the guardian *ad litem* only in prescribed cases, there is much force in the view that the rôles should always be given to different persons. Perhaps judgment on this issue should be reserved until it is known in which kinds of cases appointment by the court are prescribed. [**129**]

The Act enables regulations to be made for the establishment of panels of persons from whom guardians *ad litem* and reporting officers may be appointed. This will be considered in relation to the topic of representation of the child in care proceedings.[4] [**130**]

RESTRICTIONS ON REMOVAL OF CHILD

Section 29 of the 1975 Act amends section 34 of the Adoption Act 1958 so as to create offences[5] for wrongful removal of the child, while adoption is pending, from the custody of the person with whom the child has his home.[6] The amendments, which have operated since 26th November 1976, form part of those provisions in the Act which are designed to prevent the sudden removal of a child from a stable environment. [**131**]

---

[1] See para. [**127**], *ante*.
[2] See para. [**50**], *ante*.
[3] S. 20 (2); (Adoption Act 1976, s. 65 (2)).
[4] Chap. 12, *post*.
[5] The maximum penalty for each is three months' imprisonment or a fine of £400 or both.
[6] Since the person with whom the child has his home has "actual custody" (s. 87 (3), para. [**237**], *post*), it would have been better if s. 34 had referred to that term rather than to "custody", especially since it is a professed object of the 1975 Act to achieve uniformity in terminology. Indeed, s. 34A (3), para. [**140**], *post*, does refer to "actual custody".

Restrictions where adoption agreed or application made for freeing for adoption (Section 34)

These are imposed upon the parent or guardian.

(1) The first is substantially a re-enactment of section 34 in its original form. While an application for an adoption order is pending and the parent or guardian has agreed to an adoption order being made in favour of a specific applicant, whether or not he knows his identity, he cannot remove the child against the will of the person with whom the child has his home, unless the court gives him permission,[1] as, for example, could occur where for reasons of ill health the applicant is unable satisfactorily to look after the child.

There are two significant points about the amendment. Whereas section 34 formerly provided that there can be no removal without leave of the court, whatever the views of the person having actual custody, the effect of the amendment apparently is that, if that person is willing, the parent or guardian will be entitled to remove the child without recourse to the court. If this is the effect, it is undesirable, since there must be some risk that return to the parent or guardian will not be in the child's interests. In all cases of possible removal the matter should be considered by the court.

When section 34 (1) states that the parent or guardian "has agreed" to the making of an adoption order it must not be overlooked that he still has the right to change his mind up to the hearing of the application, even though removal is meanwhile forbidden. That right is not removed by the Act, except where the parent or guardian is willing for the child to be freed for adoption in accordance with section 14. In this respect the section in its original form is to be preferred. By referring to the parent or guardian who has "signified his consent" it seemed impliedly to recognise the right. **[132]**

(2) The second restriction relates to certain applications under section 14 of the 1975 Act affecting children who are in the care of adoption agencies. Where the child is in the care of the adoption agency which has applied for a freeing for adoption order and the application was not made with the consent of each parent or guardian, then, so long as the application is pending, no parent or guardian who did not so consent is entitled to remove the child against the will of the person with whom the child has his home, unless the court grants leave.[2]

Here, too, the restriction does not operate if the person having actual custody consents to removal, but the implication is wider than it is under section 34 (1). That person may only have temporary actual custody and may not be the eventual applicant for the adoption order. For example, he may be a short term foster parent or a house-parent in a community home (where a local authority is the agency) or in a voluntary home (where an adoption society is the agency). Because the child is in the care of the agency one might have expected the agency's consent to be essential, but section 34 is a penal section, and the Government felt that to make the agency the appropriate body for giving consent would produce a harsh rule of criminal liability. For example, the

---

[1] Adoption Act 1958, s. 34 (1); (Adoption Act 1976, s. 27 (1)). "The court" means the court which is to hear the adoption application.

[2] Adoption Act 1958, s. 34 (2); (Adoption Act 1976, s. 27 (2)). "The court" means the court which is to hear the application for a section 14 order.

foster parent or house-parent might, on his own initiative and without reference to the agency, allow the child to be taken away and the parent or guardian might reasonably believe that he had obtained consent from higher authority. Where the foster parent or house-parent is the person whom the natural parent or guardian approaches it is reasonable that the latter's conduct be judged within that context. While this rule is defensible, section 34 (2) does not require the foster parent or house-parent first to consult the agency[1] and obtain its permission before allowing the child to be removed. Instead the matter is to be left to guidance and instructions issued by the Department of Health and Social Security to agencies.[2] Its importance, it is suggested, merited enactment either in section 34 itself or through an express power to make rules governing it. **[133]**

Restrictions where applicant has provided home for five years (*Section 34A*)

These very largely affect the foster parent with whom the child has had his home for at least five years. Like those in section 34 they ought to be seen as aimed at protecting the interests of the child not those of the applicant. **[134]**

Under subsection (1) of section 34A,[3] once the foster parent applies for an adoption order, then, subject to the qualifications considered below, the position is frozen until the application is heard, as it is in cases under section 34. Under subsection (2) he can secure further protection at an earlier date. As a prospective adopter he can notify the local authority[4] of his intention to apply for an order whereupon there cannot (subject to the same qualifications) be a lawful removal before either an application for such an order is made or three months have expired since receipt of the notice by the authority, whichever first occurs. Effectively, therefore, this means that, if the application is first made, the protection afforded by subsection (1) then operates. Otherwise the foster parent cannot shelter behind subsection (2) indefinitely. Nor can he evade the time limit by issuing successive notices to the authority before the previous one expires. There must be a gap of twenty-eight days before a new notice can be served, thus enabling the child meantime to be removed by the natural parents or the local authority or a voluntary organisation, if his interests so warrant.[5] **[135]**

Under the present law subsection (2) will automatically apply in all cases of prospective adoptions save where the prospective adopter or one of them is the parent or the child is over compulsory school age, because, apart from those cases, every prospective adopter must have given, at least three months before the date of the adoption order, notice to the local authority of his intended applica-

---

[1] I.e., the local authority or, in the case of an adoption society, its body of management. Failure to consult would, however, be a breach of any undertaking to the agency.

[2] See H.C. Official Report, 1975, Standing Committee A (Eighth Sitting), cols. 410–413.

[3] Adoption Act 1976, s. 28 (1). See H.C.R., Rec. 36.

[4] I.e., the local authority within whose area he has his home. If the authority knows that the child is in the care of another local authority or a voluntary organisation it must, within seven days, inform that other authority or the organisation that they have received the prospective adopter's notice (s. 34A (4); Adoption Act 1976, s. 28 (5)).

The Department of Health and Social Security has drafted suitable forms of notice which local authorities may choose to use; see L.A.C. (76) 15, Appendix 1.

[5] Sub-s. (5); (Adoption Act 1976, s. 28 (6)).

tion for an order.[1] Although section 18 of the 1975 Act, when it comes into force, will not require notice to be given to the local authority where the child was placed by an adoption agency, the change will not have any practical effect on the rule under consideration. If a local authority placed a child, who is in their care, with foster parents over five years ago it will not have been a placement in their function as an adoption agency. Notice under section 18 will therefore be necessary. **[136]**

The position of the prospective adopter in the case of an agency placement does, however, call for comment. The 1958 Act, as amended, indirectly encourages him to apply for adoption as soon as possible after placement, because then the protection against removal by the parent operates under section 34 (1).[2] Until he does so he has no protection corresponding to that provided by section 34A (2). **[137]**

The parent or guardian or anyone else will not commit an offence if the five-year applicant or prospective adopter changes his mind and allows him to remove the child,[3] but the chances of this happening are remote. Of greater practical importance is the power of the court[4] to grant permission for removal. An order may be made not only because removal would be in the child's interests but also on a technical ground, for example, that the continuity of actual custody for five years has been broken.[5] Additionally section 34A (1) and (2) allow for removal on the arrest of the child or under authority conferred by any enactment. The kind of enactments intended are those which enable removal to a place of safety where there is actual, or immediate risk of, harm to the child. The main examples are removal on the strength of a warrant issued by a justice of the peace under section 40 of the Children and Young Persons Act 1933[6] or under section 43 of the Sexual Offences Act 1956 or on his authorisation in accordance with section 28 of the Children and Young Persons Act 1969, or, in the case of a foster child who is being kept in unsuitable surroundings, by an order of the juvenile court under section 7 of the Children Act 1958. **[138]**

---

[1] Adoption Act 1958, s. 3 (2).

[2] Note, however, the prerequisite that the parent must already have agreed to the making of an adoption order.

[3] Cf. para. [**132**], *ante*.

If the child were in the care of a local authority or voluntary organisation and boarded out with the applicant or prospective adopter, his consent to removal would be a breach of his undertaking to the authority or organisation not to hand over the child to anyone without their approval.

[4] In the case of s. 34A (1) this will be the court which is to hear the adoption application; in the case of s. 34A (2), any court authorised to make adoption orders.

[5] S. 34A (1) and (2); (Adoption Act 1976, s. 28 (1) and (2)).

See the Local Authority Circular issued by the Department of Health and Social Security; L.A.C. (76) 15, Annex A, p. 6.

Temporary absences will not break the continuity; see Children Act 1975, s. 87 (3). This rule is of special importance where the child has had a contact with the parents during the five-year period; for example on week-end or holiday visits. Were the rule otherwise it would be difficult for many foster parents to meet the requirement of continuity. The child may be in the care of the local authority and fostered out and, as part of the local authority's power to maintain contact between the child and his natural family, the foster parent may have been directed to allow the child to be removed from time to time by the parent. It is submitted that visits of this kind will not interrupt the continuity of actual custody.

[6] As amended by C.Y.P.A. 1963, Sch. 3, para. 11.

The restrictions imposed by section 34A (1) and (2) have special relevance for the local authority. Where the child is not in their care they will be able to rely on the above enactments, but where he was already in care before he began to have his home with the applicant or prospective adopter and remains in care, their power to remove him is strictly curtailed. If he is in care under section 1 of the Children Act 1948 (whether or not a resolution under section 2 is in force) or where he is the subject of a care order, the authority cannot frustrate the foster parent's actual or prospective application for adoption by invoking their powers to remove under the 1948 Act or the Children and Young Persons Act 1969.[1] Section 34A (3) provides that they can only do so in accordance with sections 35 and 36 of the Adoption Act 1958[2] or with leave of the court. In relation to section 34A (1) and (2) those two sections have rhe following consequences. **[139]**

Section 35 itself is concerned with restricting removal where the child has been placed by an adoption agency in pursuance of arrangements for adoption. It is scarcely likely that a local authority, having placed a child with a person for that purpose, will have allowed him to remain with that person for five years before the adoption application is made. However, the restrictions of section 35 also extend[3] to the child who is for the time being in the care of a local authority and who has been entrusted to the actual custody[4] of a person but not in pursuance of arrangements for adoption. It thus covers, *inter alios*, the long-term foster parent. If he gives notice to the authority that he intends not to retain actual custody, he must then within seven days return the child to the authority. Alternatively the authority may notify him of their intention not to allow him to continue to have actual custody, in which case the child must similarly be returned within seven days. However, the authority cannot give notice after the foster parent has applied for an adoption order unless the court grants leave. Consequently, viewed in relation to section 34A (3), the foster parent is in a stronger position if he has applied for an order and is not merely a "prospective adopter". In the latter circumstance the authority will have to get in their notice under section 35 before the application is made. **[140]**

The restrictive effect of section 34A (3) raises the question of what steps can be taken to remove the child in an emergency. Supposing, for example, that the foster parents have to be rushed to hospital in circumstances which prevent them from giving their consent and there is no one in the foster home to look

---

[1] It has been suggested that one of the effects of s. 34A (1) is that, where the local authority has boarded out the child under an agreement with the foster parents, on application for adoption the contract is discharged and the obligations of the local authority to pay the agreed boarding out allowance and of the foster parent to observe the terms of the agreement cease to exist; see Freeman, *op. cit.*, 72/29. *Sed quaere.* Section 34A, it is respectfully submitted, is concerned only with the question of removal of the child and does not justify the construction that the child's interests are to be prejudiced pending the hearing of the adoption application. E.g., the local authority may and should continue visits to the child. It is noteworthy that "nothing in the [Boarding out of Children Regulations 1955] brings boarding out to an end when foster parents give notice of their intention to apply for an adoption order". (Clarke Hall and Morrison, *On Children* (9th Edn.), p. 180.)

[2] Adoption Act 1976, ss. 30 and 31.

[3] By virtue of s. 36.

[4] This term replaces "care and possession" in ss. 35 and 36; see Children Act 1975, Sch. 3, para. 21 (4).

after the child. It is submitted that, since the local authority itself cannot invoke any statutory power to remove the child to a place of safety, the appropriate step would be for the police to apply under section 28 of the Children and Young Persons Act 1969 for authority so to remove the child. That section enables a justice of the peace to authorise detention for up to twenty-eight days. The interim period would then allow time for the local authority under section 34A (3) to apply for, and the court to grant, leave to remove the child. [**141**]

As with the other time-limit provisions in the Act, assessing the practical implications of section 34A is necessarily speculative, and for that reason it allows for possible amendment of the prescribed period.[1] It has been suggested[2] that the chances of the natural parent's removing the child before the effluxion of the five years are small, but the risk will be greater if foster parents should see completion of that period as a reason in itself for making an application. That attitude, if widely assumed, could move natural parents to claim back their children before the "freeze" begins to take effect. [**142**]

Return of the child who is unlawfully removed

Section 30 of the 1975 Act[3] enables the person from whose custody[4] a child has been removed in breach of section 34 or section 34A of the Adoption Act 1958 to apply to an authorised court for an order that the person who has wrongfully removed the child return him to the applicant. An application can also be made where the applicant has reasonable grounds for believing that another is intending to remove in breach of either of those sections: the court may then forbid removal.[5] In either case the court has a discretion and in exercising it must act in accordance with section 3 of the 1975 Act. In particular, where the child has already been removed the court is likely to have regard to the length of time which has evolved in tracing him. Where, exceptionally, this is a protracted period (e.g., a year) an order to return him to the applicant might not be in the child's interests. [**143**]

When the High Court or a county court has made an order under section 30 because the child has been unlawfully removed and it has not been complied with, the court has additional enforcement powers[6] to order one of its officers to search specified premises and, if the child is found, to return him to the applicant. If the section 30 order was made by a magistrates' court, and also as an alternative to the above procedure where the order was made by the High Court or a county court, search and return can be authorised by a justice of the peace if he is satisfied by information on oath that there are reasonable grounds for believing the child is in specified premises. These additional powers will therefore enable the child to be recovered from any third party to whom the person committing a breach of section 34 or 34A has entrusted actual custody of the child. [**144**]

---

[1] Sub-s. (7). The instrument requires the affirmative approval of each House of Parliament.

[2] Para. [**5**], *ante*.

[3] Adoption Act 1976, s. 29. S. 30 came into effect on 26th November 1976.

[4] I.e., actual custody; see p. 69, n. 6, *ante*.

[5] Compare s. 30 with s. 42 of the 1975 Act, paras. [**257**]–[**258**], *post*.

[6] Sub-ss. (3) and (4).

REFUSAL OF AN ADOPTION ORDER

The restrictions imposed by section 35 of the Adoption Act 1958[1] also apply when the court refuses to make an adoption order and the child has been placed for adoption by an adoption agency, but the requirement that the child must be returned to the agency concerned within seven days after notice of the refusal has been amended by the 1975 Act,[2] so that the court, if it thinks fit, can extend the period up to a maximum of six weeks. The extension accords with other provisions in the Act which are designed to avoid the abrupt removal of a child and to allow for a planned introduction into a new home. In principle it could also enable the disappointed applicant to retain the child pending an appeal, but, in the absence of a rule requiring appeals to be heard within the maximum period, the extension will not have this practical advantage. This is unfortunate if the appellate court should reverse the decision. **[145]**

When the court refuses to make an adoption order, there are a number of courses open to it. Whether there has been an agency placement or not, it can always make an interim order in favour of the applicant[3] or, when section 37 of the 1975 Act comes into operation, it will be able to grant him custodianship. Should neither of these courses be followed and the case is one of an agency placement, the court may decide to take no further action itself, leaving the rule in section 35 (3), as amended,[4] to take effect. In a non-agency case, if the court takes no further action, the child will remain with the applicant unless the natural parent reclaims him. However, both in agency and non-agency cases, the court is now empowered[5] in exceptional circumstances and if the child is under 16 to make an order placing him under the supervision of a specified local authority or of a probation officer or to commit him to the care of a specified local authority. These exceptional powers correspond to those which courts can exercise under various enactments where the upbringing of a child is in issue; for example, when a court makes a custody order under section 9 of the Guardianship of Minors Act 1971.[6] **[146]**

In relation to the refusal to grant adoption orders there are, however, circumstances to which the powers can bear no relevance. This is so in those cases where the child is already in the care of a local authority: if the foster parent is refused adoption, there will be no question of needing to invoke either of the powers. The same will be true[7] where a section 14 order is in force, and thus the parental rights and duties are already vested in the adoption agency. With regard to the latter case, it should be added that the provisions governing revocation of section 14 orders do not enable the court to exercise either of the above exceptional powers. This, it is submitted, is a serious omission. It has

---

[1] Para. [**140**], *ante*.

[2] S. 31, amending s. 35 by inserting subsection (5A); (Adoption Act 1976, s. 30 (6)). The amendment took effect on 26th November 1976.

[3] See paras. [**149**]–[**151**], *post*.

[4] Para. [**140**], *ante*.

[5] Children Act 1975, s. 17 (1); (Adoption Act 1976, s. 26 (1)). This rule has operated since 26th November 1976.

[6] See Guardianship Act 1973, s. 2. The supplementary provisions of ss. 3 and 4 of that Act apply *mutatis mutandis* to orders made under s. 17 of the 1975 Act; see s. 17 (3); operative since 26th November 1976.

[7] S. 14 is not yet operative.

been seen[1] that on revocation the parental rights and duties will revest in a particular individual, usually the parent. It may, nevertheless, be desirable exceptionally to appoint a supervisor, particularly since the child must have been away from the parent for more than twelve months.[2] [**147**]

If the child is committed to the care of the local authority, the court may order either parent to pay to the authority (in the form of weekly or other periodical payments but not a lump sum) reasonable maintenance for the child while he is in the authority's care.[3] This is one of the instances in the Act of parents envisaging the severance of all links with the child only to find themselves later liable for his maintenance.[4] It is therefore essential that the implications of the court's powers are fully explained to the parents before they agree to adoption. [**148**]

INTERIM ORDERS

Interim orders have in practice been limited to cases where the court remains doubtful about the suitability of the placement, especially in cases of adoption applications by step-parents and relatives. The improvement of agency standards, the banning of independent placements with non-relatives and the availability of custodianship will further reduce the need for such orders.[5] Nevertheless, in accordance with *Houghton*,[6] the Act retains them as exceptional measures. Section 19[7] will make certain consequential amendments to the powers to make an interim order, taking account of the changes relating to agreement to adoption, freeing for adoption, the need in non-agency placements to notify the local authority of an adoption application and the concept of legal custody. Provided the requirements thereof are complied with, an interim order will still be made for a period of not more than two years, with power to extend to that maximum if in the first instance the order is made for a lesser period. [**149**]

This probationary period is not simply designed to provide a further opportunity of assessing the character and suitability of the applicant. It can and should be used for investigating all the circumstances which bear on the welfare of the child. Thus, the court may, for the interim period, impose such terms for the maintenance of the child and otherwise, as it thinks fit. It may, for example, prescribe conditions about his education and religious upbringing. It may even allow the natural parent access.[8] Presumably, the acceptance in section 3 of a test of "first consideration" and the refusal of a "first and paramount" test will tend to strengthen any claim for access. [**150**]

---

[1] Paras. [**81**]–[**83**], *ante*.

[2] See s. 16 (1), para. [**76**], *ante*, which imposes a minimum period of twelve months from the date of the section 14 order before revocation can be sought.

[3] S. 17 (2); (Adoption Act 1976, s. 26 (2)).

[4] Cf. ss. 34 and 37, paras. [**299**] and [**282**], *post*.

[5] H.C.R., para. 310.

[6] *Ibid.*

[7] The section, which is not yet operative, will replace s. 8 of the Adoption Act 1958; (Adoption Act 1976, s. 25).

[8] *S.* v *Huddersfield Borough Council*, [1975] Fam. 113; [1974] 3 All E.R. 296 (C.A.).

One notable change is that which will confer a right of appeal against an interim order made by any court as much as against a full adoption order.[1]

[151]

---

[1] Whereas appeal from a county court lies against the making or refusal of an interim order under the present law (*Re K. (an infant)*, [1953] 1 Q.B. 117 [1952] 2 All E.R. 877), there is no appeal from a decision of a juvenile court.

For appeals generally against orders made or refused under the 1975 Act, see para. [**440**], *post*.

CHAPTER 7

CONVENTION ADOPTION ORDERS AND ADOPTION OF CHILDREN ABROAD

CONVENTION ADOPTION ORDERS

Section 24[1] is one of the sections of the 1975 Act whose value is not readily apparent. When it comes into force,[2] it will replace some of the provisions of the Adoption Act 1968, an Act which itself awaits implementation. The section is not concerned with substantial changes, but with rephrasing the earlier provisions. It can scarcely be said that it will thereby reduce their complexity. On the contrary, the fact that parts of the 1968 Act are untouched by the Children Act adds to that result. It will be as well therefore if the consolidating Adoption Act 1976 supersedes both the 1968 Act and section 24 before they ever become operative. At least the complexity will again be confined within one statute. [**152**]

The purpose of the Adoption Act 1968 is to implement the Hague Convention on Adoption (1965),[3] to which the United Kingdom Government was a signatory. It empowers the High Court (or in Scotland the Court of Session)[4] to make inter-country adoption orders. An essential feature of these "Convention adoption orders" is that the applicant either does not have the same nationality as the child or resides in a different country. This principle is partly given explicit recognition in that "the applicant or applicants and the child must not all be United Kingdom nationals living in British territory".[5] A Convention adoption order must be recognised in other contracting States and can be enforced in accordance with proceedings prescribed by the Convention. The Convention cannot take effect until ratified by at least three countries. Only Austria and Switzerland have so far done so. Ratification by the United Kingdom will be possible once the rules of procedure for the Courts have been drafted. It is to be hoped that the consolidation of adoption law in the Adoption Act 1976 will facilitate that possibility. [**153**]

---

1 Adoption Act 1976, s. 17.

2 No date has yet been fixed.

3 See Cmnd. 2613; Adoption Act 1968, s. 11 (1); Children Act 1975, s. 107 (1); (Adoption Act 1976, s. 72 (1)). For a comment on the Tenth Hague Conference, which led to the Convention, see Graveson (1965), 14 I.C.L.Q. 528.

4 Adoption Act 1968, s. 11 (1); Children Act 1975, s. 100 (5); (Adoption Act 1976, s. 62 (4)).

5 Children Act 1975, s. 24 (3); (Adoption Act 1976, s. 17 (3)).

QUALIFICATIONS OF THE PARTIES

(i) *The child*

Under section 24 (2) a child is qualified to be adopted if (a) he is a national of the United Kingdom or of a Convention country and (b) he habitually resides in British territory or a Convention country.[1] The subsection further provides that the child must never have been married, as in the case of an "internal" adoption order made under section 8 of the 1975 Act.[2] Although in re-enacting section 24 (2) the Adoption Act 1976[3] does not expressly repeat the rule concerning marriage,[4] it is submitted that the disqualification is to be implied when that Act becomes operative. To remove it would be a substantial change not warranted by a consolidating statute. The general qualifications and conditions applicable in respect of internal adoption orders are intended also to apply to Convention adoption orders except in so far as expressly excluded or modified.[5] On this basis the rule that an adoption order may be made notwithstanding that the child is already an adopted child[6] also applies to the making of Convention adoption orders as it does to internal adoption orders. **[154]**

It has already been noted[7] that the provisions in section 12 (1) of the 1975 Act relating to freeing for adoption and to parental agreement to the making of an adoption order do not apply to an application for a Convention adoption where the child is not a United Kingdom national.[8] The Hague Convention accepts the principle that consents and consultations are matters to be governed by the *lex patriae*, i.e., by the internal law[9] of the Convention country of which the child is a national.[10] The court must be satisfied that each person who consents to the order in accordance with that law does so with full understanding of what is involved. This rule is not directed at any requirement which the foreign law may impose concerning consent by or consultation with the applicant and members of his family, including his spouse.[11] The implication therefore is that English domestic law would govern, but the point is not, it is submitted, of any practical significance now that the 1975 Act has abolished the requirement that where one spouse was a sole applicant the other had to consent to adoption.[12] **[155]**

---

1 For the meaning of "habitually resides", "British territory" and "Convention country" see paras. [**164**], [**160**], [**161**], *post*.

2 S. 8 (5); (Adoption Act 1976, s. 12 (5)); see para. [**106**], ante.

3 S. 17 (2).

4 The point was also covered by the Adoption Act 1968; see the definition of "qualified infant" in s. 11 (1). However, that Act will be wholly repealed by the 1976 Act without the definition being re-enacted.

5 Cf., for example, the rule relating to consents, paras. [**155**]–[**156**], *post*.

6 Children Act 1975, s. 8 (8); (Adoption Act 1976, s. 12 (7)).

7 Para. [**56**], *ante*.

8 Children Act 1975, s. 12 (3); (Adoption Act 1976, s. 16 (3)). It must be stressed that the freeing for adoption procedure cannot be invoked where a Convention adoption order is being sought.

9 For the rules determining the internal law see para. [**163**], *post*.

10 Children Act 1975, s. 24 (6); (Adoption Act 1976, s. 17 (6)). S. 24 (6) will replace s. 3 (3) (*a*) of the Adoption Act 1968, the latter provision having already been repealed, since 1st January 1976, by the Children Act 1975, s. 108 (4) (*d*) and Part III of Sch. 4.

Note the reference in sub-s. (6) to "consents" and not "agreements"; cf. p. 34, n. 1, *ante*.

11 S. 24 (7); (Adoption Act 1976, s. 17 (7)).

12 See para. [**58**], *ante*.

The provisions in section 102 of the Act[1] concerning the admissibility of evidence of agreements and consents do not apply to Convention adoption orders. Instead, for the purpose of section 24 (6) the necessary consents may be proved in accordance with rules to be prescribed.[2] Where the foreign law allows for consents to be dispensed with, it is the High Court (or the Court of Session) which is the authority which decides whether to do so, but it must act within the limits imposed by the foreign law. However, where that law requires the attendance before the Court of any person who does not reside in Great Britain,[3] the requirement can be satisfied if he has been given a reasonable opportunity of communicating his opinion on the adoption to the proper Court official, or to an appropriate authority of the Convention country in question for transmission to the Court, provided that, if he has taken up the opportunity, his opinion has reached the court. **[156]**

(ii) *The applicant or applicants*

A husband and wife are qualified to make a joint application for a Convention adoption order if either (a) each is a national of the United Kingdom or of a Convention country and both habitually reside in Great Britain, or (b) both are United Kingdom nationals and each habitually resides in British territory or a Convention country. There must, therefore, be either common United Kingdom nationality or common residence in Great Britain. In the case of a sole applicant he must either (a) be a national of the United Kingdom or of a Convention country and habitually reside in Great Britain, or (b) be a United Kingdom national and habitually reside in British territory or a Convention country.[4] **[157]**

Where joint applicants are nationals of the same Convention country or a sole applicant is a national of a Convention country, an adoption order cannot be made if the proposed adoption is prohibited by a provision of the internal law of that country and, in pursuance of the Hague Convention, that provision is notified to the United Kingdom Government and then specified in a statutory instrument.[5] **[158]**

Section 24 requires the conditions which it imposes to be satisfied both at the time of the application and when the order is made. Thus, the requirements

---

[1] Adoption Act 1976, s. 61.

[2] S. 24 (7); (Adoption Act 1976, s. 17 (7)). S. 24 (7) will replace s. 3 (4) of the Adoption Act 1968, the latter having already been repealed by the Children Act 1975, s. 108 (4) (*d*) and Part III of Sch. 4.

[3] The foreign residence does not have to be habitual. *Semble* "resides" here means "lives". Cf. s. 24 (3), para. **[153]**, *ante*.

[4] Children Act 1975, s. 24 (4) and (5); (Adoption Act 1976, s. 17 (4) and (5)). See also the next footnote.

[5] *Ibid.* and s. 24 (8); (Adoption Act 1976, s. 17 (8)). S. 24 (4), (5) and (8) will replace s. 3 (1) and (5) and certain definitions in s. 11 (1) of the Adoption Act 1968, which have already been repealed by the Children Act 1975, s. 108 (4) (*d*) and Part III of Sch. 4.

In accordance with Art. 13 of the Hague Convention the provision may relate to any of the following matters: (a) the existence of descendants of the adopter(s); (b) the fact that a single person is applying to adopt; (c) the existence of a blood relationship between an adopter and the child; (d) the existence of a previous adoption of the child by other persons; (e) the requirement of a difference in age between the adopter(s) and the child; (f) the age of the adopter(s) and that of the child; and (g) the fact that the child does not reside with the adopter(s).

concerning the nationality and habitual residence of the applicant or applicants and of the child must be referred to both dates.[1] It follows also that, in the exceptional case where a prohibition under the foreign law is notified and then specified in a statutory instrument which is made after the application has been presented but before the order is due to be made, the notified provision cannot prevent such an order. **[159]**

DEFINITIONS AND CONCEPTS

(i) *British Territory*

The Adoption Act 1968[2] distinguishes between Great Britain and a "specified country", the latter referring to any of the following countries which are designated by order of the Secretary of State for the purposes of any provision of that Act: Northern Ireland, any of the Channel Islands, the Isle of Man and a colony. If none of these is designated, any of them may be treated as a specified country. The Children Act 1975[3] collectively refers to all of these as "British territory" for the purposes of this Act. **[160]**

(ii) *Convention country*

This means any country outside British territory, being a country for the time being designated by an order of the Secretary of State as a country in which, in his opinion, the Convention is in force.[3] **[161]**

(iii) *Nationality*

Section 9 of the 1968 Act, which is extended to the Children Act,[4] contains a number of rules for determining in doubtful cases whether a person is a national of a Convention country. First, the Secretary of State may by order specify, in accordance with information given by the Government of a Convention country, kinds of persons who are to be treated as nationals of that country. Secondly, where a person is a national of two or more countries, he is to be treated as a national of one of them according to certain rules of priority. If he is a United Kingdom national, which term is qualified by the 1968 Act[5] to mean a citizen of the United Kingdom and Colonies satisfying such conditions, if any, as the Secretary of State may specify for the purposes of the Act, he must always be so treated. If he is not, his Convention country of nationality has priority or, where there are two or more Convention countries that with which he is most closely connected. In any other case, where no Convention country is involved, it is the country of closest connection. Thirdly, a person with no, or no ascertainable, nationality is to be treated as a national of the country in which he habitually resides. **[162]**

---

1 The Adoption Act 1968 was silent about a double test being required in respect of the child. The chances of his changing nationality or habitual residence between the two dates are very remote.

2 S. 11 (1).

3 S. 107 (1); (Adoption Act 1976, s. 72 (1)).

4 Children Act 1975, s. 24 (9). S. 9 and s. 24 (9) respectively will be replaced by the Adoption Act 1976, s. 70.

5 S. 11 (1).

Where the *lex patriae* is relevant and the country of nationality contains more than one legal system (e.g., in the United States) the Court will apply the rules of selection operating in that country to determine the relevant legal system. If there are no rules, the system is that which appears to the High Court (or the Court of Session) to be the one most closely connected with the case.[1] [**163**]

(iv) *Habitual residence*

This concept has been introduced to English law over the last two decades in legislation giving effect to several Hague Conventions.[2] It has never been defined and the Hague Conventions have left each country to provide its own definition. Its meaning was considered for the first time when the High Court was considering the recognition of a foreign divorce.[3] It is submitted that habitual residence is more than ordinary residence and that it is a person's real home where he has enjoyed a regular physical presence continuing for some time. Allowance should be made for the usual absences such as holidays and business trips, provided that the period away does not substantially interrupt the continual presence. A person's intention may be indicative of the nature of the residence, but is not an essential requirement. If he establishes a sufficient connection with the country in question, then there is no need to determine his intention; but it may be relevant in deciding whether there is the requisite connection. To hold otherwise would come dangerously close to requiring the element of *animus* necessary for domicile. Whatever the quality essential for habitual residence, English private international law is not prepared to accept the continental doctrine which equates that concept with domicile.[4] [**164**]

ADOPTION OF CHILDREN ABROAD

It is normally an offence to take or send a child who is a British subject out of Great Britain to any place outside the British Islands (i.e., the United Kingdom, the Channel Islands and the Isle of Man) for the purpose of his being adopted.[5] Section 53 of the Adoption Act 1958 admits one exception by allowing a provisional adoption order to be made and thus enabling the child to be taken abroad with a view to his being adopted. Section 25 of the Children Act 1975

---

[1] Adoption Act 1968, s. 10 (1) which is extended to the Children Act 1975, by virtue of s. 24 (9) of the latter Act; (Adoption Act 1976, s. 71 (2)).

[2] See the Administration of Justice Act 1956; the Wills Act 1963; Adoption Act 1968; Recognition of Divorces and Legal Separations Act 1971; Domicile and Matrimonial Proceedings Act 1973.

[3] *Cruse* v. *Chittum* (*formerly Cruse*), [1974] 2 All E.R. 940. See Hall (1975), 24 I.C.L.Q. 1; Parry (1975), 53 Can. Bar Rev. 135.

[4] See Art. 5 of the Hague Convention to regulate Conflicts between the Law of Nationality and the Law of Domicile (1955) and the Seventh Report of the P.I.L. Committee, para. 16.

[5] Adoption Act 1958, s. 52 (1), as amended by the Children Act 1975, Sch. 3, para. 36 and Sch. 4. The amendment in so far as it alters the penalties is already operative. The maximum term of imprisonment is now three months instead of six and the maximum fine £400 instead of £100; (Adoption Act 1976, s. 56 (1)).

The restriction imposed by s. 52 does not apply if the child is to be received by a parent, guardian or relative. Note also the power of local authorities to arrange for the emigration of children in their care (Children Act 1948, s. 17).

will replace section 53,[1] but the basic purpose remains the same. The High Court or a county court[2] will be able to make, in favour of a person who is not domiciled in England and Wales or Scotland, an order vesting in him the parental rights and duties relating to the child, if the court is satisfied that the applicant intends to adopt the child under the law of, or *within the country of* the applicant's domicile.[3] Although the Houghton Committee recommended[4] the continuance of provisional adoption orders, it expressed concern over the fact that there is no way in which persons who have obtained such an order can be compelled to adopt the child under the foreign *lex domicilii*. The new enactment is unable to offer a solution. [**165**]

Section 53 of the earlier Act has been aimed at assisting persons who are ineligible to apply for a British adoption order[5] because they are not domiciled in England and Wales or Scotland. Since it has the same object, section 25 expressly provides[6] that the rules governing the domiciliary qualifications for British adoption orders,[7] shall not apply in relation to orders under section 25. However, those domiciliary qualifications have now been extended so as to include not only a person domiciled in England and Wales or Scotland, but anyone domiciled in any part of the United Kingdom or in the Channel Islands or the Isle of Man. It is submitted that this extension, coupled with section 25 and the restriction imposed by settion 52 of the Adoption Act 1958, has the following implications for a person domiciled in Northern Ireland, the Channel Islands or the Isle of Man. If, for example, he is domiciled in Northern Ireland, he can either apply for an adoption order in England and Wales or Scotland or take the child to Northern Ireland with a view to adoption there.[8] [**166**]

The requirement that the parent or guardian agrees to the making of an adoption order or that his agreement be dispensed with will apply *mutatis mutandis* to a section 25 order, and he will have to be notified of the date and place where he may be heard on the application for an order.[9] The minimum period for which the child must have had his home with the applicant before

---

[1] S. 25 (1); (Adoption Act 1976, s. 55). Section 25 is not yet operative. The Adoption Agencies Regulations 1976 apply to provisional adoption orders.

[2] But not a magistrates' court. See Children Act 1975, s. 100 (6); (Adoption Act 1976, s. 62 (6)).

[3] The words italicised probably intend to cover cases where different personal laws operate within the country of domicile.

The applicant must file expert evidence of the law of adoption in the country in which he is domiciled; Adoption (High Court) Rules 1976, r. 10; Adoption (County Court) Rules 1976, r. 22.

For the effect of an order made in Northern Ireland, the Isle of Man or any of the Channel Islands which corresponds to a section 25 order see Children Act 1975, Sch. 3, para. 44, amending the Adoption Act 1964, s. 1 (5); (Adoption Act 1976, s. 59 (3)).

[4] H.C.R., Rec. 82.

[5] I.e., one made in England and Wales or Scotland.

[6] Sub-s. (2).

[7] Children Act 1975, ss. 10 (2) and 11 (2); (Adoption Act 1976, ss. 14 (2) and 15 (2)). See paras. [**90**]–[**91**], *ante*.

[8] Note also the Children Act 1975, Sch. 1 which recognises for such purposes as the disposition and devolution of property the status of adoption conferred by an order made in Northern Ireland, the Channel Islands or the Isle of Man; (Adoption Act 1976, s. 38).

[9] Children Act 1975, s. 22 (2); (Adoption Act 1976, s. 66 (4)). Should the child be the subject of a resolution under the Children Act 1948, s. 2 (as substituted by the Children Act 1975, s. 57), it is still the agreement of the parent that is required; see *ibid.*, sub-s. (11).

an order can be made is twenty-six weeks and not the thirteen required for an adoption order. Again, the first six weeks of the child's life is to be ignored in calculating the period.[1] **[167]**

Section 25 (2) states that the provisions of Part I of the 1975 Act relating to adoptions orders will apply to orders made under the section; but the nature of the latter order necessarily means the exclusion of certain of those provisions. Thus, although the parental rights and duties vest in the applicant,[2] the child does not have the same legal status as an adopted child and the special rules governing the disposition and devolution of property where there is an adoption order do not apply[3] There is no power to make an interim order under section 19, because the court will not be in a position to make a final adoption order. Equally, section 24 which governs the making of Convention adoption orders is obviously inapplicable. **[168]**

At one stage the Children Bill provided that a section 25 order could not be made in relation to a child who is free for adoption. The restriction would have inhibited adoption agencies in making successful placements for adoption abroad of a small but vulnerable minority of children. For example, there have been instances of black American soldiers serving in England wishing to take black children to the United States with a view to adopting them. In deleting the restriction section 25 has, however, expressly excluded the provisions relating to freeing for adoption (i.e., sections 14 to 16 and 23) from applying in relation to section 25 orders. The effect is not clear. What it seems to mean is that, if a child has been freed for adoption under a section 14 order, the agency will not be prevented from placing the child with a person who intends to adopt abroad and thus to apply for a section 25 order. It is therefore important that parents consenting to the freeing for adoption procedure are made aware of the fact that their consent extends to the possibility of their child being taken abroad for adoption. However, if the child has not already been so freed, the agency will be able to place him with a view to a section 25 application without itself having first to obtain a section 14 order, but subject, of course, to the agreement to a section 25 order being given by the parents or dispensed with. **[169]**

The provisions in the Adoption Act 1958 relating to registration of adoptions[4] will apply to a section 25 order, except that any entry in the Registers of Births (or, in Scotland, the Register of Births) or the Adopted Children Register will be marked "Proposed Foreign Adoption" instead of "Provisionally adopted", as section 53 of the 1958 Act presently requires.[5] **[170]**

For the purpose of Parts III and IV of the 1958 Act an adoption order

---

[1] S. 25 (2). This essentially re-enacts the provision in s. 53 (5) of the Adoption Act 1958; (Adoption Act 1976, s. 55 (2)).

[2] I.e., by virtue of s. 25 (1) and not s. 8 (1).

[3] S. 8 (9) and Sch. 1 are excluded; see Chap. 8, *post*.

For the exclusion of ss. 10 (2) and 11 (2) see para. [**166**], *ante*.

[4] I.e., ss. 20–23, 24 (4) and (5); (Adoption Act 1976, ss. 50, 51 and Sch. 1).

[5] Children Act 1975, s. 25 (3); (Adoption Act 1976, s. 55 (3)). See also Sch. 3, para. 45, which will also apply these amendments to orders made in Northern Ireland, the Isle of Man or any of the Channel Islands which correspond to s. 25 orders; (Adoption Act 1976, Sch. 1, para. 2 (4)).

includes a section 25 order and references both in the 1958 Act and the 1975 Act to placing of children for adoption or making of arrangements for adoption include references to placements or arrangements for adoption abroad.[1] **[171]**

[1] S. 25 (4); (Adoption Act 1976, s. 55 (4)).

CHAPTER 8

THE LEGAL EFFECTS OF AN ADOPTION ORDER

The general effect of an adoption order is to create between the adopter and the child a legal relationship almost wholly the same as that between a parent and his natural, legitimate child. In restating this principle the 1975 Act is more explicit than the Adoption Act 1958, whose relevant provisions it replaces. It achieves this by (1) defining in Schedule 1[1] the status conferred by an adoption order[2] and (2) enacting for the first time the general rule that an adoption order made under the 1975 Act vests the parental rights and duties relating to the child in the applicants for adoption.[3] The defined status and the vesting rule are subject to limitations and exceptions, many of which are re-enactments of the previous law. [**172**]

A. STATUS

The adopted child is given a new status.[4] In the case of adoption by a married couple he is to be treated in law as if he had been born a child of their marriage: where there is a sole adopter, as if born in wedlock but not as a child of any actual marriage. It means, therefore, that he is included within the terms "a legitimate child" and "a child born in lawful wedlock". Indeed, it is expressly declared that he is prevented from being illegitimate. This new status[5] applies, subject to any contrary indication, for the construction of Acts or instruments whether made before or after the adoption, but only as respects things done or events after that date or after 31st December 1975, whichever

---

[1] Operative since 1st January 1976.

[2] The status, and the provisions of Sch. 1, relate not only to an adoption order made under the 1975 Act or the earlier Adoption Acts of 1950 and 1958 but also to (i) adoption by an order made in Northern Ireland, the Isle of Man or in any of the Channel Islands, (ii) an overseas adoption as defined by s. 4 (3) of the Adoption Act 1968 (Adoption Act 1976, s. 72 (2)), and (iii) an adoption recognised by English law and effected under a foreign law (Adoption Act 1976, s. 38 (1), which adds orders made in Scotland).

An "overseas adoption" means an adoption of such a description as the Secretary of State may specify. It need not be confined to "Convention adoptions".

For the recognition of foreign adoptions see Dicey and Morris, *The Conflict of Laws* (9th Edn.), pp. 477–486; Cheshire, *Private International Law* (9th Edn.), pp. 468–473.

[3] It should be noted that this vesting rule is limited to adoption orders made under s. 8 (1) of the 1975 Act (Adoption Act 1976, s. 12 (1)), including Convention adoption orders. Compare the preceding footnote.

[4] Sch. 1, paras. 3 and 4; (Adoption Act 1976, ss. 39 and 41).

[5] The relationship of adoptive parent and child may be referred to as an adoptive relationship and a male and female adopter as the adoptive father and adoptive mother. The principle extends to any other relative under an adoptive relationship. However, the fact that the word "adoptive" is omitted does not prevent the term "parent" or any other term being treated as including an adoptive relative. For example, the rule in s. 33 (4) of the Act which precludes a mother or father from applying for a custodianship order would apply to an adoptive mother or father.

is the later.[1] As will be seen,[2] there is an exception in the case of Acts and instruments concerning property. **[173]**

Notwithstanding the acquisition of the status of adoption, the child's original relationship as a child of his natural family remains relevant for the following purposes:

(i) Adoption does not affect the prohibited degrees of relationship in which the child stood to other persons before the date of adoption.[3] Additionally, the Act re-enacts the prohibition on intermarriage between the child and the adoptive parent, which continues even if the child is later adopted into another family,[4] but, in line with the recommendation of the Houghton Committee,[5] it does not extend the prohibition to intermarriage with other adoptive relatives.[6] There do not appear to be sufficiently strong social or moral pressures for such extension.[7]

(ii) Incest[8] continues to relate to the natural relationship, and the adoptive parent and child are not within the prohibited degrees for the purpose of that offence.[9]

(iii) If the adopter, or, in the case of a joint adopter, the male adopter is a citizen of the United Kingdom and Colonies and the child is not, the latter becomes such a citizen from the date of the adoption order.[10] However, without prejudice to that rule, the child is treated as not having been adopted but still related to his natural family for the purposes of any provision of (a) the British Nationality Acts 1948 to 1965 and any instrument having effect thereunder, (b) the Immigration Act 1971 and any instrument having effect thereunder, or (c) any other provision of the law for the time being in force which determines citizenship of the United Kingdom and Colonies.[11] So, a child who has that citizenship by virtue of any of those provisions will not lose it if he is adopted by a person with foreign nationality.[12]

(iv) The acquisition of the status of adoption does not exclude the natural relationship for certain purposes of the Social Security Act 1975,[13] i.e., to enable the adopted person to qualify as a near relative of a deceased person for the purpose of payment of a death grant (under section 32 of that Act); where he is an illegitimate child of a deceased person, to enable industrial death benefit to be paid to or in respect of him and his mother (under sections 70 (3) (*b*) or 73 (2));

---

[1] Sch. 1, para. 3 (5) and (6); (Adoption Act 1976, s. 39 (6) (*a*) and (*b*)). Except for possible foreign adoptions otherwise than by an order, the date of adoption is the date of the adoption order; Sch. 1, para. 1 (4); (Adoption Act 1976, s. 38 (2)).

[2] Paras. **[175]**–**[185]**, *post*.

[3] Sch. 1, para. 7 (1); (Adoption Act 1976, s. 47 (1)).

[4] Sch. 3, para. 8.

[5] Rec. 84.

[6] There is no statutory support for the *dictum* of Lord Hailsham L.C., in *Re W.*, [1971] A.C. 682 at p. 694; [1971] 2 All E.R. 49 at p. 51, that adoptive brothers and sisters are within the prohibited degrees.

[7] In its Working Paper (paras. 251–252) the Houghton Committee had suggested that an adopted child be prohibited from marrying anyone whom he would have been debarred from marrying if he had been born rather than adopted into that family.

[8] Sexual Offences Act 1956, ss. 10 and 11.

[9] Children Act 1975, Sch. 1, para. 7 (1); (Adoption Act 1976, s. 47 (1)).

[10] Adoption Act 1958, s. 19 (1); (Adoption Act 1976, s. 40 (1)).

[11] Children Act 1975, Sch. 1, para. 7 (2); (Adoption Act 1976, s. 47 (2)).

[12] British nationality is not, of course, a prerequisite to the making of an adoption order.

[13] Children Act 1975, Sch. 1, para. 7 (3)–(5); (Adoption Act 1976, s. 47 (3)-(5)).

to enable him to qualify (under section 72) as a relative of the deceased for the purpose of the latter benefit.

(v) The general provision that an adopted child is to be treated as the child of the adopters and of no other person does not affect his entitlement to a pension payable to him or for his benefit if in payment at the time of the adoption.[1] [**174**]

Dispositions of property

Ever since the Adoption Act 1949 first recognised that, for the purpose of conferring rights of succession on death and *inter vivos* dispositions, an adopted person is to be treated as a member of the adopter's family and not that of his natural parents, the relevant law has been beset with complicated time limiting factors, turning on the date from which the disposition is made to operate. [**175**]

The changes made by the 1975 Act do not apply to a disposition of property contained in any enactment or instrument existing, i.e., passed or made, before 1st January 1976, nor to any public general Act in its application to such a disposition.[2] A disposition includes the conferring of a power of appointment[3] and the creation of an entailed interest. Where the disposition is made by will or codicil it is to be regarded as having been made on the date of the testator's death and not on that of the execution of the instrument.[4] Where it is an oral disposition it is to be treated as if it were contained in an instrument when the disposition was made.[5] [**176**]

Existing instruments

For deaths occurring after 1949 but before 1st January 1976 and *inter vivos* dispositions made before that date the provisions of sections 16 and 17 of the Adoption Act 1958 still apply.[6] Under those provisions the basic rule is that the adopted child will not take as a child of the adopters unless the disposition is made after the adoption order. Thus, where a person dies intestate before 1st January 1976 but after the child has been adopted, the property devolves in all respects as if the child were a child of the adopter born in lawful wedlock and not the child of anyone else, except that this rule does not extend to entailed interests forming part of the estate.[7] [**177**]

Due to the combined effects of sections 16 (2) and 17 (2) and Schedule 5, para. 4 of the 1958 Act, together with the decision in *Re Gilpin, Hutchinson* v. *Gilpin*,[8] complicated problems may arise in applying to questions of testamentary succession the principle that the adopted child is to be treated as if

---

[1] Children Act 1975, Sch. 1, para. 8; (Adoption Act 1976, s. 48).

[2] Sch. 1, paras. 1 (5) and 5 (1); (Adoption Act 1976, s. 72 (1) and Sch. 2, para. 6 (1)). An instrument includes a private Act settling property, but not any other enactment; *ibid.*, para. 6 (6); (Adoption Act 1976, s. 42 (6)).

[3] Paras. 2 (1) and 17; (s. 46 (1) and (5)).

[4] Para. 1 (6); (s. 46 (3)).

[5] Para. 2 (2); (s. 46 (2)).

[6] Para. 5 (2); (Adoption Act 1976, Sch. 2, para. 6 (2)).

[7] Adoption Act 1958, s. 16 (1). The provisions of the law of intestate succession are to be treated as if they were contained in an instrument executed by the intestate immediately before his death; Children Act 1975, Sch. 1, para. 5 (3); (Adoption Act 1976, s. 46 (4) and Sch. 2, para. 6 (3)).

[8] [1954] Ch. 1; [1953] 2 All E.R. 1218.

he were the child of the adopter and not of his natural parents. The main rules may be summarised as follows:

1. The principle applies only to dispositions made after 1949.
2. The disposition must have been made after the adoption order.
3. Where the disposition is contained in a will or a codicil executed on or after 1st April 1959, it is deemed to have been made on the date of the testators' death.
4. Where the disposition is contained in a will or codicil executed before 1st April 1959, it is treated as having been made on the date of the execution of the document, unless that document is confirmed by a codicil executed on or after 1st April 1959, in which case rule 3 operates.
5. Where the will or codicil is executed before the date of the adoption order and is confirmed by a codicil executed after that date but before 1st April 1959 the disposition is not deemed to have been made after the date of the order.

Obviously, with the effluxion of time these rules are of diminishing practical importance. Moreover, they must be read subject to any contrary intention of the testator.[1] **[178]**

In applying sections 16 and 17 to intestacies and dispositions the child who is adopted by spouses jointly is deemed to be the brother and sister of the whole blood of any natural child or other adopted child of the spouses. In all other cases, i.e., where he is adopted by one person, he is a brother or sister of the half blood.[2] Like the legitimate child of a void marriage or a legitimated child, an adopted child cannot succeed to any dignity or title of honour or property devolving therewith.[3] **[179]**

"New" instruments

The new rules of construction, which are always subject to any contrary indication, governing instruments made on or after 1st January 1976 meet the recommendation of the Houghton Committee[4] that an adopted child should have, in respect of dispositions of property, the same rights[5] as a natural child of the adoptive family. Correspondingly, he loses these rights as a member of his natural family, except any interest vested in possession before the adoption or any interest expectant (whether immediately or not) upon an interest so vested.[6] **[180]**

---

[1] The intention may be inferred from surrounding circumstances if the evidence is cogent and convincing; *Re Jones' Will Trusts, Jones* v. *Hawtin Squire* [1965] Ch. 1124; [1965] 2 All E.R. 828; *Re Jebb, Ward-Smith* v. *Jebb*, [1966] Ch. 666; [1965] 3 All E.R. 358; *Re Brinkley's Will Trusts, Westminster Bank, Ltd.* v. *Brinkley*, [1968] Ch. 407; [1967] 3 All E.R. 805.

[2] S. 17 (1).

[3] S. 16 (3).

[4] Rec. 83.

[5] But see succession to peerages, etc., para. [**183**], *post*.

[6] Children Act 1975, Sch. 1, para. 6 (4); (Adoption Act 1976, s. 42 (4)). *Semble* a vested remainder which has not vested in possession before the date of adoption is lost; see Bromley, *Family Law* (5th Edn.), p. 581. Clearly that is the effect where the interest is contingent and so remains at the date of adoption.

One of the main changes is that which enables the child to rely on his status of adoption even where the adoption has taken place after the instrument is made. Another is that which lays down for the first time an order of seniority of children where one or more of them is adopted.[1] If a disposition depends on the date of birth of a child of the adopters, their adopted child is deemed to have been born on the date of adoption for the purpose of construing the disposition. So, if T dies in 1977 leaving a gift to "the eldest son of A", and A has a natural son, X, born in 1970 and a boy, Y, whom he adopted in 1972 when Y was 5 years old, Y is to be treated as though born in 1972 and X thus takes the gift. Where two or more children are adopted on the same date they must be treated as though they had been born on that date in the order of their actual births. For example, T dies in 1977 leaving a gift to "the eldest son of B". On the same date in 1971 B adopted two boys, C and D, then respectively 3 and 2 years old. In 1972 B had a natural son, E. C is entitled to the gift. However, the rule of seniority does not affect any reference in the instrument to the age of the child. Thus, supposing the testamentary gift is to "the first son of F to attain the age of 21". If F has a natural son, G, born in 1971 and he adopted a boy, H, in 1971, who was then 3 years old, H will be entitled.[2] [**181**]

The position of the illegitimate child who is adopted by one of his natural parents as sole adoptive parent calls for special comment.[3] In addition to providing generally that his adoption does not affect his entitlement to property depending on his relationship as the illegitimate child of his parent or as respects anything else depending on the natural relationship,[4] the Act further specifically provides[5] that his adoption in such circumstances does not affect his proprietary rights *qua* illegitimate child under Part II of the Family Law Reform Act 1969. Thus, supposing the testamentary gift is to the "eldest child of J living at my death". J has an illegitimate child, K, born in 1970 and a legitimate child, L, born in 1972. J adopts K in 1973. The testator dies in 1977. K will be entitled as J's eldest child.[6] [**182**]

In line with *Houghton* the gap between the respective proprietary rights of legitimate and adopted children is further narrowed, so far as concerns "new" instruments, by extending those of adopted children to dispositions of entailed interests.[7] However, the adopted child continues to be excluded from succession to property devolving with any peerage, dignity or title of honour, unless there is a contrary intention expressed in the instrument. Moreover, his exclusion from the peerage, dignity or title itself is now explicitly covered.[8] Given the wide status which adoption confers, it is submitted that his continued exclusion is an unjustifiable anomaly. [**183**]

Where it is necessary to determine for the purposes of a disposition of

---

[1] Para. 6 (2); (Adoption Act 1976, s. 42 (2)).

[2] See para. 6 (3) (Adoption Act 1976, s. 42 (3)) for further examples of specific phrases in wills to which the seniority rule is relevant.

[3] In view of the restrictions imposed by s. 11 (3) of the 1975 Act (Adoption Act 1976, s. 15 (3)) on adoptions by a natural parent, such instances will be rare; see paras. [**95**]–[**98**], *ante*.

[4] Para. 9; (Adoption Act 1976, s. 39 (3)).

[5] Para. 14 (1); (Adoption Act 1976, s. 43 (1)).

[6] Cf. the illustration in para. 14 (3); (Adoption Act 1976, s. 43 (2)).

[7] Para. 17; (Adoption Act 1976, s. 46 (5)).

[8] Paras. 10 and 16; (Adoption Act 1976, s. 44).

property effected by a "new" instrument whether or not a woman can have a child, it must be presumed that once a woman has reached 55 she will not adopt a child after execution of the instrument. If she does, the child will not be able to take as her child or as the child of her spouse, unless there is a contrary indication.[1] Such adoptions are likely to be rare. **[184]**

In accordance with similar protective enactments,[2] trustees and personal representatives are empowered to distribute property without first having to enquire whether (a) any adoption has been effected or revoked or (b) a person is illegitimate, or is adopted by one of his natural parents, and could be legitimated. Moreover, they are not liable in respect of any distribution which they make without regard to any of the facts in (a) and (b), if they have not *received* notice of the fact before the conveyance or distribution.[3] This protection does not extend to a third party into whose hands the property can be traced, unless he is a purchaser.[2] Like the other protective enactments, this rule does not define a purchaser, but it is submitted that it is to be construed as a purchaser in good faith for valuable consideration.[4] **[185]**

B. THE VESTING RULE

The vesting of the parental rights and duties in the adopters means, by virtue of section 85 (1) of the 1975 Act, the vesting of all the parental rights and duties which by law the mother and father have in relation to a legitimate child and his property. What constitutes the totality is not certain, but in Chapter 9 an attempt is made to list the majority of them.[5] **[186]**

An adoption order does not affect the rights and duties so far as they relate to any period preceding the date of the order.[6] Vesting operates prospectively and every right or duty which was vested in a parent or guardian immediately before that date is extinguished, except where the parent or guardian is one of the adopters.[7] In the vast majority of cases all the rights and duties will have been vested in one or both of the parents. However, any right or duty which has been vested in someone else by a court order is similarly extinguished.[8] Thus, an aunt of the child may have been granted custody or care and control in proceedings between the mother and the father under the Guardianship of Minors Act 1971[9] or in matrimonial proceedings between them under the Matri-

---

[1] Para. 6 (5); (Adoption Act 1976, s. 42 (5)).

[2] See Trustee Act 1925, s. 27 (2); Adoption Act 1958, s. 17 (3); Family Law Reform Act 1969, s. 17.

[3] Children Act 1975, Sch. 1, para. 15; (Adoption Act 1976, s. 45). Unlike s. 27 of the Trustee Act 1925, there is no initial obligation on the trustees or personal representatives to give notice of their intention to convey or distribute: the onus is entirely on the claimant to make his claim.

[4] Cf. Law of Property Act 1925, s. 205; Administration of Estates Act 1925, s. 55; Land Charges Act 1925, s. 20.

[5] Paras [**208**], *et seq*., *post*.

[6] S. 8 (2); (Adoption Act 1976, s. 12 (2)).

[7] S. 8 (3) (*a*) (i); (Adoption Act 1976, s. 12 (3) (*a*) (i)). For the date of commencement of the vesting provisions of s. 8 (1)–(4) see para. [**192**], *post*.

For reasons already considered the number of adoptions by parents will decline; see paras. [**95**]–[**103**], *ante*.

[8] S. 8 (3) (*a*) (ii); (Adoption Act 1976, s. 12 (3) (*a*) (ii)).

[9] S. 9, as amended by the Guardianship Act 1973, s. 2 and Sch. 2, Part I. See *Re R.*, [1974] 1 All E.R. 1033.

monial Causes Act 1973;[1] or she may have been given custody in domestic proceedings between the parents under the Matrimonial Proceedings (Magistrates' Courts) Act 1960[2] or care and control where there have been wardship proceedings.[3] It should be noted that in such cases extinguishment is automatic once the adoption order is made. Nevertheless, procedural steps should be taken by the court making the order to ensure that the court which made the earlier order is notified of the adoption.[4] **[187]**

When the relevant provisions come into force the rule of extinguishment will similarly operate against the custodian of a child who is adopted by someone else and against an adoption agency in whom the parental rights and duties have vested under an order freeing the child for adoption. So, too, where the rights and duties have vested in a local authority by virtue of a care order under the Children and Young Persons Act 1969, that order is discharged on adoption.[5] Where the authority has those rights and duties as the result of a resolution under section 2 of the Children Act 1948, section 8 of the 1975 Act has no relevance since there is no order of a court on which to operate, but the earlier Act, as amended by the later, ensures that the resolution ceases to have effect on the child's adoption.[6] On the other hand, in those cases where a court in exercise of various statutory powers[7] has committed the child to the care of a local authority and he is deemed to have been received into care under section 1 of the 1948 Act, section 8 does apply so as to bring the committal to an end. **[188]**

The Act specifically deals with the effect of adoption on the duty to make payments in respect of the child's maintenance, whether the duty arises from an agreement or an order of a court.[8] Adoption will not affect continued liability

---

[1] S. 42.

[2] S. 2 (1) (*d*). Under that Act a split order giving, say, care and control to the aunt but custody to a parent is not possible; see *Wild* v. *Wild*, [1969] P. 33; [1968] 3 All E.R. 608.

[3] Where the court decides that a testamentary guardian is to be a sole guardian to the exclusion of the mother or father, it is possible for the court exceptionally to grant care and control to some other person; Guardianship of Minors Act 1971, ss. 4 (4) and 10 (1) (*a*).

[4] Where the order had been made in wardship proceedings, leave of the Family Division would have been necessary to start the adoption proceedings; *F.* v. *S.* (*adoption: ward*), [1973] Fam. 203; [1973] 1 All E.R. 722.

[5] CYPA 1969, s. 21A, added by the Children Act 1975, Sch. 3, para. 70 (operative since 1st January 1976).

A care order is also discharged by making a freeing for adoption order or an order vesting the parental rights and duties in a person who intends to adopt the child under a foreign law; see *ibid*.

[6] Children Act 1948, s. 2 (8) (*a*), as substituted by the Children Act 1975, s. 57 (operative since 26th November 1976; see formerly Adoption Act 1958, s. 15 (4)).

Like a care order under CYPA 1969, a s. 2 resolution also comes to an end when an order is made under s. 14 or s. 25 of the Children Act 1975.

[7] See Matrimonial Proceedings (Magistrates' Courts) Act 1960, s. 2 (1) (*e*); Matrimonial Causes Act 1973, s. 43; Guardianship Act 1973, s. 2 (2) (*b*); Family Law Reform Act 1969, s. 7 (2); and Children Act 1975, s. 36 (3) (*a*) when the custodianship provisions take effect.

[8] S. 8 (3) (*b*); (Adoption Act 1976, s. 12 (3) (*b*)).

A court can order contributions towards the child's maintenance under, *inter alia*, the Children and Young Persons Act 1933, ss. 86–89; Children Act 1948, ss. 23, 24 and 26; Matrimonial Proceedings (Magistrates' Courts) Act 1960, s. 2 (1) (*h*); Matrimonial Causes Act 1973, s. 23 (1) (*d*) and (*e*); Family Law Reform Act 1969, s. 6; Guardianship of Minors Act 1971, ss. 9 (2) (as amended by the Guardianship Act 1973, Sch. 2), 10 and 11; and, when the custodianship provisions of the Children Act 1975 become operative, s. 34 (1) of that Act. See also Sch. 3, para. 75 (1) of the 1975 Act for a prospective amendment of s. 9 (2) of the Guardianship of Minors Act 1971.

for arrears existing at the date of the adoption order, but subsequent liability for maintenance and for payments relating to any other matter comprised in the parental duties, such as payments of school fees, is extinguished, except where the duty arises under an agreement which constitutes a trust or which expressly provides against extinguishment.[1] **[189]**

The effect of adoption of an illegitimate child on affiliation requires special note. Whereas the matter was explicitly dealt with in the Adoption Act 1958,[2] it is now left as one of the implied consequences of Schedule 1 and section 8 (1)–(3) of the 1975 Act. Thus, the father who has been liable to provide maintenance, whether by agreement[3] or under an affiliation order, will cease to be so liable from the date of adoption, and, if no affiliation order exists at that date, it will be too late to seek one. The significant difference from the former law is that extinguishment will operate even in the exceptional cases where the adoption order is made in favour of the mother. Moreover, she cannot apply for affiliation after adopting, a restriction which accords with the principle which prevents an adopted child from being illegitimate.[4] **[190]**

In view of the wide terms in which Schedule 1 defines the status of adoption and the wide effect of section 8 (1)–(3), it remains to be seen how far legislation will continue to find it necessary to refer expressly to the adopted child when providing for children. Hitherto, a number of enactments have so found it: for example, those concerned with custody, maintenance and education on breakdown of marriage and those dealing with fatal accidents claims, taxation, social insurance legislation and various statutory pension schemes. Indeed, the 1975 Act has found it necessary expressly to re-enact the rule that where an insurance policy for the payment for funeral expenses on the death of a child is taken out before the adoption order is made, the rights and liabilities thereunder pass to the adopter.[5] The general vesting rule is not wide enough to cover the point. On the other hand, the former rule,[6] which extended to adopted children the provisions of section 11 of the Married Women's Property Act 1882, is not expressly re-enacted. Section 11 allows life assurance policies to be effected so as to create a trust in favour of the spouse and children of the assured and the former rule enabled the section to operate retrospectively in favour of children adopted after the policy was effected. Apparently the terms of Schedule 1 to the 1975 Act are considered wide enough to comprehend section 11. **[191]**

Logically Schedule 1 and section 8 (1)–(4) should have been brought into effect concurrently on 1st January 1976. As it is, the postponement of the operation of the vesting rule until 26th November 1976 requires some fairly large inferences to be drawn. Thus, section 13 of the Adoption Act 1958 was repealed when Schedule 1 became operative. That section vested in the adopters all rights and duties of the parents or guardian in relation to the future custody, maintenance and education of the child. With regard to those matters it therefore fulfilled the object which is now achieved by section 8 (1)–(4). To enable an

---

[1] S. 8 (4); (Adoption Act 1976, s. 12 (4)).
[2] S. 15 (1) and (2).
[3] See *Jennings* v. *Brown* (1842), 9 M. & W. 496; Bevan, *op. cit.*, p. 454.
[4] Sch. 1, para. 3 (3); (Adoption Act 1976, s. 39 (4)).
[5] Sch. 1, para. 11 (Adoption Act 1976, s. 49), re-enacting Adoption Act 1958, s. 14 (2).
[6] Adoption Act 1958, s. 14 (3).

adoption order, made between 1st January 1976 and 26th November 1976 to have that vesting effect it is necessary to rely on the rule in the Schedule[1] that an adopted child is to be treated in law as if he were not the child of any person other than the adopter. That seems a bold conclusion. The point is, perhaps, more forcibly illustrated by reference to affiliation and the former provisions of section 15 (1) and (2) of the 1958 Act, which were also repealed when the Schedule came into effect. Suppose that an affiliation order was made in 1974 in respect of a child who was adopted in February 1976. There being at the latter date no express rule that the affiliation order thereupon ceases to have effect, is it to be inferred that that consequence nevertheless follows from the provision in the Schedule[2] that the status of adoption prevents an adopted child from being illegitimate? The alternative but doubtful possibility is to construe section 8 (1)–(4) retrospectively so that the vesting rule applies not only to adoption orders made on or since 26th November 1976, but also to those made on or since 1st January 1976. One or other of these constructions will have to be applied. Otherwise affiliation orders in the kind of case illustrated continue to be valid. **[192]**

The vesting rule is subject to the court's discretion to include conditions in an adoption order.[3] Because of the practical difficulties of enforcement it is not likely to do so, but occasionally the discretion may be exercised concerning religious education or access.[4] Although the parent in giving his agreement to adoption is no longer entitled to insist on conditions concerning the religious upbringing of the child,[5] this will not prevent the court in its discretion imposing such conditions where, exceptionally it considers this appropriate—as it may do in custody cases.[6] As for access, again exceptionally the court may on adoption grant it to the natural parent, for example, where he has maintained close contact with his child,[7] but it remains to be seen how far the enactment of section 3 of the 1975 Act will make the court more or less reluctant to grant it.[8] **[193]**

C. THE RIGHT TO OBTAIN A BIRTH CERTIFICATE

The nature of the right

Ever since 1926 when English law first allowed adoption it has been possible for an adopted person to obtain a copy of his birth certificate if he learns the name under which he was born. Such information would only likely to be forthcoming from the adoptive parents and they could well be unwilling to divulge it. The only other possibility of tracing origin has been through an order

---

[1] Para. 3 (2).

[2] Para. 3 (3).

[3] Children Act 1975, s. 8 (7); (Adoption Act 1976, s. 12 (6)).

[4] Because the 1975 Act enlarges the rights of inheritance of the adopted child, it has not been found necessary expressly to re-enact the former provision (Adoption Act 1958, s. 7 (3)) that the order may require the adopter to make financial provision for the child.

[5] See para. [**53**], *ante*.

[6] Cf. *J.* v. *C.*, [1970] A.C. 668; [1969] 1 All E.R. 788 (H.L.).

[7] *Re S. (a minor)*, [1976] Fam. 1; [1975] 1 All E.R. 109; see also *Re J.* (*Adoption Order: Conditions*), [1973] Fam. 106; [1973] 2 All E.R. 410; Cf. *Re B.* (*a minor*) (1977) *The Times*, 25th March. See Maidment, *Access and Family Adoption*, 40 M.L.R. 293.

[8] See also para. [**211**], *post* (access).

of a court directing the Registrar General to provide the necessary information.[1] The order, which is rarely sought, is intended as a means of tracing parenthood where it is relevant to claims of succession on death. The applicant may be the adopted person or someone else, e.g., personal representatives. **[194]**

Section 26 (2) of the 1975 Act, giving effect to *Houghton*,[2] introduces a major change by inserting a new section, section 20A, in the Adoption Act 1958.[3] This in effect confers on an adopted person, whose birth record is kept by the Registrar General, a right, fettered only by the restrictions of counselling, to obtain a copy of his birth certificate once he is 18 years old. The Registrar General must provide the applicant with such information as is necessary to enable him to obtain the copy.[4] Should he be under 18 but intending to marry in England or Wales, he has the right to require the Registrar General to inform him whether or not it appears from the records that he and the person whom he intends to marry may be within the degrees of relationship prohibited by Schedule 1 to the Marriage Act 1949.[5] Clearly, an application is only going to be made where the applicant has been put on his inquiry. Neither section 20A (2) nor any regulation prescribes the amount of information to which he is entitled. A mere declaration that the parties are within the prohibited degrees will therefore strictly satisfy the subsection, but it seems likely that the applicant will be told the nature of the relationship. On the other hand the information which the Registrar General is able to provide may be inconclusive. For example, it is known that the parties are the illegitimate children of different mothers, but, while it is suspected that they have the same father, the doubt cannot be resolved because the father's name is not recorded in either or both of the entries of birth. **[195]**

The conferment of the general right to have access to the record of one's birth once majority is reached is justified on the grounds that an adopted person needs to know about his origins in order to develop a proper sense of identity and that the knowledge may give him a greater degree of stability. "It is believed, too, that greater openness about a child's adoption can contribute to a closer relationship between adoptive parents and their child, based on knowledge of the true situation and full acceptance of the child as an individual with his own origins."[6] Certainly, the aphorism that "he is a wise man who

---

[1] Adoption Act 1958, s. 20 (5) as amended by the Children Act 1975, s. 26 (1); (Adoption Act 1976, s. 50 (5)). The High Court, the Westminster County Court and the court which made the adoption order are the courts with jurisdiction.

[2] H.C.R., para. 302 and 303.

[3] Operative since 26th November 1976; (Adoption Act 1976, s. 51)). See Levin, *Tracing the Birth Records of Adopted Persons*, (1977) 7 Fam. Law 104.

[4] S. 20 A (1); (Adoption Act 1976, s. 51 (1)). The section is not limited to persons born in England and Wales and will, for example, include adopted persons born abroad of British parents.

This "linking" information includes the applicant's original name, that of his natural mother and possibly the natural father, together with the name of the court where the adoption order was made.

[5] Adoption Act 1958, s. 20A (2); (Adoption Act 1976, s. 51 (2)). By its terms, the subsection does not enable a minor who is intending to marry abroad to rely on it. Thus, although he may suspect that by the foreign personal law of his fiancée, they are within the prohibited degrees (e.g., first cousins), he is left to run the risk that his marriage abroad will be void according to English conflict of laws.

[6] See Local Authority Circular (L.A.C. (76) 21, para. 3), issued by the Department of Health and Social Security.

knows his own father" has its attraction,[1] but at what risk to the welfare of others and, perhaps, to the adopted person himself? Because, although section 20A itself does no more than enable him to trace his birth record, it imposes no restriction on the use he may make of the information and, in particular, to trace his natural parents. Is, for example, the discovery that he is the issue of an incestuous union likely to promote in him a greater degree of stability? And, if the disclosure of his origins should cause harm to others, his responsibility for that consequence may in turn prove harmful to him. As for harm to others, it is not difficult to visualise the kind of problems that can occur. For example, an unmarried mother may have placed her baby for adoption apparently secure in the knowledge that all contact be irrevocably severed only to find many years later, when she has married and created a new life without disclosing her past to her husband, that the child returns into her life and that of her new family. It is ironic that, while the interests of the natural parent carried much weight in leading to the enactment of section 3 of the 1975 Act,[2] those interests were virtually ignored when it came to enacting section 20A. The only concession made to them is the rule which makes counselling compulsory in those cases where section 20A operates retrospectively, i.e., where the child was adopted before 12th November 1975, the date on which the 1975 Act was passed.[3] Where adoption occurs on or after that date the adopted person will have the choice whether or not to receive counselling. Understandably the retrospective rule was enacted under considerable protest, and parents who gave their children for adoption on the understanding that their identity would not be made accessible to the child may justifiably feel aggrieved.[4] **[196]**

The optional nature of counselling in respect of adoptions ordered on or after 12th November 1975 is justified on the ground that the natural parents will, in advance of the adoption, be informed of the adopted person's eventual right to trace his origin. This is such an important matter that one might reasonably have expected the 1975 Act itself to impose specific duties to inform. As it is, the position is unsatisfactory. It is essential that notification should be given at an early date. Where the child is deliberately being given up by the parent for adoption, the matter is partly covered by Schedule 3 to the Adoption Agencies Regulations 1976. The memorandum, which has to be given to the parent or guardian whose child is about to be adopted, tells him that the effect of the child's right to obtain his birth certificate will be that he will find out what was

---

[1] See H.L. Official Report, 1975, Vol. 356, col. 61 (Lord Bishop of Leicester).

[2] See Chap. 3, *ante*.

[3] S. 20A (6); (Adoption Act 1976, s. 51 (6)).

Even this modest concession is defective. Counselling was only introduced on 26th November 1976, when s. 20A became operative. How many natural parents, one wonders, who allowed their children to be adopted between 12th November 1975 and 26th November 1976 were made aware (1) of the right to be conferred by the section and (2) of the fact that the child would be able on majority to exercise that right without need to receive counselling?

[4] In the course of debate on the Children Bill the Government rejected an amendment which would have enabled the small and dwindling group of persons, who before 1948 had been admitted as unwanted children to the Foundling Hospital to trace their birth record It defended this denial on the ground that in the case of those persons their mothers had been given a firm pledge that their identity would not be disclosed – a pledge which had the protection of the Foundling Hospital Act 1953 – and to break that pledge would be unfair to them. Parents of children adopted before the Children Act 1975 are not likely to be persuaded by the nicety of this statutory distinction.

the parent's name and address at the date of registration of birth. It ought to go further, and spell out the consequence that there is no restriction on the child then to search out his parent, if he so desires. Parents, it is suggested, are entitled at this stage to the maximum information and warning.[1] However, it is those cases where the parent places the child with another and adoption is an ultimate but not immediate prospect that are open to major criticism. The leaflet which the Department of Health and Social Security has circulated to local authorities as guidance for use where it seems probable that a child may have to remain in care for more than six months[2] does refer to the right of the person who has had care for at least five years to start adoption proceedings without the agreement of the parent or local authority,[3] but in mentioning the effects, if adoption were ordered, omits any reference to the right of access to birth records. It is a factor which may weigh with some parents in deciding whether to allow their child to be received into, or to remain in, care. **[197]**

Mode of application and counselling

The responsibility for providing counselling services falls upon the Registrar General, each local authority and, when the new procedure for approving adoption societies comes into force,[4] each such approved society.[5] An adopted person who wishes to have access to his birth record must apply to the Registrar General for the necessary "linking" information, using the appropriate form prescribed by the Adopted Persons (Birth Records) Regulations 1976.[6] The services are available:[7]

(a) at the General Register Office, St. Catherine's House, Kingsway, London;[8] or
(b) from the local authority in whose area the applicant lives; or
(c) from the local authority in whose area the adoption order was made.

When the procedure for approving adoption societies comes into force counselling will also be available from the society which arranged the adoption. Meanwhile there is nothing to prevent a local authority drawing on the experience of voluntary organisations in adoption practice when discharging its duties of counselling. In his application the applicant must state his choice of the place at which he wishes to be interviewed, together with the details of his adoption as contained in his adoption certificate. If he is living abroad he should apply to the Registrar General. **[198]**

The role of the counsellor has been left to extra-legal guidance, but the very helpful *Notes for Counsellors* issued by the Department of Health and Social Security points out that the object of counselling is "to try to ensure (1) that the

---

[1] See para. [**38**], *ante*.
[2] L.A.C. (76) 15, Leaflet No. 2.
[3] Adoption Act 1958, s. 34A, as substituted by Children Act 1975, s. 29; (Adoption Act 1976, s. 28). See paras. [**134**]–[**144**], *ante*.
[4] Under the 1975 Act, s. 4; see para. [**19**]–[**31**], *ante*.
[5] Adoption Act 1958, s. 20A (3); (Adoption Act 1976, s. 51 (3)).
[6] Forms may be obtained from, and sent to, The General Register Office (C.A. Section), Titchfield, Fareham, Hants, Box 7, PO15 5RU.
[7] See Adoption Act 1958, s. 20 A (4) and (5); (Adoption Act 1976, s. 51 (4) and (5)).
[8] Two experienced social workers were initially appointed but the demands for counselling have necessitated the continued employment of only one.

adopted person has considered the possible effect of any enquiries on himself and on others; and (2) that the information he seeks, and to which he now has a legal right, is provided in a helpful and appropriate manner". The content and length of the counselling to be undertaken before the "linking" information is passed on by the counsellor must depend very much on the particular applicant and his needs, but the counsellor has no right to withhold that information and it seems clear from the terms of section 20A (6) that he cannot insist on a further interview before disclosure. If the applicant is intent on eliciting further information, for example, with a view to meeting his natural parents, it may well be desirable to hold additional interviews; but this will have to be by mutual agreement. In Scotland, where adopted persons aged 17 or over have since 1930 had a right to access to their birth records,[1] few have tried to trace their natural parents, being content with the details obtained from their birth certificate. Hitherto, however, counselling services have not been available to the Scottish applicant.[2] Will it be the English and Scottish experience that the availability of those services encourages applicants to trace their natural parents? **[199]**

---

[1] Adoption Act 1958, s. 22.

[2] S. 27 of the Children Act 1975 amends s. 22 of the Adoption Act 1958 so that services will be available at the option of the applicant.

PART II

CUSTODIANSHIP

CHAPTER 9

THE NATURE OF CUSTODIANSHIP

INTRODUCTION

Anyone concerned with the administration of child law is all too aware of the tangled terminology which is used to describe different legal relationships existing between an adult and a child. "Guardianship", "custody", "care", "charge", "control", "authority", "possession" are used with bewildering variety, and the law is further complicated by the fact that some of these terms bear more than one meaning.[1] It is against this confused background that the Act seeks to give effect to the *Houghton* recommendations[2] that a legal status, short of adoption, should be given to relatives and foster-parents in relation to children who are in their long-term care.[3] It achieves this by the introduction of the concept of custodianship, whose nature and scope can, it is suggested, only be fully understood within the comparative context of the concepts of custody and guardianship. [**200**]

The complexity of the relationship between custody and guardianship received the particular attention of Sachs L.J. in *Hewer* v. *Bryant*[4] in the following analysis in which guardianship, custody in its wider meaning and custody in the narrower sense of the power of physical care and control are distinguished:

> "In its wider meaning the word 'custody' is used as if it were *almost the equivalent of 'guardianship'*[5] in the fullest sense—whether the guardianship is by nature, by nurture, by testamentary disposition or by order of a court. (I use the words 'fullest sense' because guardianship may be limited to give control only over the person or only over the administration of the assets of an infant) . . . such guardianship embraces a 'bundle of rights', or to be more exact, a 'bundle of powers', . . . These include power to control education, the choice of religion, *and the administration of the infant's property.*[5] They include entitlement to veto the issue of a passport and to withhold consent to marriage. They include, also, both the personal power physically to control the infant until the years of discretion and the right (originally only if some property was concerned) to apply to the courts to exercise the powers of the Crown as *parens patriae*. It is thus clear that somewhat confusingly one of the powers conferred by custody in its wide meaning is custody in its

---

[1] See Hall, *The Waning of Parental Rights*, [1972B] C.L.J. 248.

[2] Recs. 21–29.

[3] The need for a new status was forcibly demonstrated by Rowe and Lambert in *Children Who Wait* (1973). This study showed that of 7,000 children living in the long-term care of local authorities or voluntary organisations, about 2,000 needed adoption but the other 5,000 required some secure legal relationship which did not completely sever the link between the child and his natural parents.

[4] [1970] 1 Q.B. 357, 373; [1969] 3 All E.R. 578, 585–586.

[5] Italics supplied.

limited meaning, i.e., such personal power of physical control as a parent or guardian may have. . . . The trouble is that, whilst the legislature has distinguished between guardianship and custody, the courts have tended often to use the latter word as if it were substantially the equivalent of the former, thus leading to some confusion of thought. . . . It would be a happier situation if by future legislation the courts were enabled to use the word 'guardianship' [instead of custody in its wide meaning] in orders in appropriate cases."

It has been pointed out that the wide[1] meaning of custody is of relatively recent origin and is traceable to the practice of the Divorce Court after World War II to make the "split order", which gives the care and control to one spouse (usually the wife) but leaves the custody with the other, thereby entitling him to a voice in the upbringing of the child.[2] This atomisation was soon imitated in wardship proceedings in which the High Court reserves to itself custody and delegates to an individual care and control and such other duties concerning the child's upbringing as it may determine.[3] **[201]**

The specific recommendation of *Houghton* was that the right of a parent to apply for custody under the Guardianship of Minors Act 1971[4] should be extended so that relatives and foster-parents could apply for it under the Act. Since that recommendation power has been given to the court in proceedings under that Act to grant custody to a person other than the applicant father or mother,[5] but the Act does not permit a third party to institute custody proceedings,[6] except that:

(1) a testamentary guardian who is confirmed in his guardianship to the exclusion of the surviving father or mother may apply for custody;[7] and
(2) where there is a dispute between joint guardians, one of whom is the father or mother, either or any of the guardians can apply to the court for its directions and the court may make a suitable custody order.[8] **[202]**

Houghton, therefore, was in favour of giving protection to relatives and foster-parents through the concept of custody and not through that of guardianship.[9] In its *Memorandum on the Children Bill* the Association of Directors of

---

[1] Eekelaar, *What are Parental Rights?* (1973), 89 L.Q.R. 210, 230–231.

[2] See further Bevan, *op. cit.*, pp. 263–265; Maidment, 126 New Law Jo., p. 1024. Another possibility is to make a joint custody order with care and control to one spouse; *Jussa* v. *Jussa*, [1972] 2 All E.R. 600; [1972] 1 W.L.R. 881.

[3] Eekelaar, *ibid.*, p. 231.

[4] S. 9.

[5] Guardianship of Minors Act 1971, s. 9, as amended by the Guardianship Act 1973, s. 2 and Sch. 2, Part I. See *Re R. (an infant)*, [1974] 1 All E.R. 1033. When the custodianship provisions of the 1975 Act come into operation the power will be abolished; see p. 124, n. 7, *post*.

The power to grant custody to a third party in matrimonial proceedings has a much longer history. See *D'Alton* v. *D'Alton* (1878), 4 P.D. 87, and now the Matrimonial Causes Act 1973, s. 42; the Matrimonial Proceedings (Magistrates' Courts) Act 1960, s. 2 (1) (*d*); and the Matrimonial Causes Rules 1977.

[6] But see *In re H* (1977), 74 Law Soc. Gaz. 187.

[7] Guardianship of Minors Act 1971, ss. 4 (4) and 10 (1) and (2). Cf. s. 5, p. 103, n. 1, *post*.

[8] *Ibid.*, ss. 7 and 11 (*a*) and (*c*).

[9] "For convenience" the Committee described its proposed extension of custody as "guardianship". It might have been better if the term had been avoided.

Social Services firmly supported the latter. "It is the view of this Association that the needs of children in these circumstances can only be fully met by the making of a guardianship order in the full sense of the term." This, in fact, had already been the solution proposed by the Owen Bill. It is submitted that this alternative is much to be preferred. It could have been achieved, as the Owen Bill intended, by an extension of section 5 of the Guardianship of Minors Act 1971. This section enables a court to fill a vacuum by appointing a guardian for a minor who has no parent, no guardian and no one else having parental rights with respect to him. Regrettably this power has not been invoked as often as it could be. Relatives who are caring for such children have usually been content with that state of affairs, although doubtless they would resort to section 5 if their *de facto* authority were challenged. In future, when Part II of the Act of 1975 becomes operative, they will be able in those circumstances to seek a custodianship order, but, as will be seen,[1] this will confer less extensive rights and duties, and they ought alternatively to have section 5 very much in mind.[2] **[203]**

There are at least two advantages in extending section 5 beyond the present class of cases. The first can be illustrated by reference to the step-parent. It would certainly be more intelligible to the community to confer on him the status of a guardian than to make him a custodian of the child. To have enlarged the present scope of section 5 so as to allow for his appointment as a guardian would not have involved any drastic change in the concept of guardianship. On the contrary, it would have been a realistic recognition that what was involved was a transfer of the parent's natural guardianship. Supposing, for example, that the natural father dies. The court has the power to appoint a guardian to act jointly with the surviving mother.[3] The appointee could be a step-parent. Why, then, should a step-parent be less entitled to seek appointment as a guardian where the former marriage of his spouse was terminated not by the first husband's death but by divorce?[4] **[204]**

Secondly, the sponsors of the Owen Bill were clearly aware that custody and guardianship are not identical, but they also recognised the grey area of uncertainty surrounding the concept of custody.[5] Consequently that Bill was careful to provide that, if a guardianship order were made under the proposed legislation, the person appointed would automatically be granted custody.[6] By combining guardianship and custody the widest coverage of rights and duties would be given to the relative, step-parent or foster-parent, subject to the specific exclusion of the right to give agreement to adoption and, possibly, other named rights and duties, all of which would remain vested in the natural parents. This combination would have had a double advantage. On the one hand, by

---

[1] Paras. [**231**]–[**236**], *post*.

[2] But s. 5 suffers from a major defect in that it does not empower the court to make an order concerning custody or care and control; see *Re N. (minors) (Parental Rights)*, [1974] Fam. 40; [1974] 1 All E.R. 126. Consequently, if there is likely to be a dispute between the relatives and someone else over those matters, a custodianship order will be preferable.

[3] Guardianship of Minors Act 1971, s. 3 (1) (*a*).

[4] If the first husband had been granted custody and the wife care and control, the court would have to decide whether to continue the custody order or discharge it and appoint the step-parent guardian.

[5] See Eekelaar, *op. cit.*, *passim* and especially pp. 233–234.

[6] Thus filling a gap in the present law; see n. 2, *supra*.

giving the guardian custody it would have left the courts to determine, if and when occasion demanded, the niceties of distinction between the two concepts until the whole of the law was reformulated.[1] On the other hand, by appointing the relative, step-parent or foster-parent as guardian it would have ensured that statutory references to that term would extend to him, whereas, if he were simply granted custody, it would raise difficult questions of construction of the particular statute whether the term "guardian" in its context included a person with custody. [**205**]

Regrettably such considerations did not commend themselves to the Government. Its unwillingness to expand the concept of guardianship beyond its narrow historical confines appears to have stemmed primarily from a concern that guardianship "would give rise to many problems regarding property law and other matters".[2] With respect, the argument is not convincing, if only for the basic reason that it ought to be the function of the Legislature to fulfil social needs and not to compromise them in the face of legal complexities. Admittedly, in the vast majority of cases relatives, step-parents and foster-parents are concerned with establishing a status in relation to the person of the child, and it was this aspect of the relationship which *Houghton* very largely had in mind when making its recommendations. Nevertheless, in a small minority of cases property matters may arise. The extension of guardianship would not, it is submitted, have created insurmountable problems. Granting guardianship to, say, a foster-parent would not confer on him any beneficial interest in the property of the child—the rights of intestate succession of the natural parent would remain inviolate—but it would impose on him the duty to administer it in the child's best interests.[3] Why should this not be so? Why should not the foster-parent who has been caring for the child be given the responsibility of administering his assets? If the natural parent has not been concerned in providing care over a protracted period, is it not likely to be more in the child's interests that the foster-parent, whom the court is prepared to make responsible for the person of the child, should be entrusted with that further responsibility? This reasoning, indeed, wholly accords with the existing law, for a guardian under the Guardianship of Minors Act 1971 is not only normally a guardian of the person but has also all the rights, powers and duties of a guardian of the minor's estate.[4] [**206**]

It must have been the proprietary aspects of custody[5] which similarly led to the rejection of custody in its full sense as a means of establishing a legal relationship between the child and the relative, step-parent or foster-parent. Instead the Act introduces an attenuated kind of custody, described as "legal

---

[1] See especially on this Hall, *op. cit.*, at pp. 261–264.

[2] H.C. Official Report, 1975, Standing Committee A (Tenth Sitting), col. 504 (Dr. David Owen). Nowhere in any of the Parliamentary Debates on the Children Bill are these "many problems" spelt out.

Possibly the Government may also have been influenced by the fact that the existing statutory powers of appointment of guardians depend upon at least one of the parents being dead.

[3] For the fiduciary standards imposed on the guardian see Bevan, *op. cit.*, p. 406. Where land is involved a trust would, of course, exist, since the child cannot hold the legal estate (Law of Property Act 1925, s. 1 (6)).

[4] Guardianship Act 1973, s. 7.

[5] See Sachs L.J. in *Hewer* v. *Bryant*, para. [**201**], *ante*.

custody", which can be granted to such persons in the form of a custodianship order. Its scope has to be determined in relation to "the parental rights and duties", a term generally explained but not precisely defined by the Act. [**207**]

THE SCOPE OF CUSTODIANSHIP

PARENTAL RIGHTS AND DUTIES

Unless the context otherwise requires[1] the term "parental rights and duties" means, for the purposes of the Act, all the rights and duties which by law the mother and father have in relation to a legitimate child and his property, regardless of whether or not the particular child is legitimate.[2] The inference to be drawn from the Guardianship of Minors Act 1971 is that so long as she is alive the mother of the illegitimate child exclusively has those rights and duties.[3] For its own purposes the Act puts that matter beyond doubt.[4] [**208**]

Although the term or similar ones have been used for some time in various enactments, there is no exhaustive list of parental rights and duties, and the Act, not being codifying legislation, does not repair the omission. Moreover, it is very doubtful whether this latest appearance of the term will lead the courts to undertake a detailed juristic analysis of it. More likely, it is suggested, there will be a continued willingness to treat it, at least so far as concerns "rights", as "a loose way of describing the conglomeration of rights, powers [and] liberties . . . which a parent has with respect to his child".[5] Section 85 does not attempt to limit parental rights and duties to those which vest in a mother or father *qua* mother or father. The definition includes those which rest on some wider basis; for example, the right to punish, and the statutory duty to protect, the child are based on the fact that the person exercising or performing them has care and control, not on his status. However, as will be seen,[6] it is necessary to draw the line between those rights and duties which relate to the person of the child and those which do not. No attempt is made here to examine *in extenso* all those which are commonly included in the term,[7] but they can be summarised as follows. [**209**]

Care and control

This has been described as the "personal power of physical control"[8] and includes the right to determine how and where the child spends his time. "It is a dwindling right which the courts will hesitate to enforce against the wishes of the child, and the more so the older he is. It starts with a right of control and

---

[1] As does, for example, the Children Act 1948, s. 2 (11), as substituted by the Children Act 1975, s. 57.

[2] S. 85 (1).

[3] Hall, *op. cit.*, p. 263, n. 19.

[4] S. 85 (7). As the subsection recognises, the general principle may be statutorily excluded: e.g., see Guardianship of Minors Act 1971, s. 14 (3); Family Law Reform Act 1969, s. 14 (2), para. [**223**], *post*.

[5] Eekelaar, *op. cit.*, p. 212. See also Ormrod J. in *Re N.* (*minors*) (*Parental Rights*), [1974] Fam. 40, 46; [1974] 1 All E.R. 126, 130.

[6] Para. [**231**], *post*.

[7] See Eekelaar, *op. cit.*; Hall, *op. cit.*; Bromley, *Family Law* (5th Edn.), Chap. 10.

[8] *Per* Sachs L.J. in *Hewer* v. *Bryant*, para. [**201**], *ante*.

ends with little more than advice."[1] Alternatively the right is sometimes referred to as "possession" or "custody" (in its narrow meaning). As will be seen[2] it emerges from the Children Act as "actual custody". [**210**]

Access

Where the parent does not have care and control he will, save in exceptional circumstances, be given access to the child.[3] In *M.* v. *M.*[4] the right to access was described as a right of the child rather than of the parent. It is difficult to determine why the Act should single it out for special mention.[5] Does the express reference impliedly reject the view expressed in *M.* v. *M.* and reassert that the right is "the basic right of any parent"?[6] It is better, it is suggested, to treat access as a mutual right of the parent and child to the other's companionship, of which each can only be deprived when the paramountcy of the child's welfare exceptionally so warrants.[7] [**211**]

Protection and maintenance

Consistent with the right to care and control are the duties to protect[8] and maintain the child. The common law duty to protect, which does not depend on the child's age but on the necessity for protection,[9] has very largely been replaced by statutory duties.[10] Similarly, the obligation to maintain is almost wholly a statutory one and is imposed by a "chaos of enactments".[11] Over and above these obligations there is, at least for the purpose of adoption law, "the natural and moral duty of a parent to show affection, care and interest towards his child".[12] [**212**]

Discipline

This, too, emanates from the right of care and control[13] and is a facet of the parental right to determine the child's upbringing. Its significance diminishes as the child grows older, and this is especially true with regard to the incidental rights to inflict corporal punishment and restrict liberty. The right, which must be exercised reasonably, extends to any person or body in *loco parentis*, e.g., the

---

[1] *Ibid.*, *per* Lord Denning M.R., [1970] 1 Q.B. 357, 369; [1969] 3 All E.R. 578, 582.

[2] Para. [**237**], *post*.

[3] See generally Wharam, *Access to Children*, (1972) 2 Fam. Law 101; Manchester, *Access to Child*, 123 New Law Jo. 738.

[4] [1973] 2 All E.R. 81.

[5] S. 85 (1).

[6] *Per* Willmer L.J. in *S.* v. *S. and P.*, [1962] 2 All E.R. 1, 3; [1962] 1 W.L.R. 445, 448.

[7] Some persuasive support for this conclusion may be drawn from *Re T.* (*minors*), *T.* v. *M.* (1973), 3 Fam. Law 138, where the Court of Appeal held that while the child's welfare was paramount the interests of the parent were to be considered.

[8] Cf. CYPA 1969, s. 70 (1) where, for the purposes of that Act, "care" includes "protection and guidance".

[9] *R.* v. *Shepherd* (1862), Le & Ca. 147; *R.* v. *Chattaway* (1922), 17 Cr. App. Rep. 7 (C.C.A.).

[10] Mainly to be found in Part I of the Children and Young Persons Act 1933. See generally Bevan, *op. cit.*, Chap. 6.

[11] Cretney, "*The Maintenance Quagmire*", 33 M.L.R. 662; Bromley, *op. cit.*, Chap. 16; *Bevan*, *op. cit.*, Chap. 14.

[12] *Per* Pennycuick J. in *Re P.* (*infants*), [1962] 3 All E.R. 789, 794; [1962] 1 W.L.R. 1296, 1302; see Chap. 4 para. [**55**], *ante*.

[13] Cf. CYPA 1969, s. 70 (1) where "control" includes "discipline".

school authorities. It has, indeed, been argued that parents may have a duty to punish children in that failure to do so may lead to their becoming "beyond control".[1] [**213**]

Secular education

The emphasis here is on the parental duty. This is to ensure that his child, being of compulsory school age, receives full-time education, as prescribed by section 36 of the Education Act 1944, and to secure his regular attendance.[2] Parental rights concerning secular education are strictly limited. There is the right (rarely exercised) to secure his child's education otherwise than by sending him regularly to school and that of choosing private education. With regard to State education, the local education authority must have regard to parental wishes[3] and must make sufficient schools available,[4] but this does not preclude them from taking into account other matters, the effect of which may be to defeat the parent's wishes.[5] [**214**]

Religious upbringing

There is no duty upon a parent to see that his child receives religious instruction, although the courts usually take the view that some form of religion is better than none.[6] The parental right to determine the child's religious education is invariably tied to issues over his custody and secular education. Because of the welfare principle the relevance of the right in any particular case is variable, but as a generalisation it can be stated that today it does not carry great weight and its declining significance seems to be reflected in the amendment in the 1975 Act that a parent when agreeing to an adoption order can no longer impose conditions with respect to the religious persuasion in which his child is to be brought up.[7] [**215**]

Medical treatment

As part of his statutory duty to protect, the parent must provide, or take steps to procure, essential medical aid for his child.[8] Where the treatment is not essential (for example, possible immunisation),[9] the parent of a child who is under 16[10] must normally give his consent, at least if the child is too young to be able to give it himself. The need for parental consent may, however, be overridden by considerations for the child's welfare. On the other hand, those considerations may justify refusal of treatment to which the parent has given

---

[1] Freeman, *Children Act 1975*, 72/8.

[2] Education Act 1944, s. 39.

[3] *Ibid.*, s. 76.

[4] *Ibid.*, s. 8.

[5] *Watt* v. *Kesteven County Council*, [1955] 1 Q.B. 408; [1955] 1 All E.R. 473 (C.A.); *Cumings* v. *Birkenhead Corporation*, [1972] Ch. 12; [1971] 2 All E.R. 881 (C.A.).

[6] Cf. *H.* v. *H.* (1975), 119 Sol. Jo. 590.

[7] S. 13; see para. [**53**], *ante*.

[8] Children and Young Persons Act 1933, s. 1 (1) and (2) (*a*). The duty is imposed on anyone over 16 who has "custody, charge or care" of a child under that age.

[9] See Eekelaar, *op. cit.*, pp. 224–225.

[10] Family Law Reform Act 1969, s. 8.

consent.[1] There is increasing support for the view that where the child has reached the age where he can understand the nature and the consequences of the treatment he has the right to determine the matter for himself.[2] [**216**]

Child's surname

One parent is not entitled to change the child's surname unless the other consents or a court authorises the change because it is in the child's interests.[3] So far as concerns matrimonial proceedings in a divorce court these principles are given statutory effect.[4] It seems that they are not affected by the right which a parent now has under the Guardianship Act 1973 to exercise a parental right independently of the other.[5] [**217**]

Child's services

It appears that the right of a parent to the services of his child arises not *qua* parent but as head of the domestic household. In any event, it is not enforceable against the child. The loss of the services arising from a tort is, however, actionable provided that the loss does not arise from the rape, seduction, enticement or harbouring of the child.[6] [**218**]

Passports and emigration

The "right" of a parent to veto the issue of a passport to his child is a particular incident of the right to determine the place and manner in which the child spends his time. The Passport Office impliedly recognises the right by its requirement that the parent must consent to an application for a passport by a child over 16 but under 18 and also by one under 16 where a passport separate from the parent's is sought. Since parental consent to the issue of a passport is required, it follows *a fortiori* that consent to the child's emigration is essential. [**219**]

Consent to marriage

Both parents must normally consent to the marriage of their child who, not being already a widow or widower, is between 16 and 18 years old. But where they are divorced or separated by a court order or agreement, the parent to whom custody has been granted must consent; and where one has deserted the other the latter's consent is needed.[7] [**220**]

---

[1] *Re D.*, [1976] Fam. 185; [1976] 1 All E.R. 326.

[2] See Bromley, *op. cit.*, p. 337; Eekelaar, *op. cit.*, p. 225; Skegg, *Consent to Medical Procedures on Minors*, 36 M.L.R. 370; and *Justification for Medical Procedures Performed without Consent*, 90 L.Q.R. 512, 519–523.

[3] *Re T.*, [1963] Ch. 238; [1962] 3 All E.R. 970; *Y.* v. *Y.*, [1973] Fam. 147; [1973] 2 All E.R. 574; *In re D (a minor)* (1976), 121 Sol. Jo. 35.

[4] Matrimonial Causes Rules 1977, r. 92 (8) (added by M.C. (Amendment) Rules 1974, S.I. No. 2168). This provides that, unless otherwise directed, any order giving a parent custody or care and control of a child must provide that no step (other than the institution of proceedings) can be taken to change the surname except with the leave of a judge or the consent in writing of the other parent.

[5] S. 1. (1), para. [**229**], *post*. It is difficult to believe that account was not taken of this provision when the Matrimonial Causes (Amendment) Rules 1974 were enacted.

[6] Law Reform (Miscellaneous Provisions) Act 1970, s. 5.

[7] Marriage Act 1949, s. 3 and Sch. 2, as amended by the Family Law Reform Act 1969, s. 2.

Agreement to adoption

This has already been examined.[1] [**221**]

Appointment of Guardians

Either parent may by deed or will appoint a guardian of the child after his or her death.[2] As will be seen, this calls for special consideration in relation to custodianship orders.[3] [**222**]

Succession on death

Parents have rights of intestate succession on the death of their child.[4] The normal rule that the mother of the illegitimate child alone has the parental rights and duties is excluded and the father shares equally in the succession.[5] [**223**]

Administration of assets

The right of the parent to administer his child's property is historically derived from the concept of the natural guardianship of the parent.[6] It extends to property belonging to or held in trust for the minor and to the application of the income of the property,[7] for example, for his maintenance.[8] [**224**]

Representation in legal proceedings

Apparently a parent has the right to act as "next friend", and a duty to act as guardian *ad litem*, of a child in legal proceedings. Certainly the court gives preference to a parent to act in those capacities.[9] It is clearly implicit in section 64 of the 1975 Act that he has a right to represent the child in proceedings to which that section relates.[10] [**225**]

Complaints relating to Section 2 of the Children Act 1948

A parent has the right to object to a resolution passed under section 2 of the Children Act 1948 vesting the parental rights and duties in a local authority.[11] [**226**]

As already indicated, the court may, in the interests of the child's welfare, restrict the exercise of any parental "right". Most of those listed are subject to the principle of the paramountcy of the child's welfare, prescribed by section 1 of the Guardianship of Minors Act 1971. Its application is, of course, most

---

[1] Chap. 4, *ante*.
[2] Guardianship of Minors Act 1971, s. 4 (1) and (2).
[3] Para. [**234**], *post*.
[4] Administration of Estates Act 1925, Part IV, as amended.
[5] Family Law Reform Act 1969, s. 14 (2).
[6] See Hall, *op. cit.*, p. 262, n. 14, who further points out (p. 264, n. 26) that "not even the father as natural guardian of the child can give a valid receipt for a legacy given to the child". But the conclusion rests on *Dagley* v. *Tolferry* (1715), 1 P. Wms. 285, and it is doubtful whether the decision would be followed today, particularly in the light of s. 7 (1) of the Guardianship Act 1973; see paras. [**203**]–[**206**], *ante*.
[7] See Guardianship Act 1973, s. 1 (1).
[8] Trustee Act 1925, s. 31.
[9] *Woolf* v. *Pemberton*, (1877) 6 Ch. D. 19.
[10] See further paras. [**363**], *et seq.*, *post*.
[11] On s. 2 see paras. [**329**]–[**341**], *post*.

frequent in disputes over care and control, access and religious upbringing, but it may equally be invoked in connection with discipline, medical treatment and choice of surname, while section 1 also expressly includes administration of property within its terms. It is also applicable where the appointment of a testamentary guardian is questioned[1] or where the vetoing of the issue of a passport or the withholding of consent to emigration is challenged.[2] The rights relating to consent to marriage and agreement to adoption are qualified by the court's statutory powers to dispense with them,[3] the powers being based on considerations of the child's welfare. As for representation in legal proceedings, section 64 of the 1975 Act is based on the principle that a parent shall not represent the child where there is a possible conflict of interests and, on the same basis, a court has a discretion to order that a parent shall not act as "next friend". Indeed, the only rights which have been mentioned and which are not subject to a welfare principle seem to be the parental right of intestate succession and, in so far as it is a right, the right to sue for loss of services. [**227**]

At common law an agreement to surrender parental rights is void.[4] Subject to one exception, this principle has been given statutory effect by the Guardianship Act 1973[5] which renders unenforceable "an agreement for a man or woman to give up in whole or in part, in relation to any child of his or hers, the [parental] rights and authority". Section 85 (2) of the 1975 Act, while retaining the exception, goes further because it prevents anyone from transferring any parental right or *duty* he has "as respects a child", who, therefore, may not be his own. The extension has particularly in mind a custodian under the Act. In his case, the purported transfer, apart from being void, would be a good ground for revoking the custodianship order.[6] The permitted exception is a separation agreement between husband and wife which is to operate only during their separation while married. If it provides for either spouse to give up parental rights and authority "in relation to a child of theirs" it is enforceable unless it is not for the child's benefit.[7] [**228**]

The 1975 Act also takes further another change introduced by the Guardianship Act 1973. In making the rights and authority of the mother equal with those of a father the latter Act[8] itself undermines the new principle of parity in that it allows either of them to exercise his or her rights and authority without the other. Section 85 (3) of the 1975 Act extends the power of independent action by providing that where two (or more) *persons* have a parental right or duty jointly, either may exercise or perform it in any manner without the other,

---

[1] Under the Guardianship of Minors Act 1971, s. 4.

[2] Either may be challenged by way of wardship proceedings. Alternatively, if the dispute is between the mother and father and is over the issue of a passport, application to the court to resolve it can be made under the Guardianship Act 1973, s. 1 (3). In practice the latter alternative would not, it is submitted, be available in a dispute over emigration, since that matter would inextricably be involved with the making of a custody order; see *ibid.*, s. 1 (4).

[3] Marriage Act 1949, s. 3 (1); Children Act 1975, ss. 3 and 12 (1) and (2); (Adoption Act 1976, ss. 6 and 16 (1) and (2)).

[4] *Vansittart* v. *Vansittart* (1858), 2 De G. & J. 249.

[5] S. 1 (2). The Act repeals and replaces the Custody of Infants Act 1873, s. 2.

[6] For revocation of custodianship orders see paras. [**286**]–[**288**], *post*.

[7] Guardianship Act 1973, s. 1 (2).

[8] S. 1 (1).

if the other has not signified disapproval of its exercise or performance in that manner. Like section 85 (2) this extension particularly takes account of the new concept of custodianship, but it applies as much to natural parents as to joint custodians and, with regard to the former, modifies the provisions in the Guardianship Act by its restriction concerning disapproval. However, *prima facie* the restriction is of limited effect. The primary object of subsection (3) is to enable one person to act alone in day to day affairs affecting the child or in an emergency, for example, in consenting to urgent medical treatment, but it does not attempt so to restrict its scope. As it stands, the onus is on the other person to signify disapproval. There is no duty on the one exercising the right or performing the duty to consult, or having regard to the circumstances to take reasonable steps to consult, the other. It is an open question whether the court would be willing to imply that duty. On the other hand, there are circumstances where by necessary implication subsection (3) itself is excluded; for example, in cases of consent to marriage or agreement to adoption, where normally the consent or agreement of both parents is necessary.[1] [**229**]

Where two or more persons jointly have a parental right or duty and one of them dies, it vests in the survivor(s). If the deceased had the sole right or duty it lapses on his death until someone else lawfully acquires it, for example under guardianship or custodianship proceedings. These rules apply in relation to the dissolution of a body corporate as they apply in relation to the death of an individual.[2] This last mentioned point has practical relevance where parental rights and duties are vested in a voluntary organisation, in accordance with section 60 of the Act,[3] and are shared jointly with some other person, for example, one of the parents. [**230**]

LEGAL CUSTODY

A custodianship order vests legal custody.[4] The term is so defined, in section 86, as to be limited to "so much of the parental rights and duties as relate to the person of the child", but surprisingly the Act provides minimal information on what does and what does not come within this "personal" category. There is one specified restriction. Section 86 itself precludes anyone who has legal custody, other than the parent or guardian, from effecting or arranging for the child's emigration from the United Kingdom.[5] So, where a step-parent is a custodian,[6] his or her spouse, as the parent of the child, will be responsible for making the arrangements, if the family are planning emigration. The Act also specifically refers to three parental rights which do fall within the concept of legal custody. These are the right to determine the place and manner in which the child's time is spent,[7] the right to give or withhold consent to the

---

[1] Compare with s. 85 (3), s. 1 (7) of the Guardianship Act 1973 which expressly covers this point.

[2] S. 85 (4), (5) and (6).

[3] Para. [**357**], *post*.

[4] S. 33 (1).

[5] Compare the power of local authorities to arrange for emigration of children in their care (Children Act 1948, s. 17). This is not affected by the 1975 Act.

[6] Paras. [**259**]–[**261**], *post*.

[7] S. 86, subject to the restriction concerning emigration.

marriage of the child,[1] and the right to object to a section 2 resolution under the Children Act 1948.[2] [**231**]

These apart, the Act offers no guidance for determining whether or not a parental right or duty falls within the concept of legal custody.[3] On the one hand, it can safely be said that those listed earlier in paras. [**210**]–[**216**], together with the rights to veto the issue of a passport and to represent the child in legal proceedings, do come within its scope—but subject to the power of the court, where there is a custodianship order, to make orders affecting the mother or father with regard to access and maintenance.[4] On the other hand it is obvious that the rights of succession to, and the administration of, the child's property are outside legal custody. The nature of the right to the child's services seems to be immaterial; whether "personal" or not, the custodian in his capacity of domestic head will be entitled to sue for loss. The remainder listed, namely, agreement to adoption, appointment of a testamentary guardian and changing the child's surname call for detailed comment. [**232**]

It is quite remarkable that the Act does not expressly give effect to the *Houghton* recommendation[5] that a custodian cannot give his agreement to the child's being adopted. Nevertheless, that is the necessary inference, for otherwise it would lead to the absurdity that, while a custodianship order cannot vest all the parental rights and duties in the custodian, the custodian could agree to some third person's acquiring them all without the parent's agreement. There is the further, more legalistic reason that, since an adoption order vests the proprietary as well as the personal rights and duties in the adopters, the right to give or withhold agreement to achieving that effect cannot be said to relate only to the person of the child. [**233**]

Prima facie similar reasoning leads to the conclusion that a custodian does not have the right to appoint a testamentary guardian. *Nemo dat quod non habet*. Having himself only "personal" parental rights and duties he cannot additionally confer proprietary. Moreover, a guardian under the Guardianship of Minors Act 1971 not only is guardian of the person but also has all the rights, powers and duties of a guardian of a child's estate.[6] Therefore, it is arguable that the right of appointment does not relate to the person of the child. It is submitted, however, that these arguments do not have the same cogency as their counterparts have in relation to adoption. Section 86 defines legal custody as "*so much* of the parental rights and duties as relate to the person"—not "such" or "those" rights and duties as so relate. Accordingly, the definition is open to the construction that a custodian has so much of the right to appoint as enables him to appoint a testamentary guardian of the person, and so the rule in the Guardianship of Minors Act must to that extent be qualified. Viewed

---

[1] Marriage Act 1949, s. 3 (1), as amended by the Children Act 1975, Sch. 3, para. 7.

[2] Children Act 1948, s. 4, as amended by the Children Act 1975, Sch. 3, para. 5.

[3] However, the Act does give other "rights" to the custodian. Thus, because he has legal custody he can consent to someone else applying for custodianship (s. 33 (3), para. [**246**], *post*). He can apply for an affiliation order within three years of the making of a custodianship order, provided that he is not married to the child's mother (s. 45, paras. [**302**]–[**303**], *post*).

[4] Para. [**298**], *post*.

[5] Rec. 22.

[6] Guardianship Act 1973, s. 7.

more widely the arguments are evenly balanced. On the one hand, it can be said that the conferment of such a wide right as will enable the custodian, in the event of his death, to provide for the regulation of the child's future would scarcely accord with the denial of the rights to agree to adoption and to consent to emigration. On the other hand, a right of appointment seems consistent with his right to consent to marriage. The effect of marriage of a daughter or, apparently, a son under 18 is to emancipate the child from natural guardianship.[1] If, then, the custodian has the right to withhold the termination of that guardianship, should he not be able to provide a substitute for it? It is regrettable that the Act has not clarified this matter. [**234**]

If the classification of parental rights relating to the person of the child turns on whether their subject-matter can be said to relate to the care and control and upbringing of the child, it is doubtful whether the right to change the child's surname is a "personal" right. The bearing of a name can have wider possible implications involving status and reputation.[2] Moreover, were the custodian given that right, it could create difficulties should there be revocation of the custodianship order. In the event of the parent's then resuming legal custody,[3] it would be incongruous if the child's name did not revert to the parent's. Is it in the child's interests that his name be subject to the risk of changes in this way? [**235**]

The question of changing the surname has particular practical relevance for the step-father who often wants the name of the child of his spouse by a former marriage to be changed to his own. Where he is not eligible to apply for custodianship and has to seek custody through the divorce court,[4] any change of name would be governed by the Matrimonial Causes Rule already mentioned[5] and the leave of the court would be necessary. Where he is so eligible and is appointed custodian, it will be a matter for his spouse as the natural parent to consent to the change. Indeed, even if the custodian does have a right to change the name, the consent of his spouse would be required, since in such a case the spouses jointly have the legal custody.[6] [**236**]

ACTUAL CUSTODY

This third concept essentially corresponds to the traditional, narrow meaning of custody.[7] Section 87 (1) provides that a person has actual custody of a child if he has actual possession of his person.[8] The possession may be shared with others. The use of the term "possession" in relation to children has been defended as being "more accurate than the euphemism 'care and control' which relates to distinguishable matters".[9] With respect, the advantage of "care and control" is that it recognises that these two facets are closely interwoven in the

---

[1] See Bromley, *op. cit.*, p. 309.

[2] For certain purposes the right to use a name is a proprietary right, e.g., in passing-off actions.

[3] Under s. 36 of the Act, paras. [**287**]–[**288**], *post*.

[4] See para. [**259**], *post*.

[5] Para. [**217**], *ante*.

[6] S. 44 (2), para. [**265**], *post*.

[7] See para. [**201**], *ante*.

[8] Not, perhaps, the most felicitous use of language.

[9] Eekelaar, *op. cit.*, p. 214, n. 27.

daily upbringing of the child. Apart from this reliance on "possession", the definition is to be welcomed in that it does bring home the immediacy of the relationship, and it is supplemented by the rule that, "unless the context otherwise requires, references to the person with whom a child has his home refer to the person who, disregarding absence of the child at a hospital or boarding school and any other temporary absence, has actual custody of the child".[1] So, relatives or foster parents who are caring for a child but have not sought a custodianship order have actual custody, and in that capacity they will have the same duties—but not the rights—as a custodian would have by virtue of his legal custody.[2] *Inter alia*, therefore, they will have the duty of maintaining the child. **[237]**

This section has been concerned with examining the scope of legal custody and the *parental* rights and duties which are considered to fall within it, but it must be emphasised that all legislation affecting children will have to be carefully scrutinised to see whether or not its provisions extend to the custodian. For example, it is clear that he may be eligible to claim tax allowances,[3] or child benefit.[4] **[238]**

This chapter began with a reference to the tangle of technical terminology. Few would deny the need to unravel it; but the process is a lengthy one. The 1975 Act attempts to begin this task not merely by the introduction of these new concepts but also by trying to secure their permanence as a part of child law, namely, by incorporating them into the Interpretation Act 1889 and enacting that in any future Act they shall be construed in accordance with the 1975 Act.[5] This method of enactment accords with the recommendation of the Renton Committee on the Preparation of Legislation[6] that a general Interpretation Act should increasingly be used incorporating standardised definitions.[7] While this drafting technique is to be welcomed, its use is not, it is suggested, appropriate in the present instance. The task of clearing a path through the jungle of child law ought to be seen as a protracted one involving lengthy reconnoitring—a task admirably suitable for the Law Commission. The ultimate solution, it is hoped, will be found in the three concepts of guardianship, care and control and not in those defined by the 1975 Act. **[239]**

---

[1] S. 87 (3). There may be difficulties in deciding whether or not an absence is temporary, e.g., for the purposes of s. 9 of the Act (Adoption Act 1976, s. 13 (1)); see para. [**112**], *ante*.

[2] Sub-s. (2).

[3] Income and Corporation Taxes Act 1970, s. 10 (1) (*b*).

[4] Child Benefit Act 1975, s. 3.

[5] Children Act 1975, s. 89 (1). This perpetuates the expression "the parental rights and duties", the expression "legal custody" and references to the person with whom a child has his home, but not the expression "actual custody". Nevertheless, since references to a person with whom a child has his home refer to the person having "actual custody" the latter term will to that extent also apply to future enactments.

[6] Cmnd. 6053, Chap. XIX.

[7] As originally drafted, the Children Bill provided that "in any future enactment" the concepts were to have the meaning ascribed to them by the Bill. Such legislation by reference *in futuro* would have caused serious problems for the practitioner and the risk of oversight when construing later enactments would have been high. The Government wisely abandoned the proposal in favour of s. 89 (1).

CHAPTER 10

CUSTODIANSHIP AND OTHER ORDERS

CUSTODIANSHIP ORDERS

A. QUALIFIED APPLICANTS

Eligibility to apply for a custodianship order depends partly on the kind of applicant, partly on the length of the period for which he has had actual custody of the child and partly on whether or not the application has the consent of a person who has the legal custody. The following are qualified to apply:[1]

(*a*) A relative or step-parent with whom the child has had his home for the three months preceding the making of the application, provided there is the requisite consent to the application.

(*b*) Any other person[2] with whom the child has had his home for a period or periods of at least twelve months before the making of the application, including the three preceding it, but subject to the same consent.

(*c*) Any person with whom the child has had his home for a period or periods of at least three years before the application is made, including the three months preceding that date.

Paragraph (*c*) will thus include a relative or step-parent applying without consent, but, that apart, paragraphs (*b*) and (*c*) relate to foster-parents, whether the child has been placed with them privately by the natural parents or by a local authority or voluntary society. [**240**]

The qualifications differ from those required of applicants for an adoption order in two important respects. No minimum age is imposed and joint applications are not restricted to married couples.[3] An application for a custodianship order may be made by "one or more persons" who are qualified under the above rules.[4] Thus, an order could be made in favour of a brother and sister of a much younger child where they continue to live together in the family home on the death of their parents. However, where there is more than one applicant, the court may choose to appoint only one (or some) of them as custodian.[5] Moreover, although there is no statutory minimum, the age of an applicant will be a relevant factor. In applying the principle of the paramountcy of the child's

---

[1] Children Act 1975, s. 33 (3).

[2] S. 33 (3) (*b*) refers to "any person", but, since the qualifications imposed by para. (*b*) are stricter than those of para. (*a*), relatives and step-parents will obviously always fall within the latter.

[3] Cf. ss. 10 (1) and 11 (1), para. [**93**], *ante* (Adoption Act 1976, s. 14 (1) and 15 (1)).

[4] S. 33 (1).

[5] *Ibid.* The person in whom legal custody is vested under a custodianship order may be referred to as custodian of the child (s. 33 (2)).

welfare, as it is obliged to do,[1] the court will be reluctant to make anyone under the age of 21 a custodian. [**241**]

The time limits

The period for which a child needs to have his home with someone[2] before the court can effectively reach a decision on whether or not to make an order can vary according to the individual. For some children three years can be a very long time. It is therefore arguable that each application is better left to the operation of the paramountcy principle rather than to the crude arbitrariness of minimum time limits. There is no consistent rationale underlying those prescribed. They represent a conglomeration of views and produce a compromise between the child's welfare and the rights of the natural parent. Some would see them as a safeguard against frivolous and premature applications that will protect the natural parent from being exposed to the anxiety of being involved in proceedings after only a short time.[3] While relevant to applications under paragraph (*c*), the point seems scarcely valid where an application is made with the consent of the parent either under paragraph (*a*) or (*b*), except to the extent that the consent may be too easily given.[4] The difference between the respective periods under the latter two paragraphs is justified on the ground that a longer period is needed to assess the suitability of foster-parents than that required for relatives. Generally that is so, but three months may be too short for relatives if they have had little previous contact with the child.[5] In such a case, however, the court may be unwilling to make a custodianship order, but ready to make an interim one until the child has spent a longer period with the relatives.[6] [**242**]

The twelve-month period is further defended on the ground that it gives a local authority, in whose care the child is, sufficient but not excessive time to decide whether it wants a particular fostering relationship to continue without allowing things to drift.[7] If the legal custody is still vested in the natural parent, because the child has only been received into care under section 1 of the Children Act 1948, the authority will have to decide whether or not to withdraw the child from the foster-parents before the completion of the statutory period in order to avoid an application being made with the consent of the natural parent.[8] On the other hand, there has been criticism that twelve months is too short a period, because some unsuccessful placements do not manifest themselves until the second year after placement and there is the risk that meanwhile the

---

[1] S. 33 (9).

[2] In calculating the respective periods account can be taken of the first 6 weeks of the child's life. Cf. s. 9 (1), para. [**107**], *ante* (Adoption Act 1976, s. 13 (1)).

[3] See H.C.R., para. 122.

[4] But the safeguards against this lie in the court's power to withhold an order and in the proposed practice of providing parents with explanatory leaflets.

[5] "Relative" has the same broad meaning as it has for adoption; Children Act 1975, s. 107 (1) and Adoption Act 1958, s. 57 (1); (Adoption Act 1976, s. 72 (1)).

[6] For the power to make interim orders see para. [**310**], *post*.

[7] H.C. Official Report, 1975, Standing Committee A (Tenth Sitting), cols. 490–491 (Mr. Steen).

[8] However, if the local authority were to take this step, it would be open to the parent to recover the child and then again place him with the foster-parents, as private foster-parents, with a view eventually to allowing them to apply for custodianship.

natural parent will too readily give his consent.[1] Such differing views serve to emphasise the vital role of the court and the importance of the report which the local authority will have to prepare for it.[2] **[243]**

The period of three years required by paragraph (*c*), which is to be read in conjunction with the restriction on removing the child from the applicant while the custodianship application is pending,[3] was considered by the Government to be sufficiently long to avoid any serious risk of parents being discouraged from allowing their children to be temporarily fostered. Causes for temporary fostering, such as parental illness, are likely to have disappeared before the foster-parent is in a position to apply for custodianship and the parents will be able to recover the child.[4] On the other hand, a period of five years was felt to be too long a delay in seeking vital decisions concerning the child's future. Moreover, the shorter period might even encourage some foster-parents to apply for custodianship rather than leave it until later to seek adoption. A major reason for acceptance of the three-year period was, however, the fact that a custodianship order unlike that of adoption is revocable. It is arguable that this premise is based on an over-optimistic view of the likelihood of revocation. It is to be remembered that section 1 of the Guardianship of Minors Act 1971 governs any custodianship application.[5] An order will have been made because, after consideration of all the circumstances, it accorded with the paramountcy of the child's welfare. The court will therefore require cogent evidence that his welfare now demands a revocation of the earlier decision. **[244]**

It is difficult to predict the operation of paragraph (*c*) and there is the risk of unduly reacting to its possible implications. Certain questions may be posed:

(1) *Will the provision increase short-term and reduce long-term fostering*? Both the local authority in the case of children in their care and parents in the case of private fostering may be prompted to anticipate possible custodianship applications by withdrawing the child from the foster-parents' home before the effluxion of the three years. The parent who allows his child to be received into care under section 1 of the Children Act 1948 may want to know what is the fostering policy of the particular local authority. He might even seek to make it a condition that his child is placed in a community home rather than be fostered. If this should be the approach of local authorities and parents, is it likely to be in the child's best interests?

(2) *Is a custodianship order likely to weaken or strengthen the relationship between the child and the natural parent*? It is doubtful whether many foster-parents who become custodians by virtue of having had actual custody for three years will encourage the natural parents to maintain relationships with the child. That possibility is much more likely where the parent has consented to the application for custodianship, especially if the custodian is a relative. Answers to questions of this kind will partly depend upon the degree of publicity and information given to natural and foster-parents about their respective rights.

---

[1] Para. [**242**], *ante*. See H.C. Official Report, 1975, Vol. 893, No. 142, cols. 1902–1903 (Second Reading; Mr. Whitehead).

[2] See para. [**291**], *post*.

[3] S. 41, paras. [**254**]–[**258**], *post*.

[4] On the possibility of the foster-parent's relying on wardship see para. [**326**], *post*.

[5] S. 33 (9) of the 1975 Act expressly puts the point beyond doubt.

The Act itself recognises the potential problems to which the paragraph may give rise by empowering the Secretary of State to substitute, in the light of experience, a different period for that of three years.[1] **[245]**

Consent

Usually the person whose consent will be necessary if application is made under paragraph (*a*) or (*b*) will be the natural parent or the local authority, but other possibilities will be a custodian and a voluntary organisation in whom the parental rights and duties are vested in accordance with section 60 of the Act.[2] **[246]**

The local authority in this respect occupies a special position. If the child is the subject of a resolution under section 2 of the Children Act 1948[3] or of a care order under the Children and Young Persons Act 1969, then, of course, it is the local authority and not the parent whose consent is required. The parental rights and duties are vested in it and therefore it has the legal custody. It is, however, questionable whether in such cases it is proper that the 1975 Act should automatically exclude the need for the parent's consent. A section 2 resolution, for example, is more often than not based on the neglect or ill-treatment of the child by the parent or on some other inadequacy of conduct. In cases of that kind the exclusion of any parental veto is justifiable, but there are cases where the rights and duties have been vested in the local authority and no blame can be laid at the door of the parent, for example, a section 2 resolution based on some permanent disability from which the parent suffers. Yet, the Act refuses to distinguish between the two kinds of cases. Instead it leaves it to the natural parent to make any representations through the local authority report which has to be presented to the court and through personal hearing at the application.[4] **[247]**

If the child has been received into care under section 1 of the Children Act 1948, the consent of the parent, and not of the local authority, will be needed, since the former will have retained legal custody. Nevertheless, the authority can be involved, because it is apparent from the terms of section 40 of the 1975 Act that there is nothing to prevent it from stating in the report its opposition to the application.[5] Whether this goes far enough is open to a sharp conflict of opinion. One view is that, even though the authority does not have legal custody, it ought to have an overriding veto because it has responsibilities to children whom it receives into its care and to their parents. Moreover, the advantage of a veto is that it would be less likely than later court proceedings to disturb the placement and harm the relationship between the authority and

---

[1] S. 33 (7). An order is subject to affirmative resolution by each House of Parliament. It is likely that there will be prior Government consultation with interested bodies; see H.C. Official Report, 1975, Standing Committee A (Tenth Sitting), col. 496 (Dr. David Owen).

[2] Not yet operative. See further paras. [**357**]–[**360**], *post*.

[3] As substituted by Children Act 1975, s. 57, paras. [**329**]–[**341**], *post*.

[4] It is assumed that the Rules will give the natural parent a right of audience: see para. [**251**], *post*.

[5] This point is equally relevant where there is an application under paragraph (*c*). The fact that consent is not a prerequisite does not preclude the authority, or indeed the parent, from expressing in the report their opposition.

the foster-parents, especially if the authority does not have to spell out the reasons for its objection, as it would be obliged to do if the matter came before the court.[1] This argument is, it is submitted, open to the serious objection that it pays insufficient regard to the interests of the child. If there is already conflict between the foster-parent and the authority, and the natural parent is willing to see custodianship granted, *a fortiori* the court should be made aware of the circumstances. If the authority is not happy with the proposed application, why did it allow the placement to continue? A further advantage in not giving a veto is that it may encourage an authority to make up its mind at an early stage whether or not the placement is likely to be satisfactory and whether it should be short term or long term. [**248**]

Where the child is in the care of a voluntary organisation but the parental rights and duties have not been transferred to it in accordance with section 60, its views on the custodianship application can, and should be, conveyed to the court through the local authority report. [**249**]

The requirement of consent is irrelevant, obviously, where no one has legal custody[2] or the applicant already has legal custody—as, for example, where he jointly shares legal custody and wants to become sole custodian—or where the person with legal custody cannot be found.[3] It seems clear that this last-mentioned rule is to be interpreted in the same way as the corresponding provision which enables the court to dispense with agreement to the making of an adoption order,[4] and therefore it will be necessary to ensure that every reasonable step has been taken to trace a person having legal custody. The onus will, it is submitted, lie on the applicant to do this, but because of its obligations relating to the submission of a report the local authority will necessarily be involved in the investigation.[5] If the thoroughness of inquiry usually undertaken to trace a putative father in order to notify him of an application to adopt his child is anything to go by, this will, indeed, be a heavy burden. [**250**]

The consent needed is consent to the application being made. Unlike adoption, there is no requirement that the person with legal custody must freely and with full understanding of what is involved agree unconditionally to the making of a custodianship order, unless his agreement is dispensed with on specified grounds.[6] The absence of any such requirement is partly explained on the ground that a custodianship order is revocable and does not effect a permanent severance between parent and child. Parental agreement to an order is no more essential for it than it is for a custody order. However, the absence is also, it is submitted, partly to be explained on the assumption that a person with legal custody will have the opportunity to make representations and oppose the

---

[1] See further H.C. Official Report, 1975, Standing Committee A (Tenth Sitting), cols. 484–486 (Mr. Bennett).

[2] For example, the case of an orphan with no guardian, with no one to whom custody has been granted by an order of court or, when Part II of the 1975 Act becomes operative, with no custodian.

[3] S. 33 (6).

[4] See para. [**55**], *ante*.

[5] See further para. [**252**], *post*.

[6] It follows, therefore, that a person caring for a child whose parent, for example, is incapable of giving consent to an application will have to wait until three years have passed before being eligible to apply for custodianship, unless there is some other person with legal custody who can provide the requisite consent.

making of an order. As already indicated,[1] the local authority will have to include a statement of the wishes of the mother and father regarding the application. Moreover, as also already suggested,[2] the Rules governing applications and the making of orders will give them a right of audience. It is submitted that these will run *pari passu* the Adoption Rules. It is scarcely likely that the right will be less extensive. It would, for example, be highly anomalous if a parent could be heard on the issue of custodianship where that possibility was being considered by the court of its own motion as an alternative to adoption, in accordance with section 37,[3] but not where there was only a custodianship application. [**251**]

The assumption that there is a right to be heard is, it is submitted, implicit in paragraphs (*a*) and (*b*) themselves. They require the consent of "a person", and not each person, having legal custody. Thus, where the mother and father of a legitimate child are living apart, but, there being no order of a court granting one of them custody, both are entitled to the legal custody, it will be sufficient for the applicant to rely on the consent of one of them to his application, without having to take all reasonable steps to seek out the other and satisfy the court that he cannot be found.[4] It seems likely, however, that the Rules will require the local authority to take all reasonable steps to find him in order not only to enable it to include in its report the wishes of the "missing" parent but also to notify him of his right to attend the hearing. [**252**]

Even though the requisite consent relates to the application, and not the order, being made, the two paragraphs are defective in that they do not expressly state that the consent must be given "freely and with full understanding of what is involved". One can understand the omission of those words from the requirement of consenting to a freeing for adoption application under section 14 of the Act, because the free and full understanding is a prerequisite to the giving of agreement to the making of the adoption order itself. In the present context the words will have to be imported. It is to be hoped that the courts will do so and impose on the applicant the duty of ensuring that the parent understands.[5] It would, for example, be a waste of cost and time, not to say anything about the child's welfare, if the parent did not fully understand but this was not discovered until he was later interviewed by the social worker preparing the local authority report or even later at the hearing of the application. [**253**]

Restrictions on removal of child where applicant has provided home for three years

The special protection by way of criminal sanctions which section 41 gives to the applicant for custodianship who has provided a home for the child for at least three years follows very closely the lines of the protection afforded by

---

[1] Paras. [**247**]–[**249**], *ante*.

[2] *Ibid*.

[3] See paras.]**273**]–[**282**], *post*.

[4] But the point is not entirely free from doubt. See s. 33 (6), which refers to "*the* person with legal custody cannot be found".

[5] It is suggested that the point should be covered in explanatory leaflets issued both to the natural parent and the applicant for custodianship.

section 34A of the Adoption Act 1958[1] to the applicant for adoption who has similarly provided a home for five years.[2] Once the application is made the position is frozen and the child cannot lawfully be removed from the applicant's actual custody[3] except with the leave of a court[4] or under the authority conferred by any enactment or on the arrest of the child. The kinds of circumstances which would allow removal have already been considered.[5] Additionally, it will, of course, be lawful to remove the child with the consent of the applicant. That is implicit in section 41 (1), although the possibility of its happening is remote. **[254]**

Where the child was already in the care of a local authority before he was placed with the applicant and is still in the care of a local authority, then under section 41 (2) the latter authority[6] cannot remove him from the applicant's custody[7] except with the applicant's consent or the leave of a court.[8] It has already been suggested[9] that, if the child has in an emergency to be removed from the home of the applicant and the latter is not in a position to give consent, reliance should be placed on the power of the police to remove until an application can be made by the local authority to the court. **[255]**

The protection given by section 41 lasts until the custodianship application has been heard. During the passage of the Children Bill an attempt was made to impose a maximum period of protection of 28 days from the date when the application was made, but this was resisted on the ground that it would be unduly restrictive on the applicant and his advisers in the preparation of his case. Moreover, it would not always be reasonably practicable to ensure that an application could be heard by the court within that period. At the same time, the three-year period in section 41, like its counterpart of five years in section

---

[1] Adoption Act 1976, s. 28. The maximum penalties for wrongful removal are the same as they are under sections 34 and 34A of the 1958 Act, i.e., three months' imprisonment or a fine of £400 or both; see s. 41 (3) of the 1975 Act.

[2] Note that, whereas under s. 34A the relevant period is "the five years preceding the application", for the purpose of s. 41 the three-year minimum need not be a continuous period but, in accordance with s. 33 (3) (*c*), will have to include at least the three months preceding the application.

[3] S. 41 (1) refers to "custody", but it is submitted that this is to be construed as "actual custody". Since the child has his home with the applicant, the latter by virtue of s. 87 (3) has actual custody (para. [**237**], *ante*) and there is nothing in the context which requires a different interpretation. Compare ss. 34 (1) and (2) and 34A (1) and (2) of the Adoption Act 1958 which also use the term "custody"; see p. 69, n. 6 *ante*.

[4] This, it is submitted, could include any court authorised to make custodianship orders, but in practice it will be that which would hear the application. Compare s. 34A (1) and (2) of the Adoption Act 1958, p. 72, n. 4, *ante*.

[5] Para. [**138**], *ante*.

[6] In the vast majority of cases the authority will be the same throughout, but s. 41 (2) recognises the exceptional possibility of a child being in the care of one authority when placed and boarded out and then in the care of a different authority by the time the custodianship application has been made, for example, where the foster-parents and the child have moved to another authority's area.

It was intended that the same possibility should be allowed for by s. 34A of the Adoption Act 1958, but, because of an inadvertent omission to retain an amendment in the Bill during its passage through the Commons, s. 34A (3) requires the local authority to be the same throughout. It is not intended to introduce early amending legislation.

[7] I.e., actual custody; see n. 3, *supra*, and compare s. 34A (3) which does refer to actual custody.

[8] See n. 4, *supra*. The use of the definite and indefinite article in ss. 34 and 34 A of the 1958 Act and s. 41 does not entirely follow a consistent pattern.

[9] See para. [**141**], *ante*.

34A of the 1958 Act, is intended to be experimental and is subject to possible amendment.[1] [**256**]

Apart from the preventive sanctions of the criminal law, measures are provided to enable the person whose custodianship application is pending to seek the return of the child who, in breach of section 41, has been wrongfully removed from his custody[2] or to prevent wrongful removal where he has reasonable grounds for believing that a person is intending such action.[3] The application for an order to return the child or to forbid removal must be made to an "authorised court" which, for this purpose, means the court which is to hear the custodianship application.[4] In exercising its discretion whether or not to make an order the court must act in accordance with section 1 of the Guardianship of Minors Act 1971.[5] [**257**]

These measures run parallel with those which aid the applicant or prospective applicant for adoption of a child who has had his home with him for at least five years.[6] Thus, if an order for the return of a child is not complied with and the court making the order is the High Court or a county court, it can further order one of its officers to search specified premises and, if he finds the child, to return him to the applicant.[7] If the order for return was made by a magistrates' court, and also as an alternative to the above procedure where the order was made by the High Court or a county court, a justice of the peace can authorise search and return if he is satisfied by information on oath that there are reasonable grounds for believing the child is in specified premises.[8] [**258**]

The step-parent

The position of the step-parent as an applicant for a custodianship order calls for special comment. It has already been seen[9] that, where the spouse, say the wife, of the step-parent was previously married and that marriage was dissolved or annulled, the court is more likely than not to refuse to allow them to adopt the child and will leave them to seek a remedy in the divorce court under

---

[1] S. 41 (4). Any substitution would correspond to any new period substituted for the purpose of s. 33 (3) (*c*).

[2] See p. 121, n. 3, *ante*.

[3] S. 42 (1) and (2).

[4] S. 100 (8). This provides that for the purposes of an application under s. 30 (para. [**143**], *ante*) or under s. 42 the following are authorised courts:

(a) if there is pending in respect of the child an application for an adoption order or an order under s. 14 or a custodianship order, the court in which that application is pending;

(b) in any other case, the High Court, the county court within whose district the applicant lives and the magistrates' court within whose area the applicant lives.

Para. (b) is, it is submitted, only relevant to an application under s. 30 and only then when it is made by a "prospective adopter", i.e., a person who intends to apply for an adoption order. In all other applications under s. 30 and in all applications under s. 42, para. (a) must apply. The terms of ss. 34 and 34A of the Adoption Act 1958 (Adoption Act 1976, ss. 27 and 28) and of s. 41 of the 1975 Act are such that the applications for an adoption order, s. 14 order or custodianship order, as the case may be, must be pending.

[5] See s. 33 (9).

[6] See s. 30 (Adoption Act 1976, s. 29), paras. [**143**]–[**144**], *ante*.

[7] S. 42 (3). The order to the officer may be enforced in the same manner as a warrant for committal (s. 42 (5)).

[8] *Ibid.*, sub-s. (4).

[9] Paras. [**99**]–[**103**], *ante*.

section 42 of the Matrimonial Causes Act 1973. Yet, with the court having a discretion in the matter, the step-father can at least attempt to obtain adoption, if he is so determined. In similar circumstances he is, however, normally disqualified from seeking a custodianship order and if he wishes to establish a legal relationship with the step-child, he is obliged to turn to the divorce court. Section 33 (5) of the 1975 Act provides:

> "A step-parent of the child is not qualified under any paragraph of subsection (3) if in proceedings for divorce or nullity of marriage the child was named in an order made under paragraph (*b*) or (*c*) of section 41 (1) (arrangements for welfare of children of family) of the Matrimonial Causes Act 1973."

An order will have been made under paragraph (*b*) if the divorce court was satisfied either (1) that the arrangements for the welfare of the child were satisfactory or the best that could be devised in the circumstances or (2) that it was impracticable for the parties appearing before that court to make such arrangements. An order under paragraph (*c*) will have been made where the circumstances made it desirable that the decree should be made absolute without delay notwithstanding that there were or might be children of the family and the court was unable to make a declaration in accordance with paragraph (*b*). **[259]**

The most likely circumstance to arise is where the divorce court declared its satisfaction with the arrangements concerning the step-child and granted custody to the wife and access to her former husband. Application can then be made[1] to that court for variation of the custody order in favour of the wife and the step-father jointly. The application could be made by the wife alone or, as is more likely, by her and the step-father jointly, or even by him alone.[2] The step-father is, however, likely to be a sole applicant only where the mother is dead. In that event it will still be necessary to proceed in the divorce court, since he remains ineligible for custodianship. Nor could he apply for guardianship so long as the other parent remains alive.[3] On the other hand, if that other parent is dead or cannot be found,[4] the restriction on applying for *custodianship* is lifted,[5] whether or not the parent whom the step-parent married is still alive.[6] Of course, if the natural parents were never married, no restriction under section 33 (5) could arise, unless the case were to fall within those covered by the following paragraph. **[260]**

By its terms section 33 (5) also applies to those cases where the earlier

---

[1] In accordance with s. 42 (7) of the Matrimonial Causes Act 1973.

[2] Because the 1975 Act has imposed an obligation on the step-parent to seek his remedy in the divorce court in the circumstances outlined above or to look to that court rather than seek adoption (paras. [**99**]–[**103**], *ante*), the Matrimonial Causes Rules 1977, r. 92 (3) now enables him to apply for custody in that court without any need for leave to intervene.

[3] See Guardianship of Minors Act 1971, s. 5, paras. [**203**]–[**206**], *ante*. There must, *inter alios*, be no parent alive before that section can apply.

[4] For the extent of investigation required to meet this condition see para. [**55**], *ante*.

[5] Children Act 1975, s. 33 (8) (*a*). The restriction is also removed, by s. 33 (8) (*b*), if the order made under the Matrimonial Causes Act 1973, s. 41 (1) was based on paragraph (*c*) of that subsection and it has since been determined that the child was not a child of the family to whom s. 41 applied.

[6] If that parent is also dead, the alternative possibility of guardianship is available; see n. 3, *supra*. For the effect of a custodianship order granted to a step-parent when his spouse already has custody see para. [**265**], *post*.

divorce or nullity proceedings were between the step-parent himself and the natural parent who is his spouse. An order made under section 41 (1) (*b*) or (*c*) of the Act of 1973 in respect of the child as a child of the family means that the step-parent must thereafter invoke the divorce court's jurisdiction in any claim concerning custody and is disqualified from applying for a custodianship order—not that this is really a disqualification, because the rights acquired through a custody order are wider.[1] In this context it is interesting to compare section 11 (4) of the 1975 Act.[2] Although the power to dismiss an application by the step-parent for an adoption order, leaving him to rely on section 42 of the 1973 Act, is really directed to those cases where the earlier divorce or nullity proceedings related to the former marriage of the natural parents, the terms of section 11 (4) are, it is submitted, such that in law it is possible to invoke the power of dismissal where there were such proceedings, or proceedings for judicial separation, between the natural parent and the step-parent. Supposing that the mother had been granted custody in those proceedings. If the stepfather were minded later to apply for adoption, his application would almost certainly be dismissed and he would be expected to seek his remedy in the divorce court by a variation of the custody order in his favour. [**261**]

The mother and father

The mother and father of the child are not qualified applicants for a custodianship order.[3] The reason for the exclusion is that, if either of them wishes to seek custody (in its wide meaning),[4] the appropriate jurisdiction is conferred by section 9 of the Guardianship of Minors Act 1971,[5] and duplication of custody and custodianship proceedings is to be avoided. This reasoning is readily apparent when the dispute is between the mother and the father, but what if it is with a third person? Section 9 does not expressly state that the mother or father can invoke the section in the latter circumstance, even though it does empower the court to grant custody to a third person. It is submitted that by implication the Children Act 1975 resolves any doubt in favour of the conclusion that the section is applicable so as to enable the mother or father to take proceedings against a third person. It would be strange if the mother or father were excluded from doing so both by section 9 and by the custodianship provisions of the 1975 Act, leaving them to rely solely on wardship proceedings. In the converse situation the third person's remedy against the mother or father will lie in custodianship when Part II of the Act becomes operative,[6] but additionally where the proceedings are brought by the mother or father under section 9, the present power to grant custody to the third person will be replaced by the power to grant legal custody, the court directing that the custody application by the mother or father be treated as if it had been a custodianship application made by the third person under section 33 of the 1975 Act.[7] A custodianship order

[1] See para. [**264**], *post*.
[2] For this provision see paras. [**99**]–[**104**], *ante*.
[3] Children Act 1975, s. 33 (4).
[4] Para. [**201**], *ante*.
[5] As amended by the Guardianship Act 1973, s. 2 and Sch. 2.
[6] Meanwhile he will have to continue to look to wardship jurisdiction.
[7] Children Act 1975, s. 37 (3) and Sch. 3, para. 75.

may be made in those circumstances even though the child may not have had his home with the third person for any of the minimum periods prescribed by that section. [**262**]

The *raison d'être* of this exclusion of the mother and father from applications for custodianship orders has particular significance in relation to the father of the illegitimate child. Although there is force in the criticism that section 33 ought to have stated explicitly that he, too, is barred from applying,[1] it is submitted that this is the necessary implication, since he, as much as the father of a legitimate child, has the right to apply for custody under section 9 of the 1971 Act.[2] [**263**]

B. EFFECTS OF A CUSTODIANSHIP ORDER

The general effect of a custodianship order was explained in Chapter 9, together with its specific effects in relation to certain parental rights and duties.[3] A number of other consequences need to be noted.

(1) It follows from the definition of legal custody that the rights and duties of a custodian appointed by a custodianship order will not be quite so extensive as those of a person who, not being a parent or guardian, has been granted custody of a child in proceedings under section 9 of the Guardianship of Minors Act 1971. That anomaly will disappear when the court's present power under section 9 is replaced by the power to grant legal custody,[4] but the 1975 Act has failed to close all the gaps. In matrimonial proceedings, whether under the Matrimonial Causes Act 1973 or under the Matrimonial Proceedings (Magistrates Courts) Act 1960, the courts may grant custody to a third person,[5] but no amendment is made by the 1975 Act restricting the power so that only legal custody can be granted to him in those proceedings. The omission has particular significance for the step-parent. Where he is disqualified from seeking a custodianship order and is obliged to look to the divorce court,[6] an order by that court will confer the wider rights and duties of custody, whereas in those cases where the appropriate application is for a custodianship order he will acquire the less extensive legal custody. Thus, in the case of the former order, he would be able to arrange for the child's emigration, subject in certain circumstances to the leave of the court;[7] a custodianship order would preclude that possibility. [**264**]

(2) So long as a custodianship order has effect the right of any person other than the custodian to legal custody of the child is suspended, but, subject to any further order made by any court, revives on the revocation of the custodianship order.[8] The person who normally will be affected by this rule is the parent of the child, for example the mother; but the rule will not apply where she already

---

[1] See Cretney, 126 New Law Jo. p. 57 at p. 58.
[2] Guardianship of Minors Act 1971, s. 14 (1).
[3] See paras. [**231**]–[**236**], *ante*.
[4] Para. [**262**], *ante*.
[5] See p. 102, n. 5, *ante*.
[6] Paras. [**259**]–[**261**], *ante*.
[7] Not even that would be necessary where the custody order was made by a magistrates' court under the 1960 Act, since such a court has no jurisdiction to make an order that a child shall not be removed from the jurisdiction; see *T.* v. *T.*, [1968] 3 All E.R. 321.
[8] Children Act 1975, s. 44 (1). For revocation and revival see paras. [**286**]–[**290**], *post*.

has custody and the person who becomes custodian is her husband. In such a case the spouses have the legal custody jointly.[1] Nevertheless, additionally she will still have vested in her alone, as parent, all the other parental rights and duties which legal custody does not carry. [**265**]

This last-mentioned division is not limited to the case of the step-parent who shares legal custody. Whenever anyone is appointed custodian the residual parental rights and duties remain with the person or persons in whom they were vested before the making of the custodianship order, be it a parent, a guardian, a local authority or a voluntary organisation. Thus, where at the date of the custodianship order a resolution under section 2 of the Children Act 1948 is in force,[2] it does not wholly cease to have effect,[3] but some of the residual rights and duties remain with the local authority, for example to administer any of the child's property,[4] while others, i.e., agreeing to the making of an adoption order or an order under section 25 of the Children Act 1975 or consenting to an application under section 14 of that Act, are still vested in the parents.[5] Similar consequences result where the custodianship order relates to a child who is the subject of a care order, for the former order does not bring to an end the latter.[6] On the other hand, where the child was received into care under section 1 of the Children Act 1948 without any section 2 resolution subsequently being passed, there is no transfer of parental rights and duties from the local authority to the custodian, since none as such were vested in it. Nevertheless, the effect of the custodianship order will be to relieve the authority of the duties it has under Part II of the 1948 Act to children in its care, most notably that of providing accommodation and maintenance.[7] [**266**]

The 1975 Act does not deal with the question of whether or not a custodianship order can be made, and if so its effect, while there is in force an order which has committed the care of the child to a local authority and the authority has then to treat him as if he had been received into care under section 1 of the 1948 Act. A number of enactments authorise the making of such orders,[8] and there is

---

1 *Ibid.*, sub-s. (2).

2 As substituted by s. 57 of the Children Act 1975; see para. [**329**], *et seq.*, *post.*

3 Cf. sub-s. (8) of s. 2, which provides for the termination of a resolution when the child is adopted or an order is made under s. 14 or s. 25 of the 1975 Act or a guardian is appointed under s. 5 of the Guardianship of Minors Act 1971.

4 In theory the right to arrange for the child's emigration could still be exercised by the local authority, subject to the limits imposed by s. 17 of the Children Act 1948. However, in practice so long as there is a custodian, the Secretary of State would never, it is suggested, give his consent to the emigration. The authority would first have to obtain revocation of the custodianship order.

5 See Children Act 1948, s. 2 (11).

6 S. 21A of the Children and Young Persons Act 1969 (as inserted by the Children Act 1975, Sch. 3, para. 70) provides for care orders to cease to have effect when certain other orders are made, i.e., adoption orders, orders under s. 14 or s. 25 of the 1975 Act and orders similar to a s. 25 order which are made in Northern Ireland, the Isle of Man or any of the Channel Islands. Cf. n. 3, *supra*.

On the need for the parent's agreement to the making of an adoption order where there is a s. 2 resolution, but not where there is a care order see para. [**49**], *ante*.

7 But on maintenance see para. [**271**], *post*.

8 See Matrimonial Proceedings (Magistrates' Courts) Act 1960, ss. 2 (1) (*e*) and 3; Family Law Reform Act 1969, s. 7 (2) and (3), as amended by Matrimonial Causes Act 1973, Sch. 2, para. 8 (*a*); Matrimonial Causes Act 1973, s. 43; Guardianship Act 1973, ss. 2 (2) (*b*) and 4, as amended by Children Act 1975, Sch. 3, para. 80 (amendment not yet operative); Children Act 1975, ss. 34 (4) and 36 (2) and (6) (not yet operative).

Note also the discretion of the local authority to receive into care foster children and

a provision common to all that when an order is in force the child shall continue in the care of the local authority notwithstanding any claim by a parent or other person. It is doubtful whether this restriction will prevent a foster-parent, for example, with whom the child was placed by the local authority, from seeking a custodianship order. Nor, it is submitted, will the fact that the enactments enable the foster-parent to seek a variation or discharge of the original order and an order in his or her favour be a bar to an application for a custodianship order. Under the Matrimonial Proceedings (Magistrates' Courts) Act 1960[1] he can apply for discharge and seek legal custody.[2] Under the Matrimonial Causes Act 1973 he would need leave of the court to intervene.[3] Where the order was the result of wardship proceedings, *semble* he could apply, as a person interested, for the order to be varied so as to grant him care and control. As the law stands, he is also eligible to apply for variation where the original order committing to care was made under the Guardianship Act 1973,[4] but when the amending provisions of the Children Act 1975[5] take effect, he will no longer be able to do so. This amendment clearly indicates that, at least where the original order was made under the Guardianship legislation, he will have to turn to custodianship. If he does and a custodianship order is made, it is submitted that the local authority disappears from the picture, as it does when of its own volition it receives a child under section 1 of the 1948 Act without any accompanying order and a custodianship order is later made. **[267]**

(3) The power of the court to appoint a guardian under section 5 (1) of the Guardianship of Minors Act 1971 depends on the minor's having no parent, no guardian and no other person having parental rights with respect to him. It follows, therefore, that once a person has been appointed a custodian under a custodianship order, he is not eligible for appointment as a guardian under that section,[6] unless his custodianship order is first revoked. The point is likely to be particularly relevant when a child's parents die and his custodian is a relative. **[268]**

(4) Where, prior to the making of a custodianship order, the natural parents had disagreed on a matter affecting the child's welfare and consequently the court, in accordance with the Guardianship Act 1973,[7] made an order regarding the matter, the custodian may wish to apply for a variation or discharge of the order. Supposing, for example, that the order related to the upbringing of the child in a particular religious faith and the custodian found that this was proving disturbing to the child. He would be eligible to apply as a person "having the

---

protected children who have been removed from unsuitable surroundings; see respectively Children Act 1958, s. 7 (1) and (4); Adoption Act 1958, s. 43 (1) and (3); (Adoption Act 1976, s. 34 (1) and (3)).

[1] S. 10 (1) (*e*).

[2] Legal custody is not defined but means, it is submitted, custody in the wide sense and not the narrow "legal custody" as defined by the Children Act 1975, s. 86.

[3] S. 43 (7); Matrimonial Causes Rules 1977, r. 92 (3).

[4] See Guardianship of Minors Act 1971, s. 9 (4) as extended by Guardianship Act 1973, s. 4 (3).

[5] See Children Act 1975, Sch. 3, para. 80.

[6] That would not, however, prevent the parent from appointing him a testamentary guardian in accordance with s. 4 of the 1971 Act.

[7] S. 1 (3).

custody of the minor".[1] The only limitation, it is submitted, would be where the order had not related to the person of the child but, for example, to the administration of his property, since that would not be a matter falling within the province of the custodian's rights and duties. [**269**]

(5) What is the effect of a custodianship order made in favour of an apparent step-parent when it is subsequently found that his marriage to the natural parent is void?[2] The order might, for example, have been made on the basis that a person qualified as a stepfather under section 33 (3) (*a*), the child having had his home with him for the requisite three months but for less than twelve months.[3] In *Re F.*[4] it was recently held that an adoption order granted to joint adopters whose marriage turned out to be void was itself voidable and not void. It is submitted that analogously a custodianship order would have the same effect. [**270**]

(6) Whereas a local authority is obliged through its adoption service to meet the needs of children who may be or have been adopted, their parents and the adopters or prospective adopters,[5] no corresponding obligation is imposed where a child is or may be the subject of a custodianship order. The authority's duty to provide a report[6] to the court which is to hear the application, vital though it is in assisting the court to determine what is best for the child, is obviously of limited effect, since it assists none of the interested parties once the custodianship order is made. How far is the order likely to weaken or strengthen the relationship between the child and the natural parent, especially where the latter has given his consent to the custodianship application because he believes that custodianship is in the immediate interests of the child? Where the parent is so motivated, how far will the custodian in practice encourage him to retain a relationship with his child? Questions of this kind are particularly important where, prior to the custodianship order, the child was in the care of the local authority under section 1 of the Children Act 1948 and the link with the natural parent was maintained through the social worker. The 1975 Act does not require the authority to maintain the link after the custodianship order has been made. Nor is it under a duty to commence and/or maintain contact with the custodian or to continue to provide financial aid if it has done so in the past, for example, by way of boarding out allowance paid to the custodian when he was a foster-parent. Nevertheless, a local authority has a discretion to make contributions to a custodian towards the cost of the accommodation and maintenance of the child, except where the custodian is the husband or wife of a parent of the child.[7] The hope has been expressed that a local authority will not withdraw

---

[1] *Ibid.*, sub-s. (5).

[2] The 1975 Act does not define the term step-parent. Cf. the Owen Bill, cl. 60 (1): "in relation to a minor [it] means a person who is not a parent of the minor but is or was the spouse of a parent of the minor".

[3] If in fact he had had his home with the step-father for at least twelve months, the latter would have qualified under s. 33 (3) (*b*) as "any person", notwithstanding the invalidity of the marriage.

[4] [1977] 2 All E.R. 777; [1977] 2 W.L.R. 488 (C.A.).

[5] See para. [**13**], *ante*.

[6] See para. [**291**], *post*.

[7] Children Act 1975, s. 34 (5).

financial aid simply because a custodianship order has been made which it has opposed.[1] [**271**]

Paras. [**264**]–[**271**] have been concerned with some of the effects of a custodianship order. It remains to add a comment on the consequences of not making such an order. Where the reason is not a technical one (for example, failure to satisfy the rules governing qualification to apply) but relates to the merits of the case, the child is not likely to be left with the applicant. Thus, if the order was refused because of opposition by the local authority, it may well be that the authority will recover the child from the applicant, if he is already in care. If not, then it may decide that care proceedings under section 1 of the Children and Young Persons Act 1969 are appropriate. [**272**]

C. ADOPTION OR CUSTODIANSHIP?

Section 37 of the Act is a further measure[2] designed to discourage and restrict adoptions. It does this by empowering the court on hearing an application for an adoption order (including a Convention adoption order) to make instead a custodianship order. The scope of the court's discretion depends on the kind of applicant, but a positive duty is imposed to consider the suitability of custodianship. [**273**]

(i) *Relative or step-parent*

Where the applicant is a relative or step-parent (whether the latter is applying alone or jointly with his or her spouse) and the court is satisfied that (a) the child's welfare would not be better safeguarded and protected by granting the applicant an adoption order than it would by granting him a custodianship order and (b) a custodianship order in his favour would be appropriate, then it must treat the application as if it were an application under section 33 for a custodianship order.[3] Presumably, in satisfying itself on these matters the court is governed by section 1 of the Guardianship of Minors Act 1971 and not section 3 of the 1975 Act.[4] [**274**]

(*a*) *The relative*. The number of adoptions by relatives[5] is not contained in adoption statistics but is thought to be about 1,000–1,200 a year. So, relatives

---

[1] See H.C. Official Report, 1975, Standing Committee A (Tenth Sitting), col. 517 (Dr. David Owen).

Under the Child Benefit Act 1975 a custodian will qualify for child benefit as a "person responsible" for the child; see ss. 1 (1), 3 and Sch. 1 and 2. If the local authority previously paid allowance because the child was in their care and decide to continue to give aid after a custodianship order has been made, they are certain to adjust the payment in the light of the fact that child benefit will be payable.

[2] Cf. ss. 10 (3) and 11 (4), paras. [**99**]–[**103**], *ante*.

[3] S. 37 (1). Where the adoption application is made jointly by step-parent and spouse, it is to be treated as if it were a sole custodianship application by the step-parent.

[4] Compare the Houghton Committee (H.C.R., Rec. 20): ". . . where a relative (including a step-parent applying jointly with his spouse) applies to adopt a child the law should require the court first to consider whether guardianship would be more appropriate in all the circumstances of the case, first consideration being given to the long-term welfare of the child."

[5] Relative has the same meaning as it has for the purpose of adoption law, except that it cannot, by virtue of s. 37 (6), include the father of an illegitimate child. See s. 37 (6), para. [**281**], *post*.

are more likely to apply for custodianship than adoption, but even if they apply for the latter the court is likely to invoke section 37. The main objection to allowing adoption by relatives is well known. Relationships become distorted; for example, an adoptive grandmother becomes the mother and the mother becomes a sister to her own child. Moreover, the very fact that the applicant is related to the natural parent and the child militates against a finding that his welfare will be better safeguarded by granting adoption rather than custodianship. Save in exceptional circumstances, the court is likely to be satisfied to the contrary. For example, the father may have left his child with relatives while serving a term of imprisonment. Custodianship in favour of them will probably be the appropriate order until his release when the matter can be reviewed on an application for revocation of the order. Different considerations would obtain, however, where the child's interests required severance of the parental link because of the nature of the father's crime; for example, where he had murdered the mother. [**275**]

(*b*) *The step-parent.* As already noted,[1] desire to avoid breaking the link between the child and one of his natural parents and concurrently converting the natural relationship with the other into an artificial one of adoption accounts for the restrictions imposed on the step-parent to apply for adoption. Section 37 (1) in relation to him must be read with sections 10 (3), 11 (4) and 33 (5) and (8) of the Act. [**276**]

Where there have been nullity or divorce proceedings between the natural parents, the emphasis of the Act is strongly on the step-parent's having to look to the divorce court. Thus, he is normally disqualified from seeking custodianship,[2] and, if he decides to go for adoption, his application may well be dismissed, leaving him to seek custody in the divorce court.[3] If it is not dismissed, the issue is then whether or not to make an adoption order. The court cannot rely on section 37 (1) and instead make a custodianship order.[4] Effectively, therefore, the power to invoke the section in relation to the step-parent applies to the following cases:

(1) Where there have not been divorce or nullity proceedings between the natural parents because either they were never married to one another or, if they were, their marriage was terminated by the death of that natural parent who did not marry the step-parent.

(2) Where there were such proceedings but the parent other than the one the step-parent married is dead or cannot be found.[5] [**277**]

(ii) *Persons other than a relative or step-parent*

In the case of an application for adoption by anyone who is neither a relative nor a step-parent or a joint application by a married couple who fall into neither category, the court is empowered to make a custodianship order instead of an

---

[1] Paras. [**99**]–[**103**], *ante*.
[2] S. 33 (5) and (8), paras. [**259**]–[**261**], *ante*.
[3] Ss. 10 (3) and 11 (4), paras. [**99**]–[**103**], *ante*.
[4] See *ibid.*, sub-s. (5).
[5] See s. 33 (8) (*a*).

adoption order if it is of opinion that the former is the more appropriate.[1] The court does not have to be satisfied that the child's welfare would not be better safeguarded and protected by adoption than it would by custodianship, as it must in cases under section 37 (1). This omission takes account of the fact that considerations of distortion of natural relationships and their conversion into artificial ones are here irrelevant and that the desirability of maintaining links with the natural parents carries much less weight. Accordingly, the legislative intention seems to be that a presumption in favour of custodianship is not nearly so strong.[2] [**278**]

The implications of section 37 (2) are particularly important for the long-term foster-parent with whom the child has had his home for at least three years. He will need to weigh carefully whether to seek custodianship or adoption. If the parent will not agree to adoption, a custodianship application is *prima facie* attractive, for not even parental consent to the application will be needed. If he does proceed with an adoption application, he has the double hurdle of persuading the court to dispense with parental agreement and of effectively satisfying it that it would not be more appropriate to make a custodianship order, if the court is minded to make that order.[3] Nevertheless, the advantage to the foster-parent of going for adoption is that it does in the first instance put the onus on the court to decide whether the alternative may be appropriate; it is not a matter that he has to raise. [**279**]

The duty and power of the court under section 37 (1) and (2) respectively to direct that the adoption application be treated as a custodianship application arise even though the applicant could not have qualified as an applicant for custodianship had he been proceeding under section 33.[4] For example, the child may not have had his home with the applicant for the minimum period of twelve months or three years prescribed by that section.[5] Where a direction is given under section 37, Part II of the Act then operates, just as if there had been an application under section 33. Thus, the court could, for example, make accompanying orders relating to access and maintenance.[6] The only exception to the rule is that section 40 does not apply. For obvious reasons the applicant is relieved of the duty imposed by section 40 to notify the local authority of his application, and the authority of any duty to present a report to the court.[7] The court will already have before it the report of the adoption agency in those

---

[1] S. 37 (2). There is, it is submitted, neither substantive nor semantic justification for the distinction between having to be "satisfied" under sub-s. (1) and having to be "of opinion" under sub-s. (2).

In prescribing the qualifications of applicants for adoption ss. 10 and 11 state that they are to be read subject to s. 37 (1). Why not also subject to s. 37 (2)? This seems to be a drafting oversight.

[2] See H.L. Official Report, 1975, Vol. 365, No. 157, col. 849 (Lord Wells-Pestell).

[3] The requirements of s. 12 (that the child is free for adoption and that there is parental agreement or that it has been dispensed with) or of s. 24 (6) (relating to consents and consultations under the internal law of the Convention country) must be satisfied before the court can invoke s. 37 (1) or (2).

[4] S. 37 (4).

[5] But he will have had his home with the applicant for at least three months, otherwise (except where he is a joint applicant) the requirements of s. 9 could not have been satisfied. For s. 9 see paras. [**107**], *et seq., ante.*

[6] See paras. [**298**]–[**304**], *post.*

[7] See paras. [**291**]–[**297**], *post.*

cases where the child was placed by an adoption agency with the applicant for adoption and, in all other cases, the report which the local authority has to submit in accordance with section 18 of the Act.[1] [**280**]

The restriction imposed on the mother or father alone to apply for adoption has already been noted.[2] Even where such an application is permitted, section 37 (1) and (2) cannot apply,[3] for a custodianship order cannot be made in favour of the mother or father.[4] Nor does the Act allow the court as an alternative to adoption to make a custody order. Thus, where the applicant for adoption is the father of an illegitimate child and the court regards custody as more appropriate, there will have to be a separate application made under section 9 of the Guardianship of Minors Act 1971. [**281**]

On the other hand, one effect of section 37 (1) and (2) is that the parent may have agreed to the making of an adoption order, intending to surrender, and be relieved of, all parental rights and duties, only to find that because a custodianship order has been made some of those rights and duties remain vested in him or her, coupled with the possibility of being ordered to maintain the child. It is therefore important that any explanatory leaflet issued to parents should, when Part II of the Act becomes operative, clearly explain section 37 and these possible consequences. Similarly, where the child has been freed for adoption, with the result that the parental rights and duties vest in the adoption agency,[5] and then custodianship is ordered instead of adoption, the residuary rights and duties which do not pass with legal custody remain vested in the agency. [**282**]

D. TERMINATION OF A CUSTODIANSHIP ORDER

(i) *Termination otherwise than by revocation*

A custodianship order may be made in respect of any child who is under 18,[6] but, especially since it can relate only to the person of the child, it will rarely be sought or made once he attains the age of 16.[7] Courts will almost certainly follow the practice of the divorce court in custody proceedings and recognise the unreality of an order once a child has reached that age of discretion. On the other hand once an order is made, whatever the child's age at that time, it will continue in force until he attains majority,[8] unless terminated earlier for some other reason. [**283**]

Whereas the 1975 Act expressly forbids an adoption order being made in relation to a child who is or has been married,[9] it is silent on the effect of marriage upon custodianship orders. For the reason stated in the previous paragraph the making of such an order in respect of a married child, even if permissible, is in

---

[1] See para. [**114**], *ante*.
[2] See s. 11 (3), paras. [**95**]–[**98**], *ante*.
[3] S. 37 (6).
[4] S. 33 (4).
[5] S. 14 (6).
[6] See the definition of "child" in s. 107 (1).
[7] Exceptionally an order may be desirable where the child is continuing his education beyond that age.
[8] Children Act 1975, s. 35 (6).
[9] S. 8 (5); (Adoption Act 1976, s. 12 (5)).

any event highly unlikely, since compliance with English matrimonial law will require him to be at least 16.[1] However, the point could be relevant where the child, though under that age, is validly married by the spouses' foreign personal law(s). It is arguable that, in view of the Act's silence, a custodianship order could be made in those circumstances, for example, where the child is widowed.[2] Indeed, custodianship would be most appropriate to help meet his or her needs.[3] There is, however, judicial support for the view that marriage ends parental custody over a minor daughter and apparently the same consequence attaches to marriage of a son.[4] If this be so, it would be anomalous if marriage did not have the same effect on legal custody under a custodianship order. Otherwise, it would mean that those residual rights and duties which remain vested in the parent when the order is made would cease so to remain on the child's marriage, whereas those of the custodian would still be operative. Assuming that marriage does impliedly terminate a custodianship order, it could then be argued that it would be inconsistent if marriage did not equally preclude the making of such an order. **[284]**

The Act is also silent about the effect of the death of a custodian on the order. Where he was one of joint custodians the legal custody will remain vested in the survivor or survivors.[5] What if he was the sole custodian? It will be seen[6] that on revocation of a custodianship order, the legal custody is automatically restored to the person in whom it was previously vested, unless the court otherwise orders. It seems that on death there is implied restoration to that person. It would, it is submitted, have been better if, as with revocation, the court had been given the power to review the circumstances. **[285]**

(ii) *Revocation*

An authorised court[7] may revoke a custodianship order on the application of (a) the custodian or (b) the mother or father or a guardian or (c) a local authority.[8] This power is subject to the restriction that the court cannot proceed to hear the application if the applicant was previously refused revocation, unless (a) when so refusing the court then directed that this restriction should not apply or (b) the court hearing the later application considers that because of a change in circumstances or for any other reason it is proper to proceed with the application.[9] In exercising its power to revoke or, as the case may be, to entertain a further application, the court is governed by the paramountcy of the child's welfare.[10] **[286]**

---

1 Marriage Act 1949, s. 2.

2 See Freeman, *Children Act 1975*, 72/8/5.

3 There would be power to make a care order under the Children and Young Persons Act 1969; see *Mohamed* v. *Knott*, [1969] 1 Q.B. 1; [1968] 2 All E.R. 563. *Aliter* if he or she were at least 16; see s. 1 (5) (*c*).

4 See Bromley, *op. cit.*, p. 309; Bevan, *op. cit.*, pp. 409–410.

5 By analogy with the rule that on the death of one parent custody resides solely in the other, in the absence of any testamentary guardian.

6 Paras. [**287**]–[**289**], *post*.

7 See para. [**313**], *post*.

8 S. 35 (1).

9 *Ibid.*, sub-s. (2). Compare a similar restriction on a further application for an adoption order (s. 22 (4), para. [**118**], *ante*) and a further application for revocation of a freeing for adoption order (s. 16 (4) and (5), paras. [**79**]–[**80**], *ante*).

10 See s. 33 (9).

While a custodianship order is in force the right of anyone other than the custodian to legal custody of the child is suspended, but when the order is revoked the right of that other (usually the parent) will revive, subject to any further order by the court. Obviously, therefore, it is vital for the court to know what is going to happen to the child on revocation. Section 36 (1) consequently imposes on it the duty of ascertaining who would have legal custody, if on revocation no further order were made.[1] If there is no such person and the court decides to revoke the order (for example, on the application of a local authority that the custodian is unsatisfactory), then it must commit the child to the care of a local authority.[2] There must be no possibility of any vacuum. On the other hand, if there is such a person, the court must decide whether to do nothing other than revoke the order and allow the rule of revival to operate or, in addition to revoking, either (1) allow that person to reassume legal custody but make a supervision order placing the child under the supervision of a specified local authority or of a probation officer or (2) commit the care of the child to a specified local authority.[3] Where it chooses the latter alternative it may require either parent to make weekly or other periodical payments.[4] **[287]**

Reference has already been made to the court's similar powers in custody, matrimonial and wardship proceedings to make a supervision order or commit to the care of a local authority,[5] but those powers can only be exercised in exceptional circumstances. This restriction is due to the practical consideration that otherwise undue demands would be made on local authorities and the probation service. Section 36 is a much more enlightened enactment. In deciding whether to exercise either power the court must consider what "is desirable in the interests of the welfare of the child" and in so doing it must remember that all applications under Part II of the Act are subject to the paramountcy of the child's welfare.[6] Desirability is to be understood within that principle. **[288]**

Where joint custodians have been appointed or where a natural parent is sharing legal custody jointly with a step-parent who has been appointed a custodian[7] and they cannot agree on the exercise or performance of a parental right or duty, for example concerning the religious upbringing of the child, either of them may apply to an authorised court,[8] which may make such order regarding the exercise or performance as it thinks fit.[9] However, the dispute over the child's upbringing may be general and not particular. If so, it will not be open to one of them to surrender his or her legal custody to the other,[10] even as part of the terms of a separation agreement made between them as husband and wife.

---

[1] For the power of the court to call for a report by a local authority or probation officer see para. [**297**], *post*.

[2] S. 36 (2).

[3] *Ibid.*, sub-s. (3). Sub-s. (6) further provides that ss. 3 and 4 of the Guardianship Act 1973 (which contains supplementary provisions relating to children who are subject to supervision or in the care of a local authority by virtue of orders made under s. 2 of that Act) shall apply in relation to an order made under s. 36.

[4] S. 36 (5).

[5] See p. 126, n. 8, *ante*.

[6] S. 33 (9).

[7] See s. 44 (2), para. [**265**]. *ante*.

[8] See para. [**313**], *post*.

[9] S. 38. Cf. s. 1 (3) of the Guardianship Act 1973.

[10] S. 85 (2).

Section 1 (2) of the Guardianship Act 1973, which within limits allows for the surrender of parental rights and duties under a separation agreement, only relates to "a child of theirs". Where custodianship is involved, a child can at most be only a child of one of the spouses, that being so where a natural parent is married to a custodian step-parent. In the absence of matrimonial proceedings, the appropriate step will be for one of the spouses who are joint custodians to seek revocation of the joint custodianship order and the making of a new order giving the applicant sole custodianship.[1] This would avoid any revival of the rights of those who originally had legal custody. In the case of legal custody being jointly shared by the natural parent and step-parent, the natural parent, say the mother, could seek revocation of the custodianship order granted to the stepfather, thereby leaving her with sole legal custody, together with the residual parental rights and duties which she never lost. What the 1975 Act fails to do is to provide a converse remedy for the stepfather. He will have to rely on wardship or matrimonial proceedings. The existence of the custodianship order in his favour will not, it is submitted, oust the Court's inherent jurisdiction, and he will be able to apply for the child to be made a ward of court with a view to his obtaining sole care and control. As for matrimonial proceedings, it has already been pointed out,[2] that the divorce court can make a custody order notwithstanding the existence of a similar order made by a magistrates' court under its matrimonial jurisdiction. That being so, there seems to be no reason why it could not equally make a custody order under section 42 of the Matrimonial Causes Act 1973 granting the stepfather sole custody, if there were divorce proceedings between him and the mother. Similarly, a magistrates' court in exercise of its matrimonial jurisdiction could grant the step-parent sole custody.[3] If these conclusions are correct where the matrimonial proceedings are between the natural parent and the step-parent, they would apply *mutatis mutandis* to such proceedings between joint custodians. The court would not be prevented from making a custody order in favour of either. [**289**]

Problems of this kind not only reflect some of the uncertainties to which custodianship is likely to give rise: they are, of course, also part of the wider problem of concurrent jurisdiction to make orders affecting children,[4] which will persist in the absence of a system of family courts. [**290**]

E. REPORTS

A custodianship order cannot be made unless the applicant for it has given written notice of his application to the local authority in whose area the child resides.[5] This must be done within the seven days following the making of the application unless the court or local authority extends the period.[6] The notice

---

[1] Strictly there is no power to vary the original order. S. 36 refers only to revocation of custodianship orders. Compare the power to revoke or vary orders made under s. 34; see para. [**311**], *post*.

[2] See paras. [**99**]–[**103**], *ante*.

[3] *Sed quaere* if the custodianship order has been made by the High Court.

[4] See Bevan, *op. cit.*, pp. 290–294.

[5] Ss. 40 (1) and 107 (1).

[6] An applicant who has to seek an extension will probably find it administratively more convenient to look to the local authority, relying on the court only if the authority is not amenable.

is essential to enable the local authority to discharge its duty of providing the court with a report.[1] Wisely the Act does not impose a time limit within which the report has then to be completed, but presumably the effect of this flexibility will be that the court will not fix the date of the hearing of the application until the report has been presented to it. [**291**]

This local authority duty lies at the heart of custodianship proceedings and the Act introduces the welcome provision[1] that certain matters, to be prescribed by regulations, must be included in the report. It is desirable that the social worker responsible for preparing the report should be given statutory guidance about the kinds of information he should collect,[2] but this in turn also means that the court is directed to the prescribed matters when it comes to apply the paramountcy principle in accordance with section 1 of the Guardianship of Minors Act 1971.[3] This double advantage which the Act offers could, indeed, be profitably extended to welfare reports presented in custody disputes and to social inquiry reports in the juvenile court. There is no risk of inhibiting the social worker or the court, because the matters to be prescribed are not exclusive. The report can include any other matter which is considered relevant to the custodianship application and there is nothing to preclude the local authority from expressing a view on the desirability of making a custodianship order. [**292**]

The powers of the Secretary of State to make appropriate regulations are restricted to the extent that the matters to be prescribed must include the following:[4]

(*a*) *The wishes and feelings of the child having regard to his age and understanding and all other matters relevant to the operation of section 1 of the Guardian ship of Minors Act 1971.* The express reference to the child's wishes and feelings is consistent with the wording of section 3 of the Act, but, since the facto:s which can affect the application of the principle of the paramountcy of the child's welfare are so variable, it is difficult to see how regulations could ever wholly comply with the requirement imposed in the second part of paragraph (*a*).[5] There will at least have to be a lengthy list. Will it, for example, include the child's secular education; his past religious upbringing, if any, and the applicant's reference to the question of the medical history and condition of the child and the applicant. Will the regulations follow the lines of the Adoption Rules and reference to the question of the medical history and conditions of the child and the applicant. Will the regulations follow the lines of the Adoption Rules and prescribe this as a matter to be dealt with in the report, coupled with the filing of a medical certificate? Or is it to be left to the discretion of the reporter for inclusion or, as in custody disputes, left to the parties to raise as an issue?

(*b*) *The means and suitability of the applicant.* Both this and paragraph (*c*) may be seen as matters which are relevant to the operation of section 1 of the Guardianship of Minors Act 1971 but which the 1975 Act has marked out for

---

[1] S. 40 (2).

[2] Compare the duty imposed by the Adoption Rules on the guardian *ad litem* in adoption proceedings to investigate prescribed matters.

[3] The value of directing a court's attention to specific factors has been demonstrated in the exercise of the divorce court's powers to make financial provision and property adjustment orders; see Matrimonial Causes Act 1973, ss. 23–25.

[4] S. 40 (3).

[5] Cf. ss. 18 (3) (*a*) and 22 (3), p. 63, n. 3, *ante*.

special reference. In considering the suitability of the applicant the report ought, it is suggested, also to state the reason why the applicant seeks legal custody and whether he understands the nature and obligations of a custodianship order.[1] Where, in order to comply with the time limits imposed by section 33 (3) (*b*) or (*c*), he is relying on the fact that the child has had his home with him for more than one period, that fact together with the reasons for the break in continuity should also appear in the report and the regulations ought to include them as prescribed matters.

(*c*) *Information of a kind specified in the regulations relating to members of the applicant's household.* This is in line with a provision in the respective Adoption Rules 1976,[2] but, following them, the regulations are likely also to refer to (i) particulars of the accommodation in the applicant's home and the condition of the home and (ii) in the case of an application by a married couple, the state of the marriage and whether it has the stability which is likely to provide a sound basis for a secure relationship with the child.

(*d*) *The wishes regarding the application, and the means, of the mother and father of the child.*[3] In many cases these wishes will already have been indicated, since the mother and father will both have consented to the application. However, this will not be so where they are not the persons with legal custody[4] or where only one of them has given consent. Doubtless the regulations will expressly provide that the local authority is relieved of its obligation to report where the mother or father cannot be found. [**29**]

Paragraph (*d*) raises uncertainty concerning the father of the illegitimate child. It has already been pointed out[5] that he is within the term "father" for the purpose of Part II of the Act. How far will the local authority be obliged to seek him out in order to find out his wishes? The answer would seem to turn on whether rules of court relating to the parties to custodianship proceedings and the notification of the hearing of the application are similar to those in the Adoption Rules. If so and if he already has custody by virtue of an order under the Guardianship of Minors Act 1971, he will be a respondent and his wishes will be ascertained; if he does not have custody, but is liable under an order or agreement to contribute to the child's maintenance, he will have to be notified of the hearing and again his wishes ascertained. If in any other circumstance no duty is to be imposed on the local authority to seek him but the social worker does come to learn of his whereabouts, he ought to consult him and report his wishes. [**294**]

Paragraph (*d*) refers to the means of the mother and father because the court will want information on this matter in order to assist it in deciding whether or

---

[1] Compare the similar duty of a guardian *ad litem* in an adoption application; see each Schedule 2 to the Adoption (High Court) Rules 1976, the Adoption (County Court) Rules 1976 and the Magistrates' Courts (Adoption) Rules 1976.

[2] Sch. 2.

[3] The paragraph does not require the wishes of any other person having legal custody to be reported, but the exclusion will not be serious provided rules of court make such a person a respondent to the proceedings, when he will be able to make his wishes known at the hearing. In practice it is highly likely that the report will in any event deal with the wishes of that person.

[4] For example, where the parental rights and duties are vested in a local authority or voluntary organisation.

[5] Para. [**263**], *ante*.

not to order either or both of them to pay maintenance.[1] Such an order cannot be made against the father of an illegitimate child,[2] but his financial circumstances are nevertheless relevant because, if a custodianship order is made, the custodian will then be able (and probably advised by the court) to seek an affiliation order if one is not already in existence.[3] How far the social worker will be able to elicit information about means is, however, another matter. It is more likely that this will require the energies of the court at the hearing of the custodianship application. [**295**]

Although the 1975 Act elsewhere aims to strengthen local authority supervision of private fostering,[4] the duty to report imposed by section 40 on local authorities should additionally have some beneficial effect for the child who is so fostered. The knowledge that eventually it may have to report to a court may well encourage a local authority the more strenuously to discharge its supervisory obligations. In any later application by the foster-parent for custodianship the authority's report on his suitability and on other prescribed matters may well reflect the efficacy of its supervision. [**296**]

Section 40 does not extend to an application for revocation of a custodianship order, but in such a case a duty is initially imposed on the court to request a report. Unless it already has sufficient information, it must not exercise its functions under section 36 without a report from a local authority or probation officer about the desirability of the child's returning to the legal custody of any individual if revocation were ordered.[5] Apart from this duty the court has a general discretion when dealing with any application under Part II of the Act to request a report from a local authority or probation officer and in all cases it can call for an oral or written report.[6] [**297**]

OTHER ORDERS

When a custodianship order is made, or while it is in force, the court will be able under section 34 to make certain accompanying orders relating to access and maintenance, particularly affecting the child's mother or father. There is also jurisdiction parallel with that exercised in custody cases under the Guardianship of Minors Act 1971 and 1973 which will enable the court to make supervision orders or commit the child to the care of the local authority. [**298**]

ACCESS AND MAINTENANCE BY MOTHER OR FATHER

Since a custodianship order vests in the custodian the parental rights and duties which "by law" the mother and father have in relation to the person of their legitimate child,[7] one necessary implication, it is submitted, is that the

---

[1] See paras. [**298**]–[**303**], *post*.

[2] S. 34 (3).

[3] See s. 45, paras. [**302**]–[**303**], *post*.

[4] Ss. 95 and 96, paras. [**416**], *et seq.*, *post*.

[5] S. 36 (4). The local authority need not be the local authority in whose area the child resides; cf. s. 40. It may be preferable to rely on the authority for the area in which the individual resides.

[6] S. 39 (1). For the procedure for admitting reports in a magistrates' court see paras. [**420**]–[**421**], *post*.

[7] See ss. 85 (1) and 86.

statutory duty to maintain, imposed by section 22 of the Ministry of Social Security Act 1966 on the mother and father, is transferred to the custodian. He is, however, able to look to the natural parents for possible financial assistance by applying for an order for periodical payments to be made by either or both of them.[1] The same order can also be sought against any other person in relation to whom the child was treated as a child of the family as defined by section 52 (1) of the Matrimonial Causes Act 1973,[2] but in line with that Act[3] the court, in determining whether that person should be ordered to pay, must have regard (among the circumstances of the case) to the extent, if any, to which he assumed responsibility for the child's maintenance, the basis of it, the length of time for which he discharged it and the liability of anyone else to maintain the child. Under section 25 (3) of the 1973 Act the divorce court is also specifically directed to take account of whether or not the non-parent knew that the child was not his or her own. Strangely section 34 of the 1975 Act omits any reference to this factor, but it is submitted that it is one of which the court in custodianship proceedings should take account. A person's ignorance of the true paternity of the child ought always to be highly relevant.[4] He is unlikely to be a willing payer, and it is as well that the court knows this before it makes an order. [**299**]

Apart from its power to make an order for periodical payments, the court may, under section 34, revoke or vary orders requiring the mother or father to contribute towards the child's maintenance which any other court has made.[5] Revocation is possible on the application of the mother or father; variation on the application of either of them or of the custodian. The power to vary extends to altering the amount of the contributions and to substituting the custodian for the person to whom the contributions were ordered to be made. The kinds of orders subject to these powers are those made in exercise of matrimonial jurisdiction or of jurisdiction under the Guardianship of Minors Acts 1971 and 1973 and those requiring the mother or father to contribute towards the maintenance of their children who are in care.[6] [**300**]

A notable feature of these powers is that no restriction is imposed on inferior courts to exercise them in respect of orders made by the High Court, but clearly

---

[1] S. 34 (1) (*b*). The order is a maintenance order for the purpose of registration and enforcement under the Maintenance Orders Act 1958; see Administration of Justice Act 1970, Sch. 8, para. 12, as added by Children Act 1975, Sch. 3, para. 73 (2) (*b*). See also Attachment of Earnings Act 1971, Sch. 1, para. 12, as added by Children Act 1975, Sch. 3, para. 76 (*b*).

[2] See Children Act 1975, s. 34 (2).

S. 52 (1) refers to the child who "has been treated": s. 34 (2) to the child who "was treated". Presumably the difference is deliberate and is intended to allow for the fact that the marriage of the natural parent and the step-parent may have come to an end by the time of the custodianship application. For example, a stepfather who had previously been maintaining his wife's child while they lived together may have left them but the mother may have died before divorce proceedings could be instituted. If the child was then brought up by grandparents and they seek custodianship, they could apply for a maintenance order to be made against the stepfather.

[3] See s. 25 (3). See also Matrimonial Proceedings (Magistrates' Courts) Act 1960, s. 2 (5).

[4] Cf. *W.* (*R. J.*) v. *W.* (*S. J.*), [1972] Fam. 152; [1971] 3 All E.R. 303.

[5] Sub-s. (1) (*c*) and (*d*).

[6] See Children and Young Persons Act 1933, ss. 86 and 87; Children Act 1948, ss. 23 and 24; CYPA 1963, s. 30; CYPA 1969, s. 62 and Schs. 5 and 6. For affiliation orders see paras. [**302**]–[**303**], *post*.

some administrative procedure will be necessary for registration of orders between the courts. Although the powers lie wholly within the discretion of the court exercising custodianship jurisdiction, it should remember that its own power is limited to ordering unsecured periodical payments. Thus, an existing order for secured payments ought not normally to be disturbed. On the other hand, the court might, for example, revoke an order requiring the mother or father to contribute, even though it considers that her or his application has no merit, if it feels that a new order of its own is more convenient. [**301**]

The father of the illegitimate child occupies an anomalous position in relation to section 34. While the powers of revocation and variation extend to affiliation orders, that which enables the court to make its own maintenance order does not apply to him.[1] Instead the custodian is left to take affiliation proceedings, provided he does so not more than three years after the custodianship order was made and provided he is not married to the child's mother.[2] In spite of its boldness in other respects, the Legislature was unwilling to shake custodianship free of the fetters of affiliation. Apparently it regarded the matter as part of a root and branch reform of the law affecting illegitimacy and thus outside the province of the 1975 Act. Nevertheless, the position is entirely unsatisfactory. Although the custodian makes the application, it must be by way of a summons to be served under section 1 of the Affiliation Proceedings Act 1957 and the court must proceed as on a complaint under that section.[3] So, unless paternity is admitted, the custodian will almost certainly have to call the mother to give evidence, in which event it will have to be corroborated.[4] [**302**]

There is a further possible anomaly concerning the father of the illegitimate child. The local authority's discretion to make to a custodian contributions towards the cost of the accommodation and maintenance of the child does not apply where the custodian is the husband or wife of a parent of the child. It has been pointed out that if the word "parent" is to be given its usual meaning of not including the father of an illegitimate child it "would mean that a local authority might make a contribution where the custodian was the putative father's wife, but not where he was the husband of the mother of an illegitimate child. Accordingly, the better interpretation here is that 'parent' includes the putative father".[5] [**303**]

Since one of the purposes of custodianship is to make it easier for the natural parents to retain a relationship with their children, applications by the mother or father (including the father of an illegitimate child) for access to their child, which section 34 allows,[6] are likely to be sympathetically entertained, but, as in other applications under Part II of the Act, section 1 of the Guardianship of

---

[1] See s. 34 (3).

[2] S. 45 (1) and (3). An affiliation order made under this section is a maintenance order for the purpose of registration and enforcement under the Maintenance Orders Act 1958; see Administration of Justice Act 1970, Sch. 8, para. 5, as added by Children Act 1975, Sch. 3, para. 73 (2) (*a*). See also Attachment of Earnings Act 1971, Sch. 1, para. 6, as added by Children Act 1975, Sch. 3, para. 76 (*a*).

[3] Children Act 1975, s. 45 (2).

[4] Affiliation Proceedings Act 1957, s. 4 (1) and (2) as amended by the Affiliation Proceedings (Amendment) Act 1972, s. 1 (1) and (2).

[5] Freeman, *Children Act 1975*, 72/34/5.

[6] Sub-s. (1) (*a*). An order can also be made in favour of any other applicant who treated the child as a child of the family.

Minors Act 1971 operates[1] and an order will be refused if the child's welfare so requires. The fact that the mother or father has been making financial provision or that the court when making a custodianship order also orders maintenance will immensely strengthen the case for access, but will not carry an automatic right to it, any more than it does in custody proceedings between the mother and father. [**304**]

ORDERS FOR SUPERVISION, LOCAL AUTHORITY CARE, ETC.

Following the pattern of similar enactments[2] and in particular the Guardianship Act 1973, the court can make a supervision order to accompany a custodianship order or, instead of making the latter order, commit the care of the child to a local authority.[3] These orders can, however, only be made in exceptional circumstances and provided that the child is under 16. [**305**]

Where the exceptional circumstances make a supervision order desirable, the child will be placed under the supervision of a specified local authority or of a probation officer[4] and will remain so until he reaches 16 or until the order is discharged. Section 34 of the 1975 Act adds the custodian to the list of persons qualified to apply for discharge or variation of a supervision order. Indeed, within the context of custodianship, he or the supervising authority or probation officer will in practice be the only applicants. Although either parent, including the mother or father of an illegitimate child,[5] is also qualified to apply, he or she is scarcely likely to be content with seeking revocation of the supervision order, but will want revocation of the custodianship order itself, in which event, if that is granted, the supervision order will automatically cease to have effect.[6] [**306**]

Supervision orders may have particular significance in custodianship proceedings. Any application by a custodian himself for revocation of a custodianship order[7] should always be subjected to the closest scrutiny. There may be cogent reasons for it; for example, where serious illness of the custodian prevents him from continuing to bring up the child. Much more difficult is the case of the custodian who tires of his custodianship and wishes to abnegate his responsibilities. Then the court may be reluctant to allow revocation. On the other hand, a child who is being brought up by an unwilling custodian must be at some risk. In those circumstances it could therefore well be appropriate to continue the custodianship order but to add to it a supervision order. [**307**]

Section 2 (2) (*b*) of the Guardianship Act 1973 provides:

> ". . . if it appears to the court that there are exceptional circumstances making it impracticable or undesirable for the minor to be entrusted to either

---

[1] See s. 33 (9).
[2] See para. [**267**], *ante*.
[3] Children Act 1975, s. 34 (4), extending to custodianship applications, with modifications, ss. 2 (3), (4), (6), 3 and 4 of the Guardianship Act 1973, as amended by the Children Act 1975, Sch. 3, para. 80.
[4] Guardianship Act 1973, s. 2 (2) (*a*). The local authority will in practice be that within whose area the child and custodian reside. For appointment of a probation officer see s. 3 (1).
[5] Guardianship Act 1973, s. 2 (6).
[6] Children Act 1975, s. 35 (5).
[7] See s. 35 (1).

of the parents or to any other individual, the court may commit the care of the minor to a specified local authority."[1]

In relation to section 9 of the Guardianship of Minors Act 1971, for which it was enacted, paragraph (*b*) is readily comprehensible. A custody order under that section may be made in favour of either parent, which includes for the purpose the mother or father of an illegitimate child, or any other individual, and so, if such an order is not appropriate, committal to the local authority is permitted. A custodianship order, however, can only be made in favour of the applicant. If the application is refused, Part II of the Children Act does not permit the court to entrust the child to either parent or to any other individual. Supposing the disappointed applicant is a foster-parent, the child will remain with him until some other step is taken by the parent or, if the child is in care, by the local authority to recover the child. Consequently, section 2 (2) (*b*) ought, in relation to a custodianship application, to be understood as meaning that, if it is impracticable or undesirable to entrust the child to the custodian (and therefore to make a custodianship order), the child should be committed to the care of the local authority. In the light of this construction it is difficult to see the object of the provision in section 34 of the 1975 Act that in section 2 (2) (*b*) "any reference to a parent of the minor to whom the order relates shall be construed as including a reference to any other individual". In view of the fact that paragraph (*b*) already includes the words "any other individual" the amendment might be thought to be superfluous. At least it can scarcely be described as a tidy form of amendment. [**308**]

Where the court makes an order committing the care of the child to a local authority it may further order either parent to make periodical payments to the authority towards the child's maintenance.[2] The order for payments will continue so long as the authority has care, unless meantime it is varied or discharged. This power to vary or discharge, which is new, extends also to an order committing the child to care.[3] It fills a gap in the Guardianship Act 1973 and will apply both to custody and custodianship proceedings. Periodical payments can be ordered only against either parent which for this purpose does not include the mother or father of an illegitimate child.[4] It is surprising that the Children Act does not at least enable the court to order any other person in relation to whom the child was treated as a child of the family to make payments, given that such a person can be so ordered if a custodianship order is made.[5]

---

[1] The local authority must be that in whose area the child is, in the opinion of the court, resident immediately before being so committed (s. 4 (1)).

[2] Guardianship Act 1973, s. 2 (3).

[3] Guardianship Act 1973, s. 4 (3A), as inserted by the Children Act 1975, Sch. 3, para. 80 (2) (not yet operative).

[4] See Guardianship Act 1973, s. 2 (6). For the enforcement of these orders relating to care and periodical payments see the Guardianship of Minors Act 1971, s. 13 and the Guardian ship Act 1973, s. 4 (3), as amended by the Children Act 1975, Sch. 3, para. 80 (1).

Where a person has been the subject of an order relating to care (whether as a result of custody or custodianship proceedings) either parent can be ordered to make periodical payments after he has attained majority and for any period until he reaches 21; see Guardianship of Minors Act 1971, s. 12 (2) and Guardianship Act 1973, s. 4 (3), as amended by Children Act 1975, Sch. 3, para. 80 (1).

[5] See para. [**299**], *ante*.

The omission is the more surprising in view of the court's powers where an interim order is made.[1] [**309**]

Section 2 (4) of the Guardianship Act 1973, as applied to a custodianship application, enables the court to make an interim order where it adjourns the hearing of the application for more than seven days. The order will have effect for a specified period which must not exceed three months and it can include two kinds of provisions.[2] First, "any provision regarding the custody of the minor or the right of access to the minor of the mother or father". This includes the mother or father of an illegitimate child.[3] *Semble* "custody" in relation to a custodianship application is to be understood as "legal custody" as defined by the Children Act 1975. Secondly, provision for either parent to make periodical payments to the other or to any person given the custody of the minor. For the purpose of custodianship proceedings section 34 (4) (*a*) provides that the reference to a parent includes a reference "to any other individual". So, some other individual, for example, a person in respect of whom the child was treated as a child of the family may be ordered to make payments. For the purpose of *custody* proceedings under section 9 of the Guardianship of Minors Act 1971, section 2 (4) (*a*) of the Guardianship Act 1973 does not apply to the mother or father of an illegitimate child,[3] but it is arguable that the extension which applies in custodianship proceedings enables either of them to be treated as "any other individual" and so to be ordered to make periodical payments. If this be so, it is difficult to reconcile with the rule which prevents them from being ordered to make payments when an order committing the care of the child to a local authority is made under section 2 (3). [**310**]

REVOCATION AND VARIATION OF ORDERS

Note has already been made of revocation of custodianship orders, revocation or variation of maintenance orders made by any court other than that exercising the custodianship jurisdiction, and revocation or variation of supervision orders and orders committing the care of the child to a local authority.[4] Provision is also made for revocation or variation of any order made under section 34 of the 1975 Act. Application can be made by the custodian or by any other person on whose application the order was made.[5] Thus, the application could relate to an order granting access to the mother and/or father or an order requiring either or both of them or a person in relation to whom the child was treated as a child of the family to contribute towards the child's maintenance. The person so liable to contribute can also apply for revocation or variation of that order.[6] If the custodianship order is itself revoked, any order made under section 34 is also automatically revoked.[7] Similarly, not only the custodianship order but any section 34 order will cease to have effect when the child attains 18.[8]

[**311**]

---

[1] See the following paragraph.
[2] Guardianship Act 1973, s. 2 (4).
[3] Sub-s. (6).
[4] See respectively paras. [**286**], [**300**], and [**306**], *ante*.
[5] See s. 35 (3) and (4).
[6] S. 35 (4).
[7] S. 35 (5).
[8] S. 35 (6). For the possible effect of marriage of the child see para. [**284**], *ante*.

AUTHORISED COURTS

The courts authorised to hear applications connected with custodianship are generally the same as those with jurisdiction over adoption,[1] but there are further special rules affecting particular kinds of applications. As with adoption, jurisdiction normally depends on the presence of the child in England or Wales when the application for a custodianship order is made,[2] but so far as concerns the jurisdiction of a county court or magistrates' court he must also be in the district or area respectively of those courts at the date of application.[3] [**312**]

Where there is a custodianship order in force, applications for orders under sections 34, 35 or 38 can be made whether or not the child is in England or Wales and for the purposes of those applications, the following are *also* authorised courts:[4]

(a) the court which made the custodianship order and, where that court is a magistrates' court, any other magistrates' court acting for the same petty session area;
(b) the county court within whose district the applicant is;
(c) a magistrates' court within whose area the applicant is.

Additionally where the application is made under section 35 for revocation of a custodianship order or revocation or variation of an order made under section 34 and the child's mother or father or custodian is the petitioner or respondent in proceedings for divorce, nullity or judicial separation which are pending in a court in England or Wales, that court also has jurisdiction. It is obviously appropriate that such a court, being seised of the family circumstances, should have jurisdiction to revoke the custodianship order without having to transfer the matter to some other authorised court. [**313**]

It has already been noted[5] that there are special rules prescribing the courts authorised to deal with removal or threatened removal of the child in contravention of section 41 of the Act. In those cases those courts are substituted for, and not made additional to, the courts which normally have jurisdiction. [**314**]

A magistrates' court has jurisdiction as an authorised court even though the proceedings are brought by or against a person residing outside England and Wales.[6] The court cannot make an order requiring a person to make payments towards the child's maintenance or vary an order so as to increase a person's liability unless he has been served with a summons,[7] but otherwise it can entertain an application under Part II of the Act notwithstanding that the defendant has not been served with the summons.[8] [**315**]

---

[1] See paras. [**84**]–[**88**], *ante*.
[2] S. 33 (1).
[3] S. 100 (2) (*b*) and (*d*).
[4] S. 100 (7).
[5] See p. 122, n. 4, *ante*.
[6] S. 46 (1).
[7] Sub-s. (3).
[8] Sub-s. (2). Rules may, however, prescribe matters on which the court will have to be satisfied before proceeding in such a case. Rules may also be made determining the persons to be made defendants to a complaint and providing for power to order costs where there are at least two defendants. See sub-ss. (4) and (5).

The Act includes additional methods of enforcement of custodianship orders and accompanying maintenance orders made by magistrates' courts. The custodian may, without prejudice to any other remedy, enforce his custodianship order under section 54 (3) of the Magistrates' Courts Act 1952 against anyone having the actual custody of the child requiring him to give up the child to the custodian.[1] A maintenance order made under section 34 of the 1975 Act may be enforced in the same manner as an affiliation order and the relevant enactments will correspondingly apply.[2] The person ordered to contribute must notify any change of address to the person, if any, specified in the order.[3] [**316**]

---

[1] Children Act 1975, s. 43 (1). The penalties for non-compliance under the Magistrates' Courts Act are a fine not exceeding £1 for every day in default or imprisonment for a specified period or until the default is sooner remedied, but with a maximum of £20 or two months.

[2] S. 43 (3). For the relevant enactments see the Magistrates' Courts Act. 1952, ss. 64, 74–76 and Sch. 3, para. 76 (6) and the High Court (Maintenance Orders) Act 1958, s. 21.

[3] S. 43 (2). Failure without reasonable excuse to comply with the subsection is an offence punishable by a fine not exceeding £10.

PART III

CARE

CHAPTER 11

CHILDREN IN CARE

Part III of the Act includes a number of provisions affecting the admission of children into the care of local authorities and voluntary organisations, their retention and accommodation in care and the safeguarding of their interests in care and related proceedings. These matters form the subject of this and the next chapter. [**317**]

A. CHILDREN IN CARE OF LOCAL AUTHORITIES[1]

(i) *Restrictions on removal of a child from care*

Section 3 (8) of the Children Act 1948[2] makes it an offence if anyone (a) knowingly assists or induces or persistently attempts to induce a child who is the subject of a resolution under section 2 of that Act to run away from the accommodation provided by the local authority, or (b) takes him away without lawful authority, or (c) knowingly harbours or conceals him after he has run or been taken away or prevents him from returning.[3] [**318**]

Section 56 of the 1975 Act amends section 1 of the 1948 Act[4] so as to extend the offence in relation to the child who has been in the care of a local authority[5] throughout the preceding six months[6] under section 1 but is not the subject of a section 2 resolution. No offence, however, is committed if the act, such as removing the child, is done with the consent of the local authority or by a parent or guardian who has given the authority not less than 28 days' notice of his intention to do it. Here the term "guardian" has a more restricted meaning than it has in the Children and Young Persons Acts; and is limited to a person appointed by deed or will or by the court or a person to whom custody has been given.[7] A step-parent, for example, will not therefore, simply by virtue of his status be entitled to give notice. [**319**]

The main object of the amendment is to prevent the sudden removal of the child without a planned return to the parental home. As already noted,[8] the six-month rule is a compromise between the views that the minimum period of

---

[1] For valuable analyses see J. M. Eekelaar, *Children in Care and the Children Act 1975*, 40 M.L.R. 121; M.D.A. Freeman, *Children in Care: The Impact of the Children Act 1975*, (1976) 6 Fam. Law 136.

[2] As substituted by the Children and Young Persons Act 1963, ss. 49 and 64 (1), Sch. 3, para. 38.

[3] The Children Act 1975, Sch. 3, para. 4 (already operative) increased the penalties for the offence to a fine of £400 or imprisonment up to 3 months or both. These changes are in line with the changes made in ss. 34 and 34A of the Adoption Act 1958, as substituted by s. 29 of the 1975 Act (Adoption Act 1976, ss. 27 and 28), relating to the wrongful removal of children pending adoption.

[4] By inserting two subsections, (3A) and (3B) (operative since 26th November 1976).

[5] For voluntary organisations see paras. [**355**]–[**360**], *post*.

[6] I.e., the six months preceding the act alleged to constitute the offence.

[7] Children Act 1948, ss. 6 (2) and 59 (1).

[8] Para. [**4**], *ante*.

care should be twelve months and that in all cases there should be notice of intended removal. The 1975 Act recognises the arbitrariness of its provisions in that it allows for the possibility of statutory amendment of the six-month and the twenty-eight-day periods.[1] The latter period is intended to allow the local authority some flexibility of action, but whether it is sufficiently long for rehabilitative purposes has been questioned.[2] In some cases once notice has been given the authority may consider it appropriate to return the child within a day or so; it may, indeed, have anticipated the notice and waived its requirement. In others it might prefer an initial trial period of rehabilitation in order to see the child's reaction: for example, a long week-end at home. In others it will want to consider the possibility of passing a section 2 resolution before the notice expires. It is submitted that, since the child is already in its care, it must, when deciding whether to pass a resolution, act in accordance with the new duty which the 1975 Act imposes on it.[3] This is similar to, though not identical with, that imposed on the courts and adoption agencies in the adoption process.[4] In reaching any decision relating to a child in its care it must give first consideration to the need to safeguard and promote the welfare of the child throughout his childhood and, so far as practicable, ascertain his wishes and feelings and give due consideration, having regard to his age and understanding. Although this provision forms part of Part II of the Children Act 1948, which deals with the treatment of children in care,[5] its reference to "any decision" is unqualified and would therefore appear to include decisions on the possibility of passing section 2 resolutions. The point is important, because, if this is the correct interpretation, it is essential that the body considering the resolution has before it a report on the child's attitude. However, within the present context, the duty presupposes that there is a ground for passing a resolution. Whether there is, will usually depend on the reason for the authority's having received the child into its care under section 1.[6] If the authority does decide on the need for a resolution, it will have to move quickly. One of the effects of section 56 therefore will be increased sub-delegation of powers by Social Services Committees to their Case Work Sub-Committees.[7] [**320**]

Comments in the last paragraph assume that the local authority still has the power to pass a resolution after the parent has given notice of his intention to remove the child, but the assumption has to be considered against the back-

---

1 Children Act 1948, s. 1 (3B). Cf. s. 34A (7) of the Adoption Act 1958, as substituted by s. 29 of 1975 Act (Adoption Act 1976, s. 28 (10)).

2 Freeman, *op. cit.*, at p. 137.

3 S. 59, substituting a new sub-s. (1) in s. 12 of the Children Act 1948 (operative since 1st January 1976).

4 See Chap. 3, *ante*.

5 The duty is subject to the power of the local authority to act inconsistently with the welfare principle in order to protect members of the public; for example, by restricting the child's liberty in a community home; Children Act 1948, s. 12 (1A).

6 See the close interrelationship of s. 1 (*a*) and (*b*) and s. 2 (1) (*a*) and (*b*) (as substituted by Children Act 1975, s. 57).

7 Where this happens the statutory procedures must be strictly observed; see *Re L.* (*A.C.*), [1971] 3 All E.R. 743.

For entirely different reasons, there are indications of increased use of delegation and sub-delegation in local government. Apparently some authorities are using the practice as an economy measure to reduce the frequency of meetings of their committees.

ground of doubts surrounding sections 1 and 2 of the 1948 Act which section 56 of the 1975 Act has failed to settle. **[321]**

The essence of section 1 is that it depends on the consent of the parent or guardian to the child being received into care. This voluntary nature of the reception from the parent's point of view is emphasised by subsection (3):

> "Nothing in this section shall authorise a local authority to keep a child in their care under this section if any parent or guardian desires to take over the care of the child. . . ."

A failure to recognise the purpose and limits of the section led the Court of Appeal in *Krishnan* v. *Sutton London Borough Council*[1] to affirm the proposition laid down by Pennycuick J. in *Re K.R.*[2] that section 1 (3) imposes no mandatory obligation to return the child to his parent, and led the Divisional Court in *Halvorsen* v. *Hertfordshire County Council*[3] to the conclusion that the "right to desire the return of the child was exercisable only by a parent who was not already disqualified from having the care of the child under the terms of section 1 (1) (*b*)".[4] Happily, the Court of Appeal has since recognised the real purpose of the section by holding in *Bawden* v. *Bawden*[5] that the right of a local authority to keep the child in care under section 1 ceases when a parent desires his return and *Halvorsen* must, it is submitted, be treated as having been overruled. **[322]**

It seems clear that the general rule is that the local authority's authorisation ceases from the moment the parent expresses his desire by giving notice to the local authority that he wishes to take over the care of the child.[6] Is that rule now qualified by the terms of section 1 (3A)? On the one hand, it is arguable that the words in section 1 (3), "nothing in this section", preclude subsection (3A) from having any delaying effect on the termination of the authority's authorisation—although it is another matter whether the child is, nevertheless, still in care.[7] On the other hand, it may be contended that, within the terms of subsection (3) itself, it is implicit that the parent can only "desire" if he is in a position to give notice which is capable of taking immediate effect because he has the lawful authority to take the child. Subsection (3A) denies him that authority until the 28 day period of the notice has elapsed because of its provision that:

> "for the purposes of the application of paragraph (*b*) of [section 3 (8)] in such a case a parent or guardian of the child shall not be taken to have lawful authority to take him away".

Admittedly the provision is directed to the criminal consequences of early

---

[1] [1970] Ch. 181; [1969] 3 All E.R. 1367.

[2] [1964] Ch. 455, 461; *sub nom. Re. R.* (*K.*) (*an infant*), [1963] 3 All E.R. 337, 342.

[3] (1975) 5 Fam. Law 79.

[4] For another misconception see *Cheetham* v. *Glasgow Corporation*, 1972 S.L.T. (Notes) 50, where Lord Dunpark, wrongly purporting to rely on *Krishnan*, expressed the view that s. 15 (3) of the Social Work (Scotland) Act 1968 (which is identical with s. 1 (3)) is subject to the overriding duty to keep the child in care so long as his welfare appears to the local authority to require it.

[5] (1975), 74 L.G.R. 347.

[6] That was the view of Pennycuick, J. in *Re K. R., supra.*

[7] See para. [**324**], *post.*

removal, but it would, it is submitted, be wholly incongruous if a provision which is designed to strengthen the hand of the local authority is to be ignored for the purpose of section 1 (3). [**323**]

If the latter contention is wrong, the ability of the local authority to pass a section 2 resolution during the twenty-eight-day period must depend on whether the child is still in care under section 1, notwithstanding the fact that the authority's authorisation to keep him has come to an end. It has been suggested[1] that the answer may turn upon whether the authority can still be said to have "care" of the child because it has "actual custody", as defined by the Children Act 1975[2] or whether retention of care under section 1 requires the continued existence of parental agreement, in which case the care has ended. If the former proposition is correct, the authority will be able to pass a resolution not only during but even after the twenty-eight days has elapsed, as it will at any time in respect of a child who has been in care for less than six months, notwithstanding a parental request to return the child. Cogent support for the argument that the child is still in care is to be found in section 88 of the 1975 Act. This provides that a child is in the care of a voluntary organisation if the organisation has actual custody of him or if, having had such custody, it has transferred it to an individual who does not have legal custody of him. It is arguable, therefore, that a child will still be in the care of the organisation after the parent has requested his return and that the local authority, in accordance with section 60 of the 1975 Act,[3] could still pass a resolution vesting the parental rights and duties in the organisation. It would be anomalous if the local authority were not in the same position to pass a resolution in respect of children of whom they still have actual custody.[4] [**324**]

Judicial opinion conflicts on the ability of a local authority to pass a resolution once the parental request is made.[5] In the light of section 56 of the 1975 Act it seems highly unlikely that the courts will deny to the local authority power to pass a resolution during the twenty-eight-day period, but it is submitted that they will rest that power on the fact that during that period the parent does not have lawful authority to remove the child and the local authority still has lawful authority to keep him. Once the parent's "desire" becomes effective at the end of that period no section 2 resolution is permissible. On this basis it follows that equally such a resolution is not possible in respect of a child in care for less than six months as soon as the parent gives notice reclaiming the child.[6] [**325**]

If lawful authority is the criterion for the purpose of enabling the passing of resolutions, it does not follow that when a child is reclaimed the local authority is powerless. So long as *Krishnan* remains authoritative on the point that there is no mandatory obligation to return the child to the parent, there is at least one avenue open to the local authority where it considers that the child would be

---

[1] Eekelaar, *op. cit.*, pp. 124–125.
[2] S. 87; see para. [**237**], *ante.*
[3] See para. [**357**], *post.*
[4] See Freeman, *op. cit.*, p. 137.
[5] In *Re S.*, [1965] 1 All E.R. 865, 871, Pearson L.J. said that "if the power of the local authority to keep a child in their care ceases under s. 1 (3), it is at least arguable that there is no power to make an order [*sic*] under s. 2"; but in *Krishnan*, [1970] Ch. 181, 185–186, Goff J. did not share this doubt.
[6] For a similar conclusion see Freeman, *op. cit.*, p. 138.

exposed to the risk of harm if returned, namely, wardship proceedings, because it has been held[1] that once the parental claim is made the wardship jurisdiction becomes fully effective. Not only the local authority but any interested person may apply for the child to be made a ward of court. The most likely applicant is the foster-parent with whom the child has been boarded out, especially where he is unable to satisfy the qualifications for applying for a custodianship order.[2] [**326**]

Another less likely possibility, when the relevant provisions are operative, will be an application by the local authority for a freeing for adoption order.[3] This possibility depends on the answer to the question whether the child is still in the authority's care.[4] If he is, it will have to apply for the parent's agreement to the making of an adoption order to be dispensed with. Dispensation may well be difficult to obtain. Much will rest on the reasons for the child having been received into care. [**327**]

Much more controversial is whether the local authority can apply for a place of safety order and then for a care order under section 1 (2) of the Children and Young Persons Act 1969. Although this procedure is not unknown, it has been forcibly demonstrated[5] that the provisions of the Act do not allow it. "The reason is that section 1 (2) refers to an *existing* situation, not a prognosis of possible harm." An order is not possible without proof that the child is presently suffering some impairment or neglect of his development, etc. Section 1 of that Act is aimed at *removing* the child from the parent because of the impairment or neglect and is not concerned with the child already in the care of the local authority as the result of being received under section 1 of the 1948 Act. [**328**]

(ii) *The assumption of parental rights and duties*

Section 57 of the 1975 Act substitutes a new section 2 in the Children Act 1948[6] and in so doing consolidates, with stylistic improvements, the grounds on which resolutions could formerly be passed under section 2 as it was originally enacted and extended by section 48 of the Children and Young Persons Act 1963. Account is taken of the new concept of custodianship by including within the term "parent" (on whose account a resolution can be passed) not only a guardian[7] but also a custodian.[8] So, any disability or culpability of a parent which would justify passing a resolution under s. 2 (1) (*b*) applies *mutatis mutandis* to a custodian. [**329**]

The new section 2 includes two additional grounds which take account of recommendations by *Houghton*.[9] The much wider and more controversial[10] is

---

[1] *Re K. R.*, para. [**322**], *ante*.
[2] See paras. [**242**]–[**245**], *ante*.
[3] Chap. 5, *ante*.
[4] See Children Act 1975, s. 14 (2) (*b*); (Adoption Act 1976, s. 18 (2) (*b*)).
[5] Freeman, *op. cit.*, p. 138.
[6] Operative since 26th November 1976.
[7] For the meaning of "guardian" see para. [**319**], *ante*.
[8] See s. 2 (11). Where a resolution is to be based on the fact that the parents are dead it is now a prerequisite that the child has neither a guardian nor a custodian (s. 2 (1) (*a*)).
[9] Recs. 32 and 33.
[10] S. 2 (1) (*d*).

that which enables a resolution to be passed simply on the fact that the child has throughout the three years[1] preceding the passing of the resolution been either in the care of a local authority under section 1 or partly in the care of a local authority and partly in the care of a voluntary organisation.[2] Under the latter alternative the parental rights and duties will vest in the body in whose care the child is at the time of the passing of the resolution.[3] [**330**]

This new ground, together with the restrictions on removal imposed by section 1 (3A) and on removal when applications for adoption orders or custodianship orders are made,[4] gives added importance to the duty imposed on local authorities by section 1 of the Children and Young Persons Act 1963 to prevent reception into care by making available advice, guidance and assistance to families. It also emphasises the need for proper advice and guidance to be given to the parent on the possible consequences of allowing his child to be received into care. The 1975 Act does not confer on the parent the right at the outset to be fully informed of the consequences. Instead the matter is left to the discretion of the local authority to inform by way of explanatory leaflets. The two model leaflets prepared by the Department of Health and Social Security[5] (which are intended only as guidance to local authorities in preparing their own) distinguish between the limited information which, it is felt, needs to be provided when the child is being received into care and the further information about restrictions on removal and the new "three-year" ground for passing resolutions which should gradually be communicated the longer the child remains in care. [**331**]

Before considering the other new ground[6] it is necessary to consider the changes which the 1975 Act has made on the effects of the passing of a section 2 resolution. Under the former law the general effect was to vest in the local authority "all the rights and powers which the deceased parents would have if they were still living, or, as the case may be, all the rights and powers of the person on whose account the resolution was passed". Under section 2 (1) in its present form there vests in the authority "the parental rights and duties . . . and, if the rights and duties were vested in the parent on whose account the resolution was passed jointly with another person, they shall also be vested in the local authority jointly with that other person".[7] Read with section 2 (11), which defines "parental rights and duties", the new provision raises a number of points. [**332**]

(1) Whatever may have been the position formerly with regard to the child's

---

[1] Like the other time limit provisions created by the 1975 Act the period is subject to alteration by an affirmative resolution of both Houses of Parliament; s. 2 (10).

[2] Compare the rule restricting removal from the care of a local authority (paras. [**318**]–[**319**], *ante*). There is no provision for aggregating a period in the care of a voluntary organisation with that in the care of a local authority so as to satisfy the six-month rule, even though the periods may have been continuous.

[3] See Children Act 1975, s. 60 (1), para. [**357**], *post*.

[4] See paras. [**131**] and [**254**], *ante*, respectively.

[5] With the kind permission of the Department these are included as an Appendix to this chapter, paras. [**361**] and [**362**], *post*.

[6] S. 2 (1) (*c*).

[7] Note the use of the term "other person" not "other parent" (including a guardian or custodian). The mother of an illegitimate child shares with the father rights of succession on the child's death (see p. 155, n. 3, *post*), but the father is not a parent or guardian (except where he has been granted custody by the court) for the purpose of section 2.

property—and it was strongly argued that the local authority did not acquire the parental rights therein[1]—it is clear that now it does, for "parental rights and duties" are defined by section 2 (11) as "all rights and duties which by law the mother and father have in relation to a legitimate child and his property", subject to certain exceptions noted below. Thus, it seems that, if the child dies and the resolution relates to both parents, the local authority is entitled to his estate,[2] rare though such circumstances may be. Similarly, if the section 2 resolution relates only to one parent, on the child's death the local authority and the other parent will take in equal shares.[3] These consequences are surprising. Where the resolution has been passed because of the culpability of the parent(s) there is nothing unconscionable in the estate passing to the local authority if the local authority has borne the whole of the expense of accommodating and maintaining the child, but it is unjust if the parent is to be excluded where he has contributed to the child's maintenance.[4] *A fortiori* where the resolution was made on the ground of the parent's disability and not culpability. Will such injustice persuade the courts to hold that rights of succession do not pass to a local authority, notwithstanding the explicit terms of section 2 (11)? **[333]**

(2) It would appear that the enactment of section 2 (11) is intended to be part of one of the wider objects of the 1975 Act, namely, to begin anew the formulation of basic concepts in child law,[5] but, tested against the custodian (as opposed to a parent), the effects of a resolution are far from clear. Supposing, for example, that after the death of the mother of a legitimate child a custodianship order is made in favour of X, the child's aunt, the father having consented to the application for the order. The father is now working abroad and will remain there indefinitely. Meanwhile, because of X's ill health the local authority receive the child into their care, but later pass a resolution on the ground of her mental disability. The rights and duties relating to the person of the child (legal custody) which were formerly vested in X will pass to the local authority, but, as for the proprietary rights and duties, X never shared them with the father, and, therefore, on the wording of section 2 (1) the local authority equally does not so share them. Nor would the subsequent death of the father vest them in the authority, since no resolution has been passed on his account. Nor, again, could that result be achieved by the authority's passing a new resolution under section 2 (1) (*a*) on the ground that both parents are dead and there is no guardian or custodian, since the rights of succession ended with the death of the parents.[6] **[334]**

This illustration pinpoints a larger question, namely, whether a local

---

[1] See J. M. Thomson (1974), 90 L.Q.R. 310; (1975), 91 L.Q.R. 14.

[2] See the Administration of Estates Act 1925, s. 46 (1) (iv). But, if the s. 2 resolution had been passed on the ground that both parents were dead (s. 2 (1) (*a*) of the 1948 Act), and not on any other ground, it seems in that kind of case that, because both predeceased the child, the parental rights of succession had ceased to exist before the local authority could acquire them.

[3] Administration of Estates Act 1925, s. 46 (1) (iii). Where the resolution was passed on account of the mother of an illegitimate child, the father and the local authority will share equally; see Family Law Reform Act 1969, s. 14 (2).

[4] For the duty to contribute see Children Act 1948, ss. 3 (6), 23 and 24; CYPA 1933, ss. 86 and 87; and CYPA 1963, s. 30.

[5] See paras. [**208**]–[**239**], *ante*, and especially the definition of "parental rights and duties" in s. 85 (1).

[6] Cf. n. 2, *supra*.

authority will be minded to pass a section 2 resolution in relation to a custodian or whether it will seek to rely on its right to apply for the revocation of the custodianship order[1] with a view to the court's ordering that the care of the child be committed to the authority under section 36 of the 1975 Act. In the above example it is not likely that the court would restore the legal custody to the father, but would commit the child to care. Unfortunately section 36 fails to explain the consequences of that order. It does not state, as other enactments involving custody or wardship do, that the child is to be treated as if he had been received into care under section 1 of the 1948 Act. Nor does it provide that the order is to have the same effect as a care order under the Children and Young Persons Act 1969, whereby the parental "powers and duties" vest in the local authority. [**335**]

(3) The only parental rights and duties which section 2 (11) expressly excludes from the definition of parental rights and duties for the purpose of section 2 relate to adoption.[2] It thus re-enacts in substance the former provisions in the Adoption Act 1958[3] that the rights to agree or refuse to agree to the making of an adoption order or an order under section 25 of the 1975 Act[4] (for adoption abroad) do not pass to the local authority, but it adds to those exclusions the right to consent or refuse to consent to the making of an application for a freeing for adoption order. No mention is made, however, of the right to consent to the marriage of the child and it would seem, therefore, that this does pass to the authority, although this has been doubted[5] on the ground that in amending the Marriage Act 1949 in other respects the 1975 Act did not provide for the local authority to give consent. [**336**]

(4) Whether or not access to the child is a parental right within the meaning of section 2 (11) is not free from doubt. It is expressly included as such a right for the purposes of the 1975 Act,[6] but section 2 (11) is silent about it. Nevertheless, the courts may be willing to extend the philosophy of the 1975 Act[7] to section 2. Even on the hypothesis that access is a mutual right of parent and child, it would, it is submitted, still fall within the definition in section 2 (11). *Prima facie* the point whether or not access is a parental right is important where a section 2 resolution has been passed on account of only one of the parents and the other parent is thus sharing the rights and duties with the local authority. In that event he will be entitled to visit the child or call for other arrangements to be made to see him. If the authority should deny him access, he will be entitled to resort to the court by way of proceedings under section 9 of the Guardianship of Minors Act 1971. The strength of his claim should be compared with that of the father of the illegitimate child where a section 2 resolution has been passed vesting in the authority the parental rights

---

[1] Children Act 1975, s. 35 (1) (*c*).

[2] But note also the limitation in s. 3 (7) of the 1948 Act that the local authority cannot cause the child to be brought up in any religious creed other than that in which he would have been brought up but for the resolution.

[3] See ss. 4 (3) (*c*) and 53 (4).

[4] Adoption Act 1976, s. 55.

[5] Bromley, *Family Law* (5th Edn.), p. 417, n. 3.

[6] See s. 85 (1) and para. [**211**], *ante*.

[7] Compare *Re S. (infants)*, [1977] 3 All E.R. 671, where the Court was ready to apply the philosophy of the Act in a different context; see p. 56, n. 2, *ante*.

and duties of the mother. In *Re K.*[1] it was held that on the application of the father for access under the Guardianship of Minors Act the court was left with no alternative but to decline the application and leave the discretion with regard to access to the local authority. That decision is not, it is submitted, applicable to the "other parent" situation. There he already has a right of access, not merely the right to seek it and the question is whether he shall be allowed to exercise it. The answer must depend on the strength to be given to the right in applying the principle that the child's welfare is paramount—the discretion about access is not automatically to be left to the local authority. **[337]**

(5) The other parent may not be content with access, but will want care and control of his child. Since he has not lost his right of custody he can seek lawfully to remove the child, but, if as may well be likely the local authority prevent removal, he will have to turn to the Guardianship of Minors Act, or seek care and control in wardship proceedings,[2] when, as with a dispute over access, the issue will have to be decided in the light of the paramountcy of the child's welfare.[3] **[338]**

The possibility that the other parent may remove the child in exercise of his right of custody, with the consequent risk that the parent on whose account the resolution was passed might then join them in the same household, accounts for the other additional ground on which a resolution can be passed. If, as seems to be the position, the other parent does not have to give twenty-eight days' notice of intended removal,[4] the chances of the child being removed before the local authority can prevent it may be high, and the danger therefore is that local authorities may over-react to the possibility and try to anticipate it by relying on the new ground when there is no real threat of removal. **[339]**

Whether or not that object can be achieved by the new ground is, however, open to question. Section 2 (1) (*c*) enables a resolution to be passed where a resolution under section 2 (1) (*b*) is already "in force in relation to one parent of the child who is, or is likely to become, a member of the household comprising the child and his other parent". It is difficult to resist the conclusion that an essential condition for reliance on this ground is that the child is already living with the other parent.[5] Only a strained construction of paragraph (*c*) will admit the additional possibility that the parent (say the mother), who has been deprived of her parental rights and duties and who is living or is likely to live with the father, is likely to become a member of the household comprising the child and the father, because the father is likely to remove the child and bring him to live with them. The wording of the paragraph may partially defeat one of the objects for which it was enacted. **[340]**

---

[1] [1972] 3 All E.R. 769.

[2] A further, but remote, possibility is habeas corpus proceedings.

[3] In *R.* v. *Oxford City Justices, ex parte H.*, [1974] 2 All E.R. 356 it was held that the court could entertain an application for custody by the father of an illegitimate child and the paramountcy principle would govern. It is difficult to reconcile the reasoning in *Re K.*, para. [**337**], *ante*, with this decision, but see Bagnall J. (at p. 360). See generally Maidment, 125 New Law Jo. 726.

[4] See Eekelaar, *op cit.*, pp. 133–134; Freeman, *op. cit.*, p. 139. The conclusion turns on whether after a s. 2 resolution is passed the child is in care under s. 2 and not s. 1.

[5] See Bromley, *op. cit.*, p. 416.

The 1975 Act makes certain changes concerning the jurisdiction of the juvenile court to confirm or terminate a section 2 resolution. The procedure for challenging a resolution remains unaltered.[1] Unless the parent has given his prior written consent, the local authority must, if they know his whereabouts, forthwith after passing the resolution give him written notice[2] of the fact. He is then entitled to object within a month by way of a written counter-notice. If he does so, the resolution will lapse after fourteen days from the service of the counter-notice, unless in the meantime the authority complains to a juvenile court, in which case it remains in force until the court decides whether it should lapse. This it must order unless it is satisfied on three matters:[3]

(*a*) that the grounds on which the local authority purported to pass the resolution were made out; and

(*b*) that at the time of the hearing there continue to be grounds on which a resolution could be founded; usually they will be the same grounds but this is not necessarily so; and

(*c*) that it is in the interests of the child that the court order that the resolution shall not lapse.

This third proviso is equivocal and fails to make clear the weight to be given to the child's interests.[4] Strangely, section 2 has never laid down the principle which the local authority itself should apply when deciding whether to pass a resolution. It has already been suggested[5] that the test is that now imposed by section 12 of the Children Act 1948 in which the child's interests are made the first, but not the paramount, consideration. If that is the correct test, then it is difficult to see why a different test should be applied by the court. On the other hand, it is arguable that, once the conditions of paragraphs (*b*) and (*c*) above are satisfied, the child's interests should be paramount. That would accord with section 1 of the Guardianship of Minors Act and it may be said that, because that section refers to any proceedings in any court and extends to the upbringing of the child, it applies by implication. Yet, if that is so, why enact paragraph (*c*) above? Certainly it would have been preferable if section 2 (5) had expressly adopted the paramountcy principle and the same should have been laid down for the local authority. [**341**]

Section 58 fills two serious gaps in the provisions governing confirmation and termination of resolutions. It now allows an appeal to the High Court from an order under section 2 (5) or section 4 (3) of the 1948 Act or from the refusal by the juvenile court to make such an order.[6] Thus, an appeal may be lodged by the parent(s) on whose account the resolution was passed or any person claiming to be a parent[7] where the decision of the juvenile court relates to a complaint

---

1 See Children Act 1948, s. 2 (2)–(5), and (7), as substituted by s. 57 of the 1975 Act.

2 It must inform him of his right to object. It must be sent by registered post or recorded delivery service.

3 S. 2 (5). It is here that s. 57 has made limited changes.

4 The same test applies in deciding whether to terminate a resolution; see Children Act 1948, s. 4 (3) (*b*), as substituted by Children Act 1975, Sch. 3, para. 5.

5 Para. [**320**], *ante*.

6 Children Act 1948, s. 4A, as inserted by s. 58 of the 1975 Act (operative since 26th November 1976).

7 Note that the term is being used in this chapter to include a guardian or custodian.

under section 4 (3) (*a*) of the 1948 Act [1] or by the local authority. Unfortunately section 58 does not impose an obligation on the parties to expedite appeals or, on the High Court, to ensure that they do so. It is to be hoped that the point will be met by Rules of Court. One advantage that ought in the long run to be derived from the new jurisdiction is the growth of a body of case law which will assist local authorities in discharging their responsibilities under section 2. [**342**]

Hitherto the 1948 Act has only allowed the parent to question a section 2 resolution. The child has had no *locus standi*.[2] Section 58 of the 1975 Act will partly meet this deficiency.[3] It will allow the juvenile court or the High Court, in proceedings under sections 2 (5) and 4 (3) and in appeals relating thereto, to order that the child be made a party and appoint a guardian *ad litem*. This is a discretionary power to be exercised where the court considers it necessary to safeguard the child's interests. The guardian *ad litem* will be chosen from the panel of persons which will eventually be established for the various purposes allowed by the 1975 Act.[4] His appointment and the manner in which he will be required to safeguard the child's interests are to be prescribed by Rules of Court. The Rules are likely to enable him to instruct a solicitor. Moreover, since the child will be a party, the court will be able to grant legal aid. [**343**]

New powers are given by section 67 of the 1975 Act[5] to assist local authorities to recover children who are in their care by virtue of a section 2 resolution and who have run away or unlawfully have been taken away from the place at which they are required by the local authority to live or who, having been allowed by the authority to be in the charge of a parent, guardian, relative or friend, are not returned by that person to the authority after written notice requiring him to do so has been given.[6] In any of these circumstances a justice of the peace can issue a summons requiring a person to attend and produce the child before a magistrates' court.[7] He may also issue a search warrant authorising search of specified premises where the child is reasonably believed to be. [**344**]

Similarly section 68 of the 1975 Act[5] extends the powers under section 32 of the Children and Young Persons Act 1969 for detaining absentees by adding to those conferred by section 32 the power to issue a search warrant; by increasing the penalties for offences under the section, by particularising in greater detail the application of those powers in relation to juveniles who are in a place

---

[1] I.e., in the case of a resolution passed under s. 2 (1) (*a*) because the parents are dead and there is no guardian or custodian, a complaint by a person claiming to be a parent, guardian or custodian.

[2] Compare the position in care proceedings under s. 1 of the Children and Young Persons Act 1969. There it has been his right, not the parent's, to challenge any order made. See, however, the rights which ss. 64 and 65 of the 1975 Act will give the parent in those proceedings; paras. [**404**], *et seq.*, *post.*

[3] By inserting s. 4B into the Children Act 1948 (not yet operative).

[4] S. 103. See paras. [**410**]–[**414**], *post.*

[5] Operative since 26th November 1976.

[6] I.e., under s. 49 of the Children and Young Person Act 1963.
The penalty for failing to return him is a fine of up to £100 or two months' imprisonment or both; s. 49 (1), as amended by Children Act 1975, Sch. 3, para. 42.

[7] Apart from any other possible liability, failure to comply with the summons renders the person liable to a fine of up to £100 (s. 67 (4)).

of safety and by not restricting the powers to those who are in places of safety which are community homes.[1] [**345**]

(iii) *Amendments to the Children and Young Persons Act 1969*

Apart from that just mentioned, the 1975 Act makes a number of miscellaneous amendments to the Children and Young Persons Act 1969 which take account of selective criticisms of the working of the latter Act. In the light of the Eleventh Report from the Expenditure Committee of the House of Commons[2] much still needs to be done to improve the Act. [**346**]

A new condition on which an order can be based in care proceedings under section 1 of the 1969 Act has been added.[3] It is another of the numerous changes in the 1975 Act which the Maria Colwell case inspired. Section 1 (2) (*bb*) states:

> ". . . it is probable that the conditions set out in paragraph (*a*) of this subsection will be satisfied in his case, having regard to the fact that a person who has been convicted of an offence mentioned in Schedule 1 to the [Children and Young Persons Act 1933] is, or may become, a member of the same household as the child;".

Given the range and seriousness of the scheduled offences which may be committed against a juvenile, coupled with the wide terms of section 1 (2) (*a*), there ought not to be great difficulty in satisfying the court of the probability that the juvenile's "proper development" or health will be harmed or that he will be ill-treated. It is the proof of the conviction of the offence which may cause practical difficulties, for, as has been pointed out,[4] evidence of the conviction will not readily be available, since the police are restricted in the information that they can divulge and the Legislature is not yet ready to accept the priority that risk of harm to a juvenile is more serious than risk of harm to the offender resulting from disclosure. [**347**]

The Secretary of State is empowered[5] to make regulations with respect to the exercise by a local authority of its functions as a supervisor where a supervision order has been made in care proceedings under section 1 of the 1969 Act or on the discharge of a care order under section 21 (2). Presumably regulations will be postponed until sufficient resources are available to local authorities. It remains to be seen how far regulations will be used, for example, to improve facilities for intermediate treatment, including co-operation with voluntary organisations and individuals. [**348**]

The power of the court under section 21 (2) to discharge a care order in respect of a person under the age of 18 has been restricted by the 1975 Act.[6] The amendment is self-explanatory. If it appears to the court that he is in need of care or control, discharge cannot be ordered unless the court is satisfied that

---

[1] For the definition of a place of safety see Children and Young Persons Act 1933, s. 107 (1).

[2] H.C. Paper (1975) no. 534-1.

[3] By Sch. 3, para. 67 of the 1975 Act (operative since 1st January 1976).

[4] Freeman, *op. cit.*, p. 139.

[5] CYPA 1969, s. 11A, as inserted by the Children Act 1975, Sch. 3, para. 68 (operative since 1st January 1976).

[6] Sch. 3, para. 69 (operative since 1st January 1976).

he will receive that care or control, whether through making a supervision order or otherwise. In proceedings under section 21 (2) social enquiry reports will therefore have to deal with the question of any continuing need for care or control. [**349**]

An important amendment relates to the reviewing of cases of children in the care of local authorities. Under section 27 (4) of the 1969 Act, as originally enacted, the local authority must review the case of every child who has been in its care throughout the preceding six months, if a review has not been held during that period, and where he is in care as the result of a care order they must in reviewing the case consider applying for discharge of the order. Notwithstanding the wide powers which the 1969 Act conferred on local authorities it was silent on how the duty to review was to be discharged. The 1975 Act amends section 27[1] by requiring the local authority to review the case of each child in their care in accordance with regulations to be made by the Secretary of State. These may make provision as to (a) the manner in which cases are to be reviewed; (b) the considerations to which the local authority are to have regard in reviewing; and (c) the time when a child's case is first to be reviewed and the frequency of subsequent reviews. It will be interesting to see whether, for example, the juvenile and the parent will be given the right to challenge decisions and to be legally represented and whether a person independent of the local authority will be included in the reviewing body. [**350**]

Restrictions are imposed by section 69 of the 1975 Act[2] and The Certificates of Unruly Character (Conditions) Order 1977[2] on the power of a court or a justice to issue a certificate of unruly character and commit a young person[3] to a remand centre or, if such a centre is not available, to a prison on the ground that he cannot safely be committed to the care of a local authority. The restrictions are not only the result of Parliamentary debate during the passage of the Children Bill but also partly a response to the Eleventh Report of the House of Commons Expenditure Committee, who expressed serious concern about the large number of unruly certificates being issued and, apparently in many instances, their use as a means of achieving secure accommodation. The Committee also singled out for condemnation the practice of remanding young persons to adult prisons.[4] [**351**]

A certificate can only be issued within the limits of the following conditions:

(a) the young person is charged with an offence punishable in the case of an adult with imprisonment for fourteen years or more; or

(b) he is charged with an offence of violence or has been found guilty on a previous occasion of an offence of violence; or

(c) he has persistently absconded from a community home or has seriously disrupted the running of it while resident there.

If the young person falls within either paragraph (a) or (b) one of two further conditions must be satisfied. Either (i) the court or justice is remanding him for the first time in the proceedings and is satisfied that there has not been time to obtain a written report from the local authority on the availability of suitable

---

[1] Sch. 3, para. 71 (not yet operative).
[2] Operative since 1st August 1977.
[3] I.e., a person who has attained the age of 14 and is under 17.
[4] See para. 23 of the Report (H.C. Paper (1975) no. 534).

accommodation for him in a community home, or (ii) the court or justice is satisfied on the basis of such a report that no suitable accommodation is available for him in a community home where he could be accommodated without substantial risk to himself or others. In case (c) the court or justice must be satisfied by a written report from the local authority that accommodation cannot be found for him in a suitable community home where he could be accommodated without risk of absconding or seriously disrupting the running of the home. [**352**]

The 1977 Order does not require the court or justice to state the ground on which the certificate is being issued or give the young person or his parents the right to address the court on the matter, but courts are encouraged to do this.[1] A certificate may be made by the court of its own motion, but, where application is made, advice has been given[2] that the application should be "approved at a high level", i.e., by a Director, Deputy Director, or Assistant Director of Social Services or a police officer of the rank of Inspector or above. [**353**]

Another of the criticisms of the 1969 Act has been the failure of Regional Planning Committees and local authorities to provide sufficient secure accommodation in community homes.[3] Section 71 of the 1975 Act[4] aims to meet the criticism by conferring on the Secretary of State power to make grants to local authorities for this purpose. [**354**]

B. CHILDREN IN CARE OF VOLUNTARY ORGANISATIONS

One of the purposes of the 1975 Act is to accord firmer recognition to the work of voluntary organisations[5] involved in child care, to strengthen the protection to be given to the children in the care of such bodies and to bring them closely into line with children in the care of local authorities. [**355**]

Thus, the restrictions imposed by section 56[6] on removing a child who is in the care of a local authority under section 1 of the Children Act 1948 have been extended[7] to the child not in care under that section but who is in a voluntary home[8] or is boarded out with foster-parents by a voluntary organisation in whose care he is.[9] It seems that the requirement of twenty-eight days' notice applies whether or not a resolution vesting parental rights and duties in the organisation is in force.[10] [**356**]

---

[1] See Home Office Circular 91/1977, para. 9.
[2] *Ibid.*, para. 7.
[3] See the Eleventh Report, H.C. (1975) no. 534, paras. 65–78.
[4] Inserting a new section 64A, in the Children and Young Persons Act 1969 (operative since 12th November 1975).
[5] Defined as bodies, other than a public or local authority, the activities of which are not carried on for profit; s. 107 (1). See similarly Children Act 1948, s. 59 (1) and Children Act 1958, s. 17.
[6] Paras. [**318**]–[**328**], *ante*.
[7] By s. 56 (2), inserting into the 1948 Act a new section, 33A (operative since 26th November 1976).
[8] Including a controlled community home or an assisted community home, as defined by CYPA 1969, s. 39 (3).
[9] See s. 88 of the Children Act 1975 for the circumstances in which a child is said to be in the care of a voluntary organisation.
[10] Eekelaar, *op. cit.*, p. 134, n. 94.

Of greater significance are the provisions in sections 60–63 of the 1975 Act. Section 60 enables a local authority to pass a resolution that the parental rights and duties be vested in an incorporated voluntary organisation. A number of conditions have to be satisfied. A resolution can only be passed if the organisation so requests. The child must be in the care of that organisation at the time when the resolution is passed and not in the care of any local authority, but he must be living in the authority's area. One of the conditions which would entitle a section 2 resolution to be passed must be satisfied. It must be necessary in the interests of the child's welfare for the rights and duties to be vested in the organisation. Thus, section 60 expressly refers to the child's interests, unlike section 2.[1] [**357**]

The term "parental rights and duties" has the same meaning as it has for the purpose of section 2[2] and a resolution has the same effects as a section 2 resolution. Thus, if it is made on account of one parent who has hitherto been sharing the rights and duties with the other parent, the latter will now share them with the organisation. [**358**]

Unless the aid of the court is sought, only the local authority and not the voluntary organisation can terminate the resolution. This it can do by resolving that the rights and duties are no longer to be vested in the organisation but instead in the authority. In deciding whether to do so it must have regard to the interests of the child.[3] [**359**]

The procedure for objecting to a section 2 resolution extends to a resolution made under section 60, but is not appropriate to one made under section 61.[4] However, the parent is given a right of complaint to the juvenile court by way of an "appeal", with appeals therefrom to the High Court, with respect to resolutions made under either section. He may do so either because there was no ground for making the resolution or because it should in the child's interests be determined. The Act allows for the possibility of a guardian *ad litem* in these proceedings.[5] [**360**]

---

[1] But see paras. [**320**] and [**341**], *ante*.
[2] See s. 85 (1) of the 1975 Act, which governs s. 60.
[3] Ss. 61 (1) and 62 (1). Notice of the new resolution must be given within 7 days of passing it not only to the organisation but also to each parent, guardian or custodian whose whereabouts are known (s. 61 (2)).
[4] S. 62 (3).
[5] See s. 63 (1)–(4).

Leaflet No. 1 for Parents and Guardians of Children who are being Received Voluntarily into Care of Local Authorities or Voluntary Organisations

(Name of local authority or voluntary organisation)

WHERE YOUR CHILD IS

As you know your child ....

was received into our care on ....

and is being looked after by

Mr and Mrs ....

Address..............................

....

Telephone number ....

YOUR SOCIAL WORKER:

Your social worker is ....

Address..............................

....

Telephone number ....

If you are unable to get in touch with your social worker, please ask for

....

YOUR SOCIAL WORKER WILL WANT TO:

help you so don't hesitate to discuss your problems even if they are not directly connected with your child;

discuss and plan with you about what is best for your child while* he is in care;

try to keep brothers and sisters together or at least in close touch with each other;

plan with you for your child's return home.

YOU CAN HELP BY

keeping us informed of your address. The law requires you to do so and your social worker needs to know where to get in touch with you for your child's sake. Even if you go away from home for a short time only, it would be helpful if you could write or telephone to say where you are.

* Note for authorities/voluntary organisations:
Although the texts of the models refer to the child as "he", the leaflets should be amended as appropriate for girls or for more than one child.

letting your social worker know if there are any important changes in your life so that you can talk together about how these will affect your child.

telling us all you can about your child so as to help him settle down and make him feel as much at home as possible. He will want to bring his own clothes and some of his favourite toys and possessions to remind him of you and his home. It would be nice for him to have some photographs of his family.

Some of the things you can tell us are:

What school he goes to

What clubs he goes to

Which relatives or friends you want him to keep in touch with

What food he likes or dislikes

Whether he has a special diet

What religious observance, if any, you would like him to follow

Whether he has any bedtime routines such as taking a special toy, having a favourite drink, saying prayers etc.

Whether he puts himself to bed

Whether he wets his bed

What are his favourite things, such as games, television programmes, looking after family pets?

Is there anything he is especially frightened of?

Any other matter you feel is important to him.

KEEPING IN TOUCH WITH YOUR CHILD

Your social worker will let you know how your child is getting on and will make arrangements for you to visit or meet him, will tell you how often visits may be made, at what time etc, and will help with fares if necessary. If you cannot arrange a visit, your social worker will make sure that you hear how he is getting on.

Parents often have mixed feelings about parting from their children and feel awkward about going to see them while they are being looked after by people they do not know very well. Children too may feel upset and confused no matter how carefully it has been explained to them why they are leaving home. They will miss their parents and want to see them but may also feel angry sometimes, because they have been left with strangers, and if they are too young to understand the explanations, they may think they have been deserted. So it is very important for parents to keep in close touch with their children by visiting as often as possible as well as writing and telephoning. This contact helps them to understand that they are still remembered, loved and cared for.

So if you cannot visit yourself, perhaps a close relative or a friend who knows your child well can visit instead and keep the memories of home fresh in his mind. Birthday and Christmas greetings are especially important.

Children are sometimes upset by their parents' visits. This may be distressing to the parents, too, and sometimes they feel tempted to cut out the visits or to come less often. But it is far better for children to be able to show their feelings rather than to be hurt and sad because they think they have been forgotten. It is important for parents to tell their children why they are away from home and how long this is likely to last. For your child's sake, do not promise that he can come home before you are sure you can manage.

Sometimes parents cannot visit or meet their children on the day they promised to do so. If this should happen to you, do make sure your child gets a message, either directly or through your social worker or the person caring for him, so that he doesn't feel let down.

PRACTICAL ARRANGEMENTS

Medical Attention

Your social worker will have asked for your consent to routine medical and dental inspection and to immediate medical and surgical treatment of your child if necessary. Your social worker will need to know the name of your doctor, your child's doctor and whether your child takes any medicines or is undergoing any treatment. If your child becomes seriously ill when in care, your social worker will make every effort to get in touch with you immediately to give you the fullest possible information and to get your agreement to any treatment the doctors may advise.

Money Matters

Having a child in care may affect your financial position as you may be expected to contribute to his maintenance according to your income and expenses. If you are receiving national insurance or supplementary benefit, family allowance, child benefit or family income supplement, your allowances may be affected when your child comes into our care. You should tell your local Social Security Office about your changed circumstances.

If you have any difficulties or questions about this, the Social Security Office or your social worker will help to sort them out.

YOUR CHILD'S RETURN HOME

You and your social worker will discuss when it would be best for your child to return to you and you will plan how this can be arranged. Of course you may ask for your child to be returned to you at any time, but we hope you will join us in planning ahead for his return so that he and whoever has been looking after him can make the necessary preparations. The longer a child has been in care, the more likely he is to have settled down in his new surroundings and the longer time he will need to get used to the idea of moving again, to saying goodbye to friends at school, to putting his clothes and belongings together and to saying goodbye to the people looking after him. THIS IS RECOGNISED IN LAW SO IF YOUR CHILD STAYS WITH US FOR 6 MONTHS OR MORE, YOU MUST GIVE US 28 DAYS NOTICE IN WRITING WHEN YOU WISH TO HAVE HIM BACK. However, it will often be possible for your child to be returned to you immediately or at any rate some time before the official 28 days are up.

This leaflet is intended for general guidance and must not be regarded as a full statement of the law.

Leaflet No. 2 for Parents whose Child was Received into Care Voluntarily and is likely to Remain in Care Longer than 6 Months

PART I

Name of local authority social services department ....

Your social worker is ....

Address...

Telephone number ....

If your social worker is not available you should get in touch with

....

Your child .... has now been with us since .... and seems likely to stay with us for more than 6 months.

If he is still in care on or after .... you must give us 28 days' notice in writing that you want to have him home. The law requires this because children may need a little time to get used to the idea of moving. People looking after your child also may need notice to prepare for these changes and to get his belongings together.

If you have been in constant touch with your child and with your social worker then it is very likely that your child will be able to return to you before the 28 days have passed, and in some cases almost immediately. At the latest, your child will return to you at the end of the 28 days unless there should be very special and particular circumstances.

If because of your own circumstances it seems that your child will not be able to go home in the near future, then you and your social worker must continue to talk about the best possible plans which should be made for your child's care. At regular intervals your social worker will consider your child's progress, your own circumstances and make plans and decisions for the child's future. Social workers have a duty to plan for children to return home as soon as this is in their best interest. You will be closely involved in discussion and in the making of plans and decisions.

Important points to remember

a. While your child is in our care we have a duty to give first cosideration to his welfare and interests. If your child is old enough to understand, then we must find out his wishes and feelings about any plans.

b. For the sake of your child it is important for you to keep in touch with him and with your social worker.

c. It is essential that we know where you are, so that we can get in touch with you at any time.

d. Wherever possible all decisions concerning your child will be made with your help and co-operation. If you have any problems or difficulties, we hope that you will ask your social worker to help you.

e. Your child will not be moved to another address without previous discussion with you except in unforeseen circumstances. In such a case you would be given full information as soon as possible.

f. If your child has brothers and sisters or if you have other children in care, we shall do our best to keep them together or in touch with each other.

PART II

PROTECTING CHILDREN IN SPECIAL CIRCUMSTANCES

Unexpected difficulties can happen in everybody's life. After a great deal of thought some parents may even feel that they cannot have their child back to live with them. They may therefore make the painful decision that it would be best for the child to be permanently cared for by someone else. In that event the social worker will help parents to consider such a step very carefully and will explain what has to be done legally.

In rare cases children may need protection either from being taken out of care and being placed in a situation which is likely to be harmful, or from being suddenly removed from people who have cared for them for a long time and to whom they may have become attached.

The legal position in such cases is explained below.

PARENTAL RIGHTS

The local authority can take over the rights and duties of one or both parents of a child in their care. The special circumstances in which such a decision could be made are: that the child has no parents or guardian, or that he has been "abandoned" (this means his parents have been out of touch and their address unknown for a year or more); or because of parents' serious illness or disability which make them unable to care for the child, or because of their way of life or their consistent failure to act as good parents. The local authority can also take over parental rights and duties if a child has remained in care continuously for 3 years or more and it is not in the child's interest to be removed from care at this particular time. Parents and children may grow apart from each other during such a long time, and it may be necessary to safeguard the plans that have been made for the child's future.

Parents' legal rights in such a case

If the local authority has to consider taking over parental rights and duties, parents will usually have the opportunity to discuss this fully with the social worker and may agree to this plan. The local authority is required by law to let parents know in writing if parental rights have been taken.

After receiving this official notice parents have 28 days in which to make up their minds whether to object. This has to be done in writing. After the letter has been received the local authority can agree to restore parental rights. If it does not, it must within 14 days of receiving the parents' letter, ask a juvenile court to decide the matter. Parents and the local authority would be entitled to put their case forward in the court. The parents are entitled to be legally represented.

If either the parent or the local authority is not satisfied with the decision the court makes, either of them can appeal to the High Court. In these circumstances parents should be legally represented.

While the local authority has parental rights and duties, it may allow the child to live at home under the supervision of a social worker. At any time parents can apply for their rights and duties to be restored to them and, if the local authority does not agree, parents can ask the court to decide.

Legal advice about these matters can be obtained from

a citizens' advice bureau;

a legal advice centre;

any solicitor.

Parents on a low income may apply for legal aid. Any solicitor displaying the legal aid sign will help.

WHEN CHILDREN HAVE LIVED AWAY FROM HOME FOR A LONG TIME

The longer children are away from home, the more attached they are likely to become to the people who are caring for them. What may seem a fairly short time to adults seems a very long time to children. The time may come when they want to remain with those who are looking after them. This does not necessarily mean that they have forgotten their own families.

The law says that if people have cared for a child continuously for 5 years or more, they can start adoption proceedings without the parents' or the local authority's agreement.

From the time they have notified the local authority until the adoption hearing, neither the parents, nor the local authority nor anybody else would be allowed to remove the child without the permission of the court. Such permission would be given only in very special circumstances.

THIS DOES NOT MEAN THAT THE CHILD WOULD DEFINITELY BE ADOPTED, because the parents' agreement to the making of an adoption order would normally still be needed however long the child had lived away from them. A court can only go ahead without the parents' agreement if it is satisfied that there are strong reasons for doing so. Before such a serious decision was made, parents would be able to put their case to the court and have the opportunity to be legally represented. If the court made a decision with which the parents did not agree they would have the right to appeal to a higher court. An adoption order means that the child becomes permanently and completely the child of the adopters, and takes their name. Parents then have no right of access.

The custodianship provisions described below are not yet law. They may eventually apply to children who remain in care for some time.

People who have looked after a child for periods which add up to a total of at least 3 years may apply to the court for what will be called a *custodianship order*. They will not need the parents' permission to do so. As in an application for adoption, the court will fix a date for the hearing, and until this takes place neither the parents nor the local authority nor anybody else may remove the child without the permission of the court.

Courts will not automatically grant custodianship orders. The wishes and views of the parents will be heard before the court makes a decision. Parents can be legally represented and will be able to apply for legal aid.

A custodianship order makes the person looking after the child a kind of guardian able to make all day-to-day decisions. The child's name will not be changed and the court may order that parents can continue to see the child. The court may also order parents to contribute to the child's maintenance. Parents can apply at any time to have the order cancelled. In any case a custodianship order is not as permanent as an adoption order and ends when the child is 18.

Further details about custodianship will be given to parents before it becomes law. [**362**]

CHAPTER 12

REPRESENTATION IN CARE AND RELATED PROCEEDINGS

A. INTRODUCTION

English law does not confer on the minor a general right to be represented in any court proceedings. The omission is one of the consequences of its historical failure to insist on the principle that every minor shall have a guardian, be it natural parent or other person. Instead, provision for representation has been unsystematically extended to specific kinds of proceedings, in some being mandatory, in others discretionary.[1] Thus, as a party to civil litigation he must sue by his next friend or defend by his guardian *ad litem*, who must act by a solicitor.[2] Hitherto, in all adoption proceedings the appointment of a guardian *ad litem* has been essential[3] and will so continue until the changes made by the Children Act 1975 take effect.[4] On the other hand, in wardship proceedings and proceedings under the Guardianship of Minors Acts 1971 and 1973 in the High Court the minor may be made a party and, if he is, a guardian *ad litem* (usually the Official Solicitor) is then appointed, who may instruct counsel to appear.[5] So, too, in matrimonial proceedings in that Court and in divorce county courts appointment is discretionary, although there is also the distinct power in the court to direct that the child be separately represented by a solicitor or solicitor and counsel.[6] Yet, no provision at all is made for ordering representation in proceedings under the Guardianship of Minors Acts in a county court or in those proceedings or proceedings under the Matrimonial Proceedings (Magistrates' Courts) Act 1960 in a magistrates' court.[7] Finally, in criminal and care proceedings under the Children and Young Persons Act 1969 he is a party to the case and therefore has the right to representation.[8] [**363**]

To this list the Children Act 1975 adds two very modest contributions. As already noted,[9] the Act will enable a guardian *ad litem* to be appointed where a resolution under section 2 of the Children Act 1948 is the subject of proceedings. Secondly, it aims to strengthen representation in care and related proceedings under the 1969 Act. [**364**]

---

[1] On representation generally see Levin, *The Legal Representation of Children* (1974); 4 Fam. Law 129; Cavenagh, *The Advocate in the Juvenile Court* (1973), 137 J.P.N. 633.

[2] R.S.C., Ord. 89, r. 2.

[3] Adoption Act 1958, s. 9 (7); Adoption (High Court) Rules 1976, r. 12; Adoption (County Court) Rules 1976, r. 10; Magistrates' Courts (Adoption) Rules 1976, r. 9.

[4] See para. [**124**], *ante*.

[5] R.S.C., Ord. 90, rr. 3 and 6 respectively; see also Ord. 15, r. 6 (2) (*b*).

[6] See respectively Matrimonial Causes Rules 1977, r. 115, and r. 72. Where the proceedings relate to variation of a settlement there is virtually a duty to order separate representation by solicitor or solicitor and counsel. The rules merit close scrutiny.

[7] *Semble* the inherent power of a magistrates' court to control its own proceedings in the interests of justice and a fair and expeditious trial (*Simms* v. *Moore*, [1970] 2 Q.B. 327; [1970] 3 All E.R. 1) cannot extend to ordering separate representation.

[8] See para. [**370**], *post*.

[9] Para. [**343**], *ante*.

The Owen Bill would have gone further[1] and imposed on every court when hearing a case relating to a minor the duty to consider whether it is in his interest to be separately represented and, if so, to add him as a party and provide for his representation by a solicitor or solicitor and counsel.[2] Yet, this comparatively modest reform failed to find its way into the 1975 Act, being steadfastly rejected by the Government on the ground of limited available resources, both of finance and personnel. Given the fact that the opportunity for major legislative changes in the law affecting children occurs on average about once in every eight to ten years, the rejection is much to be regretted and the reasoning for it open to question. The Government was strongly influenced by the unfortunate history of the Children and Young Persons Act 1969. Many of the criticisms of that Act are attributable to the failure to provide the facilities requisite for its effective implementation.[3] The Children Act, it was argued, must not be exposed to the same risk. The argument needs closer examination. The assurances given about the 1969 Act were that most of its provisions could be given effect within a short time, even though serious doubts about this were expressed during its enactment. Significantly, however, section 5 of that Act (which would restrict criminal proceedings in respect of young persons) has not come in for criticism on this score. It was known at the outset that it would be some years before sufficient facilities could be made available to enable its implementation and this inevitability was recognised. It is suggested that, had the Government enacted the above principle with a firm declaration that its operation would have to be postponed and only introduced piecemeal as resources became available, that policy would have found wide acceptance and would have done something to reflect the growing public concern for the need for a minor to have an independent voice to speak for him, both inside and outside the court.[4] **[365]**

Moreover, the expansion of separate representation of minors needs careful planning and the enactment of the principle would mark a significant step in that process. In particular it would have the advantage of giving notice and encouragement to lawyers to become more involved in this area of law and thus would partly meet the question of lack of personnel. As it is, the new provisions are but a pale shadow of those proposed in the Owen Bill. The most significant omission is the failure to provide for separate representation in custodianship proceedings. **[366]**

In order to assess their value it is first necessary to look at the law as it stood before the 1975 Act. It is obvious therefrom that the question of representation has never been fully thought out. In *Humberside County Council* v. *D.P.R. (an infant)*[5] Lord Widgery C.J. is reported as having described care

---

[1] Clause 52.

[2] In certain kinds of proceedings the Bill would have made the provision of separate representation virtually mandatory.

[3] See the Eleventh Report of the House of Commons Expenditure Committee (H.C. Paper (1975) no. 534).

[4] See especially the recommendation of the Justice Report on *Parental Rights and Duties and Custody Suits* (1975) that his interests be protected by a Children's Ombudsman. Cf. Bevan, *Child Protection and the Law* (1970).

[5] [1977] 3 All E.R. 964.

proceedings as "essentially non-adversary". That they ought to be "an objective examination of the position of the child", not a contest between the local authority and the parents is not open to question, but, as the learned Chief Justice observed elsewhere,[2] "in proceedings of this kind the real issue is nearly always between the local authority and the parents". Up to a point, the law before the 1975 Act reflected a three-sided contest. As will be seen,[3] the effect of the Act and the Rules thereunder is to sharpen the reflection. The most effective way to secure an objective examination of the condition of the juvenile[4] is an inquisitorial procedure, with the court being able itself to call witnesses and documentary evidence and not being confined, as it presently is, to assessing the evidence adduced by the local authority, the juvenile and the parent and only being able to call for additional information after the case has been proved.[5] Is it really too much to ask for this reform when a decision which may fundamentally affect the future life and well-being of the juvenile is involved? **[367]**

B. THE OLD LAW

The relevant law is mainly to be found in Part III of the Magistrates' Courts (Children and Young Persons) Rules 1970, but supplemented by certain provisions in the Children and Young Persons Acts, the Magistrates' Courts Act 1952, the Magistrates' Courts Rules 1968 and the Legal Aid Act 1974. Part III applies to care proceedings and to the variation and discharge of supervision orders and care orders.[6] A distinctive feature of the law is the ambivalent position occupied by the parent or guardian.[7] **[368]**

The law may be briefly summarised as follows:[8]

(1) In all the above proceedings the juvenile is a party to them.[9] In care proceedings he is always the respondent; in applications for variation or discharge of supervision or care orders he may be either the respondent or the applicant. In none of them is the parent a party. There is no unequivocal provision to that effect in the 1970 Rules or elsewhere, but the matter was recently settled in *R* v. *Worthing Justices, ex parte Stevenson*.[10] **[369]**

---

[1] *Ibid.*, at p. 966.

[2] In *R.* v. *Worthing Justices, ex parte Stevenson*, [1976] 2 All E.R. 194 at p. 196.

[3] Paras. [**381**], *et seq.*, *post.*

[4] For convenience this term will subsequently be used in this chapter collectively to describe children and young persons as they are defined for the purposes of the Children and Young Persons Acts.

[5] See CYPA 1969, s. 9 (2). It is noteworthy that the Owen Bill would have empowered any court dealing with a case relating to a minor to add as a party to the proceedings "any parent, guardian, step-parent, foster-parent or other person" and itself to summon witnesses to assist it in determining whether any order, if made, would be for the minor's welfare: see cls. 52 (3) and 53.

[6] R. 13 (1). The rule also applies to applications to remove persons in care to Borstal, but this is outside the present topic.

[7] Note the wide meaning of "guardian". It includes a person who has for the time being the charge of or control over the juvenile (CYPA 1933, s. 107 (1)), and for the purpose of Part III it includes a person who was guardian when a supervision order or care order was originally made; see r. 13 (2) and CYPA 1969, s. 70 (2). Subsequent references to the parent include a guardian.

[8] For a valuable analysis of some of the provisions of Part III, particularly in relation to the parent see B.T.H., *The Role of the Parent in Care Proceedings* (1976), 140 J.P.N. 401.

[9] Rr. 13 (2) and 19. Compare adoption which has the anomaly that the minor is a party in the High Court but not if the proceedings are in a county court or magistrates' court.

[10] [1976] 2 All E.R. 194.

(2) Because the juvenile is a party he has the right to representation and, by virtue of the Legal Aid Act 1974, the court may grant him legal aid so that he may be represented by a solicitor.[1] It cannot grant the parent legal aid, since he is not the person brought before the court. Nor can it do so under its power[2] to give legal aid at short notice when a case is already before it and the party is not represented. That power only extends to a party to the proceedings and the parent does not so qualify.[3] [**370**]

There are, however, practical difficulties to be encountered. Usually it is the parent who in practice decides whether there should be an application for legal aid. Indeed, the Act expressly gives him power to make the application on the juvenile's behalf.[4] There may be a number of reasons why this step is not taken. It may be due, for example, to ignorance or indifference or a desire himself to conduct the case[5] or a reluctance to allow a lawyer to probe into the family affairs.[6] Moreover, even where legal aid is granted to the juvenile there is the risk, especially where he is young and instructions are taken from the parent, that the latter's interests rather than the juvenile's are represented. Nevertheless, the difficulties can be exaggerated. First, the court of its own volition and without any application having been made can make a legal aid order[7] and itself appoint a solicitor to act for the juvenile.[8] Such action is particularly useful in those cases where the care proceedings are wholly or partly based on the conduct of the parent for which he has been convicted of an offence. Secondly, where the parent does himself instruct the solicitor purportedly on the juvenile's behalf, a competent advocate should be alert to the possibility of conflict between the interests of the juvenile and those of the parent. Although not trained in social work techniques, his ability to assess conflict should not be underestimated. Much will depend, however, on the assiduity of his investigations[9] and the co-operation which the local authority and the parents are prepared to give him. These comments are, of course, equally pertinent where the solicitor has independently been appointed by the court. [**371**]

(3) A number of rules illustrate the ambivalence of the parent's role.

(a) He must be given notice of the proceedings, provided his whereabouts are known to the applicant.[10] [**372**]

(b) Although the point has never been judicially tested, it is clear that in care and related proceedings he has the right to be present at the hearing as a person "directly concerned" in the case,[11] but, apart from any right, the court can insist on his presence either during the whole of the proceedings or at a

---

[1] S. 28 (3). Where the care proceedings are brought on the ground that he is guilty of an offence, representation by counsel may also be granted (s. 30 (2)).

[2] S. 2 (4).

[3] *R.* v. *Worthing Justices, ex parte Stevenson*, para. [**369**], *ante*.

[4] S. 40 (2).

[5] See para. [**375**], *post*.

[6] See Levin, *op. cit.*, pp. 129–130.

[7] Legal Aid in Criminal Proceedings (General) Regulations 1968, reg. 5.

[8] See *R.* v. *Northampton Justices, ex parte McElkennon* (1976), 120 Sol. Jo. 677.

[9] The readiness of solicitors "to go out into the field and collect evidence" has been doubted; see Harris, *Getting the balance right in child care proceedings, The Times*, 5th April 1977.

[10] Magistrates' Courts (Children and Young Persons) Rules 1970, r. 14 (2) and (3) (*b*).

[11] CYPA 1933, s. 47 (2) (*b*).

particular stage, unless it is satisfied that it would be unreasonable to require his attendance.[1] Indeed, attendance of a parent must be the normal occurrence, otherwise certain other rules would be valueless. [**373**]

(c) Thus, at the outset of the hearing the court must normally inform the juvenile himself of the general nature of the proceedings and the grounds on which they are brought.[2] If, however, because of his age and understanding or his absence, this is impracticable, any parent who is present must be informed.[3] Care proceedings can be brought in respect of a juvenile under 5 without his presence in court. The procedure is wholly within the court's discretion, but a prior condition is that either notice of the proceedings was served on the parent or he is in fact present before the court. In either event the court may direct that the proceedings continue, subject to the parent (if present) being given an opportunity to be heard.[4] [**374**]

(d) The court must allow the parent to conduct the case unless:

(i) the juvenile or his parent is legally represented, or
(ii) the proceedings are care proceedings brought at the parent's request (or under an order resulting from a request) on the ground that the juvenile is beyond his control, or
(iii) the juvenile otherwise requests[5]—an unlikely possibility but one which might occur, for example, where an independently minded sixteen-year-old applies for the discharge of a care order and both the local authority and the parent are opposed to the application.

This right normally for the parent to conduct the case is based on the assumption that he will necessarily be acting in the juvenile's interests, but in care proceedings, even more than in applications for discharge of supervision or care orders, the parent's conduct is nearly always inextricably involved and consequently he often sees the proceedings as a conflict between himself and the local authority with the need to justify his own conduct. [**375**]

(e) If the court is satisfied that in the special circumstances it is appropriate to do so, it may require a parent to withdraw from the court while the juvenile gives evidence or makes a statement.[6] The power is exercisable whether or not the parent is conducting the case on the juvenile's behalf, but, where he is, it is hardly likely that he will pursue a line of questioning—assuming his competence to do so—either in cross-examination of the local authority's witnesses or in examination-in-chief of the juvenile, which is designed to weaken his own position *vis-à-vis* the juvenile and, in particular, to elicit allegations against himself and thereby lead the court to exclude him while the juvenile gives, or continues to give, his evidence. If, however, he is excluded, then the court will have to assume the role of conducting the case on the juvenile's behalf by

---

[1] CYPA 1933, s. 34 (1), as substituted by CYPA 1963, s. 25 (1) and amended by CYPA 1969, Sch. 6.

[2] The duty to inform does not arise where he is the applicant (which, in effect, means where he is applying for variation or discharge of an order) or where the court is allowed to proceed in his absence.

[3] R. 16 (1).

[4] CYPA 1969, s. 2 (9).

[5] R. 17 (1).

[6] R. 18 (2).

examining him in chief and re-examining in the light of any cross-examination. Moreover, if the parent is excluded, how can he be expected effectively to conduct the rest of the case, for example, the examination of witnesses called on behalf of the juvenile? A clearer indication of the inadequacy of representation is scarcely conceivable. [**376**]

(f) Under the old law the parent had the right to meet any allegations which were made by the juvenile while he was so excluded,[1] but not otherwise. As will be seen,[2] this right has been extended, but it still has its defects. [**377**]

(g) The objection, already voiced,[3] that the efficacy of the parent's representation of the juvenile may be impaired if the parent is at a particular stage excluded from the court also applies to the stage where the court is considering written reports after the applicant's case has been proved. It may choose not to read aloud the report or, if it considers it necessary in the juvenile's interests, it may require him or his parent to withdraw from the court. In either event the parent must be told the substance of any part of the information given to the court which it considers to be material to the manner in which the case should be dealt with and which refers to the parent's character or conduct or to the character, conduct, home surroundings or health of the juvenile.[4] Notwithstanding this safeguard, these are restrictions on the parent and thus are difficult to reconcile with the fundamental principle that a representative is entitled to be present throughout the conduct of the proceedings. [**378**]

(h) Before finally disposing of the case the court must inform the juvenile (unless it is undesirable or impracticable to do so) and the parent, whether or not the latter is conducting the case, of the manner in which it proposes to deal with the case and allow them to make representations.[5] [**379**]

(i) On making an order the court must explain to the juvenile the general nature and effect of the order unless it appears impracticable to do so having regard to his age and understanding.[6] If that should be so, the court, strangely, is not required to explain the order to the parent, although in practice it does so. [**380**]

C. THE EFFECT OF THE CHILDREN ACT

The new provisions in the 1975 Act rest on the premise that in care and related proceedings there is an actual or potential conflict between the interests of the juvenile and those of his parent. Section 64 introduces into the Children and Young Persons Act 1969 two new sections, 32A and 32B, and these draw a distinction between what may be termed the general rule and the exceptional rule. The latter has operated since 26th November 1976, but implementation of the former is likely to be delayed for some time until the requisite additional resources are available. The Magistrates' Courts (Children and Young Persons) Rules 1970 have been amended[7] on the assumed basis that sections 32A and 32B

---

[1] See *ibid.*
[2] Para. [**406**], *post.*
[3] Para. [**376**], *ante.*
[4] R. 20 (1) and (2).
[5] R. 21 (1).
[6] R. 21 (2).
[7] By the Magistrates' Courts (Children and Young Persons) (Amendment) Rules 1976. Subsequent references refer to the 1970 Rules as so amended.

are both fully in force.[1] Certain of the amendments give rise to the general criticism that the sections have left too much to Rules of Court. It must be stressed that the sections and the amending Rules leave many of the provisions (summarised in paras. [**368**]–[**380**], *ante*) untouched and this will remain the position even when the sections have been fully implemented. [**381**]

The general rule (sections 32A (1) and 32B (2))

The rule applies to the following proceedings:

(a) care proceedings brought under section 1 of the 1969 Act;

(b) an application, other than an unopposed application, for the discharge of a supervision order, whether that order was made under section 1 (i.e., a "relevant supervision order")[2] or on the discharge of a care order which had been made under section 1 ("a relevant care order");[2]

(c) an application, other than an unopposed application, for the discharge of a care order, whether that order is a relevant care order or one which was made on the discharge of a relevant supervision order;

(Applications under paras. (b) and (c) cover both cases where the applicant is applying simply for the discharge of an order and those where he is also seeking substitution of another order, i.e., a care order for a supervision order or a supervision order for a care order.)

(d) an appeal by the juvenile to the Crown Court against an order made under section 1 proceedings, other than an order requiring his parent to enter into a recognisance to take proper care of him and exercise proper control over him;[3]

(e) an appeal by the juvenile to the Crown Court[4] (i) against the dismissal of an application for the discharge of a relevant supervision order, or (ii) against a care order which was made on the discharge either of a relevant supervision order or of a supervision order which had been made when a relevant care order was discharged; conversely,

(f) an appeal by the juvenile to the Crown Court[5] (i) against the dismissal of an application for the discharge of a relevant care order or (ii) against a supervision order which was made on the discharge either of a relevant care order or of a care order which had been made when a relevant supervision order was discharged. [**382**]

In any of the above proceedings the court may exclude the normal rule that the parent is to be treated as representing the juvenile or as otherwise being authorised to act on his behalf, and may go on to appoint a guardian *ad litem*; but the discretion is hedged about by statutory restrictions and no less than three hurdles have to be surmounted before it is certain that someone is appointed independently to safeguard the juvenile's interests. [**383**]

First, it must appear to the court that there is or may be a conflict between his interests and those of the parent on any matter relevant to the proceedings.

[1] Those currently operative will be so indicated.
[2] So defined by s. 32A (5).
[3] See CYPA 1969, s. 2 (12).
[4] Under CYPA 1969, s. 16 (8).
[5] See *ibid.*, s. 21 (4).

In principle, this obstacle to separate representation should not prove difficult. In some cases, of course, there will not be any conflict or any risk of it; for example, where the juvenile is a truant and the parent recognises the need for supervision or even a care order so as to bring home to him the consequences of his truancy. However, in the majority of proceedings under section 1 there must be a real possibility of conflict. This follows from the very terms of the section[1] and the fact that the parent is so often opposed to the proceedings. Proceedings are brought because the local authority thinks that the juvenile's welfare requires a supervision order or care order being made. The parent does not. If he did, he would agree to voluntary supervision or would allow the child to be received into care under section 1 of the Children Act 1948. It is to be hoped that the courts will exercise their discretion under section 32A (1) in this light and readily recognise the possibility of conflict of interests. [**384**]

Secondly, while the court may well be satisfied in the majority of cases that there is an actual or potential conflict, it still has a discretion whether or not to order that the parent is not to be treated as representing the juvenile. The Act offers no guidance on the factors to be taken into account in exercising this part of the discretion. [**385**]

Thirdly, even where it makes such an order, the appointment of a guardian will not automatically follow but will be made if it appears to the court that it is in his interests to do so.[2] Again, no guidance is given, but important factors in deciding whether to order appointment will be the age of the juvenile and his ability to take part in the proceedings. [**386**]

The exceptional rule (sections 32A (2) and 32B (1))[3]

This rule, which owes its origin to the Maria Colwell tragedy, applies to unopposed applications for the discharge of supervision orders or care orders. It has primarily in mind the case where the parent applies on the juvenile's behalf for discharge and the local authority does not oppose the application, but it also relates to the converse case where the authority is the applicant. Its aim is to restrict the court's discretion and the emphasis is different from that in the general rule. Nevertheless, a discretion remains and a guardian *ad litem* will not necessarily be appointed. [**387**]

Section 32A (2) provides that where there is such an application the court must order that no parent is to be treated as representing the juvenile or otherwise authorised to act on his behalf,[4] unless it is satisfied that an order is not necessary for safeguarding his interests. Where it does make an order, it must appoint a guardian *ad litem*, but this duty is also subject to the discretion not to appoint if the court is satisfied that appointment is not necessary to safeguard the juvenile's interests. The discretion not to appoint is not limited to exceptional

[1] See especially s. 1 (2) (*a*) and (*b*).

[2] R. 14A (1). Should such a vital matter on the question of representation have been left to subordinate legislation?

[3] S. 64 of the Children Act 1975, which inserts these provisions, has been modified by the Children Act 1975 (Commencement No. 1) Order 1976 to take account of the fact that s. 32A is not yet fully operative. The amendment is one of form and not substance.

[4] But such an order will not invalidate the application even though it was made by the parent on the juvenile's behalf.

circumstances. Nor is any duty imposed on the court to give reasons for not appointing. An appropriate case for not doing so could be where the court chooses to rely on its own powers to grant legal aid and itself appoint a solicitor. These powers are not modified by the 1975 Act. The court might feel, for example, that, in view of the juvenile's age and ability to instruct a solicitor the exercise of the powers would be sufficient to ensure effective representation. Again, where the unopposed application relates to a supervision order or care order made because the juvenile committed an offence and not as the result of care proceedings, the court might well feel that appointment of a guardian *ad litem* is wholly unnecessary. **[388]**

The powers to make orders under section 32A (1) and (2) and to appoint a guardian *ad item* under section 32b may be exercised before or in the course of the proceedings. Pre-hearing orders are to be preferred since they will prevent unnecessary adjournments. Where the proceedings are care proceedings or an application for discharge of a supervision or care order, as opposed to appeals therefrom,[1] the powers are exercisable before the hearing of the application, by a single justice[2] or the justices' clerk.[3] In practice they are most likely to be made by the clerk. There are, however, practical difficulties which the statutory provisions do not satisfactorily meet. What information will be available before the proceedings to enable the clerk under the general rule to reach the conclusion that there is or may be a conflict of interests, or under the exceptional rule to be satisfied that it is not necessary for safeguarding the juvenile's interests to order that the parent be not treated as representing him? Under the Magistrates' Courts (Children and Young Persons) Rules 1970, as amended, all that the applicant proposing to bring the proceedings has to do is to send to the clerk a notice specifying the grounds for the proceedings together with the names and addresses of the persons to whom he, the applicant, has to send a copy of the notice.[4] There is no duty to submit any documentary evidence which would support the making of orders under sections 32A and 32B. Nor has the clerk power to call for such evidence from the applicant or from the local authority (if not the applicant) or a probation officer.[5] Consequently, the only information he is likely to have before him is a record of the earlier care proceedings indicating the ground on which the order was made and the age of the child. In an unopposed application under the exceptional rule this information is hardly likely to be sufficient to justify not making orders under sections 32A (2) and 32B (1).

---

[1] If an order is made under s. 32A (1) or (2) in relation to care proceedings or an application for discharge of a supervision or care order, it will then have effect also for the purposes of an appeal to the Crown Court; see s. 32A (3). If, however, no order under s. 32A was made in respect of the original proceedings, the Crown Court may on the appeal make such an order.

[2] Ss. 32A (4) and 32B (1) and (2) and the Magistrates' Courts (Children and Young Persons) Rules 1970, r. 14A (4).

[3] The Justices' Clerks Rules 1970, rr. 13 and 14 (as inserted by the Justices' Clerks (Amendment) Rules 1976) and the Magistrates' Courts (Children and Young Persons) Rules 1970, r. 14 A (4).

[4] R. 14 (1).

[5] The Justices' Clerks (Amendment) Rules 1976 extend to a justices' clerk the power conferred by s. 6 (1) of the Guardianship Act 1973 to call for a report from a local authority or probation officer so as to enable him to do so before the hearing of any application to which s. 6 (1) relates. That subsection does not, however, relate to applications made under the Children and Young Persons Act 1969.

Much will depend on the recorded note, if any, of the earlier case. One possible improvement would be a requirement that the notice of application includes information indicating what has happened to the juvenile since the original order. Another would be a power to call for a report from the local authority or a probation officer. [**389**]

The functions of the guardian ad litem

Like the guardian *ad litem* in adoption proceedings he is appointed to safeguard the juvenile's interests before the court.[1] This means not only protecting them *vis-à-vis* the parent. The juvenile may also be in conflict with the local authority. For example, the authority may have applied for discharge of a care order because they consider it best for the juvenile to return permanently to his parents, whereas the foster-parents may be convinced that termination of the authority's care is not in his interests. [**390**]

The Rules governing his functions do not prescribe a lengthy list of duties as they do for his counterpart in adoption. Possibly the Secretary of State will review the matter in the light of experience of the operation of the exceptional rule and lay down further specific duties when the general rule is brought into effect. Those which the present Rules[2] impose on him are:

(a) So far as is reasonably practicable, he must investigate all circumstances relevant to the proceedings and for that purpose interview such persons and inspect such records as he thinks appropriate. Although discharging this duty may involve duplication of enquiries which may already have been made by other agencies, this possibility should not deter the guardian *ad litem* from undertaking the fullest investigations so as to enable him to come to an independent conclusion on what is best for the juvenile. [**391**]

He is not statutorily required to interview all the persons to whom copy of the notice of the proceedings has to be sent,[3] but invariably he will have to do so if he is to investigate all relevant circumstances. Obviously he will see the juvenile and, where old enough, ascertain his wishes and feelings. This may involve a number of interviews while he gains the juvenile's confidence. The interviews may show, in the case of an application for discharge of a care order, that the juvenile does not want the order discharged. The guardian *ad litem* will also want to hear the views of the foster-parent or other person with whom the juvenile has had his home.[4] His views are particularly important in cases of unopposed applications made by the parent on the juvenile's behalf. The foster-parent will also be able to indicate from his own observations the child's own wishes and feelings. Where the application is for discharge of a supervision order the supervisor should be consulted and in all proceedings the guardian *ad litem* should approach the school authorities for a report on the juvenile. Indeed, in this way he might be able to glean information which would not necessarily

---

[1] S. 32B (3).

[2] Magistrates' Courts (Children and Young Persons) Rules 1970, r. 14A (6) and (7).

[3] See r. 14 (2) and (3). Compare the duty of the guardian *ad litem* in adoption proceedings to interview specified persons.

[4] The foster-parent or other person will have had notice of the proceedings if the child has had his home with him for a period of not less than six weeks ending not more than six months before the date of the application; see r. 14 (3) (*bb*).

appear in the school report to the court. Where he considers it necessary, he may also obtain an independent medical report on the juvenile. [**392**]

The extent of co-operation which he might receive from the parent or guardian[1] will vary considerably and, where it is not forthcoming, the guardian *ad litem* should report the fact to the court. How far the appropriate local authority will allow its files to be inspected and its officers to be interviewed is still speculative, but the Department of Health and Social Security has requested that authorities make their records freely available to guardians *ad litem*.[2] Social workers' reports are privileged documents,[3] but if the juvenile's welfare is to be the paramount consideration, the juvenile court should have the power to order discovery and also to authorise the guardian *ad litem* to inspect. As it is, if a local authority declines to make its records available, the guardian *ad litem* should so report to the court. [**393**]

(b) In the light of his investigation the guardian *ad litem* must consider whether it is in the juvenile's best interests that the application to which the proceedings relate should succeed. [**394**]

(c) In the light of that consideration, he must decide how the case should be conducted on behalf of the juvenile and, where appropriate, instruct a solicitor to represent the juvenile. [**395**]

The combined effect of these duties seems to be that, if the guardian *ad litem* should reach the considered conclusion that the application should succeed, he is not obliged to draw the court's attention to a specific matter which might militate against that result. For example, in an unopposed application for discharge of a care order, he might conclude that it is best for the juvenile to return to his parent's home, even though he has certain reservations about the parent's character or conduct. [**396**]

Where the guardian *ad litem* decides that a solicitor should represent the juvenile, he himself strictly cannot apply on the juvenile's behalf for legal aid, since he is not a "guardian" within the meaning of the relevant statutory provisions.[4] What he can do, however, is to invite the court to exercise its power of its own motion to make a legal aid order.[5] In practice the distinction should prove academic. [**397**]

(d) Where the juvenile is not legally represented, the guardian *ad litem* must conduct the case on behalf of the juvenile unless he otherwise requests. Should the guardian *ad litem* already know that the local authority and the parent are to be legally represented, it is very likely that he will also instruct a solicitor, but no guidance is given by the Rules on the factors which should weigh with him in deciding whether or not there should be legal representation. It is suggested that before deciding the matter he should explain the alternatives to the juvenile if he is old enough to understand. If the juvenile does not want the guardian *ad litem* to conduct the case but the latter declines to instruct a solicitor, the juvenile can insist on instructing a solicitor himself. Moreover, the

---

[1] See p. 173, n. 7, *ante*, for the wide meaning of this term.

[2] See L.A.C. (76) 20, para. 29.

[3] *R.* v. *Greenwich Juvenile Court, ex parte Greenwich London Borough Council* (1977), *The Times*, 10th May.

[4] See Legal Aid Act 1974, s. 40 (2); Legal Aid in Criminal Proceedings (General) Regulations 1968, reg. 1 (1); CYPA 1933, s. 107 (1); CYPA 1969, s. 70 (2).

[5] See para. [**370**], *ante*.

decision of a guardian *ad litem* to conduct the case does not, it is submitted, exclude the court's power to grant legal aid and appoint a solicitor, although such a step is likely to be exceptional. [**398**]

Paragraph (d) does, however, raise the wider question of whether the guardian *ad litem* should act as advocate. The most effective representation is the professionally trained advocate acting on the instructions of an expert in social work techniques. Although the guardian *ad litem* may himself acquire skills in advocacy, his role as an advocate is inappropriate in the light of his other functions. It is, for example, a possible source of embarrassment if he has to cross-examine persons whom he has earlier interviewed in his investigatory role. If, for reasons of economy and inadequacy of resources, there has to be a compromise of the principle of legal representation in all cases, then in those cases where the guardian *ad litem* decides not to instruct a solicitor, he should be *obliged* to submit a report to the court,[1] giving his reasons for not so instructing and adding his own representations. Unfortunately the Rules provide that his report is only to be considered after the case has been proved.[2] It is suggested that it ought to be made available to the clerk to the justices or a single justice before the hearing so that he may then advise the court whether it should invoke its power to appoint a solicitor. [**399**]

(e) Where he thinks it would assist the court the guardian *ad litem* must make a written report to it. The court must take the report into consideration, but the rules governing disclosure differ from those in adoption proceedings. In the latter the report is confidential[3] except in so far as the court thinks fit to disclose its contents.[4] In care and related proceedings it may be received and considered without being read aloud,[5] but, if it is not read aloud, the substance of any part of it which affects the character or conduct of the juvenile or of the parent and which is material to the manner in which the case should be dealt with must be explained to the juvenile or the parent respectively.[6] [**400**]

This function differs in two other respects from that of the guardian *ad litem* in adoption proceedings. First, it leaves the guardian *ad litem* in care and related proceedings with a discretion whether or not to submit a report. Secondly, it does not authorise him to make interim reports to the court with a view to obtaining the directions of the court on any particular matter, a surprising omission in the light of the following duty which he has to discharge. [**401**]

(f) The guardian *ad litem* must perform such other duties as the court shall direct. In view of the primary role of representing the juvenile in the proceedings, whether by conducting the case or instructing a solicitor, which the guardian *ad litem* has in care and related proceedings, it would seem that this function is more likely to arise after the case has been proved and the court directs the guardian *ad litem* to make further inquiries before reaching its decision on the application. [**402**]

(g) When the court has finally disposed of the case the guardian *ad litem*

---

[1] Under the Rules submission is discretionary; see paras. [**400**]–[**401**], *post*.
[2] See para. [**401**], *post*.
[3] Adoption (High Court) Rules 1976, r. 13 (4); Adoption (County Court) Rules 1976, r. 11 (4); Magistrates' Courts (Adoption) Rules 1976, r. 10 (4).
[4] *Re J. S. (an infant)*, [1959] 3 All E.R. 856; [1959] 1 W.L.R. 1218; *Re G. (an infant)*, [1963] 2 Q.B. 73; [1963] 1 All E.R. 20 (C.A.).
[5] Magistrates' Courts (Children and Young Persons) Rules 1970, r. 20 (1) (*a*), as amended.
[6] See r. 20 (2) for fuller details.

must consider whether it would be in the juvenile's best interests to appeal to the Crown Court, and, if he considers that it would be, he must give notice of appeal on the juvenile's behalf. The Rules say nothing, however, about any power in the guardian *ad litem* in respect of appeal by way of case stated. Is he entitled on the juvenile's behalf to invoke the appropriate procedure? [**403**]

The parent

The 1975 Act and the amendments to the Magistrates' Courts (Children and Young Persons) Rules 1970 allow the parent a more effective participation in care and related proceedings, but leave him occupying a position somewhere between being a party to the proceedings and being a witness with additional limited rights. The compromise demonstrates the need for a new basic approach to care and related proceedings along inquisitorial lines. There are two main changes. [**404**]

The first enables the parent to be granted legal aid. Where the court makes an order under section 32A affecting him he may be granted legal aid for the purpose of taking such part in the proceedings as the 1970 Rules allow.[1] This therefore means that at present such aid is only possible where there is an unopposed application for discharge of a supervision order or care order. Where legal aid is granted the parent will only be assessed for the purpose of determining any grant to himself and not also in respect of a grant to the juvenile, but, until the parent becomes eligible for aid for all other care and related proceedings, it seems that his means will continue to be assessed for the purpose of any grant to the juvenile. [**405**]

The Rules allow the parent to take part in the proceedings before the case is proved to the following extent:[2]

(1) Under Rule 14B he may meet any allegations made against him in the course of the proceedings by calling or giving evidence.[3] This amended Rule applies to all care and related proceedings and is already fully operative. It is not confined to cases where a section 32A order is made. The amendment removes an injustice and anomaly. Previously the right was limited to meeting allegations which the juvenile had made against him while the parent was excluded from the court.[4] Thus, under the former law, if the juvenile made allegations, however serious, while the parent was in court or formally admitted allegations made by the local authority, the parent was powerless to challenge them. [**406**]

Still the extended right has its limitations. The parent must call or give his evidence at the conclusion of the evidence for the respondent and the evidence, if any, for the applicant in rebuttal but before the respondent or the applicant addresses the court. There is no right to cross-examine the evidence already adduced respectively by the parties to the proceedings. But has the parent the right to address the court before the respondent or the applicant does so? The answer would seem to depend upon the remaining terms of Rule 14B and the construction to be placed upon Rule 21 (1). [**407**]

---

[1] Children Act 1975, s. 65, amending s. 28 of the Legal Aid Act 1974.

[2] On his right to be heard and informed after the case has been proved see para. [**379**], *ante*.

[3] R. 14B (*a*).

[4] See para. [**377**], *ante*.

(2) Rule 14B further provides[1] that where the court has made an order under section 32A the parent is entitled to make representations to the court.[2] This he will be able to do whether or not he has adduced evidence to refute allegations against himself. However, the express reference to representations only where a section 32A order is made implies that no such representations are possible without that order, even though the parent has adduced evidence. Can he, in the latter circumstances, rely on Rule 21 (1)? As already noted,[3] before finally disposing of the case the court must inform him, if present, of the manner in which it proposes to deal with the case and allow him to make representations. It seems that this Rule only becomes relevant after the case has been proved and the court is determining the appropriate order. If so, the parent will not be able to make representations in the light of the evidence he gave or called to refute allegations, unless, which must be doubted, the court feels bold enough to invoke its inherent power to control its own proceedings in the interests of justice and a fair and expeditious trial.[4] The uncertainties to which the Rules give rise firmly indicate the need for enactment of a clear code of procedure in care and related proceedings. The need is the greater with the appearance of the guardian *ad litem*, especially since he has the right himself to conduct the case on the juvenile's behalf. [**408**]

THE APPOINTMENT OF GUARDIANS AD LITEM

The Children Act 1975 leaves wholly to Rules of Court the question of the eligibility and qualifications of persons for appointment as guardians *ad litem* in care and related proceedings,[5] in proceedings concerning the continuation or termination of section 2 resolutions under the Children Act 1948[6] and in adoption proceedings;[7] save that in adoption, section 20 (2) of the 1975 Act[8] itself disqualifies a person who is employed by the adoption agency involved. Subject to those disqualifications, Rules of Court are also to determine the appointment of reporting officers.[9] [**409**]

The criteria and the kinds of suitable persons are therefore a matter of Departmental policy (although it is arguable that this is an unduly wide delegation of legislative powers), and the 1975 Act[10] empowers the Secretary of State to provide for the establishment of a panel of persons from whom guardians *ad litem* for the purpose of any of the above proceedings, and reporting officers

---

[1] R. 14B (*b*).
[2] This must also be done after the respondent and applicant have completed their evidence but before they address the court.
[3] Para. [**379**], *ante*.
[4] *Simms* v. *Moore*, [1970] 2 Q.B. 327; [1970] 3 All E.R. 1.; see p. 171,n . 7, *ante*.
[5] See s. 64, inserting provisions into s. 32B (1) and (2) of the Children and Young Persons Act 1969.
[6] Children Act 1975, s. 58, inserting s. 4B (1) into the Children Act 1948.
[7] Children Act 1975, s. 20 (1); (Adoption Act 1976, s. 65 (1)).
[8] Adoption Act 1976, s. 65 (2).
[9] The Rules may provide for a reporting officer to be appointed before the application is made for an adoption order, freeing for adoption order, revocation of a freeing for adoption order or an order in respect of a child to be adopted abroad; see s. 20 (3); see para. [**127**] *ante*.
[10] S. 103 (1).

for adoption, may be appointed. Panels have not yet been established[1] and the appointment of guardians *ad litem* in adoption proceedings are still governed by the Adoption Rules 1976 of the High Court, county courts and magistrates' courts.[2] [**410**]

In unopposed applications for the discharge of supervision orders or care orders the guardian *ad litem* is, until panels are established, to be some "suitable person", provided that he is not a member, officer or servant of a local authority or of the National Society for the Prevention of Cruelty to Children, which is a party to the proceedings.[3] This proviso will also operate when the panels have been set up. Ideally, no one connected with a local authority should be eligible for appointment, even though it is not the authority involved in the proceedings. Local authorities are the linchpin in the operation of the law regulating children in care. To ask a local authority social worker to discharge this function of guardian *ad litem* runs the risk of making unreasonable demands on professional loyalties. However, in the foreseeable future the limited number of suitable persons available prevents that ideal from being realised. Local authority social workers will, indeed, be the main source of appointments. [**411**]

The present Rules go no further and do not prescribe categories of suitable persons or qualifications for appointment. Instead the matter has been left to guidance by Departmental Circular,[4] pending the establishment of panels. Courts have been advised that in the interim period they might consider it appropriate to appoint persons who are recommended by the Director of Social Services of a local authority (other than one involved in the proceedings) or a probation officer nominated by the Chief Probation Officer but not being one who is already supervising the juvenile or other member of the household. Those recommended by the local authority may include not only existing members of staff but exceptionally retired social workers or other suitable persons such as a person employed by a voluntary organisation working in child care. Clearly, liaison between local authorities and the Probation Service would be particularly helpful, but, since the appointment of a guardian *ad litem* is a matter for the court, it has, it is suggested, complete discretion whether to look to the local authority or the Probation and After-Care Committee. [**412**]

The following qualifications have been recommended for persons suitable for appointment:[5]

> "Persons required to undertake guardian *ad litem* duties should have practical experience of social work with families and children under stress, as well as with children needing to live temporarily or permanently apart from their parents. The ability to communicate effectively with children of

---

[1] The timetable is to be arranged between the Department of Health and Social Security and local authority associations in the light of availability of resources. Although appointment of a guardian *ad litem* is made by the court, the panels, it seems, will not be attached to the courts.

[2] See respectively, r. 12, r. 10 and r. 9.

[3] Magistrates' Courts (Children and Young Persons) Rules 1970, r. 14A (2). Notice of appointment must be given to the guardian *ad litem*, the applicant and the persons to whom notice of the proceedings has to be given (r. 14A (5)). The court may revoke an appointment and make a new one (r. 14A (3)).

[4] See L.A.C. (76) 20.

[5] *Ibid.*, para. 22.

all ages is of primary importance in the selection of persons to act as guardians *ad litem*. Bearing in mind that guardians *ad litem* will be required to examine social work records and will need to have the status necessary to give their social work colleagues and courts confidence in their advice, they should normally be experienced social workers or probation officers. Ideally they should be people with professional casework training plus relevant post training experience. Experience of court work in care and related proceedings will be especially important."

The interim measures will give further opportunity for consideration of the qualities needed for appointment to the proposed panels. Experience may show, for example, that persons with experience as guardians *ad litem* in adoption proceedings are not necessarily suitable for appointment for care and related proceedings. [**413**]

The present Rules are open to the serious objection that they fail to ensure that sufficient resources will be made available to enable the guardian *ad litem* to discharge his duties. The availability of support services and funds to meet expenses depends upon the extent to which local authorities and Probation and After-Care Committees are prepared to provide them. There is no statutory duty to do so and the 1975 Act is cautious about the future; regulations may provide for expenses incurred by members of the panel to be defrayed by local authorities.[1] It does not prescribe specific kinds of services that have to be made available. Nor does it deal with the consequences of not providing a particular service. For example, supposing the guardian *ad litem* considers that an independent medical report is needed, but the local authority firmly believes it is not. In such circumstances it is suggested that he should inform the court so that it may order a report. [**414**]

---

[1] S. 103 (2).

PART IV

MISCELLANEOUS

CHAPTER 13

MISCELLANEOUS MATTERS

A. FOSTER CHILDREN

Except in so far as it relates to adoption and custodianship the practice and control of private fostering did not receive the attention of the Houghton/Stockdale Committee or of the Children Bill initially, and it was only in the later stages of the Bill that it was decided to give the Secretary of State power to make regulations covering certain aspects of private fostering and the control exercised by local authorities under the Children Act 1958, as substantially amended by the Children and Young Persons Act 1969. [**415**]

One of the matters affected is the visiting of foster-children. The 1969 Act widened the local authority's discretion, making it necessary for its officers to visit "from time to time" all foster-children but only "so far as appears to the authority to be appropriate".[1] The 1975 Act tightens up the provision by removing the discretion. Section 95[2] imposes on the local authority an absolute duty which is to be carried out in accordance with regulations to be made under section 2A of the Children Act 1958. This new section enables the Secretary of State to make regulations[3] requiring foster-children to be visited by an officer of the local authority on specified occasions or within specified periods. Thus, local authority discretion gives way to Central Government directive. Nevertheless, in specifying the occasions and periods account will have to be taken of the resources which local authorities can reasonably be expected to provide. [**416**]

The basic problem about the supervision of private fostering arrangements is ensuring that the local authority is made aware of them. Section 3 (1) of the 1958 Act requires the foster-parent to notify the local authority of the arrangements, but, either through ignorance or by design, this frequently does not happen. Moreover, as section 3 presently stands,[4] it is not necessary for him to notify the authority of every child whom he intends to foster and of every foster-child who has ceased to be in his care. All that is needed is that a person gives notice when he becomes, and when he ceases to be, a foster-parent. The 1975 Act seeks in two complementary ways to strengthen the local authority control. First, when the new regulations under section 2A are made, every person who is maintaining a foster-child[5] and who has not already given notice under section 3 (1) in respect of the child will be obliged to do so within eight weeks of the date on which the regulations are made.[6] The intended emphasis is on notice in

---

[1] Children Act 1958, s. 1, as substituted by CYPA 1969, s. 51.

[2] See sub-ss. (1) and (3). The section is not yet in force.

[3] By statutory instrument subject to the annulment procedure of either House of Parliament. See s. 2A (1) and (3).

[4] See sub-s. (2A).

[5] For the definition of a foster-child see s. 2 of the 1958 Act.

[6] Children Act 1958, s. 2A (2), as inserted by Children Act 1975, s. 95 (3).

respect of each child[1] and when the regulations come into force the rule that a foster-parent need only give notice when he becomes, and when he ceases to be, a foster-parent will be abolished.[2] The 1975 Act does not, however, give any indication of the way in which the new provision is to be given greater efficacy than has been the experience of section 3 (1). It seems that this difficulty is to be a matter for further consultation and study.[3] Presumably an essential feature will be planned publicity of the enactment of the regulations. [**417**]

The same publicity is no doubt intended for the other change designed to strengthen the authority's control.[4] This enables regulations to be made requiring parents whose children are, or are going to be, maintained as foster-children to give notice to the authority. Possibly those regulations and those under section 2A might include administrative arrangements whereby local authorities are informed of child benefits paid to persons other than a parent. [**418**]

Hitherto restrictions on advertisements concerning private fostering have been strictly limited. Under section 37 of the 1958 Act the only limitation is that, if a person advertises that he will undertake, or will arrange for, the care and maintenance of a child, he must truly state his name and address. The 1975 Act[5] empowers the Secretary of State to make regulations controlling advertisements not only by prospective foster-parents or persons willing to arrange fostering but also by parents or guardians. A distinctive feature of the new power is the flexibility it allows. The regulations may make different provision for different cases or classes of cases and may exclude certain cases or classes of cases. No doubt, these, like the regulations to be made under sections 2A and 3A, will take account of current studies into private fostering. [**419**]

B. PROVISION OF REPORTS IN CERTAIN PROCEEDINGS

Sections 90 and 91 of the 1975 Act have introduced procedural changes[6] in the submission and disclosure of reports made to *magistrates' courts* by a local authority officer or a probation officer in certain proceedings under the Guardianship of Minors Act 1971 and in proceedings under the Matrimonial Proceedings (Magistrates' Courts) Act 1960.[7] Their objects are to save time in cases where the report is lengthy and nothing is added by its narration in court, and to avoid unnecessary repetition of embarrassing and private information. Thus, unless the court rules otherwise, it is no longer necessary for the report to be read

---

[1] See also the amendments made by s. 95 (4) (*a*) and (*b*) of the 1975 Act to s. 3 (5A) and (5B) of the 1958 Act where notice of ceasing to maintain is required in respect of each particular child.

[2] Children Act 1958, s. 3 (8), as inserted by Children Act 1975, s. 95 (4) (*c*).

[3] See H.C. Official Report, Standing Committee A, cols. 752–753; 14th Sitting; 5th August 1975 (Dr. David Owen).

[4] See s. 96 of the 1975 Act inserting a new s. 3A in the 1958 Act.

[5] S. 97 (1), inserting sub-ss. (1A), (1B) and (1C) into s. 37 of the 1958 Act (not yet operative). *Semble* guardian is to be understood in its most common meaning, namely a person so appointed by deed, will or by the court.

The penalties for a breach of s. 37 are imprisonment for up to six months or a fine not exceeding £400 or both; sub-s. (2), as amended by Children Act 1975, s. 97 (2) and Sch. 3, para. 20.

[6] Operative since 1st January 1976.

[7] See respectively s. 90 (1) substituting new sub-ss. (2), (3) and (3A) in s. 6 of the Guardianship Act 1973 and s. 91 (1) substituting new sub-ss. (3), (4) and (4A) in s. 4 of the 1960 Act.

aloud at the hearing provided that it is in writing and a copy has been given to each party to the proceedings or his legal representative before or during the hearing. Moreover, the officer who makes the report is not required to give evidence of, or with respect to, the matters referred to in the report, unless the court or any party so requires. If evidence is given, a party remains entitled to give evidence on the report or on the officer's evidence. Clearly, in order to avoid unnecessary attendance of the social worker or probation officer, a copy of his report should, whenever possible, be sent to a party before the hearing, requesting him to indicate whether or not attendance is neccessary. [**420**]

The power to call for reports under section 6 (1) of the Guardianship Act 1973 extends to applications under section 9 of the Guardianship of Minors Act 1971 for a custody order and to applications for the variation or discharge of a supervision order which was made when custody was granted under section 9[1] and, as already indicated, the provisions mentioned in the preceding paragraph will apply if the court hearing the application is a magistrates' court. However, the 1975 Act extends those provisions also to a magistrates' court which requires a report in applications under Part II of the Act relating to custodianship and the revocation of custodianship orders,[2] and to a juvenile court requiring a report in proceedings for the confirmation or termination of resolutions made under section 2 of the Children Act 1948.[3] In order to avoid unnecessary delays at the hearing of the application, a single justice[4] or a clerk to the justices[5] is empowered to request a report in any of the proceedings mentioned in this paragraph provided the request is made before the hearing of the application. [**421**]

C. REGISTRATION OF BIRTHS

Abandoned children

Section 92 of the 1975 Act[6] amends the Births and Deaths Registration Act 1953 by providing for a special Register for the births of abandoned children. Already before the amendment section 3 of the latter Act imposed a duty on any person finding or having charge of an abandoned child to give the registrar of births and deaths, within 42 days of finding the child, such information concerning the child's birth as the informant possessed. In addition, a new section, 3A, now enables the person who has charge of the child[7] and who does not know and cannot ascertain the child's place and date of birth to apply to the Registrar General for the birth to be registered. Provided that either (a) the Registrar General is satisfied that the child was born in England or Wales, or (b) the child has not been adopted by a court order made in the United Kingdom, the Isle of Man or the Channel Islands or (c) subject to section 3A (5),[8] the child's

---

[1] See Guardianship Act 1973, ss. 2 (2) (*a*) and 3 (3).
[2] See ss. 36 (4) and (7), 39 (1) and (2) and 40 (2) and (4).
[3] Children Act 1948, s. 4B (3), as inserted by Children Act 1975, s. 58. See also Children Act 1975, s. 63 (4).
[4] Guardianship of Minors Act 1971, s. 6 (6), as added by Children Act 1975, s. 90 (2).
[5] Justices' Clerk (Amendment) Rules 1976, r. 2.
[6] Operative since 1st January 1977. See also Sch. 4, Part VI.
[7] I.e., "actual custody" within the meaning of s. 87 (1) of the 1975 Act.
[8] Para. [**424**], *post*.

birth is not known to have been previously registered under the 1953 Act, the Registrar General must register the child at the General Register Office. [**422**]

The following particulars must be registered:

(a) as the child's place of birth, the registration district and sub-district where he was found, if he was found by the applicant or by any person from whom he directly or indirectly took charge of the child, or, in any other case, where the child was abandoned;

(b) as the child's date of birth, the date which appears to the Registrar General the most likely date of birth;

(c) and other particulars as may be prescribed.[1]

The 1975 Act[2] also fills a gap by allowing anyone over 18 who has not been adopted and who cannot trace his birth entry in any register to apply to the Registrar General for his birth to be registered under section 3A. [**423**]

It is provided in section 1 of the 1953 Act that where a living newly born child is found exposed and no information about the place of birth is available, the birth must be registered by the registrar for the sub-district in which the child is found. Section 3A (5) now provides that, on the application of a person having the charge of such a child or on the application of any such child who has attained 18, the Registrar General shall re-register the birth under section 3A, with a marginal reference to the re-registration being made in the original entry of registration. [**424**]

Illegitimate children

More significant are the amendments made by section 93 of the 1975 Act[3] concerning the registration of births of illegitimate children. These allow (1) for the registration of the father at the mother's request and without his consent, and (2) for re-registration of the child's birth where the original entry made no reference to the father. [**425**]

Previously, section 10 of the 1953 Act only allowed registration of the name of the father at his and the mother's joint request or at the request of the mother alone on production of a declaration by her that the man is the father, together with a statutory declaration by him acknowledging paternity. In no case was registration possible where he disputed paternity. Section 10 (*c*) now additionally allows for registration of the father's name at the mother's request where the man has been named as the putative father in an affiliation order.[4] Where the child has attained the age of 16 his written consent to the registration of the father's name is also required. A certified copy of the affiliation order must be produced to the registrar. In addition it should be confirmed that the affiliation order has not been quashed. A Home Office Circular[5] states that on the receipt of each application for registration in the father's name the General Register Office will send to the court that made the affiliation order a letter of enquiry

---

[1] See the Registration of Births (Abandoned Children) Regulations 1976.

[2] S. 92, inserting s. 3A (4) into the 1953 Act.

[3] Operative since 1st January 1977. See also Registration of Births, Deaths, and Marriages (Amendment) Regulations 1976.

[4] Inserted by s. 93 (1) of the 1975 Act.

[5] H.O.C. 80/1977.

to establish whether or not there was an appeal against the order and, if so, the result of the appeal. [**426**]

Where the birth was originally registered without the father's name, section 10A[1] allows for re-registration so as to include it, provided any of the three above conditions which would enable registration under section 10 are satisfied. The re-registration must be in the prescribed manner and with the authority of the Registrar General.[2] [**427**]

In view of the new power to register the father's name on the authority of an affiliation order, it is clearly important that both parties to an application for such an order should be fully informed about the new provisions, especially about the father's consent not being required. As a temporary measure the Home Office has prepared an appropriate notice for issue to the parties before the hearing, but the possibility of including notes in the summons and in the affiliation order is under consideration. The present notice states that if the birth has been registered before the affiliation order is made, application for inclusion of the father's name should be made to the Registrar General, enclosing the order and a certificate of the child's birth. If the order is made before the birth is registered, it should be produced to the registrar at the time of registration. Authority for inclusion of the father's name will not be given until 21 days has elapsed from the date of the order or, if an appeal against the finding of paternity is lodged, until the result of the appeal is known. [**428**]

D. INQUIRIES

Section 98 of the 1975 Act[3] empowers the Secretary of State to order the holding of an inquiry into any of the following:

(a) the functions of a local authority's social services committee which relate to children;
(b) the functions of an adoption agency;
(c) the functions of a voluntary organisation in so far as they relate to voluntary homes;
(d) a home maintained by the Secretary of State for the accommodation of children in the care of local authorities and who are in need of the particular facilities and services provided in the home;
(e) the detention of a child under section 53 of the Children and Young Persons Act 1933 (detention for a grave crime).

This is yet another section in the Act resulting from the Maria Colwell Report, which drew attention to the lack of statutory authority for the holding of an inquiry into cases of this kind. Under the former law any such inquiry was non-statutory, which meant that the committee of inquiry was not authorised to subpoena witnesses, take evidence on oath or require the production of

---

[1] Inserted by s. 93 (2) of the 1975 Act.

[2] For the persons who are required to sign the register see s. 10A (2). S. 9 of the 1953 Act, which enables the information required to be given to the registrar to be given to other persons, is extended (by the addition of new sub-ss. (4) and (5)) to include a request under ss. 10 and 10A.

[3] Operative since 1st January 1976; see s. 108 (4).

documents. Now such powers are exercisable in an inquiry conducted under section 98.[1] Section 98 is not likely to be often invoked. Where it is, the inquiry must be held in public, unless the Secretary of State directs it be held in private or, failing that, the person holding it directs that it or part of it is to be in private.[2] [**429**]

E. LEGITIMATION

In Chapter 8 attention was drawn to the changes made by Schedule 1 of the 1975 Act relating to the effects of adoption on dispositions of property. Comparable provisions for legitimation were also there included, but these have been repealed and re-enacted in the Legitimacy Act 1976.[3] [**430**]

A number of the rules affecting adoption apply *mutatis mutandis* to legitimation.[4] Thus, the changes relating to legitimation do not apply to a disposition contained in an instrument[5] made before 1st January 1976. A disposition includes the conferring of a power of appointment[6] and the creation of an entailed interest,[7] but the legitimated child continues to be excluded from succession to any peerage, dignity or title of honour and, unless there is a contrary intention expressed in the instrument, from succession to property devolving therewith.[8] Except where the context otherwise requires, the death of the testator is the date at which a will or codicil is to be regarded as made, and an oral disposition is to be deemed to be contained in an instrument when the disposition was made.[9] For the purposes of succession by legitimated persons, provisions of the law of intestate succession applicable to the estate of a deceased person shall be treated as if contained in an instrument executed by him (while of full capacity) immediately before his death.[10] Protection, similar to that in adoption, is given to trustees and personal representatives who distribute property without first having enquired whether a person is illegitimate or is adopted by one of his natural parents and could be legitimated.[11] [**431**]

The improved property rights relate to children who are legitimated under the Legitimacy Acts 1926 and 1976 by the subsequent marriage of their parents, whether by virtue of English municipal law[12] or of a foreign law,[13] or whose legitimation (whether or not by virtue of subsequent marriage of the parents[14])

---

[1] See s. 98 (3), extending to such an inquiry the provisions of s. 250 (2)–(5) of the Local Government Act 1972.

[2] S. 98 (2).

[3] This consolidating Act has been in force since 22nd August 1976. Subsequent references herein are to that Act, except where otherwise indicated.

[4] Cf. paras. [**175**]–[**176**]. *ante*.

[5] An "existing" instrument; see s. 10 (1). An instrument includes a private Act settling property but not any other enactments; see s. 5 (7).

[6] S. 10 (1).

[7] S. 10 (4).

[8] Legitimacy Act 1976, Sch. 1, para. 4 (2) and (3). Cf. para. [**183**], *ante*.

[9] S. 10 (3) (*a*) and (*b*).

[10] S. 5 (2).

[11] S. 7; see para. [**185**], *ante*.

[12] Legitimacy Act 1926, s. 1; (Legitimacy Act 1976, s. 2).

[13] Legitimacy Act 1926, s. 8; (Legitimacy Act 1976, s. 3).

[14] See, e.g., *Re Luck's Settlement*, [1940] Ch. 864.

is recognised by English law[1] and effected under the law of any other country.[2] Legitimation includes, where the context admits, legitimations effected or recognised before the passing of the Children Act 1975.[3] [**432**]

Before the changes introduced by the 1975 Act, persons legitimated under the Legitimacy Act 1926 or recognised as legitimated under section 8 of that Act were entitled to succeed as if born legitimate, but only in respect of any interest in the estate of an intestate dying after the legitimation or under any disposition coming into operation after that date.[4] In the case of a foreign legitimation recognised at common law, a legitimated person could succeed under English law as if he were legitimate, notwithstanding that the deed, will or intestacy came into operation before the date of legitimation.[5] The advantage of being recognised as legitimated at common law was minimised by the Family Law Reform Act 1969 which provides[6] that, in respect of dispositions made on or after 1st January 1970, any reference to the child of any person shall, unless the contrary intention appears, be construed as including an illegitimate child. Illegitimate children include reference to legitimated children.[7] [**433**]

The effect of the change made by the Children Act is embodied in the Legitimacy Act 1976 to remove the restriction imposed by the 1926 Act that legitimation must precede the date on which the disposition comes into operation. The change relates to instruments made on or after 1st January 1976. In respect of deaths on or after that date and settlements made on or after it a legitimated person, and any other person, shall be entitled to take any interest as if the legitimated person had been born legitimate.[8] [**434**]

However, in the light of the provisions of the Family Law Reform Act 1969, the change is of limited significance and will only be of importance in relation to wills made before 1st January 1970 where the death is on or after 1st January 1976 or in those cases where there is a gift before legitimation expressing a contrary intention. For example, a gift is made in 1975 to the "lawful" children of A. Z is A's illegitimate child and is legitimated in 1976. Z cannot claim, whereas he could if the gift is made in 1976. [**435**]

The new rules apply subject to any contrary indication. Thus, while a gift to "lawful" children will include legitimated children—such being able to take as if born legitimate—a gift to "children born in lawful wedlock" will presumably not. [**436**]

A disposition which depends on the date of birth of a child shall be construed as if a legitimated child had been born on the date of legitimation. If two children are legitimated on the same day, they are to be treated as though born on that date in the order of their actual births.[9] For example, T dies in 1976 leaving a gift to "the eldest lawful son of A". A has by B two illegitimate sons, X and Y, born in 1972 and 1973 respectively. He also has a legitimate son

---

[1] See Dicey & Morris, *The Conflict of Laws* (9th Edn.), pp. 447–459; Cheshire's, *Private International Law* (9th Edn.), pp. 452–459.

[2] Legitimacy Act 1976, s. 10 (1).

[3] S. 10 (2).

[4] Legitimacy Act 1926, s. 3 (1).

[5] *Re Hurll, Angelini* v. *Dick*, [1952] Ch. 722.

[6] S. 15.

[7] S. 15 (4).

[8] S. 5 (3).

[9] S. 5 (4).

Z, born in 1974. Z's mother dies in 1975, whereupon A marries B. Z will take. Had Z not been born, X would have taken.[1] As with adoption, this provision does not affect any reference to the age of a child nor entitlement under Part II of the Family Law Reform Act 1969.[2] **[437]**

No longer is an illegitimate person or a person adopted by one of his parents, who dies before his parents marry and who would otherwise have been legitimated, prevented from becoming a legitimated person so as to take an interest by, or in succession to his spouse, children and remoter issue. He is treated as if he had been legitimated by virtue of the marriage.[3] **[438]**

Special rules apply to the legitimation of adopted children.[4] Paragraph 3 of Schedule 1 to the Children Act which prevents an adopted child from being illegitimate does not prevent an adopted child being legitimated if either natural parent is the sole adopter. Where such a child is legitimated the child will still be treated in law as if he were the child of the other natural parent.[5] If the adoption order is revoked in consequence of the legitimation,[6] the child's rights under any instrument made before the date of legitimation are unaffected.[7] **[439]**

F. APPEALS AND TRANSFER OF CASES

Section 101 of the 1975 Act lays down three general rules concerning appeals and transfer of cases heard under the Act.[8]

(1) Where an application has been made under this Act to a county court, the High Court has power, at the instance of any party to the application, to order that the application be removed to the High Court and there proceeded with on such terms as to costs as it thinks proper.[9] This power, may, for example, be useful in adoption where an order under section 25 of the Act[10] is sought and complicated problems may arise over the foreign *lex domicilii*, but transfers under this provision are not likely to be frequent.[11]

(2) Where on an application to a magistrates' court under the Act the court makes or refuses to make an order, appeal lies to the High Court.

(3) Where an application is made to a magistrates' court under the Act but the court considers that the matter would more conveniently be dealt with by the High Court, the magistrates' court must refuse to make an order. In that case no appeal lies to the High Court. It is very doubtful whether this rule will often be invoked. Rarely are corresponding provisions in other enactments relied on.[12] **[440]**

---

[1] Further examples of phrases in wills on which the rule can operate are set out in s. 5 (5).
[2] S. 6 (1).
[3] S. 5 (6).
[4] S. 4.
[5] S. 4 (2) (*a*).
[6] Adoption Act 1976, s. 52 (1).
[7] S. 4 (2) (*b*).
[8] These are embodied in the Adoption Act 1976, s. 63 (1)–(3), so far as concerns adoption proceedings; for exceptions see sub-s. (4).
[9] Cf. Guardianship of Minors Act 1971, s. 16 (1).
[10] Adoption Act 1976, s. 55.
[11] Cf. (3), below.
[12] See Guardianship of Minors Act 1971, s. 16 (4); Matrimonial Proceedings (Magistrates' Courts) Act 1960, s. 5.

CHAPTER 14

THE ADOPTION ACT 1976

The provisions relating to the law of adoption which are unaffected by the new Act[1] have been consolidated, along with those provisions of the 1975 Act relating to adoption, in the Adoption Act 1976,[2] which also repeals the Adoption Acts 1960, 1964, and 1968.[3] The provisions which are unaffected by the 1975 Act and which therefore remain operative until the 1976 Act is brought into force are largely contained in the Adoption Act 1958. Brief note is made of them in this chapter so that they may be read in conjunction with the adoption provisions in Part I of the 1975 Act. These provisions mainly govern nationality, registration amendment and revocation of adoption orders, regulation of adoption agencies and inspection of books, return of children, protected children, prohibition of payments and restrictions upon advertisements.[4] [**441**]

NATIONALITY

The acquisition and determination of nationality have already been considered.[5] [**442**]

REGISTRATION, AMENDMENT AND REVOCATION OF ADOPTION ORDERS

Every adoption must be registered by the Registrar General in the Adopted Children Register in accordance with the particulars given by the adoption order.[6] The court which made the adoption order may, on the application of the adopter or the adopted person, amend it by correcting any error in the particulars;[7] for example, the date of the child's birth.[8] It may also substitute

---

1 See the Adoption Acts 1958, 1960, 1964 and 1968.

2 Not yet in force. See Adoption Act 1976, s. 74 (2). The Act does not extend to Scotland except sections 22, 23, 51, 73 (2), 74 and Sch. 3, Part II; see s. 74 (3). Neither does it extend to Northern Ireland except section 40 and Sch. 4 in so far as that Schedule repeals s. 19 of the 1958 Act, s. 1 (3) of the 1964 Act and ss. 9 (5) and 14 of the 1968 Act; see s. 74 (4).

3 For the Adoption Act 1960, see Adoption Act 1976, s. 52 (2) and (4); for the Adoption Act 1964, see Adoption Act 1976, ss. 59 (3) and 60 and Sch. 1, para. 2 (2)–(5); for the Adoption Act 1968, see Adoption Act 1976, ss. 40 (3) and Children Act 1975, Sch. 3, para. 63, 52 (3), 53, 54, 59 (1), 67 (1), (2), (4) and (5), 70, 71, 72 (1), (2) and (4) and Sch. 1, paras. 1 (2), 3, 4 (5) and 5 (2).

4 See also Adoption Act 1976, s. 66 (1), (2), (5) and (6) (replacing Adoption Act 1958, s. 9 (3), (4)); s. 67 (1), (2), (3), (5) and (6) (replacing Adoption Act 1958, s. 56 (1), 34A (7), 32 (4) and 56 (2)); s. 68 (replacing Adoption Act 1958, s. 54 (1)); s. 69 (replacing Adoption Act 1958, s. 55); s. 72 (1), (3) and (4) (replacing Adoption Act 1958, s. 57 (1), (2) and (4)); Sch. 2, paras. 4, 5 (4) and (8) (replacing Adoption Act 1958, Sch. 5, paras. 10, 7 and 5).

5 See paras. [**162**]–[**163**] and [**174**], *ante*.

6 Adoption Act 1958, ss. 20 and 21, as amended by Children Act 1975, Sch. 3, para. 24; see Adoption Act 1976, s. 50 and Sch. 1, para. 1 (1), (3), (4) and (5). See Bevan, *Law Relating to Children*, p. 363 *et seq*.

7 Adoption Act 1958, s. 24; see Adoption Act 1976, Sch. 1, paras. 2 (1), 4 (1)–(4) and (6), 5 (2) and (3).

8 *R.* v. *Chelsea Juvenile Court Justices* (*Re an infant*), [1955] 1 All E.R. 38; [1955] 1 W.L.R. 52.

or add any new name which was given to the adopted person within the first year of the order. There is also power to revoke the order if it was made in favour of the mother or father alone and the child is subsequently legitimated by the marriage of his parents.[1] [**443**]

REGULATION OF ADOPTION AGENCIES AND INSPECTION OF BOOKS

Section 32 of the 1958 Act[2] has been amended by the Children Act 1975[3] to enable the Secretary of State to make regulations prohibiting unincorporated bodies applying for approval as adoption societies under section 4 of the 1975 Act.[4] The section also empowers him to make regulations relating to an approved adoption society's exercise of its functions[5] and regulations with regard to the functions of a local authority as an adoption agency.[6] [**444**]

So that a local authority may check that an approved adoption society is performing its function of making arrangements for the adoption of children, the authority has a general power to call for the production of the society's books for inspection on the giving of written notice at any time.[7] Failure to comply is an offence.[8] [**445**]

RETURN OF CHILDREN

While an application for an adoption order is pending where the child was placed by an adoption agency and the applicant later decides either before or after making his application that he does not wish to go on with it, he may give written notice to the agency that he does not intend to retain custody of the child.[9] If so he must return the child to the agency within seven days.[10] The same duty to return arises if the application is refused[11] or if the period specified

---

[1] Adoption Act 1976, s. 52 (1) and (4) and Sch. 1, para. 6, replacing Adoption Act 1958, s. 26, as amended by Children Act 1975, Sch. 3, para. 26. On revocation generally see Bevan, *op. cit.*, p. 364. For the provisions relating to re-registration of birth on legitimation see Adoption Act 1976, Sch. 1, para. 5 (1), replacing Adoption Act 1958, s. 27.

[2] Adoption Act 1976, s. 9.

[3] Sch. 3, para. 27 (*a*); see paras. [**20**] and [**30**], *ante*.

[4] Adoption Act 1976, s. 3; see paras. [**19**]–[**31**], *ante*.

[5] Adoption Act 1976, s. 9 (2), replacing Adoption Act 1958, s. 32 (1A), as inserted by Children Act 1975, Sch. 3, para. 27 (*a*). Contravention or failure to comply with regulations under the subsection is an offence. The penalty is a fine not exceeding £400; s. 9 (4) replacing Adoption Act 1958, s. 32 (2), as amended by Children Act 1975, Sch. 3, para. 27 (*b*).

[6] Adoption Act 1976, s. 9 (3), replacing Adoption Act 1958, s. 32 (3).

[7] Adoption Act 1976, s. 10 (1), replacing Adoption Act 1958, s. 33 (1), as amended by Children Act 1975, Sch. 3, para. 28 (*a*). Any such notice may require the information to be verified in a manner specified; s. 10 (2), replacing Adoption Act 1958, s. 33 (2), as amended by Children Act 1975, Sch. 3, para. 28 (*b*).

[8] The penalty is imprisonment for up to 3 months and/or a fine not exceeding £50; s. 10 (3), replacing Adoption Act 1958, s. 33 (3).

[9] I.e., presumably actual custody. The Adoption Act 1976, s. 30 (1) (*a*), which refers to custody, replaces Adoption Act 1958, s. 35 (1) (*a*), as amended by Children Act 1975, Sch. 3, para. 21 (3) and (4), the latter referring to "actual custody".

[10] Adoption Act 1976, s. 30 (3); (Adoption Act 1958, s. 35 (3)). Delivery to, and receipt by, a suitable person nominated by the adoption agency is sufficient compliance; s. 30 (5); (s. 35 (5)).

[11] Note the court's power on refusal to extend the period up to a maximum of 6 weeks; Adoption Act 1976, s. 30 (6); (Adoption Act 1958, s. 35 (5A), as inserted by Children Act 1975, s. 31). See para. [**145**], *ante*.

in an interim order[1] expires without an adoption order having been made[2] or if the agency gives the applicant written notice that it does not intend to allow him to continue to have custody[3] of the child.[4] Failure to return the child is an offence punishable by up to three months' imprisonment or up to £400 fine or both and the convicting court may order the child to be returned to the parent or guardian or the agency.[5] [**446**]

These rules also apply where the child has not been placed by an adoption agency but was for the time being in the care of a local authority when notice of intention to adopt was given under section 18 (1) of the Children Act 1975.[6] In this kind of case, however, if the application is refused by the court or withdrawn the child need not be returned to the authority unless the authority so require.[7] Further, until the application has been made and disposed of the local authority's right to the return of the child is limited to that in section 30 of the 1976 Act.[8] During the period of actual custody contributions by the father and mother towards maintenance are not payable,[9] but this rule ceases to operate if after twelve weeks from the date of giving notice no application has been made or, if it has, once it has been refused or withdrawn.[10] [**447**]

PROTECTED CHILDREN

A protected child is one in respect of whom a person has given notice to the local authority[11] that he intends to apply for an adoption order. The child is a protected child while he has his home with the prospective applicant. Protection is not, as previously, limited to children under the upper school age limit who have been placed with someone other than the parent, guardian or relative.[12] A protected child is subject to the supervision of the local authority during the period of "protection" which continues until (a) the appointment of a guardian for him under the Guardianship of Minors Act 1971; (b) the notification to the local authority that the application for an adoption order has been withdrawn; (c) the making of an adoption order, an order under section 17 of the Children

---

[1] For interim orders generally see paras. [**149**]–[**151**], *ante*.

[2] Adoption Act 1976, s. 30 (4); (Adoption Act 1958, s. 35 (4)).

[3] I.e., presumably actual custody see also s. 30 (1) (*a*), p. 198, n. 9, *ante*.

[4] Adoption Act 1976, s. 30 (1) (*b*); (Adoption Act 1958, s. 35 (1) (*b*), as amended by Children Act 1975, Sch. 3, para. 21 (3) and (4)).

If application for an adoption order has been made leave of the court seised of the application, must be obtained; Adoption Act 1976, s. 30 (2); (Adoption Act 1958, s. 35 (2)).

[5] Adoption Act 1976, s. 30 (7); (Adoption Act 1958, s. 35 (6), as amended by Children Act 1975, Sch. 3, para. 29).

[6] Adoption Act 1976, s. 22 (1).

[7] Adoption Act 1976, s. 31 (1), replacing Adoption Act 1958, s. 36 (1), as amended by Children Act 1975, Sch. 3, para. 30 (*a*). If the notice is given to an authority other than that which has the temporary care of the child that other must be told of the notice within 7 days; s. 22 (4), replacing Adoption Act 1958, s. 36 (3), as amended by Children Act 1975, Sch. 3, para. 30 (*b*).

[8] Adoption Act 1976, s. 31 (2), replacing Adoption Act 1958, s. 36 (2).

[9] Under s. 86 of the Children and Young Persons Act 1933.

[10] Adoption Act 1976, s. 31 (3), replacing Adoption Act 1958, s. 36 (2).

[11] See Children Act 1975, s. 18, para. [**114**], *ante*; (Adoption Act 1976, s. 22).

[12] See Bevan, *op. cit.*, p. 332. The Adoption Act 1958, s. 37 (1), as amended by Children Act 1975, Sch. 3, para. 31; see now Adoption Act 1976, s. 32 (1). A protected child under s. 37 of the Adoption Act 1958 is deemed to be a protected child, *ibid.* s. 32 (2).

Act 1975,[1] a custodianship order,[2] an order under section 42, 43 or 44 of the Matrimonial Causes Act 1973; or (d) he attains 18, whichever first occurs.[3] [**448**]

The local authority must ensure that the child is visited from time to time by its officers who must be satisfied about the child's well-being and must give advice about his care and maintenance. Such officers are also authorised to inspect any premises in the authority's area where the child is being kept.[4] [**449**]

A local authority may complain to a juvenile court that the child is being kept, or is about to be received by, a person who is unfit to have his care or in premises or an environment detrimental to him.[5] The court[6] may order the child to be removed to a place of safety until he can be restored to a parent, relative or guardian or until other arrangements can be made, including the possibility of the local authority receiving him into their care under s. 1 of the Children Act 1948, even if he appears to be over 17.[7] In a case of imminent danger to the health or well-being of the child a justice of the peace may make an order for removal on the application of an officer of the local authority. Where a child is removed under this section the local authority shall, if practicable, inform the child's parent or guardian.[8] The person who maintains the protected child is deemed to have no interest in the child's life for the purposes of the Life Assurance Act 1774.[9] [**450**]

PROHIBITION ON PAYMENTS

The prohibitions contained in section 50 of the Adoption Act 1958 as amen-

---

[1] Adoption Act 1976, s. 26.

[2] See Chap. 10, *ante*.

[3] Adoption Act 1958, s. 37 (4), as amended by Children Act 1975, Sch. 3, para. 31 (*b*); see now Adoption Act 1976 ,s. 32 (4).

Even if notice of intended adoption is given a child does not come within this term while (a) he is in the care of any person in any school, home or institution as is mentioned in Children Act 1958, s. 2 (3) or (5); (b) he is resident in a residential home for the mentally disordered as defined in the Mental Health Act 1959, s. 19; (c) he is liable to be detained or subject to guardianship under the Mental Health Act 1959 (s. 32 (3), replacing Adoption Act 1958, s. 37 (3)). In the event of the child's death the prospective adopter must notify the local authority within forty-eight hours (s. 35 (2), replacing Adoption Act 1958, s. 40 (5)).

[4] Adoption Act 1958, ss. 38 and 39; see now Adoption Act 1976, s. 33. Refusal to allow the visiting of a protected child is an offence punishable by imprisonment for up to three months and/or a fine of up to £400 (s. 36 (1) (*b*) and (2), replacing Adoption Act 1958, s. 44 (1) (*b*) and (2)). It also justifies the issue of a warrant to search for and remove the child (s. 37 (1), replacing Adoption Act 1958, s. 45). If the prospective adopter moves he must notify the local authority at least two weeks in advance, or in the case of an emergency within one week of the change. The notified authority will in turn notify any new authority into whose area he has moved giving details of the child's birth, name and sex and the name and address of any parent or guardian (s. 35 (1), replacing Adoption Act 1958 s. 40 (4) and (6), as amended by Children Act 1975, Sch. 3, para. 32). Failure to comply is an offence punishable by imprisonment for up to three months and/or a fine of up to £400 (s. 36 (1) (*a*) and (2), replacing Adoption Act 1958, s. 44 (1) (*a*) and (2)).

[5] Adoption Act 1958, s. 43 (1); see now Adoption Act 1976, s. 34 (1).

[6] The usual restrictions on the sittings of juvenile courts do not apply here and proceedings are held in open court. Appeal lies to the Crown Court. See s. 37 (3) and (4); (replacing Adoption Act 1958, ss. 47 and 48).

[7] S. 34 (3); (replacing Adoption Act 1958, s. 43 (3)). Failure to comply with an order is an offence (s. 36 (1) (*c*) and (2), replacing Adoption Act 1958, s. 44 (1) (*d*) and (2)). An order may be executed by any person authorised to visit protected children or by any constable (s. 34 (2), replacing Adoption Act 1958, s. 43 (2)).

[8] Adoption Act 1976, s. 34 (4); (replacing Adoption Act 1958, s. 43 (4)).

[9] Adoption Act 1976, s. 37 (2); (replacing Adoption Act 1958, s. 46).

ded[1] have already been considered.[2] Section 57 of the 1976 Act will replace section 50 of the 1958 Act. [**451**]

Adoption agencies have increasingly been prepared to make certain payments to cover legal and medical expenses connected with applications for an adoption order. Such expenses can be substantial and therefore beyond the resources of the prospective adopters. Also, in order to find prospective adopters for children with special needs, agencies frequently use one another's resources as well as the services of specialist agencies, and pay inter-agency fees. Similarly, many agencies belong to the Adoption Resource Exchange to which they pay linking fees for its services.[3] [**452**]

The doubts about the legality of such payments have been removed by the Criminal Law Act 1977 which amends the Adoption Acts 1958 and 1976.[4] The new provisions ensure the legality of three types of payment made by adoption agencies:

(1) payment made to adoptive parents in respect of legal or medical expenses incurred by them in connection with the adoption;
(2) payment made to another adoption agency which has found an adoptive home for a child whose placement was sought by the paying agency;
(3) payment made to an approved voluntary organisation by an adoption agency which was seeking an adoptive home for a child, as a fee for the organisation's services in putting that adoption agency into contact with another adoption agency with a view to arrangements being made for the child's adoption. [**453**]

ADVERTISING

It is an offence[5] to cause to be published or knowingly publish any advertisement that the parent or guardian wishes to have a child adopted or that a person wishes to adopt a child or that anyone other than an adoption agency is willing to make arrangements for the adoption of a child.[6] [**454**]

---

[1] By the Children Act 1975, Sch. 3, paras. 21 (2), 21 (4) and 34 (*a*).
[2] See paras. [**119**]-[**123**], *ante*. See also Home Office Circular No. 141/1977.
[3] See Local Authority Circular (77) 18.
[4] By inserting a new sub-s. (3A) in s. 50 of the 1958 Act (Adoption Act 1976, s. 57). The 1977 Act also corrects a printing error in section 28 (8) of the Adoption Act 1976. See Criminal Law Act 1977, Sch. 12. These provisions have been operative since 8th September 1977.
[5] The penalty is a fine not exceeding £400; Adoption Act 1976, s. 58 (2), replacing Adoption Act 1958, s. 51 (2), as amended by Children Act 1975, Sch. 3, para. 35.
[6] Adoption Act 1976, s. 58 (1), replacing Adoption Act 1958, s. 51 (1).

THE CHILDREN ACT 1975

(1975 c. 72)

ARRANGEMENT OF SECTIONS

PART I

ADOPTION

PART II

CUSTODY

PART V

MISCELLANEOUS AND SUPPLEMENTAL

SCHEDULES

An Act to make further provision for children [12th November 1975]

PART I

ADOPTION

PROSPECTIVE REPEAL

This Part (ss. 1–32) is repealed with savings by the Adoption Act 1976, s. 73 and Sch. 4, A.L.S. Vol. 244, as from a day to be appointed, and replaced as noted in the destination table, para. [**589**], *post*.

The Adoption Services

1. Establishment of Adoption Services

(1) It is the duty of every local authority to establish and maintain within their area a service designed to meet the needs, in relation to adoption, of—

(*a*) children who have been or may be adopted,
(*b*) parents and guardians of such children, and
(*c*) persons who have adopted or may adopt a child,

and for that purpose to provide the requisite facilities, or secure that they are provided by approved adoption societies.

(2) The facilities to be provided as part of the service maintained under subsection (1) include—

(*a*) temporary board and lodging where needed by pregnant women, mothers or children;
(*b*) arrangements for assessing children and prospective adopters, and placing children for adoption;
(*c*) counselling for persons with problems relating to adoption.

(3) The facilities of the service maintained under subsection (1) shall be provided in conjunction with the local authority's other social services and with approved adoption societies in their area, so that help may be given in a co-ordinated manner without duplication, omission or avoidable delay.

(4) The services maintained under subsection (1) by local authorities in England and Wales may be collectively referred to as "the Adoption Service" and those maintained by local authorities in Scotland, as "the Scottish Adoption Service", and a local authority or approved adoption society may be referred to as an adoption agency. [**455**]

EFFECT OF SECTION

For the effect of this section see paras. [**13**]–[**17**], *ante*.

COMMENCEMENT

At the time of going to press this section was not yet in force; see s. 108 (2), para. [**541**], *post*.

2. Local authorities' social services

The social services referred to in section 1 (3) are the functions of a local authority which stand referred to the authority's social services committee or, in Scotland, social work committee, including, in particular but without prejudice to the generality of the foregoing, a local authority's functions relating to—

(*a*) the promotion of the welfare of children by diminishing the need to receive children into care or keep them in care, including (in exceptional circumstances) the giving of assistance in cash;
(*b*) the welfare of children in the care of a local authority;
(*c*) the welfare of children who are foster children within the meaning of the Children Act 1958;
(*d*) children who are subject to supervision orders made in matrimonial proceedings;
(*e*) the provision of residential accommodation for expectant mothers and young children and of day-care facilities;
(*f*) the regulation and inspection of nurseries and child minders;
(*g*) care and other treatment of children through court proceedings and children's hearings. **[456]**

EFFECT OF SECTION
For the effect of this section see para. [**18**], *ante*.

COMMENCEMENT
At the time of going to press this section was not yet in force; see s. 108 (2), para. [**541**], *post*.

3. Duty to promote welfare of child

In reaching any decision relating to the adoption of a child, a court or adoption agency shall have regard to all the circumstances, first consideration being given to the need to safeguard and promote the welfare of the child throughout his childhood; and shall so far as practicable ascertain the wishes and feelings of the child regarding the decision and give due consideration to them, having regard to his age and understanding. **[457]**

EFFECT OF SECTION
For the effect of this section see paras. [**32**]–[**45**], *ante*.

COMMENCEMENT
This section came into force on 1st January 1976; see s. 108 (4), para. [**541**], *post*.

4. Approval of adoption societies

(1) A body desiring to act as an adoption society or, if it is already an adoption society, desiring to continue to act as such in England and Wales or in Scotland may, in the manner specified by regulations made by the Secretary of State, apply to the Secretary of State for his approval to its doing so.

(2) On an application under subsection (1), the Secretary of State shall take into account the matters relating to the applicant specified in subsections (3) to (5) and any other relevant considerations, and if, but only if, he is satisfied that the applicant is likely to make, or, if the applicant is an approved adoption society, is making, an effective contribution to the Adoption Service or, as the case may be, to the Scottish Adoption Service he shall by notice to the applicant give his approval, which shall be operative from a date specified in the notice or, in the case of a renewal of approval, from the date of the notice.

(3) In considering the application, the Secretary of State shall have regard, in relation to the period for which approval is sought, to the following—

(*a*) the applicant's adoption programme, including, in particular, its ability to make provision for children who are free for adoption,

(*b*) the number and qualifications of its staff,

(*c*) its financial resources, and

(*d*) the organisation and control of its operations.

(4) Where it appears to the Secretary of State that the applicant is likely to operate extensively within the area of a particular local authority he shall ask the authority whether they support the application, and shall take account of any views about it put to him by the authority.

(5) Where the applicant is already an approved adoption society or, whether before or after the passing of this Act, previously acted as an adoption society, the Secretary of State, in considering the application, shall also have regard to the record and reputation of the applicant in the adoption field, and the areas within which and the scale on which it is currently operating or has operated in the past.

(6) If after considering the application the Secretary of State is not satisfied that the applicant is likely to make or, as the case may be, is making an effective contribution to the Adoption Service or, as the case may be, to the Scottish Adoption Service, the Secretary of State shall, subject to section 6 (1) and (2), by notice inform the applicant that his application is refused.

(7) If not withdrawn earlier under section 5, approval given under this section shall last for a period of three years from the date on which it becomes operative, and shall then expire or, in the case of an approved adoption society whose further application for approval is pending at that time, shall expire on the date that application is granted, or, as the case may be, refused. [**458**]

EFFECT OF SECTION

For the effect of this section see paras. [**19**]–[**23**], *ante*.

COMMENCEMENT

At the time of going to press this section was not yet in force; see s. 108 (2), para. [**541**], *post*.

5. Withdrawal of approval

(1) If, while approval of a body under section 4 is operative, it appears to the Secretary of State that the body is not making an effective contribution to the Adoption Service or, as the case may be, to the Scottish Adoption Service, he shall subject to section 6 (3) and (4) by notice to the body withdraw the approval from a date specified in the notice.

(2) If an approved adoption society fails to provide the Secretary of State with information required by him for the purpose of carrying out his functions under subsection (1), or fails to verify such information in the manner required by him, he may by notice to the society withdraw the approval from a date specified in the notice.

(3) Where approval is withdrawn under subsection (1) or (2) or expires the Secretary of State may direct the body concerned to make such arrangements as to children who are in its care and other transitional matters as seem to him expedient. [**459**]

EFFECT OF SECTION

For the effect of this section see paras. [**23**]–[**24**], *ante*.

COMMENCEMENT

At the time of going to press this section was not yet in force; see s. 108 (2), para. [**541**], *post*.

6. Procedure on refusal to approve, or withdrawal of approval from, societies

(1) Before notifying a body which has applied for approval that the application is refused in accordance with section 4 (6) the Secretary of State shall serve on the applicant a notice—

(*a*) setting out the reasons why he proposes to refuse the application;
(*b*) informing the applicant that he may make representations in writing to the Secretary of State within 28 days of the date of service of the notice.

(2) If any representations are made by the applicant in accordance with subsection (1), the Secretary of State shall give further consideration to the application taking into account those representations.

(3) The Secretary of State shall, before withdrawing approval of an adoption society in accordance with section 5 (1), serve on the society a notice—

(*a*) setting out the reasons why he proposes to withdraw the approval; and
(*b*) informing the society that they may make representations in writing to the Secretary of State within 28 days of the date of service of the notice.

(4) If any representations are made by the society in accordance with subsection (3), the Secretary of State shall give further consideration to the withdrawal of approval under section 5 (1) taking into account those representations.

(5) This section does not apply where the Secretary of State, after having considered any representations made by the applicant in accordance with this section, proposes to refuse approval or, as the case may be, to withdraw approval for reasons which have already been communicated to the applicant in a notice under this section. [**460**]

EFFECT OF SECTION

For the effect of this section see paras. [**22**]–[**23**], *ante*.

COMMENCEMENT

At the time of going to press this section was not yet in force; see s. 108 (2), para. [**541**], *post*.

7. Inactive or defunct adoption societies

(1) If it appears to the Secretary of State that an approved adoption society, or one in relation to which approval has been withdrawn under section 5 or has expired, is inactive or defunct he may, in relation to any child who is or was in the care of the society, direct what appears to him to be the appropriate local authority to take any such action as might have been taken by the society or by the society jointly with the authority; and if apart from this section the authority would not be entitled to take that action, or would not be entitled to take it without joining the society in the action, it shall be entitled to do so.

(2) Before giving a direction under subsection (1) the Secretary of State shall, if practicable, consult both the society and the authority. [**461**]

EFFECT OF SECTION

For the effect of this section see paras. [**25**]–[**29**], *ante*.

COMMENCEMENT

At the time of going to press this section was not yet in force; see s. 108 (2), para. [**541**], *post*.

Adoption orders

8. Adoption orders

(1) An adoption order is an order vesting the parental rights and duties relating to a child in the adopters, made on their application by an authorised court.

(2) The order does not affect the parental rights and duties so far as they relate to any period before the making of the order.

(3) The making of the order operates to extinguish—

(*a*) any parental right or duty relating to the child which—

(i) is vested in a person (not being one of the adopters) who was the parent or guardian of the child immediately before the making of the order, or

(ii) is vested in any other person by virtue of the order of any court; and

(*b*) any duty arising by virtue of an agreement or the order of a court to make payments, so far as the payments are in respect of the child's maintenance for any period after the making of the order or any other matter comprised in the parental duties and relating to such a period.

(4) Subsection (3) (*b*) does not apply to a duty arising by virtue of an agreement—

(*a*) which constitutes a trust, or

(*b*) which expressly provides that the duty is not to be extinguished by the making of an adoption order.

(5) An adoption order may not be made in relation to a child who is or has been married.

(6) (*Applies to Scotland.*)

(7) An adoption order may contain such terms and conditions as the court thinks fit.

(8) An adoption order may be made notwithstanding that the child is already subject to any British or foreign adoption order.

(9) Schedule 1 contains for England and Wales further provisions about the effect of adoption . . .

(10) (*Applies to Scotland.*) [**462**]

EFFECT OF SECTION

For the effect of this section see paras. [**106**] and [**172**]–[**193**], *ante*.

COMMENCEMENT

Sub-ss. (9) and (10) came into force on 1st January 1976; see s. 108 (4), para. [**541**], *post*. Sub-ss. (1)–(5) and (7)–(8) were brought into force on 26th November 1976 by the Children Act 1975 (Commencement No. 1) Order 1976, S.I. 1976 No. 1744, made under s. 108 (2), para. [**541**], *post*.

AMENDMENT

The words omitted in sub-s. (9) were repealed by the Legitimacy Act 1976, s. 11 (2) and Sch. 2, A.L.S. Vol. 244.

9. Child to live with adopters before order made

(1) Where—

(*a*) the applicant, or one of the applicants, is a parent, step-parent or relative of the child, or

(*b*) the child was placed with the applicants by an adoption agency or in pursuance of an order of the High Court,

an adoption order shall not be made unless the child is at least 19 weeks old and at all times during the preceding 13 weeks had his home with the applicants or one of them.

(2) Where subsection (1) does not apply, an adoption order shall not be made unless the child is at least twelve months old and at all times during the preceding twelve months had his home with the applicants or one of them.

(3) An adoption order shall not be made unless the court is satisfied that sufficient opportunities to see the child with the applicant or, in the case of an application by a married couple, both applicants together in the home environment have been afforded—

(*a*) where the child was placed with the applicant by an adoption agency, to that agency, or

(*b*) in any other case, to the local authority within whose area the home is.

[**463**]

EFFECT OF SECTION

For the effect of this section see paras. [**107**]–[**113**], *ante*.

COMMENCEMENT

At the time of going to press this section was not yet in force; see s. 108 (2), para. [**541**], *post*.

10. Adoption by married couple

(1) Subject to sections 37 (1) and 53 (1) an adoption order may be made on the application of a married couple where each has attained the age of 21 but an adoption order shall not otherwise be made on the application of more than one person.

(2) An adoption order shall not be made on the application of a married couple unless—

(*a*) at least one of them is domiciled in a part of the United Kingdom, or in the Channel Islands or the Isle of Man, or

(*b*) the application is for a Convention adoption order and section 24 is complied with.

(3) Where the application is made to a court in England or Wales and the married couple consist of a parent and step-parent of the child, the court shall dismiss the application if it considers the matter would be better dealt with under section 42 (orders for custody etc.) of the Matrimonial Causes Act 1973.

[**464**]

EFFECT OF SECTION

For the effect of this section see paras. [**89**]–[**105**], *ante*.

COMMENCEMENT

This section was brought into force on 26th November 1976 by the Children Act 1975 (Commencement No. 1) Order 1976, S.I. 1976 No. 1744, made under s. 108 (2), para. [**541**], *post*.

11. Adoption by one person

(1) Subject to sections 37 (1) and 53 (1) an adoption order may be made on the application of one person where he has attained the age of 21 and—

(*a*) is not married, or

(*b*) is married and the court is satisfied that—

(i) his spouse cannot be found, or

(ii) the spouses have separated and are living apart, and the separation is likely to be permanent, or

(iii) his spouse is by reason of ill health, whether physical or mental, incapable of making an application for an adoption order.

(2) An adoption order shall not be made on the application of one person unless—

(*a*) he is domiciled in a part of the United Kingdom, or in the Channel Islands or the Isle of Man, or

(*b*) the application is for a Convention adoption order and section 24 is complied with.

(3) An adoption order shall not be made on the application of the mother or father of the child alone unless the court is satisfied that—

(*a*) the other natural parent is dead or cannot be found, or

(*b*) there is some other reason justifying the exclusion of the other natural parent,

and where such an order is made the reason justifying the exclusion of the other natural parent shall be recorded by the court.

(4) Where the application is made to a court in England or Wales and the applicant is a step-parent of the child, the court shall dismiss the application if it considers the matter would be better dealt with under section 42 (orders for custody etc.) of the Matrimonial Causes Act 1973. **[465]**

EFFECT OF SECTION

For the effect of this section see paras. [**58**] and [**89**]–[**105**], *ante*.

COMMENCEMENT

This section was brought into force on 26th November 1976 by the Children Act 1975 (Commencement No. 1) Order 1976, S.I. 1976 No. 1744, made under s. 108 (2), para. [**541**], *post*.

12. Parental agreement

(1) An adoption order shall not be made unless—

(*a*) the child is free for adoption; or

(*b*) in the case of each parent or guardian of the child the court is satisfied that—

(i) he freely, and with full understanding of what is involved, agrees unconditionally to the making of the adoption order (whether or not he knows the identity of the applicants), or

(ii) his agreement to the making of the adoption order should be dispensed with on a ground specified in subsection (2).

(2) The grounds mentioned in subsection (1) (*b*) (ii) are that the parent or guardian—

(*a*) cannot be found or is incapable of giving agreement;

(*b*) is withholding his agreement unreasonably;

(*c*) has persistently failed without reasonable cause to discharge the parental duties in relation to the child;
(*d*) has abandoned or neglected the child;
(*e*) has persistently ill-treated the child;
(*f*) has seriously ill-treated the child (subject to subsection (5)).

(3) Subsection (1) does not apply in any case where the child is not a United Kingdom national and the application for the adoption order is for a Convention adoption order.

(4) Agreement is ineffective for the purposes of subsection (1) (*b*) (i) if given by the mother less than six weeks after the child's birth.

(5) Subsection (2) (*f*) does not apply unless (because of the ill-treatment or for other reasons) the rehabilitation of the child within the household of the parent or guardian is unlikely.

(6) A child is free for adoption if he is the subject of an order under section 14 and the order has not been revoked under section 16. [**466**]

EFFECT OF SECTION
For the effect of this section see paras. [**46**]–[**57**], *ante*.

COMMENCEMENT
This section was brought into force on 26th November 1976 by the Children Act 1975 (Commencement No. 1) Order 1976, S.I. 1976 No. 1744, made under s. 108 (2), para. [**541**], *post*.

13. Religious upbringing of adopted child

An adoption agency shall in placing a child for adoption have regard (so far as is practicable) to any wishes of the child's parents and guardians as to the religious upbringing of the child. [**467**]

EFFECT OF SECTION
For the effect of this section see para. [**53**], *ante*.

COMMENCEMENT
This section came into force on 1st January 1976; see s. 108 (4), para. [**541**], *post*.

14. Freeing child for adoption

(1) Where, on an application by an adoption agency, an authorised court is satisfied in the case of each parent or guardian of the child that—
(*a*) he freely, and with full understanding of what is involved, agrees generally and unconditionally to the making of an adoption order, or
(*b*) his agreement to the making of an adoption order should be dispensed with on a ground specified in section 12 (2),
the court shall, subject to subsection (5), make an order declaring the child free for adoption.

(2) No application shall be made under subsection (1) unless—
(*a*) it is made with the consent of a parent or guardian of the child, or
(*b*) the adoption agency is applying for dispensation under subsection (1) (*b*) of the agreement of each parent or guardian of the child, and the child is in the care of the adoption agency.

(3) No agreement required under subsection (1) (*a*) shall be dispensed with under subsection (1) (*b*) unless the child is already placed for adoption or the court is satisfied that it is likely that the child will be placed for adoption.

(4) An agreement by the mother of the child is ineffective for the purposes of this section if given less than six weeks after the child's birth.

(5) (*Applies to Scotland.*)

(6) On the making of an order under this section, the parental rights and duties relating to the child vest in the adoption agency, and subsections (2) and (3) of section 8 apply as if the order were an adoption order and the agency were the adopters.

(7) Before making an order under this section the court shall satisfy itself that each parent or guardian who can be found has been given an opportunity of making, if he so wishes, a declaration that he prefers not to be involved in future questions concerning the adoption of the child; and any such declaration shall be recorded by the court.

(8) Before making an order under this section in the case of an illegitimate child whose father is not its guardian, the court shall satisfy itself in relation to any person claiming to be the father that either—

(*a*) he has no intention of applying for custody of the child under section 9 of the Guardianship of Minors Act 1971 or under section 2 of the Illegitimate Children (Scotland) Act 1930, or

(*b*) if he did apply for custody under either of those sections the application would be likely to be refused. [**468**]

EFFECT OF SECTION

For the effect of this section see paras. [**60**]–[**72**], *ante*.

COMMENCEMENT

At the time of going to press this section was not yet in force; see s. 108 (2), para. [**541**], *post*.

15. Progress reports to former parent

(1) This section and section 16 apply to any person ("the former parent") who was required to be given an opportunity of making a declaration under section 14 (7) but did not do so.

(2) Within the 14 days following the date twelve months after the making of the order under section 14, the adoption agency in which the parental rights and duties were vested on the making of the order, unless it has previously by notice to the former parent informed him that an adoption order has been made in respect of the child, shall by notice to the former parent inform him—

(*a*) whether an adoption order has been made in respect of the child, and (if not)

(*b*) whether the child has his home with a person with whom he has been placed for adoption.

(3) If at the time when the former parent is given notice under subsection (2) an adoption order has not been made in respect of the child, it is thereafter the duty of the adoption agency to give notice to the former parent of the making of an adoption order (if and when made), and meanwhile to give the former parent notice whenever the child is placed for adoption or ceases to have his home with a person with whom he has been placed for adoption.

(4) If at any time the former parent by notice makes a declaration to the adoption agency that he prefers not to be involved in future questions concerning the adoption of the child—

(*a*) the agency shall secure that the declaration is recorded by the court which made the order under section 14, and

(*b*) the agency is released from the duty of complying further with subsection (3) as respects that former parent. [**469**]

EFFECT OF SECTION

For the effect of this section see paras. [**73**]–[**75**], *ante*.

COMMENCEMENT

At the time of going to press this section was not yet in force; see s. 108 (2), para. [**541**], *post*.

16. Revocation of section 14 order

(1) The former parent, at any time more than twelve months after the making of the order under section 14 when—

(*a*) no adoption order has been made in respect of the child, and

(*b*) the child does not have his home with a person with whom he has been placed for adoption,

may apply to the court which made the order for a further order revoking it on the ground that he wishes to resume the parental rights and duties.

(2) While the application is pending the adoption agency having the parental rights and duties shall not place the child for adoption without the leave of the court.

(3) Where an order freeing a child for adoption is revoked under this section—

(*a*) the parental rights and duties relating to the child are vested in the individual or, as the case may be, the individuals in whom they vested immediately before that order was made;

(*b*) if the parental rights and duties, or any of them, vested in a local authority or voluntary organisation immediately before the order freeing the child for adoption was made, those rights and duties are vested in the individual or, as the case may be, the individuals in whom they vested immediately before they were vested in the authority or organisation; and

(*c*) any duty extinguished by virtue of section 8 (3) (*b*) is forthwith revived,

but the revocation does not affect any right or duty so far as it relates to any period before the date of the revocation.

(4) Subject to subsection (5), if the application is dismissed on the ground that to allow it would contravene the principle embodied in section 3—

(*a*) the former parent who made the application shall not be entitled to make any further application under subsection (1) in respect of the child, and

(*b*) the adoption agency is released from the duty of complying further with section 15 (3) as respects that parent.

(5) Subsection (4) (*a*) shall not apply where the court which dismissed the application gives leave to the former parent to make a further application under subsection (1), but such leave shall not be given unless it appears to the court that because of the change in circumstances or for any other reason it is proper to allow the application to be made. [**470**]

EFFECT OF SECTION

For the effect of this section see paras. [**76**]–[**83**], *ante*.

COMMENCEMENT

At the time of going to press this section was not yet in force; see s. 108 (2), para. [**541**], *post*.

17. Care, etc., of child on refusal of adoption order

(1) Where on an application for an adoption order in relation to a child under the age of 16 the court refuses to make the adoption order then—

(*a*) if it appears to the court that there are exceptional circumstances making it desirable that the child should be under the supervision of an independent person, the court may order that the child shall be under the supervision of a specified local authority or under the supervision of a probation officer;

(*b*) if it appears to the court that there are exceptional circumstances making it impracticable or undesirable for the child to be entrusted to either of the parents or to any other individual, the court may by order commit the child to the care of a specified local authority.

(2) Where the court makes an order under subsection (1) (*b*) the order may require the payment by either parent to the local authority, while it has the care of the child, of such weekly or other periodical sum towards the maintenance of the child as the court thinks reasonable.

(3) Sections 3 and 4 of the Guardianship Act 1973 (which contain supplementary provisions relating to children who are subject to supervision, or in the care of local authorities, by virtue of orders made under section 2 of that Act) apply in relation to an order under this section as they apply in relation to an order under section 2 of that Act.

(4) (*Applies to Scotland.*) [**471**]

EFFECT OF SECTION

For the effect of this section see paras. [**146**]–[**148**], *ante*.

COMMENCEMENT

Sub-ss. (1)–(3) were brought into force on 26th November 1976 by the Children Act 1975 (Commencement No. 1) Order 1976, S.I. 1976 No. 1744, made under s. 108 (2), para. [**541**], *post*.

18. Need to notify local authority of adoption application

(1) An adoption order shall not be made in respect of a child who was not placed with the applicant by an adoption agency unless the applicant has, at least three months before the date of the order, given notice to the local authority within whose area he has his home of his intention to apply for the adoption order.

(2) On receipt of such a notice the local authority shall investigate the matter and submit to the court a report of their investigation.

(3) Under subsection (2), the local authority shall in particular investigate—

(*a*) so far as is practicable the suitability of the applicant, and any other matters relevant to the operation of section 3 in relation to the application, and

(*b*) whether the child was placed with the applicant in contravention of section 29 of the 1958 Act. [**472**]

EFFECT OF SECTION

For the effect of this section see paras. [**114**]–[**115**], *ante.*

COMMENCEMENT

At the time of going to press this section was not yet in force; see s. 108 (2), para. [**541**], *post.*

19. Interim orders

(1) Where on an application for an adoption order the requirements of sections 12 (1) and 18 (1) are complied with the court may postpone the determination of the application and make an order vesting the legal custody of the child in the applicants for a probationary period not exceeding two years upon such terms for the maintenance of the child and otherwise as the court thinks fit.

(2) Where the probationary period specified in an order under subsection (1) is less than two years, the court may by a further order extend the period to a duration not exceeding two years in all. [**473**]

EFFECT OF SECTION

For the effect of this section see paras. [**149**]–[**151**], *ante.*

COMMENCEMENT

At the time of going to press this section was not yet in force; see s. 108 (2), para. [**541**], *post.*

20. Guardian ad litem and reporting officer

(1) For the purpose of any application for an adoption order or an order under section 14, 16 or 25, rules shall provide for the appointment, in such cases as are prescribed,—

(*a*) of a person to act as guardian ad litem of the child upon the hearing of the application, with the duty of safeguarding the interests of the child in the prescribed manner;

(*b*) of a person to act as reporting officer for the purpose of witnessing agreements to adoption and performing such other duties as the rules may prescribe.

(2) A person who is employed—

(*a*) in the case of an application for an adoption order, by the adoption agency by whom the child was placed; or

(*b*) in the case of an application under section 14, by the adoption agency by whom the application was made; or

(*c*) in the case of an application under section 16, by the adoption agency with the parental rights and duties relating to the child,

shall not be appointed to act as guardian ad litem or reporting officer for the purposes of the application but, subject to that, the same person may if the court thinks fit be both guardian ad litem and reporting officer.

(3) Rules may provide for the reporting officer to be appointed before the application is made.

(4) (*Applies to Scotland.*) [**474**]

EFFECT OF SECTION

For the effect of this section see paras. [**124**]–[**130**], *ante.*

COMMENCEMENT

At the time of going to press this section was not yet in force; see s. 108 (2), para. [**541**], *post.*

21. Hearings of applications, etc., in private

(1) Proceedings in the High Court under this Part may be disposed of in chambers.

(2) All proceedings in the county court under this Part shall be heard and determined in camera.

(3) Proceedings in the magistrates' court under this Part shall be domestic proceedings for the purposes of the Magistrates' Courts Act 1952 but section 57 (2) (*d*) of that Act shall not apply in relation to any proceedings under this Part.

(4) (*Applies to Scotland.*) [**475**]

EFFECT OF SECTION

For the effect of this section see para. [**87**], *ante*.

COMMENCEMENT

Sub-ss. (1)–(2) were brought into force on 26th November 1976 by the Children Act 1975 (Commencement No. 1) Order 1976, S.I. 1976 No. 1744, made under s. 108 (2), para. [**541**], *post*. At the time of going to press sub-s. (3) was not yet in force.

22. Making of order

(1) In the case of—

(*a*) an application for an adoption order in relation to a child who is not free for adoption;

(*b*) an application for an order under section 14,

rules shall require every person who can be found and whose agreement or consent to the making of the order is required to be given or dispensed with under this Act to be notified of a date and place where he may be heard on the application and of the fact that, unless he wishes or the court requires, he need not attend.

(2) In the case of an application under section 25 rules shall require every person who can be found and whose agreement to the making of the order would be required if the application were for an adoption order (other than a Convention adoption order) to be notified as aforesaid.

(3) Where an application for an adoption order relates to a child placed by an adoption agency, the agency shall submit to the court a report on the suitability of the applicants and any other matters relevant to the operation of section 3, and shall assist the court in any manner the court may direct.

(4) The court shall not proceed to hear an application for an adoption order in relation to a child where a previous application for a British adoption order made in relation to the child by the same persons was refused by any court unless—

(*a*) in refusing the previous application the court directed that this sub-section should not apply, or

(*b*) it appears to the court that because of a change in circumstances or for any other reason it is proper to proceed with the application.

(5) The court shall not make an adoption order in relation to a child unless it is satisfied that the applicants have not, as respects the child, contravened section 50 of the 1958 Act (prohibition of certain payments in relation to adoption).

(6) (*Applies to Scotland.*) [**476**]

EFFECT OF SECTION

For the effect of this section see paras. [**116**]–[**119**], *ante*.

COMMENCEMENT

Sub-ss. (4)–(5) were brought into force on 26th November 1976 by the Children Act 1975 (Commencement No. 1) Order 1976, S.I. 1976 No. 1744, made under s. 108 (2), para. [**541**], *post*. At the time of going to press sub-ss. (1)–(3) were not yet in force.

23. Transfer of parental rights and duties between adoption agencies

On the joint application of an adoption agency in which the parental rights and duties relating to a child who is in Great Britain are vested under section 14 (6) or this section and any other adoption agency, an authorised court may if it thinks fit by order transfer the parental rights and duties to the latter agency. **[477]**

COMMENCEMENT

At the time of going to press this section was not yet in force; see s. 108 (2), para. [**541**]. *post*.

24. Convention adoption orders

(1) An adoption order shall be made as a Convention adoption order if the application is for a Convention adoption order and the following conditions are satisfied both at the time of the application and when the order is made.

(2) The child—

(*a*) must be a United Kingdom national or a national of a Convention country, and

(*b*) must habitually reside in British territory or a Convention country, and

(*c*) must not be, or have been, married.

(3) The applicant or applicants and the child must not all be United Kingdom nationals living in British territory.

(4) If the application is by a married couple, either—

(*a*) each must be a United Kingdom national or a national of a Convention country, and both must habitually reside in Great Britain, or

(*b*) both must be United Kingdom nationals, and each must habitually reside in British territory or a Convention country,

and if the applicants are nationals of the same Convention country the adoption must not be prohibited by a specified provision (as defined in subsection (8)) of the internal law of that country.

(5) If the application is by one person, either—

(*a*) he must be a United Kingdom national or a national of a Convention country, and must habitually reside in Great Britain, or

(*b*) he must be a United Kingdom national, and must habitually reside in British territory or a Convention country,

and if he is a national of a Convention country the adoption must not be prohibited by a specified provision (as defined in subsection (8)) of the internal law of that country.

(6) If the child is not a United Kingdom national the order shall not be made—

(*a*) except in accordance with the provisions, if any, relating to consents and consultations of the internal law relating to adoption of the Convention country of which the child is a national, and (*b*) unless the court is satisfied that each person who consents to the order in accordance with that internal law does so with full understanding of what is involved.

(7) The reference to consents and consultations in subsection (6) does not include a reference to consent by and consultation with the applicant and members of the applicant's family (including his or her spouse), and for the purposes of subsection (6) consents may be proved in the manner prescribed by rules and the court shall be treated as the authority by whom, under the law mentioned in subsection (6), consents may be dispensed with and the adoption in question may be effected; and where the provisions there mentioned require the attendance before that authority of any person who does not reside in Great Britain, that requirement shall be treated as satisfied for the purposes of subsection (6) if—

(*a*) that person has been given a reasonable opportunity of communicating his opinion on the adoption in question to the proper officer or clerk of the court, or to an appropriate authority of the country in question, for transmission to the court; and

(*b*) where he has availed himself of that opportunity, his opinion has been transmitted to the court.

(8) In subsections (4) and (5) "specified provision" means a provision specified in an order of the Secretary of State as one notified to the Government of the United Kingdom in pursuance of the provisions of the Convention which relate to prohibitions on an adoption contained in the national law of the Convention country in question.

(9) Sections 9 and 10 (1) (ascertainment of nationality, and internal law of foreign country) of the Adoption Act 1968 shall apply with any necessary modifications for the purposes of this section as they apply for the purposes of that Act. [**478**]

EFFECT OF SECTION

For the effect of this section see paras. [**152**]–[**164**], *ante*.

COMMENCEMENT

At the time of going to press this section was not yet in force; see s. 108 (2), para. [**541**], *post*.

25. Adoption of children abroad

(1) Where on an application made in relation to a child by a person who is not domiciled in England and Wales or Scotland an authorised court is satisfied that he intends to adopt the child under the law of or within the country in which the applicant is domiciled, the court may, subject to the following provisions of this section, make an order vesting in him the parental rights and duties relating to the child.

(2) The provisions of this Part relating to adoption orders, except sections 8 (1), (9) and (10), 10 (2), 11 (2), 14 to 16, 19, 22 (1), 23 and 24, shall apply in relation to orders under this section as they apply in relation to adoption orders subject to the modification that in section 9 (1) for "19" and "13" there are substituted "32" and "26" respectively.

(3) Sections 20 to 23 and 24 (4) and (5) of the 1958 Act shall apply in relation to an order under this section as they apply in relation to an adoption order except that any entry in the Registers of Births, the Register of Births or the Adopted Children Register which is required to be marked in consequence of the

making of an order under this section shall, in lieu of being marked with the word "Adopted" or "Re-adopted" (with or without the addition of the word "(Scotland)" or "(England)") be marked with the words "Proposed Foreign Adoption" or "Proposed Foreign Re-adoption", as the case may require.

(4) References in Parts III and IV of the 1958 Act to an adoption order include references to an order under this section, and references in this Act and in the 1958 Act to the placing of children for adoption or to the making of arrangements for adoption include references to the placing of children for adoption abroad or the making of arrangements for adoption abroad. **[479]**

EFFECT OF SECTION

For the effect of this section see paras. [**165**]–[**171**], *ante*.

COMMENCEMENT

At the time of going to press this section was not yet in force; see s. 108 (2), para. [**541**], *post*.

Amendments of Adoption Act 1958

26. Obtaining of birth certificate by adopted person

(1) In section 20 of the 1958 Act, in subsection (5), after the word "except" there are inserted the words "in accordance with section 20A of this Act or".

(2) The following section is inserted in the 1958 Act after section 20—

"20A. Disclosure of birth records of adopted persons

(1) Subject to subsections (4) and (6) of this section, the Registrar General shall on an application made in the prescribed manner by an adopted person a record of whose birth is kept by the Registrar General and who has attained the age of 18 years supply to that person on payment of the prescribed fee (if any) such information as is necessary to enable that person to obtain a certified copy of the record of his birth.

(2) On an application made in the prescribed manner by an adopted person under the age of 18 years a record of whose birth is kept by the Registrar General and who is intending to be married in England or Wales, and on payment of the prescribed fee (if any), the Registrar General shall inform the applicant whether or not it appears from information contained in the registers of live births or other records that the applicant and the person whom he intends to marry may be within the prohibited degrees of relationship for the purposes of the Marriage Act 1949.

(3) It shall be the duty of the Registrar General and each local authority and approved adoption society to provide counselling for adopted persons who apply for information under subsection (1) of this section.

(4) Before supplying any information to an applicant under subsection (1) of this section, the Registrar General shall inform the applicant that counselling services are available to him—

(*a*) at the General Register Office; or

(*b*) from the local authority for the area where the applicant is at the time the application is made; or

(*c*) from the local authority for the area where the court which made the adoption order relating to the applicant; or

(*d*) if the applicant's adoption was arranged by an adoption society which is approved under section 4 of the Children Act 1975, from that society.

(5) If the applicant chooses to receive counselling from a local authority or an adoption society under subsection (4) the Registrar General shall send to the authority or society of the applicant's choice the information to which the applicant is entitled under subsection (1).

(6) The Registrar General shall not supply a person who was adopted before the date on which the Children Act 1975 was passed with any information under subsection (1) of this section unless that person has attended an interview with a counsellor either at the General Register Office or in pursuance of arrangements made by the local authority or adoption society from whom the applicant is entitled to receive counselling in accordance with subsection (4).

(7) In this section "prescribed" means prescribed by regulations made by the Registrar General.". [**480**]

EFFECT OF SECTION

For the effect of this section see paras. [**194**]–[**199**], *ante*.

COMMENCEMENT

This section was brought into force on 26th November 1976 by the Children Act 1975 (Commencement No. 1) Order 1976, S.I. 1976 No. 1744, made under s. 108 (2), para. [**541**], *post*

27. (*Applies to Scotland.*)

28. Restriction on arranging adoption and placing of children

In section 29 of the 1958 Act—

(*a*) the following subsection is substituted for subsections (1) and (2)—

"(1) A person other than an adoption agency shall not make arrangements for the adoption of a child, or place a child for adoption, unless—

(*a*) the proposed adopter is a relative of the child, or
(*b*) he is acting in pursuance of an order of the High Court";

(*b*) the following subsections are inserted after subsection (1)—

"(2) An adoption society approved under the Children Act 1975 only as respects England and Wales shall not act as an adoption society in Scotland, except to the extent that it considers it necessary to do so in the interests of a person mentioned in section 1 (1) of that Act.

(2A) An adoption society approved under the Children Act 1975 only as respects Scotland shall not act as an adoption society in England or Wales except to the extent that it considers it necessary to do so in the interests of a person mentioned in section 1 (1) of that Act.";

(*c*) in subsection (3)—

(i) the following is inserted after paragraph (*b*)—

"or

(*c*) receives a child placed with him in contravention of subsection (1) of this section";

(ii) for the words "six months" there are substituted the words "three months" and for the words "one hundred pounds" there are substituted the words "£400";

(*d*) the following subsection is substituted for subsection (5)—

"(5) Section 17 of the Children Act 1975 shall apply where a person is convicted of a contravention of subsection (1) of this section as it applies where an application for an adoption order is refused.". [**481**]

EFFECT OF SECTION

For the effect of this section see paras. [**108**]–[**110**], *ante*.

COMMENCEMENT

Para. (*c*) (ii) was brought into force on 26th November 1976 by the Children Act 1975 (Commencement No. 1) Order 1976, S.I. 1976 No. 1744, made under s. 108 (2), para. [**541**], *post*. At the time of going to press the remainder of this section was not yet in force.

29. Restrictions on removal of child pending adoption

The following sections are substituted for section 34 of the 1958 Act—

"34. Restrictions on removal where adoption agreed or application made under section 14 of Children Act 1975

(1) While an application for an adoption order is pending in a case where a parent or guardian of the child has agreed to the making of the adoption order (whether or not he knows the identity of the applicant), the parent or guardian is not entitled, against the will of the person with whom the child has his home, to remove the child from the custody of that person except with the leave of the court.

(2) While an application is pending for an order under section 14 of the Children Act 1975 and—

(*a*) the child is in the care of the adoption agency making the application, and

(*b*) the application was not made with the consent of each parent or guardian of the child,

no parent or guardian of the child who did not consent to the application is entitled, against the will of the person with whom the child has his home, to remove the child from the custody of that person except with the leave of the court.

(3) Any person who contravenes subsection (1) or (2) of this section commits an offence and shall be liable on summary conviction to imprisonment for a term not exceeding three months or a fine not exceeding £400 or both.

34A. Restrictions on removal where applicant has provided home for five years

(1) While an application for an adoption order in respect of a child made by the person with whom the child has had his home for the five years preceding the application is pending, no person is entitled, against the will of the applicant, to remove the child from the applicant's custody

except with the leave of the court or under authority conferred by any enactment or on the arrest of the child.

(2) Where a person ("the prospective adopter") gives notice in writing to the local authority within whose area he has his home that he intends to apply for an adoption order in respect of a child who for the preceding five years has had his home with the prospective adopter, no person is entitled, against the will of the prospective adopter, to remove the child from the prospective adopter's custody, except with the leave of a court or under authority conferred by any enactment or on the arrest of the child before—

(*a*) the prospective adopter applies for the adoption order, or
(*b*) the period of three months from the receipt of the notice by the local authority expires,

whichever occurs first.

(3) In any case where subsection (1) or (2) of this section applies, and—

(*a*) the child was in the care of the local authority before he began to have his home with the applicant or, as the case may be, the prospective adopter, and
(*b*) the child remains in the care of the authority,

the authority shall not remove the child from the actual custody of the applicant or of the prospective adopter except in accordance with sections 35 and 36 of this Act or with the leave of the court.

(4) A local authority which receives such notice as aforesaid in respect of a child whom the authority know to be in the care of another local authority or of a voluntary organisation shall, not more than seven days after the receipt of the notice, inform that other authority or the organisation in writing that they have received the notice.

(5) Subsection (2) of this section does not apply to any further notice served by the prospective adopter on any local authority in respect of the same child during the period referred to in paragraph (*b*) of that subsection or within 28 days after its expiry.

(6) Any person who contravenes subsection (1) or (2) of this section commits an offence and shall be liable on summary conviction to imprisonment for a term not exceeding three months or a fine not exceeding £400 or both.

(7) The Secretary of State may by order made by statutory instrument a draft of which has been approved by each House of Parliament amend subsection (1) or (2) of this section to substitute a different period for the period of five years mentioned in that subsection (or the period which, by a previous order under this subsection, was substituted for that period).

(8) (*Applies to Scotland.*)". [**482**]

EFFECT OF SECTION

For the effect of this section see paras. [**131**]–[**142**], *ante*.

COMMENCEMENT

This section was brought into force on 26th November 1976 by the Children Act 1975 (Commencement No. 1) Order 1976, S.I. 1976 No. 1744, made under s. 108 (2), para. [**541**], *post*.

30. Return of child taken away in breach of section 34 or 34A of 1958 Act

(1) An authorised court may on the application of a person from whose custody a child has been removed in breach of section 34 or 34A of the 1958 Act order the person who has so removed the child to return the child to the applicant.

(2) An authorised court may on the application of a person who has reasonable grounds for believing that another person is intending to remove a child from the applicant's custody in breach of section 34 or 34A of the 1958 Act by order direct that other person not to remove the child from the applicant's custody in breach of the said section 34 or 34A.

(3) If, in the case of an order made by the High Court under subsection (1), the High Court or, in the case of an order made by a county court under subsection (1), a county court is satisfied that the child has not been returned to the applicant, the court may make an order authorising an officer of the court to search such premises as may be specified in the order for the child and, if the officer finds the child, to return the child to the applicant.

(4) If a justice of the peace is satisfied by information on oath that there are reasonable grounds for believing that a child to whom an order under subsection (1) relates is in premises specified in the information, he may issue a search warrant authorising a constable to search the premises for the child; and if a constable acting in pursuance of a warrant under this section finds the child, he shall return the child to the person on whose application the order under subsection (1) was made.

(5) An order under subsection (3) may be enforced in like manner as a warrant for committal.

(6) Subsections (3), (4) and (5) do not apply to Scotland. [**483**]

EFFECT OF SECTION

For the effect of this section see paras. [**143**]–[**144**], *ante*.

COMMENCEMENT

This section was brought into force on 26th November 1976 by the Children Act 1975 (Commencement No. 1) Order 1976, S.I. 1976 No. 1744, made under s. 108 (2), para. [**541**], *post*.

31. Return of child on refusal of adoption order

In section 35 of the 1958 Act, the following subsection is inserted after subsection (5)—

> "(5A) Where an application for an adoption order is refused the court may, if it thinks fit, at any time before the expiry of the period of seven days mentioned in subsection (3) of this section order that period to be extended to a duration, not exceeding six weeks, specified in the order.".

[**484**]

EFFECT OF SECTION

For the effect of this section see para. [**145**], *ante*.

COMMENCEMENT

This section was brought into force on 26th November 1976 by the Children Act 1975 (Commencement No. 1) Order 1976, S.I. 1976 No. 1744, made under s. 108 (2), para. [**541**], *post*.

32. Payment of allowances to adopters

In section 50 (prohibition of certain payments in relation to adoption) of the 1958 Act, the following subsections are inserted at the end—

"(4) If an adoption agency submits to the Secretary of State a scheme for the payment by the agency of allowances to persons who have adopted or intend to adopt a child where arrangements for the adoption were made, or are to be made, by that agency, and the Secretary of State approves the scheme, this section shall not apply to any payment made in accordance with the scheme.

(5) The Secretary of State, in the case of a scheme approved by him under subsection (4) of this section, may at any time—

(*a*) make, or approve the making by the agency of, alterations to the scheme;

(*b*) revoke the scheme.

(6) The Secretary of State shall, within seven years of the date on which section 32 of the Children Act 1975 comes into force and, thereafter, every five years, publish a report on the operation of the schemes since that date or since the publication of the last report.

(7) Subject to the following subsection, subsection (4) of this section shall expire on the seventh anniversary of the date on which it comes into force.

(8) The Secretary of State may by order made by statutory instrument at any time before the said anniversary, repeal subsection (7) of this section.

(9) An order under subsection (8) of this section shall not be made unless—

(*a*) a report has been published under subsection (6) of this section, and

(*b*) a draft of the order has been laid before Parliament and approved by resolution of each House.

(10) Notwithstanding the expiry of subsection (4) of this section or the revocation of a scheme approved under this section, subsection (1) of this section shall not apply in relation to any payment made, whether before or after the expiry of subsection (4) or the revocation of the scheme, in accordance with a scheme which was approved under this section to a person to whom such payments were made, where the scheme was not revoked, before the expiry of subsection (4) or, if the scheme was revoked, before the date of its revocation." [**485**]

EFFECT OF SECTION

For the effect of this section see paras. [**120**]–[**123**], *ante*.

COMMENCEMENT

At the time of going to press this section was not yet in force; see s. 108 (2), para. [**541**], *post*.

Part II

Custody

Custodianship orders

33. Custodianship orders

(1) An authorised court may on the application of one or more persons qualified under subsection (3) make an order vesting the legal custody of a child in the

applicant or, as the case may be, in one or more of the applicants if the child is in England or Wales at the time the application is made.

(2) An order under subsection (1) may be referred to as a custodianship order, and the person in whom legal custody of the child is vested under the order may be referred to as the custodian of the child.

(3) The persons qualified to apply for a custodianship order are—

(*a*) a relative or step-parent of the child—

(i) who applies with the consent of a person having legal custody of the child, and

(ii) with whom the child has had his home for the three months preceding the making of the application;

(*b*) any person—

(i) who applies with the consent of a person having legal custody of the child, and

(ii) with whom the child has had his home for a period or periods before the making of the application which amount to at least twelve months and include the three months preceding the making of the application;

(*c*) any person with whom the child has had his home for a period or periods before the making of the application which amount to at least three years and include the three months preceding the making of the application.

(4) The mother or father of the child is not qualified under any paragraph of subsection (3).

(5) A step-parent of the child is not qualified under any paragraph of subsection (3) if in proceedings for divorce or nullity of marriage the child was named in an order made under paragraph (*b*) or (*c*) of section 41 (1) (arrangements for welfare of children of family) of the Matrimonial Causes Act 1973.

(6) If no person has legal custody of the child, or the applicant himself has legal custody or the person with legal custody cannot be found, paragraphs (*a*) and (*b*) of subsection (3) apply with the omission of sub-paragraph (i).

(7) The Secretary of State may by order a draft of which has been approved by each House of Parliament amend subsection (3) (*c*) to substitute a different period for the period of three years mentioned in that paragraph (or the period which, by a previous order under this subsection, was substituted for that period).

(8) Subsection (5) does not apply—

(*a*) if the parent other than the one the step-parent married is dead or cannot be found, or

(*b*) if the order referred to in subsection (5) was made under subsection (1) (*c*) of section 41 of the Matrimonial Causes Act 1973 and it has since been determined that the child was not a child of the family to which that section applied.

(9) For the avoidance of doubt, it is hereby declared that the provisions of section 1 of the Guardianship of Minors Act 1971 apply to applications made under this Part of this Act.

(10) This section and sections 34 to 46 do not apply to Scotland. [**486**]

EFFECT OF SECTION

For the effect of this section see paras. [**240**]–[**253**] and [**259**]–[**272**], *ante*.

COMMENCEMENT

At the time of going to press this section was not yet in force; see s. 108 (2), para. [**541**], *post*.

34. Access and maintenance

(1) An authorised court may, on making a custodianship order or while a custodianship order is in force, by order—

(*a*) on the application of the child's mother or father make such provision as it thinks fit requiring access to the child to be given to the applicant;

(*b*) on the application of the custodian, require the child's mother or father (or both) to make to the applicant such periodical payments towards the maintenance of the child as it thinks reasonable;

(*c*) on the application of the child's mother or father, revoke an order requiring the applicant to contribute towards the child's maintenance made (otherwise than under this section) by any court;

(*d*) on the application of the child's mother or father or the custodian vary an order made (otherwise than under this section) by any court requiring the mother or father to contribute towards the child's maintenance—

(i) by altering the amount of the contributions;

(ii) by substituting the custodian for the person to whom the contributions were ordered to be made.

(2) References in subsection (1) to the child's mother or father include any person in relation to whom the child was treated as a child of the family (as defined in section 52 (1) of the Matrimonial Causes Act 1973) but the court in deciding whether to make an order under subsection (1) (*b*) against a person who is not the child's mother or father shall have regard (among the circumstances of the case)—

(*a*) to whether that person had assumed any responsibility for the child's maintenance and, if he did, to the extent to which and the basis on which he did so, and to the length of time during which he discharged that responsibility;

(*b*) to the liability of any other person to maintain that child.

(3) No order shall be made under subsection (1) (*b*) requiring the father of an illegitimate child to make any payments to the child's custodian.

(4) Subsections (2), (3), (4) and (6) (orders as to supervision, local authority care, maintenance etc. of children) of section 2 of the Guardianship Act 1973 and sections 3 and 4 of that Act (supplementary provisions) shall apply to an application for a custodianship order as they apply to an application under section 9 of the Guardianship of Minors Act 1971 subject to the following modifications, that is to say—

(*a*) in section 2 (2) (*b*) and (4) (*a*) of the Guardianship Act 1973 any reference to a parent of the minor to whom the order relates shall be construed as including a reference to any other individual;

(*b*) section 3 (3) of that Act shall have effect as if the words "or the custodian" were inserted after the words "application of either parent".

(5) A local authority may make contributions to a custodian towards the cost of the accommodation and maintenance of the child, except where the custodian is the husband or wife of a parent of the child. [**487**]

EFFECT OF SECTION

For the effect of this section see paras. [**298**]–[**311**], *ante*.

COMMENCEMENT

At the time of going to press this section was not yet in force; see s. 108 (2), para. [**541**], *post*.

35. Revocation and variation of orders

(1) An authorised court may by order revoke a custodianship order on the application of—

(*a*) the custodian, or
(*b*) the mother or father, or a guardian, of the child, or
(*c*) any local authority in England or Wales.

(2) The court shall not proceed to hear an application made by any person for the revocation of a custodianship order where a previous such application made by the same person was refused by that or any other court unless—

(*a*) in refusing the previous application the court directed that this subsection should not apply, or
(*b*) it appears to the court that because of a change in circumstances or for any other reason it is proper to proceed with the application.

(3) The custodian of a child may apply to an authorised court for the revocation or variation of any order made under section 34 in respect of that child.

(4) Any other person on whose application an order under section 34 was made, or who was required by such an order to contribute towards the maintenance of the child, may apply to an authorised court for the revocation or variation of that order.

(5) Any order made under section 34 in respect of a child who is the subject of a custodianship order shall cease to have effect on the revocation of the custodianship order.

(6) A custodianship order made in respect of a child, and any order made under section 34 in respect of the child, shall cease to have effect when the child attains the age of 18 years. [**488**]

EFFECT OF SECTION

For the effect of this section see paras. [**283**]–[**286**], *ante*.

COMMENCEMENT

At the time of going to press this section was not yet in force; see s. 108 (2), para. [**541**], *post*.

36. Care etc., of child on revocation of custodianship order

(1) Before revoking a custodianship order the court shall ascertain who would have legal custody of the child, if, on the revocation of the custodianship order, no further order were made under this section.

(2) If the child would not be in the legal custody of any person, the court shall, if it revokes the custodianship order, commit the care of the child to a specified local authority.

(3) If there is a person who would have legal custody of the child on the revocation of the custodianship order, the court shall consider whether it is desirable in the interests of the welfare of the child for the child to be in the legal custody of that person and—

(*a*) if the court is of the opinion that it would not be so desirable, it shall on revoking the custodianship order commit the care of the child to a specified local authority;

(*b*) if it is of the opinion that while it is desirable for the child to be in the legal custody of that person, it is also desirable in the interests of the welfare of the child for him to be under the supervision of an independent person, the court shall on revoking the custodianship order, order that the child shall be under the supervision of a specified local authority or of a probation officer.

(4) Before exercising its functions under this section the court shall, unless it has sufficient information before it for the purpose, request—

(*a*) a local authority to arrange for an officer of the authority, or

(*b*) a probation officer,

to make to the court a report, orally or in writing, on the desirability of the child returning to the legal custody of any individual, and it shall be the duty of the local authority or probation officer to comply with the request.

(5) Where the court makes an order under subsection (3) (*a*), the order may require the payment by either parent to the local authority, while it has the care of the child, of such weekly or other periodical sum towards the maintenance of the child as the court thinks reasonable.

(6) Sections 3 and 4 of the Guardianship Act 1973 (which contain supplementary provisions relating to children who are subject to supervision, or in the care of local authority, by virtue of orders made under section 2 of that Act) apply in relation to an order under this section as they apply in relation to an order under section 2 of that Act.

(7) Subsections (2) to (6) of section 6 of the Guardianship Act 1973 shall apply in relation to reports which are requested by magistrates' courts under this section as they apply to reports under subsection (1) of that section. [**489**]

EFFECT OF SECTION

For the effect of this section see paras. [**287**]–[**288**], *ante*.

COMMENCEMENT

At the time of going to press this section was not yet in force; see s. 108 (2), para. [**541**], *post*.

37. Custodianship order on application for adoption or guardianship

(1) Where on an application for an adoption order by a relative of the child or by the husband or wife of the mother or father of the child, whether alone or jointly with his or her spouse, the requirements of section 12 or, where the application is for a Convention adoption order, section 24 (6) are satisfied, but the court is satisfied—

(*a*) that the child's welfare would not be better safeguarded and promoted by the making of adoption order in favour of the applicant, than it would be by the making of a custodianship order in his favour, and

(*b*) that it would be appropriate to make a custodianship order in the applicant's favour, the court shall direct the application to be treated as if it has been made by the applicant under section 33, but if the application was made jointly by the father or mother of the child and his or her spouse, the court shall direct the application to be treated as if made by the father's wife or the mother's husband alone.

(2) Where on an application for an adoption order made—

(*a*) by a person who is neither a relative of the child nor the husband or wife of the mother or father of the child; or

(*b*) by a married couple neither of whom falls within paragraph (*a*),

the said requirements are satisfied but the court is of opinion that it would be more appropriate to make a custodianship order in favour of the applicant, it may direct the application to be treated as if it had been made by the applicant under section 33.

(3) Where on an application under section 9 (orders for custody and maintenance on application of mother or father) of the Guardianship of Minors Act 1971 the court is of opinion that legal custody should be given to a person other than the mother or father, it may direct the application to be treated as if it had been made by that person under section 33.

(4) Where a direction is given under this section the applicant shall be treated (if such is not the case) as if he were qualified to apply for a custodianship order and this Part, except section 40, shall have effect accordingly.

(5) Subsection (1) does not apply to an application made by a step-parent whether alone or jointly with another person in any case where the step-parent is prevented by section 33 (5) from being qualified to apply for a custodianship order in respect of the child.

(6) Subsections (1) and (2) do not apply to an application for an adoption order made by the child's mother or father alone. [**490**]

EFFECT OF SECTION

For the effect of this section see paras. [**273**]–[**282**], *ante*.

COMMENCEMENT

At the time of going to press this section was not yet in force; see s. 108 (2), para. [**541**], *post*.

PROSPECTIVE AMENDMENT

Sub-s. (1) is amended by the Adoption Act 1976, s. 73 (2) and Sch. 3, para. 19, A.L.S. Vol. 244, as from a day to be appointed.

38. Disputes between joint custodians

If two persons have a parental right or duty vested in them jointly by a custodianship order or by virtue of section 44 (2) but cannot agree on its exercise or performance, either of them may apply to an authorised court, and the court may make such order regarding the exercise of the right or performance of the duty as it thinks fit. [**491**]

EFFECT OF SECTION

For the effect of this section see paras. [**289**]–[**290**], *ante*.

COMMENCEMENT

At the time of going to press this section was not yet in force; see s. 108 (2), para. [**541**], *post*.

39. Reports by local authorities and probation officers

(1) A court dealing with an application made under this Part, or an application which is treated as if made under section 33, may request—

(*a*) a local authority to arrange for an officer of the authority, or
(*b*) a probation officer,

to make to the court a report, orally or in writing, with respect to any specified matter which appears to the court to be relevant to the application, and it shall be the duty of the local authority or probation officer to comply with the request.

(2) Subsections (2) to (6) of section 6 of the Guardianship Act 1973 shall apply in relation to reports which are requested by magistrates' courts under this section as they apply to reports under subsection (1) of that section. **[492]**

EFFECT OF SECTION

For the effect of this section see para. [**297**], *ante*.

COMMENCEMENT

At the time of going to press this section was not yet in force; see s. 108 (2), para. [**541**], *post*.

40. Notice of application to be given to local authority

(1) A custodianship order shall not be made unless the applicant has given notice of the application for the order to the local authority in whose area the child resides within the seven days following the making of the application, or such extended period as the court or local authority may allow.

(2) On receipt of a notice given by the applicant under subsection (1) the local authority shall arrange for an officer of the authority to make a report to the court (so far as is practicable) on the matters prescribed under subsection (3) and on any other matter which he considers to be relevant to the application.

(3) The Secretary of State shall by regulations prescribe matters which are to be included in a report under subsection (2) and, in particular, but without prejudice to the generality of the foregoing, the prescribed matters shall include—

(*a*) the wishes and feelings of the child having regard to his age and understanding and all other matters relevant to the operation of section 1 (principle on which questions relating to custody are to be decided) of the Guardianship of Minors Act 1971 in relation to the application;
(*b*) the means and suitability of the applicant;
(*c*) information of a kind specified in the regulations relating to members of the applicant's household;
(*d*) the wishes regarding the application, and the means, of the mother and father of the child.

(4) Subsections (2), (3) and (3A) of section 6 of the Guardianship Act 1973 shall apply to a report under this section which is submitted to a magistrates' court. **[493]**

EFFECT OF SECTION

For the effect of this section see paras. [**291**]–[**297**], *ante*.

COMMENCEMENT

At the time of going to press this section was not yet in force; see s. 108 (2), para. [**541**], *post*.

41. Restriction on removal of child where applicant has provided home for three years

(1) While an application for a custodianship order in respect of a child made by the person with whom the child has at the time the application is made had his home for a period (whether continuous or not) amounting to at least three years is pending, another person is not entitled, against the will of the applicant, to remove the child from the applicant's custody except with the leave of a court or under authority conferred by any enactment or on the arrest of the child.

(2) In any case where subsection (1) applies, and

(*a*) the child was in the care of a local authority before he began to have his home with the applicant, and

(*b*) the child remains in the care of a local authority,

the authority in whose care the child is shall not remove the child from the applicant's custody except with the applicant's consent or the leave of a court.

(3) Any person who contravenes subsection (1) commits an offence and shall be liable on summary conviction to imprisonment for a term not exceeding three months or a fine not exceeding £400 or both.

(4) The Secretary of State may by order a draft of which has been approved by each House of Parliament amend subsection (1) to substitute a different period for the period mentioned in that subsection (or the period which, by a previous order under this subsection, was substituted for that period). [**494**]

EFFECT OF SECTION

For the effect of this section see paras. [**254**]–[**258**], *ante*.

COMMENCEMENT

At the time of going to press this section was not yet in force; see s. 108 (2), para. [**541**], *post*.

42. Return of child taken away in breach of section 41

(1) An authorised court may on the application of a person from whose custody a child has been removed in breach of section 41 order the person who has so removed the child to return the child to the applicant.

(2) An authorised court may on the application of a person who has reasonable grounds for believing that another person is intending to remove a child from the applicant's custody in breach of section 41 by order direct that other person not to remove the child from the applicant's custody in breach of that section.

(3) If, in the case of an order made by the High Court under subsection (1), the High Court or, in the case of an order made by a county court under subsection (1), a county court is satisfied that the child has not been returned to the applicant, the court may make an order authorising an officer of the court to search such premises as may be specified in the order for the child and, if the officer finds the child, to return the child to the applicant.

(4) If a justice of the peace is satisfied by information on oath that there are reasonable grounds for believing that a child to whom an order under subsection (1) relates is in premises specified in the information, he may issue a search warrant authorising a constable to search the premises for the child; and if a constable acting in pursuance of a warrant under this section finds the child, he shall return the child to the person on whose application the order under subsection (1) was made.

(5) An order under subsection (3) may be enforced in like manner as a warrant for committal. [**495**]

EFFECT OF SECTION

For the effect of this section see paras. [**257**]–[**258**], *ante*.

COMMENCEMENT

At the time of going to press this section was not yet in force; see s. 108 (2), para. [**541**], *post*.

43. Enforcement of orders made by magistrates' courts

(1) If at a time when the custodian is entitled to actual custody of the child by virtue of a custodianship order made by a magistrates' court any other person has actual custody of him, a copy of the custodianship order may be served on that person and thereupon the order may, without prejudice to any other remedy open to the custodian, be enforced under section 54 (3) of the Magistrates' Courts Act 1952 as if it were an order of a magistrates' court requiring that person to give up the child to the custodian.

(2) Any person for the time being under an obligation to make payments in pursuance of any order for the payment of money made by a magistrates' court under section 34 shall give notice of any change of address to such person (if any) as may be specified in the order; and if he fails without reasonable excuse to give such a notice he commits an offence and shall be liable on summary conviction to a fine not exceeding £10.

(3) An order for the payment of money made by a magistrates' court under section 34 may be enforced in like manner as an affiliation order, and the enactments relating to affiliation orders shall apply accordingly with the necessary modifications. [**496**]

EFFECT OF SECTION

For the effect of this section see para. [**316**], *ante*.

COMMENCEMENT

At the time of going to press this section was not yet in force; see s. 108 (2), para. [**541**], *post*.

44. Effect of custodianship order on existing custody

(1) While a custodianship order has effect in relation to a child the right of any person other than the custodian to legal custody of the child is suspended, but, subject to any further order made by any court, revives on the revocation of the custodianship order.

(2) Subsection (1) does not apply where the person already having custody is a parent of the child and the person who becomes custodian under the order is the husband or wife of the parent; and in such a case the spouses have the legal custody jointly. [**497**]

EFFECT OF SECTION

For the effect of this section see paras. [**265**]–[**266**], *ante*.

COMMENCEMENT

At the time of going to press this section was not yet in force; see s. 108 (2), para. [**541**], *post*.

45. Affiliation order on application by custodian

(1) Where a custodianship order subsists in respect of an illegitimate child, and no affiliation order relating to the child has been made under the Affiliation Proceedings Act 1957, the custodian of the child may apply to a justice of the

peace acting for the petty sessions area in which the child or the child's mother resides for a summons to be served under section 1 of that Act.

(2) The court shall proceed on the application as on a complaint under that section, but the person entitled to any payments under an affiliation order made on the application shall be the custodian.

(3) An application may not be made under subsection (1)—

(*a*) if the custodian is married to the child's mother, or

(*b*) more than three years after the custodianship order was made. **[498]**

EFFECT OF SECTION

For the effect of this section see paras. [**302**]–[**303**], *ante*.

COMMENCEMENT

At the time of going to press this section was not yet in force; see s. 108 (2), para. [**541**], *post*.

46. Procedure in magistrates' courts

(1) It is hereby declared that any jurisdiction conferred on a magistrates' court by virtue of this Part is exercisable notwithstanding that the proceedings are brought by or against a person residing outside England and Wales.

(2) A magistrates' court may, subject to subsection (3), proceed on an application for an order under this Part notwithstanding that the defendant has not been served with the summons, and rules may prescribe matters as to which the court is to be satisfied before proceeding in such a case.

(3) A magistrates' court shall not—

(*a*) make an order under this Part requiring a person to make payments towards the maintenance of a child, or

(*b*) vary an order under this Part so as to increase a person's liability to make payments towards the maintenance of a child,

unless the person has been served with the summons.

(4) Rules may make provision as to the persons who are to be made defendants to a complaint for an order under this Part, and where there are two or more defendants to such a complaint the power of the court under section 55 (1) of the Magistrates' Courts Act 1952 (power to award costs etc.) shall be deemed to include power, whatever adjudication the court makes, to order any of the parties to pay the whole or part of the costs of all or any of the parties.

(5) In this section "rules" means rules made under section 15 of the Justices of the Peace Act 1949. **[499]**

EFFECT OF SECTION

For the effect of this section see para. [**315**], *ante*.

COMMENCEMENT

At the time of going to press this section was not yet in force; see s. 108 (2), para. [**541**], *post*.

Custody in Scotland

47. Granting of custody

(1) Without prejudice to any existing enactment or rule of law conferring a—

(*a*) right to apply for custody of a child;

(*b*) power to grant custody of a child;

any relative, step-parent or foster parent of the child is qualified to apply for, and subject to subsection (2) may be granted, such custody in the same manner as any person so qualified before the commencement of this Act.

(2) Except in the case of an application under section 2 of the Illegitimate Children (Scotland) Act 1930, custody of a child shall not be granted in any proceedings to a person other than a parent or guardian of the child unless that person—

(*a*) being a relative or step-parent of the child, has the consent of a parent or guardian of the child and has had care and possession of the child for the three months preceding the making of the application for custody; or

(*b*) has the consent of a parent or guardian of the child and has had care and possession of the child for a period or periods, before such application, which amounted to at least twelve months and included the three months preceding such application; or

(*c*) has had care and possession of the child for a period or periods before such application which amounted to at least three years and included the three months preceding such application; or

(*d*) while not falling within paragraph (*a*), (*b*) or (*c*), can show cause, having regard to section 1 of the Guardianship of Infants Act 1925 (the principle on which questions relating to custody, upbringing etc. of children are to be decided) why an order should be made awarding him custody of the child.

(3) Nothing in this section shall prejudice any ancillary power of the court in any proceedings relative to custody.

(4) The Secretary of State may by order a draft of which has been approved by each House of Parliament amend subsection (2) (*c*) to substitute a different period for the period of three years mentioned in that paragraph (or the period which by a previous order under this subsection was substituted for that period).

(5) In relation to a grant of custody to which this section applies,

(*a*) "guardian" has the same meaning as in the 1958 Act;

(*b*) "foster parent" means a person who, at the commencement of the proceedings in which the grant is made, has had care and possession of the child for a period or periods amounting to at least 12 months, whether or not that person continues to have care and possession of the child;

(*c*) "relative" has the same meaning as in the 1958 Act, except that, where the child is illegitimate, "relative" does not include the father of the child.

(6) The form and manner of any consent required in terms of subsection (2) (*a*) or (*b*) may be prescribed by act of sederunt. [**500**]

48. (*Applies to Scotland only.*)

49. Notice to local authority of certain custody applications

(1) Where an applicant for custody of a child is a relative, step-parent or foster parent of the child, an order awarding custody to that applicant shall not except on cause shown be made unless the applicant—

(*a*) in any case where at the time of the application he resided in Scotland, has, within the seven days following the making of the application, given notice thereof to the local authority within whose area he resided at that time;

(*b*) in any other case, has within such time as the court may direct given, to such local authority in Scotland as the court may specify, notice of the making of the application.

(2), (3). (*Apply to Scotland only.*) **[501]**

50-52. (*Apply to Scotland only.*)

53. Custody order on application for adoption in Scotland

(1) Without prejudice to the provisions of section 19 (power to make an interim order giving custody), where on an application for an adoption order in respect of a child the applicant is a person qualified to apply for custody of the child, and the court is of the opinion—

(*a*) in the case of an applicant who is a relative of the child or a husband or wife of the mother or father of the child (whether applying alone or jointly with his or her spouse)—

(i) that the child's welfare would not be better safeguarded and promoted by the making of an adoption order in favour of the applicant than it would be by the making of a custody order in his favour; and

(ii) that it would be appropriate to make a custody order in favour of the applicant; or

(*b*) in any other case, that the making of a custody order in favour of the applicant would be more appropriate than the making of an adoption order in his favour,

the court shall direct that the application is to be treated as if it had been made for custody of the child; but where such a direction is made the court shall not cease to have jurisdiction by reason only that it would not have had jurisdiction to hear an application by the applicant for custody of the child.

(2), (3). (*Apply to Scotland only.*) **[502]**

54. Jurisdiction of Scottish courts in certain applications for custody

(1) Without prejudice to any existing grounds of jurisdiction, the court shall have jurisdiction in proceedings for custody of a child if at the time of application for such custody—

(*a*) the child resides in Scotland; and

(*b*) the child is domiciled in England and Wales; and

(*c*) the person applying for custody is a person qualified, in terms of subsections (3) to (8) of section 33 of this Act, to apply in England or Wales for a custodianship order in respect of the child.

(2) For the purposes of this section, "the court" means—

(*a*) the Court of Session; or

(*b*) the sheriff court of the sheriffdom within which the child resides.

[503]

55. Interpretation and extent of sections 47 to 55

(1) In sections 47 to 54 "child" means a person under the age of sixteen.

(2) Sections 47 to 54 and this section apply to Scotland only. **[504]**

PART III

CARE

Children in care of local authorities

56. Restriction on removal of child from care

(1) In section 1 of the Children Act 1948, the following subsections are inserted after subsection (3)—

"(3A) Except in relation to an act done—

(*a*) with the consent of the local authority, or

(*b*) by a parent or guardian of the child who has given the local authority not less than 28 days' notice of his intention to do it,

subsection (8) (penalty for taking away a child in care) of section 3 of this Act shall apply to a child in the care of a local authority under this section (notwithstanding that no resolution is in force under section 2 of this Act with respect to the child) if he has been in the care of that local authority throughout the preceding six months; and for the purposes of the application of paragraph (*b*) of that subsection in such a case a parent or guardian of the child shall not be taken to have lawful authority to take him away.

(3B) The Secretary of State may by order a draft of which has been approved by each House of Parliament amend subsection (3A) of this section by substituting a different period for the period of 28 days or of six months mentioned in that subsection (or the period which, by a previous order under this subsection, was substituted for that period)."

(2) The following section is inserted after section 33 of the Children Act 1948—

"33A. Restriction on removal of child from care of voluntary organisation

(1) Section 3 (8) of this Act shall apply in relation to children who are not in the care of local authorities under section 1 of this Act but who are in voluntary homes or are boarded out, as it applies by virtue of subsection (3A) of the said section 1 to children in the care of the local authority, except that in the case of a child who is not in the care of a local authority the references in subsection (3A) to a local authority shall be construed as references to the voluntary organisation in whose care the child is.

(2) For the purposes of this section—

(*a*) a child is boarded out if he is boarded out, by the voluntary organisation in whose care he is, with foster parents to live in their home as a member of their family;

(*b*) "voluntary home" includes a controlled community home and an assisted community home.". [**505**]

EFFECT OF SECTION

For the effect of this section see paras. [**318**]–[**328**], *ante*.

COMMENCEMENT

This section was brought into force on 26th November 1976 by the Children Act 1975 (Commencement No. 1) Order 1976, S.I. 1976 No. 1744, made under s. 108 (2), para. [**541**], *post*.

57. Substitution of s. 2 of Children Act 1948

The following section is substituted for section 2 of the Children Act 1948.

"2. Assumption by local authority of parental rights and duties

(1) Subject to the provision of this Part of this Act, if it appears to a local authority in relation to any child who is in their care under the foregoing section—

(*a*) that his parents are dead and he has no guardian or custodian; or

(*b*) that a parent of his—

(i) has abandoned him, or

(ii) suffers from some permanent disability rendering him incapable of caring for the child, or

(iii) while not falling within sub-paragraph (ii) of this paragraph, suffers from a mental disorder (within the meaning of the Mental Health Act 1959), which renders him unfit to have the care of the child, or

(iv) is of such habits or mode of life as to be unfit to have the care of the child, or

(v) has so consistently failed without reasonable cause to discharge the obligations of a parent as to be unfit to have the care of the child; or

(*c*) that a resolution under paragraph (*b*) of this subsection is in force in relation to one parent of the child who is, or is likely to become, a member of the household comprising the child and his other parent; or

(*d*) that throughout the three years preceding the passing of the resolution the child has been in the care of a local authority under the foregoing section, or partly in the care of a local authority and partly in the care of a voluntary organisation,

the local authority may resolve that there shall vest in them the parental rights and duties with respect to that child, and, if the rights and duties were vested in the parent on whose account the resolution was passed jointly with another person, they shall also be vested in the local authority jointly with that other person.

(2) In the case of a resolution passed under paragraph (*b*), (*c*) or (*d*) of subsection (1) of this section, unless the person whose parental rights and duties have under the resolution vested in the local authority has consented in writing to the passing of the resolution, the local authority, if that person's whereabouts are known to them, shall forthwith after the passing of the resolution serve on him notice in writing of the passing thereof.

(3) Every notice served by a local authority under subsection (2) of this section shall inform the person on whom the notice is served of his right to object to the resolution and the effect of any objection made by him.

(4) If, not later than one month after notice is served on a person under subsection (2) of this section, he serves a counter-notice in writing on the local authority objecting to the resolution, the resolution shall, subject to the provisions of subsection (5) of this section, lapse on the expiry of fourteen days from the service of the counter-notice.

(5) Where a counter-notice has been served on a local authority under subsection (4) of this section, the authority may not later than fourteen days after the receipt by them of the counter-notice complain to a juvenile court having jurisdiction in the area of the authority, and in that event the resolution shall not lapse until the determination of the complaint; and the court may on the hearing of the complaint order that the resolution shall not lapse by reason of the service of the counter-notice:

Provided that the court shall not so order unless satisfied—

(*a*) that the grounds mentioned in subsection (1) of this section on which the local authority purported to pass the resolution were made out, and

(*b*) that at the time of the hearing there continued to be grounds on which a resolution under subsection (1) of this section could be founded, and

(*c*) that it is in the interests of the child to do so.

(6) While a resolution passed under subsection (1) (*b*), (*c*) or (*d*) of this section is in force with respect to a child, section 1 (3) of this Act shall not apply in relation to the person who, but for the resolution, would have the parental rights and duties in relation to the child.

(7) Any notice under this section (including a counter-notice) may be served by post, so however that a notice served by a local authority under subsection (2) of this section shall not be duly served by post unless it is sent by registered post or recorded delivery service.

(8) A resolution under this section shall cease to have effect if—

(*a*) the child is adopted;

(*b*) an order in respect of the child is made under section 14 or 25 of the Children Act 1975; or

(*c*) a guardian of the child is appointed under section 5 of the Guardianship of Minors Act 1971.

(9) Where, after a child has been received into the care of a local authority under the foregoing section, the whereabouts of any parent of his have remained unknown for twelve months, then, for the purposes of this section, the parent shall be deemed to have abandoned the child.

(10) The Secretary of State may by order a draft of which has been approved by each House of Parliament amend subsection (1) (*d*) of this section to substitute a different period for the period mentioned in that paragraph (or the period which, by a previous order under this subsection, was substituted for that period).

(11) In this section—

"parent", except in subsection (1) (*a*), includes a guardian or custodian;

"parental rights and duties", in relation to a particular child, means all rights and duties which by law the mother and father have in relation to a legitimate child and his property except the right to consent or refuse to consent to the making of an application under section 14 of the Children Act 1975 and the right to agree or refuse to agree to the making of an adoption order or an order under section 25 of that Act". [**506**]

EFFECT OF SECTION

For the effect of this section see paras. [**329**]–[**341**], *ante*.

COMMENCEMENT

This section was brought into force on 26th November 1976 by the Children Act 1975 (Commencement No. 1) Order 1976, S.I. 1976 No. 1744, made under s. 108 (2), para. [**541**], *post*.

58. Supplementary provisions relating to care proceedings

In the Children Act 1948, the following sections are inserted after section 4—

"4A. Appeal to High Court

An appeal shall lie to the High Court from the making by a juvenile court of an order under section 2 (5) or section 4 (3) of this Act (orders confirming or terminating local authority resolutions under section 2 (1) of this Act), or from the refusal by a juvenile court to make such an order.

4B. Guardians ad litem and reports in care proceedings

(1) In any proceedings under section 2 (5) or 4 (3) or 4A of this Act, a juvenile court or the High Court may, where it considers it necessary in order to safeguard the interests of the child to whom the proceedings relate, by order make the child a party to the proceedings and appoint, subject to rules of court, a guardian ad litem of the child for the purposes of the proceedings.

(2) A guardian ad litem appointed in pursuance of this section shall be under a duty to safeguard the interests of the child in the manner prescribed by rules of court.

(3) Section 6 of the Guardianship Act 1973 shall apply in relation to complaints under section 2 (5) or 4 (3) of this Act as it applies in relation to applications under section 3 (3) of the said Act of 1973." [**507**]

EFFECT OF SECTION

For the effect of this section see paras. [**342**]–[**343**], *ante*.

COMMENCEMENT

This section, in so far as it provides for the insertion of the Children Act 1948, s. 4A, was brought into force on 26th November 1976 by the Children Act 1975 (Commencement No. 1) Order 1976, S.I. 1976 No. 1744, made under s. 108 (2), para. [**541**], *post*. At the time of going to press the remainder of this section was not yet in force.

59. General duty of local authority in care cases

In section 12 of the Children Act 1948, the following subsections are substituted for subsection (1)—

"(1) In reaching any decision relating to a child in their care, a local authority shall give first consideration to the need to safeguard and promote the welfare of the child throughout his childhood; and shall so far as practicable ascertain the wishes and feelings of the child regarding the decision and give due consideration to them, having regard to his age and understanding.

(1A) If it appears to the local authority that it is necessary, for the purpose of protecting members of the public, to exercise their powers in relation to a particular child in their care in a manner which may not be consistent with their duty under the foregoing subsection, the authority may, notwithstanding that duty, act in that manner." [**508**]

EFFECT OF SECTION

For the effect of this section see para. [**320**], *ante*.

COMMENCEMENT

This section came into force on 1st January 1976; see s. 108 (4), para. [**541**], *post*.

Children in care of voluntary organisations in England and Wales

60. Transfer of parental rights and duties to voluntary organisations

(1) Where it appears to a local authority as respects a child in the care of a voluntary organisation which is an incorporated body—

(*a*) that the child is not in the care of any local authority; and

(*b*) that a condition specified in section 2 (1) of the Children Act 1948 is satisfied; and

(*c*) that it is necessary in the interests of the welfare of the child for the parental rights and duties to be vested in the organisation,

the authority may, subject to subsections (5) and (6), resolve that there shall vest in the organisation the parental rights and duties with respect to that child.

(2) While a resolution under this section is in force the parental rights and duties shall vest in the organisation in whose care the child is when the resolution is passed.

(3) If, immediately before the resolution is passed, the parental rights and duties are vested in the parent in relation to whom the resolution is passed jointly with any other person, then on the passing of the resolution the parental rights and duties shall vest jointly in that other person and the organisation in whose care the child is.

(4) In determining, for the purposes of subsection (1) of this section, whether the condition specified in section 2 (1) (*b*) (i) of the Children Act 1948 is satisfied, if the whereabouts of any parent of the child have remained unknown for twelve months, that parent shall be deemed to have abandoned the child.

(5) A resolution under subsection (1) may not be passed by a local authority in respect of any child unless—

(*a*) the child is living in the area of the authority either in a voluntary home or with foster parents with whom he has been boarded by the organisation in whose care he is; and

(*b*) that organisation has requested the authority to pass the resolution.

(6) The parental rights and duties which may vest in an organisation by virtue of this section do not include the right to consent or refuse to consent to the making of an application under section 14 and the right to agree or refuse to agree to the making of an adoption order or an order under section 25; and regulations made under section 33 (1) of the Children Act 1948 shall apply to the emigration of a child notwithstanding that the parental rights and duties relating to the child are vested in the voluntary organisation.

(7) Subsection (8) of section 2 of the Children Act 1948 shall apply in relation to a resolution under subsection (1) as if it were a resolution under the said section 2. [**509**]

EFFECT OF SECTION

For the effect of this section see paras. [**357**]–[**360**], *ante*.

COMMENCEMENT

At the time of going to press this section was not yet in force; see s. 108 (2), para. [**541**], *post*.

PROSPECTIVE AMENDMENT

Sub-s. (6) is amended by the Adoption Act 1976, s. 73 (2) and Sch. 3, para. 20, A.L.S. Vol. 244, as from a day to be appointed.

61. Duty of local authorities to assume parental rights and duties

(1) If it appears to a local authority, having regard to the interests of the welfare of a child living within their area, the parental rights and duties with respect to whom are by virtue of a resolution under section 60 vested in a voluntary organisation, that it is necessary that the parental rights and duties should no longer be vested in the organisation, the local authority shall resolve that there shall vest in them the parental rights and duties relating to the child.

(2) The local authority shall within seven days of passing a resolution under subsection (1) by notice in writing inform the organisation and each parent, guardian or custodian of the child whose whereabouts are known to them that the resolution has been passed. **[510]**

EFFECT OF SECTION

For the effect of this section see para. [**359**], *ante*.

COMMENCEMENT

At the time of going to press this section was not yet in force; see s. 108 (2), para. [**541**], *post*.

62. Effect of resolutions under sections 60 and 61

(1) A resolution under subsection (1) of section 60 shall cease to have effect on the passing of a resolution under subsection (1) of section 61.

(2) Section 6 of the Children Act 1948 shall have effect in relation to a resolution under subsection (1) of section 60 as it has effect in relation to a resolution under section 2 of that Act.

(3) A resolution under subsection (1) of section 61 shall be deemed to be a resolution under section 2 of the Children Act 1948 except that sections 2 (2) to (7) and 4 (3) of that Act shall not apply. **[511]**

EFFECT OF SECTION

For the effect of this section see paras. [**359**]–[**360**], *ante*.

COMMENCEMENT

At the time of going to press this section was not yet in force; see s. 108 (2), para. [**541**], *post*.

63. Appeals by parents, etc.

(1) Subsections (2) to (5) and (7) of section 2 of the Children Act 1948 shall apply to a resolution under section 60 as they apply to a resolution under the said section 2, with the substitution for the reference in subsection (2) to the vesting of parental rights and duties in the local authority of a reference to the vesting of parental rights and duties in the voluntary organisation.

(2) An appeal may be made—

(*a*) where the complaint relates to a resolution under section 60, by a person deprived of parental rights and duties by the resolution, or

(*b*) where the complaint relates to a resolution under section 61, by a person who but for that resolution and an earlier resolution under section 60 would have parental rights and duties,

to a juvenile court having jurisdiction in the area of the authority which passed the resolution, on the ground that—

(i) there was no ground for the making of the resolution, or

(ii) that the resolution should in the interests of the child be determined.

(3) An appeal shall lie to the High Court against the decision of a juvenile court under this section.

(4) Section 4B of the Children Act 1948 shall apply in relation to proceedings under this section. **[512]**

EFFECT OF SECTION

For the effect of this section see para. [**360**], *ante*.

COMMENCEMENT

At the time of going to press this section was not yet in force; see s. 108 (2), para. [**541**], *post*.

Conflict of interest between parent and child

64. Addition of new sections to Children and Young Persons Act 1969

The following heading and sections are inserted after section 32 of the Children and Young Persons Act 1969—

"Conflict of interest between parent and child or young person

32A. Conflict of interest between parent and child or young person

(1) If before or in the course of proceedings in respect of a child or young person—

(*a*) in pursuance of section 1 of this Act, or

(*b*) on an application under section 15 (1) of this Act for the discharge of a relevant supervision order or a supervision order made under section 21 (2) of this Act on the discharge of a relevant care order; or

(*c*) on an application under section 21 (2) of this Act for the discharge of a relevant care order or a care order made under section 15 (1) of this Act on the discharge of a relevant supervision order; or

(*d*) on an appeal to the Crown Court under section 2 (12) of this Act, or

(*e*) on an appeal to the Crown Court under section 16 (8) of this Act against the dismissal of an application for the discharge of a relevant supervision order or against a care order made under section 15 (1) on the discharge of—

(i) a relevant supervision order; or

(ii) a supervision order made under section 21 (2) on the discharge of a relevant care order; or

(*f*) on an appeal to the Crown Court under section 21 (4) of this Act against the dismissal of an application for the discharge of a relevant care order or against a supervision order made under section 21 (2) on the discharge of—

(i) a relevant care order; or

(ii) a care order made under section 15 (1) on the discharge of a relevant supervision order,

it appears to the court that there is or may be a conflict, on any matter relevant to the proceedings, between the interests of the child or young person and those of his parent or guardian, the court may order that in relation to the proceeding the parent or guardian is not to be treated as representing the child or young person or as otherwise authorised to act on his behalf.

(2) If an application such as is referred to in subsection (1) (*b*) or (*c*) of this section is unopposed, the court, unless satisfied that to do so is not necessary for safeguarding the interests of the child or young person, shall order that in relation to proceedings on the application no parent or guardian of his shall be treated as representing him or as otherwise authorised to act on his behalf; but where the application was made by a parent or guardian on his behalf the order shall not invalidate the application.

(3) Where an order is made under subsection (1) or (2) of this section for the purposes of proceedings on an application within subsection (1) (*a*), (*b*) or (*c*) of this section, that order shall also have effect for the purposes of any appeal to the Crown Court arising out of those proceedings.

(4) The power of the court to make orders for the purposes of an application within subsection (1) (*a*), (*b*) or (*c*) of this section shall also be exercisable, before the hearing of the application, by a single justice.

(5) In this section—

'relevant care order' means a care order made under section 1 of this Act;

'relevant supervision order' means a supervision order made under section 1 of this Act.

32B. Safeguarding of interests of child or young person where section 32A order made

(1) Where the court makes an order under section 32A (2) of this Act the court, unless satisfied that to do so is not necessary for safeguarding the interests of the child or young person, shall in accordance with rules of court appoint a guardian ad litem of the child or young person for the purposes of the proceedings.

In this subsection 'court' includes a single justice.

(2) Rules of court shall provide for the appointment of a guardian ad litem of the child or young person for the purposes of any proceedings to which an order under section 32A (1) of this Act relates.

(3) A guardian ad litem appointed in pursuance of this section shall be under a duty to safeguard the interests of the child or young person in the manner prescribed by rules of court.". **[513]**

EFFECT OF SECTION

For the effect of this section see paras. [**363**]–[**414**], *ante*.

COMMENCEMENT

This section, in so far as it provides for the insertion of the Children and Young Persons Act 1969, ss. 32A (2)–(5) and 32B (1) and (3), was brought into force on 26th November 1976 by the Children Act 1975 (Commencement No. 1) Order 1976, S.I. 1976 No. 1744, made under s. 108 (2), para. [**541**], *post*. At the time of going to press the remainder of this section was not yet in force. See as to transitional provisions, Sch. 3 to the Commencement No. 1 Order.

65. Legal aid for parents where order made under new s. 32A of 1969 Act

In section 28 (power to order legal aid to be given) of the Legal Aid Act 1974—

(*a*) in subsection (1), for "subsections (3) and (6)" there is substituted "subsections (3), (6) and (6A)", and (*b*) the following subsection is inserted after subsection (6)—

"(6A) Where a court makes an order under section 32A of the Children and Young Persons Act 1969 affecting the parent or guardian of a person in relation to any proceedings, it may order that the parent or guardian shall be given legal aid for the purpose of taking such part in the proceedings as may be allowed by rules of court.

In this subsection 'guardian' has the same meaning as in the Children and Young Persons Act 1933." [**514**]

EFFECT OF SECTION

For the effect of this section see paras. [**404**]–[**405**], *ante*.

COMMENCEMENT

This section was brought into force on 26th November 1976 by the Children Act 1975 (Commencement No. 1) Order 1976, S.I. 1976 No. 1744, made under s. 108 (2), para. [**541**], *post*.

66. (*Applies to Scotland.*)

Absence from care and children in need of secure accommodation

67. Recovery of children in care of local authorities

(1) This section applies to a child—

(*a*) who is in the care of a local authority under section 1 of the Children Act 1948; and

(*b*) with respect to whom there is in force a resolution under section 2 of that Act; and

(*c*) who—

(i) has run away from accommodation provided for him by the local authority under Part II of the said Act; or

(ii) has been taken away from such accommodation contrary to section 3 (8) of the said Act; or

(iii) has not been returned to the local authority as required by a notice served under section 49 of the Children and Young Persons Act 1963 on a person under whose charge and control the child was, in accordance with section 13 (2) of the said Act of 1948, allowed to be.

(2) If a justice of the peace is satisfied by information on oath that there are reasonable grounds for believing that a person specified in the information can produce the child to whom this section applies, he may issue a summons directed to the person so specified and requiring him to attend and produce the child before a magistrates' court acting for the same petty sessions area as the justice.

(3) Without prejudice to the powers under subsection (2) above, if a justice of the peace is satisfied by information on oath that there are reasonable grounds for believing that a child to whom this section applies is in premises specified in the information, he may issue a search warrant authorising a person named in the warrant, being an officer of the local authority in whose care the child is, to search the premises for the child; and if the child is found, he shall be placed in such accommodation as the local authority may provide for him under Part II of the Children Act 1948.

(4) A person who, without reasonable excuse, fails to comply with a sum-

mons under subsection (2) shall, without prejudice to any liability apart from this subsection, be guilty of an offence and liable on summary conviction to a fine not exceeding £100. [**515**]

EFFECT OF SECTION

For the effect of this section see para. [**344**], *ante*.

COMMENCEMENT

This section was brought into force on 26th November 1976 by the Children Act 1975 (Commencement No. 1) Order 1976, S.I. 1976 No. 1744, made under s. 108 (2), para. [**541**], *post*.

68. Extension of powers under s. 32 of the Children and Young Persons Act 1969

(1) Section 32 of the Children and Young Persons Act 1969 (detention of absentees) shall have effect subject to the following provisions of this section.

(2) In subsection (1) of the said section 32, paragraph (*b*) shall cease to have effect.

(3) After subsection (1) of the said section 32, there is inserted the following subsection—

"(1A) If a child or young person is absent from a place of safety to which he has been taken in pursuance of section 2 (5), 16 (3) or 28 of this Act without the consent of—

(*a*) the person who made the arrangements for his detention in the place of safety in pursuance of the said section 2 (5) or 16 (3), or

(*b*) the person on whose application an authorisation relating to the child or young person has been issued under the said section 28,

he may be arrested by a constable anywhere in the United Kingdom or the Channel Islands without a warrant, and shall, if so arrested, be conducted to the place of safety at the expense of the person referred to in paragraph (*a*) or (*b*) (as the case may be) of this subsection.".

(4) In subsection (2) of the said section 32, after the words "subsection (1)" there are inserted the words "or (1A)", and for the words "twenty pounds" there is substituted the word "£100".

(5) After the said subsection (2), the following subsections are inserted—

"(2A) Without prejudice to its powers under subsection (2) of this section, a magistrates' court (within the meaning of that subsection) may, if it is satisfied by information on oath that there are reasonable grounds for believing that a person who is absent as mentioned in subsection (1) or (1A) of this section is in premises specified in the information, issue a search warrant authorising a constable to search the premises for that person.

(2B) A court shall not issue a summons or search warrant under subsection (2) or (2A) of this section in any case where the person who is absent is a person to whom subsection (1A) of this section applies, unless the information referred to in the said subsection (2) or (2A) is given by the person referred to in subsection (1A) (*a*) or (*b*) (as the case may be) of this section."

(6) In subsection (3) of the said section 32, for the words "one hundred pounds" there is substituted the word "£400".

(7) In subsection (4) of the said section 32, for the words "subsection (1)"

there are substituted the words "subsections (1), (1A) and (2A)", and for the words "that subsection" there are substituted the words "subsection (1)". **[516]**

EFFECT OF SECTION

For the effect of this section see paras. [**344**]–[**345**], *ante*.

COMMENCEMENT

This section was brought into force on 26th November 1976 by the Children Act 1975 (Commencement No. 1) Order 1976, S.I. 1976 No. 1744, made under s. 108 (2), para. [**541**], *post*.

69. Certificates of unruly character

The court shall not certify under section 22 (5) or section 23 (2) or (3) of the Children and Young Persons Act 1969 (committals to remand centres or prison) that a child is of so unruly a character that he cannot safely be committed to the care of a local authority unless the conditions prescribed by order made by the Secretary of State are satisfied in relation to that child.

In this section, "court" includes a justice. **[517]**

EFFECT OF SECTION

For the effect of this section see paras. [**351**]–[**353**], *ante*.

COMMENCEMENT

This section was brought into force on 1st August 1977 by the Children Act 1975 (Commencement No. 2) Order 1977, S.I. 1977 No. 1036, made under s. 108 (2), para. [**541**], *post*.

70. (*Applies to Scotland.*)

71. Grants in respect of secure accommodation for children in England and Wales

The following section is inserted after section 64 of the Children and Young Persons Act 1969—

> **"64A. Grants in respect of secure accommodation**
>
> (1) The Secretary of State may make to local authorities out of moneys provided by Parliament grants of such amount and subject to such conditions as he may with the consent of the Treasury determine in respect of expenditure incurred by the authorities in providing secure accommodation in community homes other than assisted community homes.
>
> (2) The Secretary of State may with the consent of the Treasury require the local authority to repay the grant, in whole or in part, if the secure accommodation in respect of which the grant was made (including such accommodation in a controlled community home) ceases to be used as such.
>
> (3) In this section "secure accommodation" means accommodation provided for the purposes of restricting the liberty of children in a community home". **[518]**

EFFECT OF SECTION

For the effect of this section see para. [**354**], *ante*.

COMMENCEMENT

This section came into force on the passing of this Act on 12th November 1975; see s. 108 (3), para. [**541**], *post*.

72-84. (*Apply to Scotland.*)

PART IV

FURTHER AMENDMENTS OF LAW OF ENGLAND AND WALES

Explanation of concepts

85. Parental rights and duties

(1) In this Act, unless the context otherwise requires, "the parental rights and duties" means as respects a particular child (whether legitimate or not), all the rights and duties which by law the mother and father have in relation to a legitimate child and his property; and references to a parental right or duty shall be construed accordingly and shall include a right of access and any other element included in a right or duty.

(2) Subject to section 1 (2) of the Guardianship Act 1973 (which relates to separation agreements between husband and wife), a person cannot surrender or transfer to another any parental right or duty he has as respects a child.

(3) Where two or more persons have a parental right or duty jointly, any one of them may exercise or perform it in any manner without the other or others if the other or, as the case may be, one or more of the others have not signified disapproval of its exercise or performance in that manner.

(4) From the death of a person who has a parental right or duty jointly with one other person, or jointly with two or more other persons, that other person has the right or duty exclusively or, as the case may be, those other persons have it jointly.

(5) Where subsection (4) does not apply on the death of a person who has a parental right or duty, that right or duty lapses, but without prejudice to its acquisition by another person at any time under any enactment.

(6) Subsections (4) and (5) apply in relation to the dissolution of a body corporate as they apply in relation to the death of an individual.

(7) Except as otherwise provided by or under any enactment, while the mother of an illegitimate child is living she has the parental right and duties exclusively. **[519]**

EFFECT OF SECTION

For the effect of this section see paras. [**208**]–[**230**], *ante*.

COMMENCEMENT

This section came into force on 1st January 1976; see s. 108 (4), para. [**541**], *post*.

86. Legal custody

In this Act, unless the context otherwise requires, "legal custody" means, as respects a child, so much of the parental rights and duties as relate to the person of the child (including the place and manner in which his time is spent); but a person shall not by virtue of having legal custody of a child be entitled to effect or arrange for his emigration from the United Kingdom unless he is a parent or guardian of the child. **[520]**

EFFECT OF SECTION

For the effect of this section see paras. [**231**]–[**236**], *ante*.

COMMENCEMENT

This section came into force on 1st January 1976; see s. 108 (4), para. [**541**], *post*.

87. Actual custody

(1) A person has actual custody of a child if he has actual possession of his person, whether or not that possession is shared with one or more other persons.

(2) While a person not having legal custody of a child has actual custody of the child he has the like duties in relation to the child as a custodian would have by virtue of his legal custody.

(3) In this Act, unless the context otherwise requires, references to the person with whom a child has his home refer to the person who, disregarding absence of the child at a hospital or boarding school and any other temporary absence, has actual custody of the child. **[521]**

EFFECT OF SECTION

For the effect of this section see para. [**237**], *ante*.

COMMENCEMENT

This section came into force on 1st January 1976; see s. 108 (4), para. [**541**], *post*.

88. Child in care of voluntary organisation

A child is in the care of a voluntary organisation if—

(*a*) the organisation has actual custody of him, or

(*b*) having had actual custody of him, the organisation has transferred that custody to an individual who does not have legal custody of him. **[522]**

EFFECT OF SECTION

For the effect of this section see para. [**356**], *ante*.

COMMENCEMENT

This section came into force on 1st January 1976; see s. 108 (4), para. [**541**], *post*.

89. Amendment of Interpretation Act 1889

(1) In the Interpretation Act 1889 after section 19 there is inserted the following section—

"19A. Meaning of expressions relating to children

In any Act passed after the Children Act 1975, unless the contrary intention appears—

(*a*) the expression 'the parental rights and duties',

(*b*) the expression 'legal custody' (as respects a child) and

(*c*) references to the person with whom a child has his home,

shall be construed in accordance with Part IV of the Children Act 1975.

(2) This section does not extend to Scotland or Northern Ireland." **[523]**

EFFECT OF SECTION

For the effect of this section see para. [**239**], *ante*.

COMMENCEMENT

This section came into force on 1st January 1976; see s. 108 (4), para. [**541**], *post*.

Reports in guardianship and matrimonial proceedings

90. Procedure in guardianship proceedings

(1) The following subsections are substituted for subsections (2) and (3) of section 6 of the Guardianship Act 1973:—

"(2) A report made in pursuance of subsection (1) above to a magistrates' court shall be made to the court at a hearing of the application unless it is in writing in which case—

(*a*) a copy of the report shall be given to each party to the proceedings or to his counsel or solicitor either before or during a hearing of the application; and

(*b*) if the court thinks fit, the report, or such part of the report as the court requires, shall be read aloud at a hearing of the application.

(3) A magistrates' court may and, if requested to do so at the hearing by a party to the proceedings or his counsel or solicitor, shall, require the officer by whom the report was made to give evidence of or with respect to the matters referred to in the report and if the officer gives such evidence, any party to the proceedings may give or call evidence with respect to any such matter or any matter referred to in the officer's evidence.

(3A) A magistrates' court may take account of—

(*a*) any statement contained in a report made at a hearing of the application or of which copies have been given to the parties or their representatives in accordance with subsection (2) (*a*) above; and

(*b*) any evidence given by the officer under subsection (3) above,

in so far as the statement or evidence is, in the opinion of the court, relevant to the application notwithstanding any enactment or rule of law to the contrary."

(2) The following subsection is added after subsection (5) of the said section 6—

"(6) A single justice may request a report under subsection (1) of this section before the hearing of the application, but in such a case the report shall be made to the court which hears the application, and the foregoing provisions of this section shall apply accordingly." [**524**]

EFFECT OF SECTION

For the effect of this section see paras. [**420**]–[**421**], *ante*.

COMMENCEMENT

This section came into force on 1st January 1976; see s. 108 (4), para. [**541**], *post*.

91. Procedure in matrimonial proceedings

(1) The following subsections are substituted for subsections (3) and (4) of section 4 of the Matrimonial Proceedings (Magistrates' Courts) Act 1960—

"(3) A report made in pursuance of subsection (2) of this section shall be made to the court at a hearing of the complaint unless it is in writing in which case—

(*a*) a copy of the report shall be given to each party to the proceedings or to his counsel or solicitor either before or during a hearing of the complaint; and

(*b*) if the court thinks fit, the report, or such parts of the report as the court requires, shall be read aloud at a hearing of the complaint.

(4) The court may and, if requested to do so at the hearing by a party to the proceedings or his counsel or solicitor, shall, require the officer by whom the report was made to give evidence on or with respect to the

matters referred to in the report and if the officer gives such evidence, any party to the proceedings may give or call evidence on or with respect to any such matter or any matter referred to in the officer's evidence.

(4A) Subject to the next following subsection, the court may take account of—

(*a*) any statement contained in a report made at a hearing of the complaint or of which copies have been given to the parties or their representatives in accordance with subsection (3) (*a*) of this section; and

(*b*) any evidence given by the officer under subsection (4) of this section,

in so far as the statement or evidence relates to the matters specified by the court under subsection (2) of this section, notwithstanding any enactment or rule of law to the contrary."

(2) In subsection (5) of the said section 4, for "subsection (4)" there is substituted "subsections (4) and (4A)". [**525**]

EFFECT OF SECTION

For the effect of this section see para. [**420**], *ante*.

COMMENCEMENT

This section came into force on 1st January 1976; see s. 108 (4), para. [**541**], *post*.

Registration of births

92. Registration of births of abandoned children

The following section is inserted after section 3 of the Births and Deaths Registration Act 1953—

"3A. Registration of births of abandoned children

(1) Where the place and date of birth of a child who was abandoned are unknown to, and cannot be ascertained by, the person who has charge of the child, that person may apply to the Registrar General for the child's birth to be registered under this section.

(2) On an application under this section the Registrar General shall enter in a register maintained at the General Register Office—

(*a*) as the child's place of birth, if the child was found by the applicant or by any person from whom (directly or indirectly) the applicant took charge of the child, the registration district and sub-district where the child was found, or, in any other case, where the child was abandoned;

(*b*) as the child's date of birth, the date which, having regard to such evidence as is produced to him, appears to him to be the most likely date of birth of the child, and

(*c*) such other particulars as may be prescribed.

(3) The Registrar General shall not register a child's birth under this section if—

(*a*) he is satisfied that the child was not born in England or Wales; or

(*b*) the child has been adopted in pursuance of a court order made in the United Kingdom, the Isle of Man or the Channel Islands; or

(*c*) subject to subsection (5) below, the child's birth is known to have been previously registered under this Act.

(4) If no entry can be traced in any register of births relating to a person who has attained the age of 18 and has not been adopted as aforesaid, that person may apply to the Registrar General for his birth to be registered under this section.

(5) On the application of—

(*a*) a person having the charge of a child whose birth had been registered under this Act by virtue of the proviso to section 1 of this Act (as originally enacted), or

(*b*) any such child who has attained the age of 18 years,

the Registrar General shall re-register the birth of the child under this section, and shall direct the officer having custody of the register of births in which the entry relating to the child was previously made to enter in the margin of the register a reference to the re-registration of the birth."

[**526**]

EFFECT OF SECTION

For the effect of this section see paras. [**422**]–[**424**], *ante*.

COMMENCEMENT

This section was brought into force on 1st January 1977 by the Children Act 1975 (Commencement No. 1) Order 1976, S.I. 1976 No. 1744, made under s. 108 (2), para. [**541**], *post*.

93. Registration of father of illegitimate child

(1) At the end of paragraph (*b*) of section 10 of the Births and Deaths Registration Act of 1953 (which makes provision for the registration of fathers of illegitimate children) there is added "or

(*c*) at the request of the mother (which shall be made in writing) on production of—

(i) a certified copy of an order made under section 4 of the Affiliation Proceedings Act 1957 naming that person as the putative father of the child, and

(ii) if the child has attained the age of 16 years, the written consent of the child to the registration of that person as his father."

(2) After the said section 10 there is inserted the following section—

"10A. Re-registration of births of illegitimate children

(1) Where the birth of an illegitimate child has been registered under this Act but no person has been registered as the child's father, the registrar shall re-register the birth so as to show a person as the father—

(*a*) at the joint request of the mother and of that person; or

(*b*) at the request of the mother on production of—

(i) a declaration in the prescribed form made by the mother stating that that person is the father of the child; and

(ii) a statutory declaration made by that person acknowledging himself to be the father of the child; or

(*c*) at the request of the mother (which shall be made in writing) on production of—

(i) a certified copy of an order made under section 4 of the Affiliation Proceedings Act 1957 naming that person as the putative father of that child, and

(ii) if the child has attained the age of 16 years, the written consent of the child to the registration of that person as his father;

but no birth shall be re-registered under this section except in the prescribed manner and with the authority of the Registrar General.

(2) On the re-registration of a birth under this section—

(*a*) the registrar and the mother shall sign the register;

(*b*) in the case of a request under paragraph (*a*) of subsection (1) of this section, the other person making the request shall also sign the register; and

(*c*) if the re-registration takes place more than three months after the birth, the superintendent registrar shall also sign the register."

(3) In section 9 of the said Act of 1953 (which enables information required to be given to the registrar to be given to other persons) after subsection (3) there are added the following subsections—

"(4) A request made under section 10 of this Act may be included in a declaration under subsection (1) of this section, and, if the request is made under paragraph (*b*) or (*c*) of that section, the documents required by that paragraph to be produced shall be produced to the officer in whose presence the declaration is made and sent by him with the declaration to the registrar.

(5) A request made under section 10A of this Act instead of being made to the registrar may be made by making and signing in the presence of and delivering to a prescribed officer a statement in the prescribed form and producing to the officer any documents required to be produced by that section, and—

(*a*) the officer shall send the request together with those documents, if any, to the registrar who shall with the authority of the Registrar General re-register the birth as if the request had been made to him; and

(*b*) the person or persons who sign the statement shall be deemed to have signed the register as required by subsection (2) of that section." [**527**]

EFFECT OF SECTION

For the effect of this section see paras. [**425**]–[**428**], *ante*.

COMMENCEMENT

This section was brought into force on 1st January 1977 by the Children Act 1975 (Commencement No. 1) Order 1976, S.I. 1976 No. 1744, made under s. 108 (2), para. [**541**], *post*.

Extent of Part IV

94. Extent of Part IV

This Part does not extend to Scotland. [**528**]

COMMENCEMENT

This section came into force on 1st January 1976; see s. 108 (4), para. [**541**], *post*.

Part V

Miscellaneous and Supplemental

Foster children

95. Visiting of foster children

(1) In section 1 of the Children Act 1958 (visiting of foster children), the words

"so far as appears to the authority to be appropriate" shall cease to have effect, and for the words "from time to time" there are substituted the words "in accordance with regulations made under section 2A of this Act".

(2) (*Applies to Scotland.*)

(3) The following section is inserted in the said Act after section 2—

"2A. Visits to foster children

(1) The Secretary of State may make regulations requiring foster children in a local authority's area to be visited by an officer of the local authority on specified occasions or within specified periods of time.

(2) Every person who is maintaining a foster child within the area of a local authority on the date on which regulations made under subsection (1) of this section come into operation, and who before that date has not given notice in respect of the child to the local authority under section 3 (1) of this Act, shall within eight weeks of that date give written notice that he is maintaining the child to the local authority.

(3) Regulations under this section shall be made by statutory instrument which shall be subject to annulment in pursuance of a resolution of either House of Parliament."

(4) In section 3 of the said Act as it applies to England and Wales (duty of persons maintaining foster children to notify local authority)—

(*a*) in subsection (5A), for the words "one or more foster children" there are substituted the words "a foster child", and for the words "foster children" and "any foster children" there are substituted the words "that foster child";

(*b*) in subsection (5B) for the words "foster children" there are substituted the words "a foster child", and for the words "any of them as a" there is substituted the word "that"; and

(*c*) the following subsection is added at the end—

"(8) Subsection (2A) of this section shall cease to have effect on the date regulations made under section 2A of this Act come into operation.". [**529**]

EFFECT OF SECTION

For the effect of this section see paras. [**416**]–[**418**], *ante*.

COMMENCEMENT

At the time of going to press this section was not yet in force; see s. 108 (2), para. [**541**], *post*.

96. Notification by parents

(1) The following section is inserted in the Children Act 1958 after section 3—

"3A. Notification by parents

(1) The Secretary of State may by regulations made by statutory instrument make provision for requiring parents whose children are or are going to be maintained as foster children to give to the local authority for the area where the children are, or are going to be, living as foster children, such information about the fostering as may be specified in the regulations.

(2) Regulations under this section—

(*a*) may include such incidental and supplementary provisions as the Secretary of State thinks fit;

(*b*) shall be subject to annulment in pursuance of a resolution of either House of Parliament."

(2) In section 14 of the said Act (offences), in subsection (1) (*a*), after the words "this Part of this Act" there are inserted the words "or under regulations made under section 3A of this Act". **[530]**

EFFECT OF SECTION

For the effect of this section see paras. [**417**]–[**418**], *ante*.

COMMENCEMENT

At the time of going to press this section was not yet in force; see s. 108 (2), para. [**541**], *post*.

97. Advertisements relating to foster children

(1) In section 37 of the Children Act 1958 the following subsections are inserted after subsection (1)—

"(1A) The Secretary of State may by regulations prohibit the parent or guardian of any child from publishing or causing to be published an advertisement indicating that foster parents are sought for the child.

(1B) The Secretary of State may by regulations prohibit—

(*a*) a member of a class of persons specified in the regulations, or

(*b*) a person other than a person, or other than a member of a class of persons, specified in the regulations,

from publishing or causing to be published any advertisement indicating that he is willing to undertake, or to arrange for, the care and maintenance of a child.

(1C) Regulations made under this section—

(*a*) may make different provision for different cases or classes of cases, and

(*b*) may exclude certain cases or classes of cases, and shall be made by statutory instrument,

subject to annulment in pursuance of a resolution of either House of Parliament."

(2) In subsection (2) of the said section 37, after the words "this section" there are inserted the words "or of regulations made under this section". **[531]**

EFFECT OF SECTION

For the effect of this section see para. [**419**], *ante*.

COMMENCEMENT

At the time of going to press this section was not yet in force; see s. 108 (2), para. [**541**], *post*.

Inquiries

98. Inquiries in England and Wales

(1) The Secretary of State may cause an inquiry to be held into any matter relating to—

(*a*) the functions of the social services committee of a local authority, in so far as those functions relate to children;

(*b*) the functions of an adoption agency;

(*c*) the functions of a voluntary organisation in so far as those functions relate to voluntary homes;

(*d*) a home maintained by the Secretary of State for the accommodation of children who are in the care of local authorities and are in need of the particular facilities and services provided in the home;

(*e*) the detention of a child under section 53 of the Children and Young Persons Act 1933.

(2) The Secretary of State may, before an inquiry is commenced, direct that it shall be held in private, but where no such direction has been given, the person holding the inquiry may if he thinks fit hold it or any part of it in private.

(3) Subsections (2) to (5) of section 250 of the Local Government Act 1972 (powers in relation to local inquiries) shall apply in relation to an inquiry under this section as they apply in relation to a local inquiry under that section.

(4) In this section—

"functions" includes powers and duties which a person has otherwise than by virtue of any enactment;

"voluntary home" means a home or other institution for the boarding, care and maintenance of poor children which is supported wholly or partly by voluntary contributions, but does not include a mental nursing home or residential home for mentally disordered persons within the meaning of Part III of the Mental Health Act 1959.

(5) This section does not apply to Scotland. [**532**]

EFFECT OF SECTION

For the effect of this section see para. [**429**], *ante*.

COMMENCEMENT

This section came into force on 1st January 1976; see s. 108 (4), para. [**541**], *post*.

PROSPECTIVE AMENDMENT

Sub-s. (1) (*b*) is amended by the Adoption Act 1976, s. 73 (2) and Sch. 3, para. 21, A.L.S. Vol. 244, as from a day to be appointed.

99. (*Applies to Scotland.*)

Supplemental

100. Courts

(1) In this Act "authorised court", as respects an application for an order relating to a child, shall be construed as follows.

(2) If the child is in England or Wales when the application is made, the following are authorised courts—

(*a*) the High Court;

(*b*) the county court within whose district the child is and, in the case of an application under section 14, any county court within whose district a parent or guardian of the child is;

(*c*) any other county court prescribed by rules made under section 102 of the County Courts Act 1959;

(*d*) a magistrates' court within whose area the child is and, in the case of an application under section 14, a magistrates' court within whose area a parent or guardian of the child is.

(3) If the child is in Scotland when the application is made, the following are authorised courts—

(*a*) the Court of Session;

(*b*) the sheriff court of the sheriffdom within which the child is.

(4) If in the case of an application for an adoption order or an order under

section 14 the child is not in Great Britain when the application is made, the following are authorised courts—

(*a*) the High Court;

(*b*) the Court of Session.

(5) In the case of a Convention adoption order paragraphs (*b*), (*c*) and (*d*) of subsection (2) or, as the case may be, paragraph (*b*) of subsection (3) do not apply.

(6) In the case of an order under section 25, paragraph (*d*) of subsection (2) does not apply.

(7) Subsection (2) applies in the case of an application for an order under section 34, 35 or 38 relating to a child who is subject to a custodianship order whether or not the child is in England or Wales and for the purposes of such an application the following are also authorised courts—

(*a*) the court which made the custodianship order and where that court is a magistrates' court, any other magistrates' court acting for the same petty session area;

(*b*) the county court within whose district the applicant is;

(*c*) a magistrates' court within whose area the applicant is;

(*d*) where the application is made under section 35 and the child's mother or father or custodian is the petitioner or respondent in proceedings for a decree of divorce, nullity or judicial separation which are pending in a court in England or Wales, that court.

(8) Subsection (2) does not apply in the case of an application under section 30 or 42 but for the purposes of such an application the following are authorised courts—

(*a*) if there is pending in respect of the child an application for an adoption order or an order under section 14 or a custodianship order, the court in which that application is pending;

(*b*) in any other case, the High Court, the county court within whose district the applicant lives and the magistrates' court within whose area the applicant lives.

(9) (*Applies to Scotland.*) **[533]**

EFFECT OF SECTION

For the effect of this section see paras. [**84**]–[**88**] and [**312**]–[**316**], *ante*.

COMMENCEMENT

This section came into force on 1st January 1976; see s. 108 (4), para. [**541**], *post*.

PROSPECTIVE REPEAL

Sub-ss. (4)–(6) are repealed by the Adoption Act 1976, s. 73 and Sch. 4, A.L.S. Vol. 244, as from a day to be appointed, and replaced as noted in the destination table, para. [**589**], *post*.

101. Appeals, etc.

(1) Where any application has been made under this Act to a county court, the High Court may, at the instance of any party to the application, order the application to be removed to the High Court and there proceeded with on such terms as to costs as it thinks proper.

(2) Subject to subsection (3), where on an application to a magistrates' court under this Act the court makes or refuses to make an order, an appeal shall lie to the High Court.

(3) Where an application is made to a magistrates' court under this Act,

and the court considers that the matter is one which would more conveniently be dealt with by the High Court, the magistrates' court shall refuse to make an order, and in that case no appeal shall lie to the High Court. [**534**]

EFFECT OF SECTION

For the effect of this section see para. [**440**], *ante*.

COMMENCEMENT

This section was brought into force on 26th November 1976 by the Children Act 1975 (Commencement No. 1) Order 1976, S.I. 1976 No. 1744, made under s. 108 (2), para. [**541**], *post*.

102. Evidence of agreement and consent

(1) Any agreement or consent which is required by Part I, except section 24 (6), or Part II to be given to the making of any order or application for an order may be given in writing, and, if the document signifying the agreement or consent is—

(*a*) in the case of an adoption order or an application for an order under section 14, witnessed in accordance with rules, or

(*b*) in the case of an application made under Part II, witnessed in accordance with rules of court,

it shall be admissible in evidence without further proof of the signature of the person by whom it was executed.

(2) A document signifying such agreement or consent which purports to be witnessed in accordance with rules or, as the case may be, with rules of court shall be presumed to be so witnessed, and to have been executed and witnessed on the date and at the place specified in the document, unless the contrary is proved.

(3) (*Applies to Scotland.*) [**535**]

EFFECT OF SECTION

For the effect of this section see para. [**127**], *ante*.

COMMENCEMENT

At the time of going to press this section was not yet in force; see s. 108 (2), para. [**541**], *post*.

PROSPECTIVE REPEAL

Sub-s. (1) is repealed in part by the Adoption Act 1976, s. 73 and Sch. 4, A.L.S. Vol. 244, as from a day to be appointed, and replaced as noted in the destination table, para. [**589**], *post*.

103. Panel for guardians ad litem and reporting officers

(1) The Secretary of State may by regulations make provision for the establishment of a panel of persons from whom—

(*a*) guardians ad litem and reporting officers may in accordance with rules or rules of court be appointed for the purposes of—

(i) section 20 of this Act;

(ii) section 32B of the Children and Young Persons Act 1969;

(iii) section 4B of the Children Act 1948;

(*b*) (*applies to Scotland*).

(2) Regulations under subsection (1) may provide for the expenses incurred by members of the panel to be defrayed by local authorities.

(3) (*Applies to Scotland.*) [**536**]

EFFECT OF SECTION

For the effect of this section see paras. [**410**]–[**414**], *ante*.

COMMENCEMENT

This section came into force on 1st January 1976; see s. 108 (4), para. [**541**], *post*.

PROSPECTIVE AMENDMENT

Sub-s. (1) (*a*) (i) is substituted by the Adoption Act 1976, s. 73 (2) and Sch. 3, para. 22, A.L.S. Vol. 244, as from a day to be appointed.

104. Saving for powers of High Court

Nothing in this Act shall restrict or affect the jurisdiction of the High Court to appoint or remove guardians, or otherwise in respect of children. [**537**]

COMMENCEMENT

This section came into force on 1st January 1976; see s. 108 (4), para. [**541**], *post*.

105. Periodic review of Act

The Secretary of State shall, within three years of the first of the dates appointed by order by the Secretary of State under section 108 (2) and, thereafter, every five years lay before Parliament a report on the operation of those sections of the Act which are in force at that time; and the Secretary of State shall institute such research as is necessary to provide the information for these reports. [**538**]

COMMENCEMENT

This section came into force on 1st January 1976; see s. 108 (4), para. [**541**], *post*.

106. Regulations and orders

(1) Where a power to make regulations or orders is exercisable by the Secretary of State by virtue of this Act, regulations or orders made in the exercise of that power shall be made by statutory instrument and may—

(*a*) make different provision in relation to different cases or classes of case, and

(*b*) exclude certain cases or classes of case.

(2) A statutory instrument containing regulations made by the Secretary of State under section 103 shall be subject to annulment in pursuance of a resolution of either House of Parliament.

(3) Any power conferred on the Secretary of State by this Act to make orders include powers to vary or revoke an order so made. [**539**]

COMMENCEMENT

This section came into force on 1st January 1976; see s. 108 (4), para. [**541**], *post*.

107. Interpretation

(1) In this Act, unless the context otherwise requires—

"adoption order" means an order under section 8 (1);

"adoption society" has the same meaning as in the 1958 Act;

"approved adoption society" means an adoption society approved under Part I;

"area", in relation to a magistrates' court, means the commission area (within the meaning of section 1 of the Administration of Justice Act 1973) for which the court is appointed;

"authorised court" shall be construed in accordance with section 100;

"British adoption order" means an adoption order, or any provision for the adoption of a child effected under the law of Northern Ireland or any British territory outside the United Kingdom;

"British territory" means, for the purposes of any provision of this Act, any of the following countries, that is to say, the United Kingdom, the Channel Islands, the Isle of Man and a colony, being a country designated for the purposes of that provision by order of the Secretary of State or, if no country is so designated, any of those countries;

"child", except where used to express a relationship, means a person who has not attained the age of 18;

"the Convention" means the Convention relating to the adoption of children concluded at The Hague on 15th November 1965 and signed on behalf of the United Kingdom on that date;

"Convention adoption order" means an adoption order made as mentioned in section 24 (1);

"Convention country" means any country outside British territory, being a country for the time being designated by an order of the Secretary of State as a country in which, in his opinion, the Convention is in force;

"guardian" means—

(*a*) a person appointed by deed or will in accordance with the provisions of the Guardianship of Infants Acts 1886 and 1925 or the Guardianship of Minors Act 1971 or by a court of competent jurisdiction to be the guardian of the child, and

(*b*) in relation to the adoption of an illegitimate child, includes the father where he has custody of the child by virtue of an order under section 9 of the Guardianship of Minors Act 1971, or under section 2 of the Illegitimate Children (Scotland) Act 1930;

"home" shall be construed in accordance with section 87 (3);

"local authority" means in relation to England and Wales the council of a county (other than a metropolitan county), a metropolitan district, a London borough or the Common Council of the City of London;

"notice" means a notice in writing;

"relative" has the same meaning as in the 1958 Act;

"rules" means, in England and Wales, rules made under section 9 (3) of the 1958 Act or made by virtue of section 9 (4) of the 1958 Act under section 15 of the Justices of the Peace Act 1949;

"the 1958 Act" means the Adoption Act 1958;

"United Kingdom national" means, for the purposes of any provision of this Act, a citizen of the United Kingdom and Colonies satisfying such conditions, if any, as the Secretary of State may by order specify for the purposes of that provision;

"voluntary organisation" means a body other than a public or local authority the activities of which are not carried on for profit.

(2) In this Act, in relation to Scotland, unless the context otherwise requires—

"actual custody" means care and possession;

"legal custody" means custody;

"local authority" means a regional or islands council; and

"rules" means rules made by act of sederunt.

(3) Except so far as the context otherwise requires, any reference in this Act to an enactment shall be construed as a reference to that enactment as amended by or under any other enactment, including this Act.

(4) In this Act, except where otherwise indicated—

(*a*) a reference to a numbered Part, section or Schedule is a reference to the Part or section of, or the Schedule to, this Act so numbered, and

(*b*) a reference in a section to a numbered subsection is a reference to the subsection of that section so numbered, and

(*c*) a reference in a section, subsection or Schedule to a numbered paragraph is a reference to the paragraph of that section, subsection or Schedule so numbered. [**540**]

COMMENCEMENT

This section came into force on 1st January 1976; see s. 108 (4), para. [**541**], *post*.

PROSPECTIVE REPEAL

In sub-s. (1) the definitions of "adoption order", "adoption society", "approved adoption society", "British adoption order", "British territory", "the Convention", "Convention adoption order", "Convention country" and "United Kingdom national", and, in the definition "guardian", para. (*b*), are repealed by the Adoption Act 1976, s. 73 and Sch. 4, A.L.S. Vol. 244, as from a day to be appointed, and replaced as noted in the destination table, para. [**589**], *post*.

108. Amendments, repeals, commencement and transitory provisions

(1) Subject to the following provisions of this section—

(*a*) the enactments specified in Schedule 3 shall have effect subject to the amendments specified in that Schedule (being minor amendments or amendments consequential on the preceding provisions of this Act), and

(*b*) the enactments specified in Schedule 4 are repealed to the extent shown in column 3 of that Schedule.

(2) This Act, except the provisions specified in subsections (3) and (4), shall come into force on such date as the Secretary of State may by order appoint and different dates may be appointed for, or for different purposes of, different provisions.

(3) Sections 71, 72 and 82, this section, section 109 and paragraph 57 of Schedule 3 shall come into force on the passing of this Act.

(4) The following provisions of this Act shall come into force on 1st January 1976—

(*a*) sections 3, 8 (9) and (10), 13, 59, 83–91, 94, 98–100, and 103–107;

(*b*) Schedules 1 and 2;

(*c*) In Schedule 3, paragraphs 1, 2, 3, 4, 6, 8, 9, 13 (6), 15, 17, 18, 19, 20, 21 (1), (2), (4), 22–25, 27 (*b*), 29, 33, 34 (*b*), 35, 36 (*b*), 38, 39 (*c*), (*d*), (*e*), 40, 43, 48, 49, 51 (*a*), 52 (*f*) (ii) and (*g*) (ii), 54, 55, 58 to 63, 65 to 70, 75 (3), 77, 78, 81 and 83.

(*d*) Parts I, II and III of Schedule 4.

(5) Until the date appointed under subsection (2) for sections 4 to 7, in this Act and in the 1958 Act "adoption agency" means a local authority or a registered adoption society within the meaning of the 1958 Act.

(6) Until the date so appointed for section 12, section 5 (1) of the 1958 Act shall, in relation to an application made after 31st December 1975 for an adoption order, have effect with the addition at the end of paragraph (*b*) of the following words "or

(*c*) has seriously ill-treated the child and that (whether because of the ill-treatment or for other reasons) the rehabilitation of the child within the household of that person is unlikely."

(7) Until the date so appointed for section 18, section 21A of the Children and Young Persons Act 1969 shall have effect as if for references to section 25 there were substituted references to section 53 of the 1958 Act.

(8) An order under subsection (2) may make such transitional provision as appears to the Secretary of State to be necessary or expedient in connection with the provisions thereby brought into force, including such adaptations of those provisions or any provision of this Act then in force or any provision of the 1958 Act as appear to him to be necessary or expedient in consequence of the partial operation of this Act. [**541**]

ORDERS UNDER THIS SECTION

The Children Act 1975 (Commencement No. 1) Order 1976, S.I. 1976 No. 1744; and the Children Act 1975 (Commencement No. 2) Order 1977, S.I. 1977 No. 1036.

109. Short title and extent

(1) This Act may be cited as the Children Act 1975.

(2) This Act, except—

(*a*) section 68;

(*b*) paragraphs 10, 11 and 63 of Schedule 3; and

(*c*) Schedule 4 in so far as it repeals—

(i) the words "or adoption" in section 9 (5) of the Adoption Act 1968, and

(ii) the references in that Act to section 19 of the Adoption Act 1958,

does not extend to Northern Ireland.

(3) Subsection (1) of section 68 extends to the Channel Islands. [**542**]

COMMENCEMENT

This section came into force on the passing of this Act on 12th November 1975; see s. 108 (3), para. [**541**], *ante*.

SCHEDULES

SCHEDULE 1

Section 8

STATUS CONFERRED BY ADOPTION OR LEGITIMATION IN ENGLAND AND WALES

PART I

INTERPRETATION

1.—(1) This Part applies for the construction of this Schedule, except where the context otherwise requires.

(2) "Adoption" means adoption—

(*a*) by an adoption order as defined in section 107,

(*b*) by an adoption order made under the 1958 Act or the Adoption Act 1950 or any enactment repealed by the Adoption Act 1950,

(*c*) by an order made in Northern Ireland, the Isle of Man or in any of the Channel Islands,

(*d*) which is an overseas adoption as defined by section 4 (3) of the Adoption Act 1968, or

(*e*) which is an adoption recognised by the law of England and Wales, and effected under the law of any other country.

and cognate expressions shall be construed accordingly.

(3) (*Repealed by the Legitimacy Act 1976, s. 11 (2), Sch. 2, A.L.S. Vol. 244.*)

(4) [This definition of adoption includes], where the context admits, [an adoption effected] before the passing of this Act, and the date of an adoption effected by an order is the date of the making of the order.

(5) "Existing", in relation to any enactment or other instrument, means one passed or made before 1st January 1976 (and whether or not before the passing of this Act).

(6) The death of the testator is the date at which a will or codicil is to be regarded as made.

Dispositions of property

2.—(1) In this Schedule—

"disposition" includes the conferring of a power of appointment and any other disposition of an interest in or right over property;

"power of appointment" includes any discretionary power to transfer a beneficial interest in property without the furnishing of valuable consideration.

(2) This Schedule applies to an oral disposition of property as if contained in an instrument made when the disposition was made. [**543**]

COMMENCEMENT

This Schedule came into force on 1st January 1976; see s. 108 (4), para. [**541**], *ante*.

AMENDMENT

The words in square brackets in para. 1 (4) were inserted by the Legitimacy Act 1976, s. 11 (1) and Sch. 1, para. 7, A.L.S. Vol. 244.

PROSPECTIVE REPEAL

This Schedule is repealed by the Adoption Act 1976, s. 73 and Sch. 4, A.L.S. Vol. 244, as from a day to be appointed, and replaced as noted in the destination table, para. [**589**], *post*.

Part II

Adoption Orders

Status conferred by adoption

3.—(1) An adopted child shall be treated in law—

(*a*) where the adopters are a married couple, as if he had been born as a child of the marriage (whether or not he was in fact born after the marriage was solemnized);

(*b*) in any other case, as if he had been born to the adopter in wedlock (but not as a child of any actual marriage of the adopter).

(2) An adopted child shall be treated in law as if he were not the child of any person other than the adopters or adopter.

(3) It is hereby declared that this paragraph prevents an adopted child from being illegitimate.

(4) This paragraph has effect—

(*a*) in the case of an adoption before 1st January 1976, from that date, and

(*b*) in the case of any other adoption, from the date of the adoption.

(5) Subject to the provisions of this Part, this paragraph applies for the construction of enactments or instruments passed or made before the adoption or later, and so applies subject to any contrary indication.

(6) Subject to the provisions of this Part, this paragraph has effect as respects things done, or events occurring, after the adoption, or after 31st December 1975, whichever is the later.

Vocabulary

4. A relationship existing by virtue of paragraph 3 may be referred to as an adoptive relationship, and—

(*a*) a male adopter may be referred to as the adoptive father;
(*b*) a female adopter may be referred to as the adoptive mother;
(*c*) any other relative of any degree under an adoptive relationship may be referred to as an adoptive relative of that degree.

but this paragraph does not prevent the term "parent", or any other term not qualified by the word "adoptive", being treated as including an adoptive relative.

Instruments and enactments concerning property

5.—(1) Paragraph 3—

(*a*) does not apply to an existing instrument or enactment so far as it contains a disposition of property, and
(*b*) does not apply to any public general Act in its application to any disposition of property in an existing instrument or enactment.

(2) The repeal by this Act of sections 16 and 17 of the 1958 Act, and of provisions containing references to those sections, does not affect their application in relation to a disposition of property effected by an existing instrument.

(3) For the purposes of this paragraph, and of paragraph 6, provisions of the law of intestate succession applicable to the estate of a deceased person shall be treated as if contained in an instrument executed by him (while of full capacity) immediately before his death.

6.—(1) Subject to any contrary indication, the rules of construction contained in this paragraph apply to any instrument, other than an existing instrument, so far as it contains a disposition of property.

(2) In applying paragraph 3 (1) to a disposition which depends on the date of birth of a child or children of the adoptive parent or parents, the disposition shall be construed as if—

(*a*) the adopted child had been born on the date of adoption,
(*b*) two or more children adopted on the same date had been born on that date in the order of their actual births,

but this does not affect any reference to the age of a child.

(3) Examples of phrases in wills on which sub-paragraph (2) can operate are—

1. Children of A "living at my death or born afterwards".
2. Children of A "living at my death or born afterwards before any one of such children for the time being in existence attains a vested interest, and who attain the age of 21 years".
3. As in example 1 or 2, but referring to grandchildren of A, instead of children of A.
4. A for life "until he has a child", and then to his child or children.

Note: Sub-paragraph (2) will not affect the reference to the age of 21 years in example 2.

(4) Paragraph 3 (2) does not prejudice any interest vested in possession in the adopted child before the adoption, or any interest expectant (whether immediately or not) upon an interest so vested.

(5) Where it is necessary to determine for the purposes of a disposition of property effected by an instrument whether a woman can have a child, it shall be presumed that once a woman has attained the age of fifty-five she will not adopt a child after execution of the instrument, and notwithstanding paragraph 3 if she does so the child shall not be treated as her child or as the child of her spouse (if any) for the purposes of the instrument.

(6) In this paragraph "instrument" includes a private Act settling property, but not any other enactment.

(7) Paragraph 3 (6) has effect subject to this paragraph.

Other enactments and instruments

7.—(1) Paragraph 3 does not apply for the purposes of the table of kindred and affinity in Schedule 1 to the Marriage Act 1949 or sections 10 and 11 (incest) of the Sexual Offences Act 1956.

(2) Paragraph 3 does not apply for the purposes of any provision of—

(*a*) the British Nationality Acts 1948 to 1965,
(*b*) the Immigration Act 1971,
(*c*) any instrument having effect under an enactment within paragraph (*a*) or (*b*), or
(*d*) any other provision of the law for the time being in force which determines citizenship of the United Kingdom and Colonies.

(3) Paragraph 3 shall not prevent a person being treated as a near relative of a deceased person for the purposes of section 32 of the Social Security Act 1975 (payment of death grant), if apart from paragraph 3 he would be so treated.

(4) Paragraph 3 does not apply for the purposes of section 70 (3) (*b*) or section 73 (2) of the Social Security Act 1975 (payment of industrial death benefit to or in respect of an illegitimate child of the deceased and the child's mother).

(5) Subject to regulations made under section 72 of the Social Security Act 1975 (entitlement of certain relatives of deceased to industrial death benefit), paragraph 3 shall not affect the entitlement to an industrial death benefit of a person who would, apart from paragraph 3, be treated as a relative of a deceased person for the purposes of the said section 72.

Pensions

8. Paragraph 3 (2) does not affect entitlement to a pension which is payable to or for the benefit of a child and is in payment at the time of his adoption.

Adoption of child by natural parents

9. In the case of a child adopted by one of its natural parents as sole adoptive parent, paragraph 3 (2) has no effect as respects entitlement to property depending on relationship to that parent, or as respects anything else depending on that relationship.

Peerages, etc.

10. An adoption does not affect the descent of any peerage or dignity or title of honour.

Insurance

11. Where a child is adopted whose natural parent has effected an insurance with a friendly society or a collecting society or an industrial insurance company for the payment on the death of the child of money for funeral expenses, the rights and liabilities under the policy shall by virtue of the adoption be transferred to the adoptive parents who shall for the purposes of the enactments relating to such societies and companies be treated as the person who took out the policy. [**544**]

COMMENCEMENT

This Schedule came into force on 1st January 1976; see s. 108 (4), para. [**541**], *ante*.

AMENDMENT

Para. 3 is restricted by the Legitimacy Act 1976, s. 4, A.L.S. Vol. 244.

PROSPECTIVE REPEAL

This Schedule is repealed by the Adoption Act 1976, s. 73 and Sch. 4, A.L.S. Vol. 244, as from a day to be appointed, and replaced as noted in the destination table, para. **[589]**, *post.*

PART III

LEGITIMATION

(*This part of this Schedule was repealed by the Legitimacy Act 1976, s. 11* (*2*), *Sch. 2, A.L.S. Vol. 244; see now that Act, ss. 4, 5, 11* (*1*) *and Sch. 1.*) **[545]**

PART IV

SUPPLEMENTAL

Dispositions depending on date of birth

14.—(1) Where a disposition depends on the date of birth of a child who was born illegitimate and who—

(*a*) is adopted by one of the natural parents as sole adoptive parent,

(*b*) (*Repealed by the Legitimacy Act 1976, s. 11* (*2*), *Sch. 2, A.L.S. Vol. 244.*)

paragraph 6 (2) and paragraph 12 (4) do not affect entitlement under Part II of the Family Law Reform Act 1969 (illegitimate children).

(2) (*Repealed by the Legitimacy Act 1976, s. 11* (*2*), *Sch. 2, A.L.S. Vol. 244.*)

(3) This paragraph applies for example where—

(*a*) a testator dies in 1976 bequeathing a legacy to his eldest grandchild living at a specified time,

(*b*) his daughter has an illegitimate child in 1977 who is the first grandchild,

(*c*) his married son has a child in 1978,

(*d*) subsequently the illegitimate child is adopted by the mother as sole adoptive parent . . . ,

and in all those cases the daughter's child remains the eldest grandchild of the testator throughout.

Protection of trustees and personal representatives

15.—(1) A trustee or personal representative is not under a duty, by virtue of the law relating to trusts or the administration of estates, to enquire, before conveying or distributing any property, whether—

(*a*) any adoption has been effected or revoked,

(*b*) (*Repealed by the Legitimacy Act 1976, s. 11* (*2*), *Sch. 2, A.L.S. Vol. 244.*)

if that fact could affect entitlement to the property.

(2) A trustee or personal representative shall not be liable to any person by reason of a conveyance or distribution of the property made without regard to any such fact if he has not received notice of the fact before the conveyance or distribution.

(3) This paragraph does not prejudice the right of a person to follow the property, or any property representing it, into the hands of another person, other than a purchaser, who has received it.

Property devolving with peerages, etc.

16.—(1) This Schedule shall not affect the devolution of any property limited (expressly or not) to devolve (as nearly as the law permits) along with any peerage or dignity or title of honour.

(2) This paragraph applies only if and so far as a contrary intention is not expressed in the instrument, and shall have effect subject to the terms of the instrument.

Entails

17. It is hereby declared that references in this Schedule to dispositions of property include references to a disposition by the creation of an entailed interest. [**546**]

COMMENCEMENT

This Schedule came into force on 1st January 1976; see s. 108 (4), para. [**541**], *ante.*

AMENDMENT

The words omitted in para. 14 (3) (*d*) were repealed by the Legitimacy Act 1976, s. 11 (2) and Sch. 2, A.L.S. Vol. 244.

PROSPECTIVE REPEAL

This Schedule is repealed by the Adoption Act 1976, s. 73 and Sch. 4, A.L.S. Vol. 244, as from a day to be appointed, and replaced as noted in the destination table, para. [**589**], *post.*

PART V

EXTENT

18. This Schedule does not apply to Scotland. [**547**]

COMMENCEMENT

This Schedule came into force on 1st January 1976; see s. 108 (4), para. [**541**], *ante.*

PROSPECTIVE REPEAL

This Schedule is repealed by the Adoption Act 1976, s. 73 and Sch. 4, A.L.S. Vol. 244, as from a day to be appointed, and replaced as noted in the destination table, para. [**589**], *post.*

(*Sch.* 2 *applies to Scotland.*)

SCHEDULE 3

Section 108.

MINOR AND CONSEQUENTIAL AMENDMENTS

Children and Young Persons Act 1933 (23 *and* 24 *Geo.* 5 *c.* 12)

1. In section 1 (1) (*b*), for the words "one hundred pounds" there are substituted the words "£400". [**548**]

COMMENCEMENT

Para. 1 came into force on 1st January 1976; see s. 108 (4), para. [**541**], *ante.*

2. (*Applies to Scotland.*)

Education Act 1944 (*c.* 31)

3. In section 106, the following subsection is substituted for subsection (4)—

"(4) In this section 'guardian' means the person having legal custody of the child or young person, as defined by section 86 of the Children Act 1975." [**549**]

COMMENCEMENT

Para. 3 came into force on 1st January 1976; see s. 108 (4), para. [**541**], *ante.*

Children Act 1948 (*c.* 43)

4. In section 3 (8) for the words "twenty pounds" and "two months" there are substituted respectively the words "£400" and "three months".

5. In section 4—

(*a*) in subsection (3) (*a*) after the words "parent or guardian" there are inserted the words "or custodian";

(*b*) for subsection (3) (*b*) there is substituted— "(*b*) in the case of a resolution passed by virtue of paragraph (*b*), (*c*) or (*d*) of subsection (1) of the said section 2, by the person who, but for the resolution, would have the parental rights and duties in relation to the child,".

6. In section 43 (1), for the words "and the Adoption Act 1968" there are substituted the words "the Adoption Act 1968 and the Children Act 1975". [**550**]

COMMENCEMENT

Paras. 4 and 6 came into force on 1st January 1976; see s. 108 (4), para. [**541**], *ante*. Para. 5 (*b*) was brought into force on 26th November 1976 by the Children Act 1975 (Commencement No. 1) Order 1976, S.I. 1976 No. 1744, made under s. 108 (2), para. [**541**], *ante*. At the time of going to press, para. 5 (*a*) was not yet in force.

PROSPECTIVE REPEAL

Para. 6 is repealed by the Adoption Act 1976, s. 73 and Sch. 4, A.L.S. Vol. 244, as from a day to be appointed, and replaced as noted in the destination table, para. [**589**], *post*.

Marriage Act 1949 (*c.* 76)

7. In section 3 (1), after the words "shall be required" there are inserted the words "unless the infant is subject to a custodianship order, when the consent of the custodian and, where the custodian is the husband or wife of a parent of the infant, of that parent shall be required".

8. In Part I of Schedule 1—

(*a*) after "Mother" there is inserted "Adoptive mother or former adoptive mother";

(*b*) after "Daughter" there is inserted "Adoptive daughter or former adoptive daughter";

(*c*) after "Father" there is inserted "Adoptive father or former adoptive father";

(*d*) after "Son" there is inserted "Adoptive son or former adoptive son".

9. In Schedule 2 in paragraph 2 (*b*) after the words "deceased parent" there are inserted the words "or by the court under section 3 of the Guardianship of Minors Act 1971". [**551**]

COMMENCEMENT

Paras. 8 and 9 came into force on 1st January 1976; see s. 108 (4), para. [**541**], *ante*. At the time of going to press. para. 7 was not yet in force.

Maintenance Orders Act 1950 (*c.* 37)

10. In section 15, after the words "Maintenance Orders (Reciprocal Enforcement) Act 1972" there are inserted the words "or sections 33 to 45 of the Children Act 1975".

11. In section 16 (2) (*a*), after sub-paragraph (v) there are inserted the following sub-paragraphs—

"(vi) section 4 of the Affiliation Proceedings Act 1957 on an application made under section 45 of the Children Act 1975;

(vii) section 34 (1) (*b*) of the Children Act 1975;". [**552**]

COMMENCEMENT

At the time of going to press, paras. 10 and 11 were not yet in force; see s. 108 (2), para. [**541**], *ante*.

Magistrates' Courts Act 1952 (*c.* 55)

12. In section 56 (1) (meaning of "domestic proceedings"), the following paragraph is inserted after paragraph (*e*)—

"(*f*) under the Adoption Act 1958 or Part I or II of the Children Act 1975", and there are added at the end the following words "or proceedings on an information". [**553**]

COMMENCEMENT

At the time of going to press, para. 12 was not yet in force; see s. 108 (2), para. [**541**], *ante*.

Births and Deaths Registration Act 1953 (*c.* 20)

13.—(1) For "living new-born child" in each place where it occurs, except sections 6, 7, 8, 34 (3) and 36, there is substituted "still-born child".

(2) In section 1 (2) after paragraph (*d*) there is added—

"(*e*) in the case of a still-born child found exposed, the person who found the child."

(3) In section 14 (1) (*a*) after "section 10" there is inserted "or 10A".

(4) In section 30 after subsection (1) there is inserted the following subsection—

"(1A) The Registrar General shall cause an index to be made and kept in the General Register Office of the entries in the register kept by him under section 3A of this Act."

(5) In section 34—

(*a*) in subsection (2) after paragraph (*c*) there is added the following paragraph—

"(*d*) in relation to the re-registration of a birth under section (5) of this Act";

(*b*) in subsection (3) after "new-born child" there is inserted "or still-born child".

(6) In section 41—

(*a*) after the definition of "disposal" there is inserted the following definition—

"'father', in relation to an adopted child, means the child's natural father;";

(*b*) after the definition of "the Minister" there is inserted the following definition—

"'mother', in relation to an adopted child, means the child's natural mother;". [**554**]

COMMENCEMENT

Para. 13 (6) came into force on 1st January 1976; see s. 108 (4), para. [**541**], *ante*. Para. 13 (1)–(5) was brought into force on 1st January 1977 by the Children Act 1975 (Commencement No. 1) Order 1976, S.I. 1976 No. 1744, made under s. 108 (2), para. [**541**], *ante*.

Affiliation Proceedings Act 1957 (*c.* 55)

14. In section 5 (2) there is inserted at the end the following paragraph—

"(*e*) section 45 of the Children Act 1975 (which enables the custodian of a child to apply for an affiliation order under this Act within three years after the making of the custodianship order)." [**555**]

COMMENCEMENT

At the time of going to press, para. 14 was not yet in force; see s. 108 (2), para. [**541**], *ante*.

Housing Act 1957 (*c.* 56)

15. In Schedule 2, in paragraph 4 (7) for the words "any illegitimate son or daughter, and any adopted son or daughter" there are substituted the words "and any illegitimate son or daughter". [**556**]

COMMENCEMENT

Para. 15 came into force on 1st January 1976; see s. 108 (4), para. [**541**], *ante*.

Children Act 1958 (6 & 7 *Eliz.* 2 *c.* 65)

16. In section 2, as it applies in England and Wales,—

(*a*) in subsection (1), after the word "guardian" there is inserted the word "custodian";

(*b*) in subsection (4A),—

(i) for the words "registered adoption society as is referred to in Part II of the Adoption Act 1958" there are substituted the words "adoption society approved under Part I of the Children Act 1975", and

(ii) for the words "that Act" there are substituted the words "the Adoption Act 1958".

17. (*Applies to Scotland.*)

18. In section 6 for the words "obtained their consent" there are substituted the words "obtained their written consent".

19. In section 14 (2), for the words "one hundred pounds" there are substituted the words "£400".

20. In section 37 (2), for the words "one hundred pounds" there are substituted the words "£400". [**557**]

COMMENCEMENT

Paras. 17–20 came into force on 1st January 1976; see s. 108 (4), para. [**541**], *ante*. At the time of going to press, para. 16 was not yet in force; see s. 108 (2), para. [**541**], *ante*.

PROSPECTIVE REPEAL

Paras. 16 (*b*) and 17 are repealed by the Adoption Act 1976, s. 73 and Sch. 4, A.L.S. Vol. 244, as from a day to be appointed, and replaced as noted in the destination table, para. [**589**], *post*.

Adoption Act 1958 (7 & 8 *Eliz.* 2 *c.* 5)

21.—(1) For "Adoption Rules" in each place where it occurs there is substituted "rules".

(2) For "infant" and "infants" in each place where they occur there are respectively substituted "child" and "children".

(3) For "registered adoption society" in each place where it occurs there is substituted "approved adoption society".

(4) For "care and possession" in each place where it occurs there is substituted "actual custody".

22. In section 9 (3), for "this Part of this Act" in each place where it occurs there is substituted "the relevant provisions", and at the end there is inserted—

"In this subsection 'the relevant provisions' means this Part, Part III and Part V of this Act and Part I of the Children Act 1975."

23. (*Applies to Scotland.*)

24. In section 21 (1) for the words from "the form" to the end there is substituted "such form as the Registrar General may by regulations specify".

25. (*Applies to Scotland*).

26. In section 26 (2) after the words "adoption order" there are inserted the words "other than a Convention adoption order".

27. In section 32—

(*a*) the following subsections are substituted for subsection (1)—

"(1) The Secretary of State may by regulations prohibit unincorporated bodies from applying for approval under section 4 of the Children Act 1975 (Approval of adoption societies); and he shall not approve any unincorporated body whose application is contrary to regulations made under this subsection.

(1A) The Secretary of State may make regulations for any purpose relating to the exercise of its functions by an approved adoption society.";

(*b*) in subsection (2) for "(1)" there is substituted "(2)" and for the words from "twenty-five pounds" to the end of the subsection there is substituted the word "£400".

(*c*) the following subsection is added after subsection (3)—

"(4) Regulations under this section may make different provisions in relation to different cases or classes of cases and may exclude certain cases or classes of cases."

28. In section 33—

(*a*) in subsection (1)—

(i) for "registered by the authority under this Part of this Act" there is substituted "approved under Part I of the Children Act 1975";

(ii) for "the exercise of" to the end there is substituted "its own information or that of the Secretary of State";

(*b*) in subsection (2), for "by statutory declaration" there is substituted "in a manner specified in the notice".

29. In section 35 (6) for the word "six" there is substituted the word "three" and for the words "one hundred pounds" there are substituted the words "£400".

30. In section 36—

(*a*) in subsection (1) for the words "subsection (2) of section 3 of this Act" there are substituted the words "section 18 (1) of the Children Act 1975"; and

(*b*) for subsection (3), there is substituted the following—

"(3) A local authority which receives such notice as aforesaid in respect of a child whom the authority know to be in the care of another local authority shall, not more than seven days after the receipt of the notice, inform that other authority in writing that they have received the notice."

31. In section 37—

(*a*) in subsection (1), for the words "subsection (2) of section 3 of this Act" there are substituted the words "section 18 (1) of the Children Act 1975";

(*b*) the following subsections are substituted for subsection (4)—

"(4) A protected child ceases to be a protected child—

(*a*) on the appointment of a guardian for him under the Guardianship Act 1971;

(*b*) on the notification to the local authority for the area where the child has his home that the application for an adoption order has been withdrawn;

(*c*) on the making of any of the following orders in respect of the child—

(i) an adoption order;

(ii) an order under section 17 of the Children Act 1975;

(iii) a custodianship order;

(iv) an order under section 42, 43 or 44 of the Matrimonial Causes Act 1973; or

(*d*) on his attaining the age of 18, whichever first occurs.

(4A) (*Applies to Scotland.*)

32. In section 40 (6) for the words from the beginning to "that is to say" there are substituted the following words "The particulars referred to in subsection (4) of this section are".

33. In section 44 (2), for the word "six" there is substituted the word "three" and for the words "one hundred pounds" there are substituted the words "£400".

34. In section 50—

(*a*) in subsection (1) in paragraph (*b*), for "any consent" there is substituted "any agreement or consent";

(*b*) in subsection (2), for the word "six" there is substituted the word "three" and for the words "one hundred pounds" there are substituted the words "£400";

(*c*) in subsection (3), for "adoption society" there is substituted "approved adoption society".

35. In section 51 (2), for the words "fifty pounds" there is substituted the word "£400".

36. In section 52 (1)—

(*a*) for the words "fifty-three of this Act" there are substituted the words "twenty-five of the Children Act 1975"; and

(*b*) for the word "six" there is substituted the word "three" and for the words "one hundred pounds" there are substituted the words "£400".

37. In section 55, after the words "this Act" there are inserted the words "or Part I of the Children Act 1975".

38. For section 56 there is substituted the following section—

"56. Rules and regulations

(1) Any power to make rules or regulations conferred by this Act on the Lord Chancellor, the Secretary of State, the Registrar General or the Registrar General for Scotland shall be exercisable by statutory instrument which shall be subject to annulment in pursuance of a resolution of either House of Parliament.

(2) The Registrar General shall not make regulations under section 20 or 21 of this Act except with the approval of the Secretary of State.

(3), (4) (*Apply to Scotland.*)

39. In section 57 (1)—

(*a*) for the definition of "adoption order" there is substituted " 'adoption order' means an order under section 1 of this Act or section 8 (1) of the Children Act 1975;",

(*b*) there are inserted after the definition of "adoption society" the words " 'approved adoption society' means an adoption society approved under Part I of the Children Act 1975;",

(*c*) after the definition of "body of persons" there are inserted the following definitions—

"child", except where used to express a relationship, means a person who has not attained the age of 18;

"Convention adoption order" has the same meaning as in the Children Act 1975;",

(*d*) for the definition of "guardian" there is substituted " 'guardian' means—

(*a*) a person appointed by deed or will in accordance with the provisions of the Guardianship of Infants Acts 1886 and 1925 or the Guardianship of Minors Act 1971 or by a court of competent jurisdiction to be the guardian of the child, and

(*b*) in the case of an illegitimate child, includes the father where he has custody of the child by virtue of an order under section 9 of the Guardianship of Minors Act 1971, or under section 2 of the Illegitimate Children (Scotland) Act 1930;",

(*e*) after the definition of "relative" there is inserted the following definition—

" "voluntary organisation" means a body other than a public or local authority the activities of which are not carried on for profit."

40. (*Applies to Scotland.*) [**558**]

COMMENCEMENT

Paras. 21 (1), (2) and (4), 22–25, 27 (*b*), 29, 33, 34 (*b*), 35, 36 (*b*), 38, 39 (*c*), (*d*) and (*e*) and 40 came into force on 1st January 1976; see s. 108 (4), para. [**541**], *ante*. Paras. 30 (*b*), 31 (*b*), in so far as it provides for the substitution of the Adoption Act 1958, s. 37 (4), 34 (*a*), 37 and 39 (*a*) were brought into force on 26th November 1976 by the Children Act 1975 (Commencement No. 1) Order 1976, S. I. 1976 No. 1744, made under s. 108 (2) para. [**541**] *ante*. At the time of going to press, paras. 21 (3), 36, 27 (*a*) and (*c*), 28, 30 (*a*), 31 (*a*), 31 (*b*), so far as not already in force, 32, 34 (*c*), 36 (*a*) and 39 (*b*) were not yet in force.

PROSPECTIVE REPEAL

Paras. 21–40 are repealed by the Adoption Act 1976, s. 73 and Sch. 4, A.L.S. Vol. 244, as from a day to be appointed, and replaced as noted in the destination table, para. [**589**], *post*.

County Courts Act 1959 (*c.* 22)

41. In section 109 (2) the following paragraph is inserted after paragraph (*g*)—

"(*h*) any proceedings under the Guardianship of Minors Acts 1971 and 1973 or the Children Act 1975." [**559**]

COMMENCEMENT

Para. 41 was brought into force on 26th November 1976 by the Children Act 1975 (Commencement No. 1) Order 1976, S.I. 1976 No. 1744, made under s. 108 (2), para. [**541**], *ante*.

Children and Young Persons Act 1963 (*c.* 37)

42. In section 49 (1), for the words "twenty pounds" there are substituted the words "£100". [**560**]

COMMENCEMENT

Para. 42 was brought into force on 26th November 1976 by the Children Act 1975 (Commencement No. 1) Order 1976, S.I. 1976 No. 1744, made under s. 108 (2), para. [**541**], *ante*.

Perpetuities and Accumulations Act 1964 (*c.* 55)

43. In section 4, the following subsection is inserted at the end—

"(7) For the avoidance of doubt it is hereby declared that a question arising under section 3 of this Act or subsection (1) (*a*) above of whether a disposition would be void apart from this section is to be determined as if subsection (6) above had been a separate section of this Act." [**561**]

COMMENCEMENT

Para. 43 came into force on 1st Janury 1976; see s. 108 (4), para. [**541**], *ante*.

Adoption Act 1964 (*c.* 57)

44. In section 1, the following subsection is substituted for subsection (5)—

"(5) Section 8 (3) and (4) of, and paragraph 11 of Schedule 1 and paragraph 3 of Schedule 2 to, the Children Act 1975 apply in relation to a child who is the subject of an order which is similar to an order under section 25 of that Act and is made (whether before or after this subsection has effect) in Northern Ireland, the Isle of Man or any of the Channel Islands, as they apply in relation to a child who is the subject of an adoption order."

45. In section 3 (3)—

(*a*) for the words "section 53 of the said Act of 1958" there are substituted the words "section 25 of the Children Act 1975";

(*b*) for the words from "the word 'Provisionally' " to the end of the subsection there are substituted the words "the words 'Proposed Foreign Adoption' " or, as the case may require, " 'Proposed Foreign Re-adoption' followed by the name, in brackets, of the country in which the order was made."

[562]

COMMENCEMENT

At the time of going to press, paras. 44 and 45 were not yet in force; see s. 108 (2), para. [**541**], *ante*.

PROSPECTIVE REPEAL

Paras. 44 and 45 are repealed by the Adoption Act 1976, s. 73 and Sch. 4, A.L.S. Vol. 244, as from a day to be appointed, and replaced as noted in the destination table, para. [**589**], *post*.

Health Services and Public Health Act 1968 (*c.* 46)

46. For section 64 (3) (*a*) there is substituted—

"(*a*) 'the relevant enactments' means—

(i) Parts III and IV of the Children and Young Persons Act 1933,
(ii) the National Health Service Act 1946,
(iii) Part III of the National Assistance Act 1948,
(iv) the Children Act 1948,
(v) the Adoption Act 1958,
(vi) the Children Act 1958,
(vii) section 9 of the Mental Health Act 1959,
(viii) section 10 of the Mental Health Act 1959, so far as it relates to cases mentioned in paragraph (*a*) of that section,
(ix) section 2 (1) (*f*) of the Matrimonial Proceedings (Magistrates' Courts) Act 1960,
(x) the Children and Young Persons Act 1963 except Part II and section 56,
(xi) this Act,
(xii) the Adoption Act 1968,
(xiii) section 7 (4) of the Family Law Reform Act 1969,
(xiv) the Children and Young Persons Act 1969, except so far as it relates to any voluntary home designated as mentioned in section 39 (1) of that Act as a controlled or assisted community home,
(xv) section 43 of the Matrimonial Causes Act 1973,
(xvi) the National Health Service Reorganisation Act 1973,
(xvii) the Children Act 1975."

47. For section 65 (3) (*b*) there is substituted—

"(*b*) 'the relevant enactments' means—

(i) Parts III and IV of the Children and Young Persons Act 1933,
(ii) Part III of the National Health Service Act 1946,
(iii) Part III of the National Assistance Act 1948,

(iv) the Children Act 1948,
(v) the Adoption Act 1958,
(vi) section 3 of the Disabled Persons (Employment) Act 1958,
(vii) the Children Act 1958,
(viii) section 9 of the Mental Health Act 1959,
(ix) section 10 of the Mental Health Act 1959, so far as it relates to cases mentioned in paragraph (*a*) of that section,
(x) section 2 (1) (*f*) of the Matrimonial Proceedings (Magistrates' Courts) Act 1960,
(xi) the Children and Young Persons Act 1963, except Part II and section 56,
(xii) this Act,
(xiii) the Adoption Act 1968,
(xiv) section 7 (4) of the Family Law Reform Act 1969,
(xv) the Children and Young Persons Act 1969,
(xvi) section 43 of the Matrimonial Causes Act 1973,
(xvii) the National Health Service Reorganisation Act 1973,
(xviii) the Children Act 1975." [**563**]

COMMENCEMENT

Paras. 46 and 47 were brought into force on 26th November 1976 by the Children Act 1975 (Commencement No. 1) Order 1976, S.I. 1976 No. 1744, made under s. 108 (2), para. [**541**], *ante*.

Social Work (Scotland) Act 1968 (*c*. 49)

48–57. (*Apply to Scotland only*.)

58. In section 69—

(*a*) In subsection (1), at the end there are added the following words—

"; and a court, if satisfied that there are reasonable grounds for believing that the child is within any premises, may grant a search warrant authorising a constable to search those premises for the child."

(*b*) for subsection (5) there is substituted—

"(5) In this and the next following section any reference—

(*a*) to a child absconding includes a reference to his being unlawfully taken away;

(*b*) to a child absconding from a place or from the control of a person includes a reference to his absconding while being taken to, or awaiting being taken to, that place or that person as the case may be."

59. In section 70, at the end there are added the following words—

"; and a court, if satisfied that there are reasonable grounds for believing that the child is within any premises, may grant a search warrant authorising a constable to search those premises for the child.".

60. In section 71, for the words "one hundred pounds" there is substituted "£400". [**564**]

COMMENCEMENT

Paras. 58–60 came into force on 1st January 1976; see s. 108 (4), para. [**541**], *ante*.

Adoption Act 1968 (*c*. 53)

61. In section 8 (2)—

(*a*) for the words "form set out in Schedule 1 to the Act of 1958, as modified by this subsection" there are substituted the words "form specified for the purposes of this subsection in regulations made by the Registrar General under section 21 of the Act of 1958"; and

(*b*) the words from "and for the purposes" to the end are repealed.

62. (*Applies to Scotland.*)

63. In section 9 (5), for the words "a specified order or an overseas adoption" there are substituted the words "or a specified order".

64. In section 11 (1)—

(*a*) for the definition of "adoption order" there is substituted the following definition—

" "adoption order" means an order made under section 8 of the Children Act 1975 as a Convention adoption order;";

(*b*) in the definition of "specified order" for the words "section 1 of this Act" there are substituted the words "sections 8 (1) and 24 of the Children Act 1975".

65. In section 12 (2), for the words from "made by virtue of" to "any of those provisions)" there are substituted the words "containing rules made by the Lord Chancellor under subsection (1) of this section". [**565**]

COMMENCEMENT

Paras. 61, 63 and 65 came into force on 1st January 1976; see s. 108 (4), para. [**541**], *ante*. Para. 64 was brought into force on 26th November 1976 by the Children Act 1975 (Commencement No. 1) Order 1976, S.I. 1976 No. 1744, made under s. 108 (2), para. [**541**], *ante*.

PROSPECTIVE REPEAL

Paras. 61–65 are repealed by the Adoption Act 1976, s. 73 and Sch. 4, A.L.S. Vol. 244, as from a day to be appointed, and replaced as noted in the destination table, para. [**589**], *post*.

Housing Act 1969 (*c*. 33)

66. In section 86 (2) for the words "any illegitimate son or daughter and any adopted son or daughter" there are substituted the words "and any illegitimate son or daughter". [**566**]

COMMENCEMENT

Para. 66 came into force on 1st January 1976; see s. 108 (4), para. [**541**], *ante*.

Children and Young Persons Act 1969 (*c*. 54)

67. In section 1 (2) the following paragraph is inserted after paragraph (*b*)—

"(*bb*) it is probable that the condition set out in paragraph (*a*) of this subsection will be satisfied in his case, having regard to the fact that a person who has been convicted of an offence mentioned in Schedule 1 to the Act of 1933 is, or may become, a member of the same household as the child;".

68. The following section is inserted after section 11—

"11A. Local authority functions under certain supervision orders

The Secretary of State may make regulations with respect to the exercise by a local authority of their functions in a case where a person has been placed under their supervision by an order made under section 1 (3) (*b*) or 21 (2) of this Act."

69. In section 21—

(*a*) the following subsection is inserted after subsection (2)—

"(2A) A juvenile court shall not make an order under subsection (2) of this section in the case of a person who has not attained the age of 18 and appears to the court to be in need of care or control unless the court is satisfied that, whether through the making of a supervision order or otherwise, he will receive that care or control.";

(*b*) in subsection (3) for "the preceding subsection" there is substituted "subsection (2) of this section".

70. The following section is inserted aft. . section 21—

"**21A. Termination of care order on adoption, etc.**

A care order relating to a child shall cease to have effect—

(*a*) on the adoption of the child;
(*b*) if an order under section 14 or section 25 of the Children Act 1975 is made in relation to the child;
(*c*) if an order similar to an order under section 25 of the Children Act 1975 is made in Northern Ireland, the Isle of Man or any of the Channel Islands in relation to the child."

71. In section 27—

(*a*) in subsection (3), for the words "their general duty aforesaid" there are substituted the words "their general duty under section 12 (1) of the Children Act 1948";
(*b*) the following subsections are substituted for subsection (4)—

"(4) Without prejudice to their general duty under the said section 12, it shall be the duty of a local authority to review the case of each child in their care in accordance with regulations made under the following subsection.

(5) The Secretary of State may by regulations make provision as to—

(*a*) the manner in which cases are to be reviewed under this section;
(*b*) the considerations to which the local authority are to have regard in reviewing cases under this section; and
(*c*) the time when a child's case is first to be reviewed and the frequency of subsequent reviews under this section."

72. In section 58 (1), the following passage is inserted after paragraph (*b*)—

"(*bb*) premises in which a child is living with a person other than his parent, guardian, relative or custodian, with whom he has been placed by an adoption agency (within the meaning of section 1 of the Children Act 1975);". [**567**]

COMMENCEMENT

Paras. 67–70 came into force on 1st January 1976; see s. 108 (4), para. [**541**], *ante*. At the time of going to press, paras. 71 and 72 were not yet in force; see s. 108 (2), para. [**541**], *ante*.

Administration of Justice Act 1970 (*c*. 31)

73.—(1) In Schedule 1—

(*a*) after "*Appellate Business*" there is inserted the following paragraph—

"Proceedings on appeal under section 4A of the Children Act 1948;";

(*b*) at the end there is inserted the following paragraph—

"Proceedings on appeal under the Children Act 1975".

(2) In Schedule 8—

(*a*) in paragraph 5, after the words "Social Security Act 1966" there are inserted the words "or section 45 of the Children Act 1975";

(*b*) after paragraph 11, there is inserted the following paragraph—

"12. An order under section 34 (1) (*b*) of the Children Act 1975 (payments of maintenance in respect of a child to his custodian).". [**568**]

COMMENCEMENT

Para. 73 (1) was brought into force on 26th November 1976 by the Children Act 1975 (Commencement No. 1) Order 1976, S.I. 1976 No. 1744, made under s. 108 (2), para. [**541**], *ante*. At the time of going to press, para. 73 (2) was not yet in force.

Local Authority Social Services Act 1970 (*c*. 42)

74. In Schedule 1—

(*a*) at the end of the entry relating to the Adoption Act 1958 there are added the following words "Counselling services for adopted persons";

(*b*) the following is inserted at the end—

"Children Act 1975 (c. 72.)

Part I	..	Maintenance of Adoption Service; function of local authority as adoption agency; applications for orders freeing children for adoption; inquiries carried out by local authorities in adoption cases.
Part II	..	Application by local authority for revocation of custodianship order; inquiries carried out by local authority in custodianship cases.". [**569**]

COMMENCEMENT

Para. 74 (*a*) was brought into force on 26th November 1976 by the Children Act 1975 (Commencement No. 1) Order 1976, S.I. 1976 No. 1744, made under s. 108 (2), para. [**541**], *ante*. At the time of going to press, para. 74 (*b*) was not yet in force.

PROSPECTIVE REPEAL

Para. 74 (*a*) is repealed by the Adoption Act 1976, s. 73 and Sch. 4, A.L.S. Vol. 244, as from a day to be appointed, and replaced as noted in the destination table, para. [**589**], *post*.

Guardianship of Minors Act 1971 (*c*. 3)

75.—(1) In section 9—

(*a*) in subsection (2) for "any person (whether or not one of the parents)" there is substituted "one of the parents" and the words "or either of the parents" are repealed;

(*b*) in subsection (3), the proviso is repealed;

(*c*) in subsection (4), the words from "or (before or after the death of either parent)" to the end are repealed;

(*d*) the following subsections are inserted after subsection (4)—

"(5) An order shall not be made under subsection (1) of this section giving custody to a person other than the mother or father.

(6) An order shall not be made under subsection (1) of this section at any time when the minor is free for adoption (within the meaning of section 12 (6) of the Children Act 1975)."

(2) In section 13 (2), after the words "order for the payment of money" there are inserted the words "made by a magistrates' court".

(3) In section 16—

(*a*) in subsection (1) for "the High Court shall" there is substituted "the High Court may";

(*b*) in subsection (4) for "the magistrates' court may" there is substituted "the magistrates' court shall".

(*c*) in subsection (5), for the words from "section 9" to "so given" there are substituted the words "section 3 (3) or 4 (3A) of the Guardianship Act 1973 for the discharge of variation of a supervision order or, as the case may be, an order giving the care of a minor to a local authority or an order requiring payments to be made to an authority to whom care of a minor is so given". [**570**]

COMMENCEMENT

Para. 75 (3) came into force on 1st January 1976; see s. 108 (4), para. [**541**], *ante*. At the time of going to press. para. 75 (1) and (2) was not yet in force.

Attachment of Earnings Act 1971 (*c*. 32)

76. In Schedule 1—

(*a*) in paragraph 6, after the words "Social Security Act 1966" there are inserted the words "or section 45 of the Children Act 1975";

(*b*) after paragraph 11, there is inserted the following paragraph—

"12. An order under section 34 (1) (*b*) of the Children Act 1975 (payments of maintenance in respect of a child to his custodian)." [**571**]

COMMENCEMENT

At the time of going to press, para. 76 was not yet in force; see s. 108 (2), para. [**541**], *ante*.

Parliamentary and Other Pensions Act 1972 (*c*. 48)

77. In section 15 (6) for the words "a stepchild or adopted child" there are substituted the words "or a stepchild". [**572**]

COMMENCEMENT

Para. 77 came into force on 1st January 1976; see s. 108 (4), para. [**541**], *ante*.

Matrimonial Causes Act 1973 (*c*. 18)

78. In section 44 (1) for the words "custody of any person" there are substituted the words "care of any person".

79. In section 50 (1) at the end of paragraph (*e*) there are inserted the following words—

"or

(*f*) proceedings to which section 100 (7) (*d*) of the Children Act 1975 applies (certain applications for revocation and variation of custodianship, etc. orders);". [**573**]

COMMENCEMENT

Para. 78 came into force on 1st January 1976; see s. 108 (4), para. [**541**], *ante*. At the time of going to press, para. 79 was not yet in force; see s. 108 (2), para. [**541**], *ante*.

Guardianship Act 1973 (*c*. 29)

80.—(1) In section 4 (3) for the words from "the following provisions" to the end there are substituted the following words "sections 12 (2) and 13 of the Guardianship of Minors Act 1971 shall apply as if the order made under section 2 of this Act were an order under section 9 of the Guardianship of Minors Act 1971.

(2) After section 4 (3) there is inserted the following subsection—

"(3A) An order under section 2 (2) (*b*) or (3) above relating to a minor may be varied or discharged by a subsequent order made on the application of either parent or after the death of either parent on the application of any guardian under the Guardianship of Minors Act 1971 or on the application of the local authority to whose care the minor was committed by the order under section 2 (2) (*b*)."

81. In section 6 (1), for "section 9 of the Guardianship of Minors Act 1971 or section" there is substituted "section 5 or 9 of the Guardianship of Minors Act 1971 or section 1 (3) or". [**574**]

COMMENCEMENT

Para. 81 came into force on 1st January 1976; see s. 108 (4), para. [**541**], *ante*. At the time of going to press, para. 80 was not yet in force.

Legal Aid Act 1974 (*c*. 4)

82. In Schedule 1—

(*a*) for paragraph 3 (*d*), there is substituted—

"(*d*) proceedings in which the making of an order under Part I of the Children Act 1975 is opposed by any party to the proceedings;";

(*b*) the following paragraphs are inserted after paragraph 3 (*e*)—

"(*f*) proceedings under Part II of the Children Act 1975;

(*g*) proceedings under section 63 (2) of the Children Act 1975". [**575**]

COMMENCEMENT

Para. 82 (*a*) was brought into force on 26th November 1976 by the Children Act 1975 (Commencement No. 1) Order 1976, S.I. 1976 No. 1744, made under s. 108 (2), para. [**541**], *ante*. At the time of going to press, para. 82 (*b*) was not yet in force.

Housing Act 1974 (*c*. 44)

83. In section 129 (4) for the words "any illegitimate son or daughter and any adopted son or daughter" there are substituted the words "and any illegitimate son or daughter". [**576**]

COMMENCEMENT

Para. 83 came into force on 1st January 1976; see s. 108 (4), para. [**541**], *ante*.

Section 108

SCHEDULE 4

FURTHER REPEALS

PART I

STATUS OF ADOPTED CHILD

Chapter	Short Title	Extent of Repeal
16 & 17 Geo. 5 c. 29	Adoption of Children Act 1926	The whole Act so far as unrepealed.
3 & 4 Geo. 6 c. 42	Law Reform (Miscellaneous Provisions) (Scotland) Act 1940	Section 2 (1) and (3).
11 & 12 Geo. 6 c. 43	Children Act 1948	In section 59 (1), in the definition of "parent", paragraph (*a*).

Chapter	Short Title	Extent of Repeal
11 & 12 Geo. 6 c. 53	Nurseries and Child-Minders Regulation Act 1948	In section 13 (2), in the definition of "relative" (as inserted by section 13 of the Adoption of Children Act 1949), paragraph (*a*).
12 & 13 Geo. 6 c. 76	Marriage Act 1949	In section 68 (3), the words from "includes" to "but".
12, 13 & 14 Geo. 6 c. 98	Adoption of Children Act 1949	Section 13 (1) (*a*).
14 & 15 Geo. 6 c. 11	Administration of Justice (Pensions) Act 1950	Section 26 (2).
1 & 2 Eliz. 2 c. 20	Births and Deaths Registration Act 1953	In section 41, in the definition of "relative" the words from "and in relation to" to the end.
3 & 4 Eliz. 2 c. 18	Army Act 1955	In section 150 (5), in the paragraph relating to a child of a person, the words "or adopted" and the words from "and in this paragraph" to the end of the paragraph.
3 & 4 Eliz. 2 c. 19	Air Force Act 1955	In section 15 (5), in the paragraph relating to a child of a person, the words "or adopted" and the words from "and in this paragraph" to the end of the paragraph.
4 & 5 Eliz. 2 c. 69	Sexual Offences Act 1956	In section 28 (4), in paragraph (*a*) the words from "has been adopted" to "a girl who" and the words "(and has not been so adopted)".
4 & 5 Eliz. 2 c. 70	Marriage (Scotland) Act 1956	In section 1 (5), paragraph (*a*) and the words "or adoptive parent" in paragraph (*b*).
6 & 7 Eliz. 2 c. 65	Children Act 1958	In section 17, the definition of "parent".
6 & 7 Eliz. 2 c. 40	Matrimonial Proceedings (Children) Act 1958	In section 7 (1) (*b*), the words "or an adopted". Section 7 (3).
7 & 8 Eliz. 2 c. 5	Adoption Act 1958	Sections 13 and 14. Sections 15 (1), (2) and (3). Sections 16 and 17. Section 18 (1). Section 25. In section 52 (1) the words "(whether in law or in fact)". In section 57 (1), in the definition of "relative" paragraph (*a*). Section 58 (2) and (3). In Schedule 5, paragraphs 1 to 4.
7 & 8 Eliz. 2 c. 65	Fatal Accidents Act 1959	In section 1, subsection (2) (*a*) and subsection (3).

Chapter	Short Title	Extent of Repeal
7 & 8 Eliz. 2 c. 72	Mental Health Act 1959	In section 49, in subsection (2) the words from "an adopted person" to "as aforesaid", and subsection (5).
8 & 9 Eliz. 2 c. 48	Matrimonial Proceedings (Magistrates' Courts) Act 1960	In section 16 (1), the words "or adopted" and "but does not include a child adopted by some other person or persons", and the words from "and 'adopted'" to the end.
8 & 9 Eliz. 2 c. 59	Adoption Act 1960	Section 1 (2).
8 & 9 Eliz. 2 c. 61	Mental Health (Scotland) Act 1960	In section 45, in subsection (2) the words from "adopted person" to "person; and"; and subsection (5).
1964 c. 57	Adoption Act 1964	Section 1 (1), (2) and (4).
1965 c. 49	Registration of Births, Deaths and Marriages (Scotland) Act 1965	In section 56 (1), in the definition of "relative" the words from "and in relation to" to the end.
1965 c. 53	Family Allowances Act 1965	Section 17 (4).
1967 c. 29	Housing Subsidies Act 1967	In section 24 (3) (*c*), the word "adopted".
1967 c. 81	Companies Act 1967	In section 30 (2), the words "and adopted son" and "and adopted daughter". In section 31 (5), the words "and adopted son" and "and adopted daughter".
1967 c. 88	Leasehold Reform Act 1967	In section 7 (7), the words "and any adopted son or daughter". In section 18 (3), the words "and any adopted son or daughter".
1968 c. 49	Social Work (Scotland) Act 1968	In section 94 (1), in the definition of "parent", paragraph (*a*).
1968 c. 53	Adoption Act 1968	Section 4 (1) and (2). Section 10 (2) and (3).
1968 c. 71	Race Relations Act 1968	In section 7 (4) the words "and any adopted son or daughter".
1971 c. 56	Pensions (Increase) Act 1971	In section 3 (7), the words from "and includes" to the end.
1973 c. 16	Education Act 1973	In section 3 (5), the words from "and a child" to the end.
1973 c. 18	Matrimonial Causes Act 1973	In section 52 (1), the definition of "adopted" and, in the definition of "child", the words "or adopted".
1973 c. 45	Domicile and Matrimonial Proceedings Act 1973	In section 4 (5), the words from "and in its application" to the end.
1975 c. 14	Social Security Act 1975	In section 32 (3) (*c*), the words "the same relationship by adoption and to include also".

Chapter	Short Title	Extent of Repeal
1975 c.14—*contd.*	Social Security Act 1975—*contd.*	In section 71 (6), the words "and a parent by adoption". In section 161 (2), the words "a son or daughter by adoption and". In Schedule 20, in the definition of "relative" the words "or adoption".
1975 c. 61	Child Benefit Act 1975	Section 24 (3) (*c*).

The repeals of sections 16 and 17 of the 1958 Act, and of provisions containing references to those sections, have effect subject to paragraph 5 (2) of Schedule 1, and the other repeals in this Part have effect as respect things done, or events occurring after 31st December 1975. [**577**]

COMMENCEMENT

This Part of this Schedule came into force on 1st January 1976; see s. 108 (4), para. [**541**], *ante*.

PART II

LEGITIMATION

Chapter	Short Title	Extent of Repeal
16 & 17 Geo. 5 c. 60	Legitimacy Act 1926	Section 1 (3). Sections 3 to 5. In section 8 (2), the words from "and to the taking" to "of a legitimated person". In section 11, the definitions of "disposition", "intestate" and "entailed interest".
1969 c. 46	Family Law Reform Act 1969	Section 14 (8). Section 15 (4) and (6).

These repeals have effect subject to paragraph 12 (9) of Schedule 1. [**578**]

COMMENCEMENT

This Part of this Schedule came into force on 1st January 1976; see s. 108 (4), para. [**541**], *ante*.

PART III

MISCELLANEOUS

Chapter	Short Title	Extent of Repeal
23 and 24 Geo. 5 c. 12	Children and Young Persons Act 1933	In section 1, in subsection (1) (*a*), the words "not exceeding one hundred pounds", and in subsection (5), the words from "the maximum" to "pounds, and".

Chapter	Short Title	Extent of Repeal
1937 c. 37	Children and Young Persons (Scotland) Act 1937	In section 12, in subsection (1) (*a*), the words "not exceeding one hundred pounds", and in subsection (5) (*a*) the words from "the maximum" to "pounds, and".
7 & 8 Eliz. 2 c. 5	Adoption Act 1958	In section 4 (2), the words from "(either" to "brought up)". Section 7 (1) (*b*) and (2). In section 20 (4), the words from "pursuant to" to "in force". Section 21 (3). Section 49. In section 57 (1) the definition of "infant". Schedules 1 and 2.
1963 c. 37	Children and Young Persons Act 1963	Section 54.
1965 c. 49	Registration of Births, Deaths and Marriages (Scotland) Act 1965	Section 54 (1) (*d*).
1968 c. 22	Legitimation (Scotland) Act 1968	In section 6 (3), the words "or to subsection (1) of that section".
1968 c. 53	Adoption Act 1968	Sections 1 to 3. In section 9 (5), the words "or adoption". In section 11 (1), the definitions of "qualified infant", "qualified person" and "qualified spouses". In section 12 (1), the words "or under Part I of the Act of 1958 in its application to adoption orders and proposed adoption orders", the words "or the said Part I" in both places where they occur and the words from "and the rules" to the end. In section 14 (3), the words from "except the" to "1958 and".
1969 c. 54	Children and Young Persons Act 1969	Section 27 (2).
1973 c. 29	Guardianship Act 1973	Section 3 (5).

These repeals take effect on 1st January 1976. [**579**]

COMMENCEMENT

This Part of this Schedule came into force on 1st January 1976; see s. 108 (4), para. [**541**], *ante*.

Part IV

Adoption Orders

Chapter	Short Title	Extent of Repeal
7 & 8 Eliz. 2 c. 5	Adoption Act 1958	Sections 1 and 2. Sections 4 and 5. Section 7 (1) (*a*) and (*c*) and (3). Section 9 (1) and (5). Section 10. Section 11 (1) and (3). Section 12. Section 21 (2).
1966 c. 19	Law Reform (Miscellaneous Provisions) (Scotland) Act 1966	Section 4.
1971 c. 3	Guardianship of Minors Act 1971	Section 16 (2).

These repeals take effect on the date section 8 (1) comes into force. [**580**]

COMMENCEMENT

This Part of this Schedule, except in so far as it relates to the provisions of the Adoption Act 1958, ss. 4 (3) (other than paras. (*c*) and (*d*)), 9 (5) and 12 (3) was brought into force on 26th November 1976 by the Children Act 1975 (Commencement No. 1) Order 1976, S.I. 1976 No. 1744, made under s. 108 (2), para. [**541**], *ante*. At the time of going to press the remaining provisions of this Part of this Schedule were not yet in force, and the footnote to Part IV above is consequently amended by Sch. 3 to the Commencement No. 1 Order.

Part V

Children in Care of Local Authorities

Chapter	Short Title	Extent of Repeal
10 & 11 Geo. 6 c. 43	Children Act 1948	Section 3 (1) and (2).
7 & 8 Eliz. 2 c. 5	Adoption Act 1958	Section 15 (4) and (5).
7 & 8 Eliz. 2 c. 72	Mental Health Act 1959	In Schedule 7, the entry relating to the Children Act 1948.
1963 c. 37	Children and Young Persons Act 1963	Section 48.
1968 c. 49	Social Work (Scotland) Act 1968	Section 17 (1) and (2). In section 18 (4) the words "but where on such an application the court appoints a guardian the resolution shall cease to have effect".
1971 c. 3	Guardianship of Minors Act 1971	In section 5 (2) the words from "but where" to the end.

These repeals take effect on the date sections 57 and 74 come into force. [**581**]

COMMENCEMENT

This Part of this Schedule was brought into force on 26th November 1976 by the Children Act 1975 (Commencement No. 1) Order 1976, S.I. 1976 No. 1744, made under s. 108 (2), para. [**541**], *ante*.

Part VI

Registration of Births

Chapter	Short Title	Extent of Repeal
1953 c. 20	Births and Deaths Registration Act 1953	In section 3, the words "and of any person in whose charge the child may be placed" and the proviso. In section 6, the words "or finding" and in that section and in section 7 the words "or from the date when any living new-born child is found exposed". In section 8, the words "or, in the case of a living new-born child found exposed, from the date of the finding". In section 36 (*a*), the words "or any living new-born child".
1969 c. 46	Family Law Reform Act 1969	Section 27 (2), (3), (4) and (5).

These repeals take effect on the date section 92 comes into force. [**582**]

COMMENCEMENT

This Part of this Schedule was brought into force on 1st January 1977 by the Children Act 1975 (Commencement No. 1) Order 1976, S.I. 1976 No. 1744, made under s. 108 (2), para. [541], *ante*.

Part VII

Adoption Agencies

Chapter	Short Title	Extent of Repeal
7 & 8 Eliz. 2 c. 5	Adoption Act 1958	Section 28 (2). Sections 30 and 31. In section 32 (3) the words from "children" to the end. In section 57 (1) the definitions of "charitable association" and "registered adoption society". Schedule 3.
1970 c. 42	Local Authority Social Services Act 1970	In column 2 of Schedule 1, the words "Making etc. arrangements for the adoption of children; regulation of adoption societies."

These repeals take effect on the date section 4 comes into force. [**583**]

COMMENCEMENT

At the time of going to press, this Part of this Schedule was not yet in force; see s. 108 (2), para. [541], *ante*.

Part VIII

Adoption: Evidence of Agreement and Guardians Ad Litem

Chapter	Short Title	Extent of Repeal
7 & 8 Eliz. 2 c. 5	Adoption Act 1958	Section 6. Section 9 (7) and (8). Se ction 11 (4) and (5).

These repeals take effect on the date section 20 comes into force. [**584**]

COMMENCEMENT

At the time of going to press, this Part of this Schedule was not yet in force; see s. 108 (2), para. [**541**], *ante*.

Part IX

Inquiries etc. by Adoption Agencies

Chapter	Short Title	Extent of Repeal
7 & 8 Eliz. 2 c. 5	Adoption Act 1958	Section 3. Section 8. Section 53. In section 57 (1), the definition of "Compulsory School age".

These repeals take effect on the date section 18 comes into force. [**585**]

COMMENCEMENT

At the time of going to press, this Part of this Schedule was not yet in force; see s. 108 (2), para. [**541**], *ante*.

Part X

Grants etc. for Voluntary Organisations

Chapter	Short Title	Extent of Repeal
10 & 11 Geo. 6 c. 43	Children Act 1948	Section 45 (2). Section 46.
1969 c. 54	Children and Young Persons Act 1969	Section 65 (2).

These repeals take effect on the date paragraphs 46 and 47 of Schedule 3 come into force. [**586**]

COMMENCEMENT

This Part of this Schedule was brought into force on 26th November 1976 by the Children Act 1975 (Commencement No. 1) Order 1976, S.I. 1976 No. 1744, made under s. 108 (2), para. [**541**], *ante*.

Part XI
Protected Children

Chapter	Short Title	Extent of Repeal
7 & 8 Eliz. 2 c. 5	Adoption Act 1958	In section 37 (1), paragraph (*a*), the words "of the person first mentioned in paragraph (*a*) of this subsection or, as the case may be," and the words "but is not a foster child within the meaning of Part I of the Children Act 1958". Section 37 (2) and (5). Section 40 (1), (2) and (3). Sections 41 and 42. In section 43 (1), the words from "or in contravention" to "of this Act".

These repeals take effect on the date paragraph 31 of Schedule 3 comes into force. [**587**]

COMMENCEMENT
At the time of going to press, this Part of this Schedule was not yet in force; see s. 108 (2), para. [541], ***ante*****.**

Part XII
Custodianship

Chapter	Short Title	Extent of Repeal
1973 c. 29	Guardianship Act 1973.	In section 2, in subsection (2) (*b*), the words "or to any other individual" and in subsection (4) (*a*) the words "or to any person given the custody of the minor". In section 3 (3), the words from "or (before" to "section 9 (1) of that Act" and the words from "and section 16 (5)" to the end.

These repeals take effect on the date section 33 comes into force. [**588**]

COMMENCEMENT
At the time of going to press, this Part of this Schedule was not yet in force; see s. 108 (2), para. [541], ***ante*****.**

DESTINATION TABLE

This table shows in column (1) the provisions of the Children Act 1975 and Legitimacy Act 1976 repealed by the Adoption Act 1976 and in column (2) the provisions of the Act corresponding thereto.

In certain cases the enactment in column (1), though having a corresponding provision in column (2) is not, or is not wholly, repealed as it is still required, or partly required, for the purposes of other legislation.

(1)	(2)
Children Act 1975 (c. 72)	Adoption Act 1976 (c. 36)
ss. 1, 2	ss. 1, 2
s. 3	s. 6
ss. 4–6	ss. 3–5
s. 7	s. 8
8 (1)–(5)	12 (1)–(5)
(6)	Applies to Scotland
(7), (8)	s. 12 (6), (7)
(9)	——
(10)	Applies to Scotland
ss. 9–11	ss. 13–15
s. 12 (1)–(5)	s. 16
(6)	(1) (*a*)
13	7
14 (1)–(4)	18 (1)–(4)
(5)	Applies to Scotland
(6)–(8)	s. 18 (5)–(7)
ss. 15, 16	ss. 19, 20
s. 17 (1)–(3)	s. 26
(4)	Applies to Scotland
18	s. 22 (1)–(3)
19	25
20 (1), (2)	65
(3)	——
(4)	Applies to Scotland
21 (1)–(3)	s. 64
(4)	Applies to Scotland
22 (1), (2)	s. 66 (3), (4)
(3)	23
(4), (5)	24
(6)	Applies to Scotland
23	s. 21
24 (1), (2) (*a*), (*b*)	17 (1), (2)
(2) (*c*)	12 (5)
(3)–(8)	17 (3)–(8)
(9)	ss. 70, 71 (2)
25	s. 55
26 (1)	50 (5)
(2)	51
27	Applies to Scotland
28 (*a*)	s. 11 (1)
(*b*) (so far as relating to sub-s. (2))	Applies to Scotland
(*b*) (so far as relating to sub-s. (2A))	s. 11 (2)
(*c*), (*d*)	(3), (5)
29 (so far as relating to substituted s. 34)	27 (1)–(3)

(1)	(2)
Children Act 1975 (c. 72)	Adoption Act 1976 (c. 36)
s. 29 (so far as relating to substituted s. 34A)	ss. 28 (1)–(3), (5) (7), (10), 67 (1), (3)
30 (1)–(5)	s. 29
(6)	Applies to Scotland
31	s. 30 (6)
32	ss. 57 (4)–(10), 67 (3)
100 (1)*, (2)*	s. 62 (1), (2)
(4) (*a*)	(3)
(*b*)	Applies to Scotland
(5), (6)	s. 62 (4), (6)
(8)*	(5)
101*	63
102 (1)† (2)*	61
106 (1)*	67 (1), (5)
(2)*	(2)
(3)*	(4)
107 (1)†	72 (1)
(3)*	s. 72 (4)
(4)*	(5)
Sch. 1, para. 1 (1), (2)	s. 38 (1)
(3)‡	——
(4)	s. 38 (2)
(5)	72 (1)
(6)	46 (3)
2	(1), (2)
3	39 (1), (2), (4)–(6)
4	41
5 (1), (2)	Sch. 2, para. 6
(3)	s. 46 (4)
6 (1)–(6)	42
(7)	——
paras. 7, 8	ss. 47, 48
para. 9	s. 39 (3)
10	44 (1)
11	49
paras. 12‡, 13‡	——
para. 14 (1) (*a*)	43 (1)
(*b*)‡ (2)‡	——
(3)	43 (2)
15 (1) (*a*)	45 (1)
(*b*)‡	——
(2), (3)	45 (2), (3)
16	44 (2), (3)
17	46 (5)
18	——
2	Applies to Scotland
3, para. 6	——

† Repealed in part.   * Not repealed.

‡ These provisions of the Children Act 1975 are replaced by provisions of the Legitimacy Act 1976, A.L.S. Vol. 244.

DESTINATION TABLE

(1)	(2)	(1)	(2)
Children Act 1975 (c. 72)	Adoption Act 1976 (c. 36)	Children Act 1975 (c. 72)	Adoption Act 1976 (c. 36)
Sch. 3, para. 16 (*b*)	——	Sch. 3, para, 36	56 (1)
17	Applies to Scotland	37	69
21	Passim	38	67 (1), (2), (6)
22	s. 66 (1), (6)	39	72 (1)
23	Applies to Scotland	40	Applies to Scotland
24	Sch. 1, para. 1 (1)	44	s. 59 (3)
25	Applies to Scotland	45	Sch. 1, para. 2 (4)
26	Sch. 1, para. 6	61	Sch. 1, para. 3
27	ss. 9 (1), (2), (4), 67 (5)	62	Applies to Scotland
28	s. 10 (1), (2)	63	s. 40 (3)
29	30 (7)	64	72 (1)
30 (*a*)	31 (1)	65	67 (1)
(*b*)	22 (4)	74 (*a*)	——
31 (*a*)	32 (1)		
(*b*)	(4)		
32	35 (1)	Legitimacy Act 1976 (c. 31)	
33	36 (2)		
34	57 (1)–(3)		
35	58 (2)	Sch. 1, para. 7	38 (2)

[**589**]

INDEX

References in this index are to paragraph numbers.
The letter "n" indicates a reference to a footnote.

References are to paragraph numbers

References are to paragraph numbers

References are to paragraph numbers

References are to paragraph numbers

References are to paragraph numbers

References are to paragraph numbers

References are to paragraph numbers

UNIVERSITY LIBRARY
LIVERPOOL